D0909357

SOCIAL WORK PRACTICE: PEOPLE AND ENVIRONMENTS

SOCIAL WORK PRACTICE:
PEOPLE AND ENVIRONMENTS
AN ECOLOGICAL PERSPECTIVE

CAREL B. GERMAIN

EDITOR

NEW YORK
COLUMBIA UNIVERSITY PRESS

ST. PHILIPS COLLEGE LIBRARY

362.973
S 678

Library of Congress Cataloging in Publication Data

Main entry under title:

Social work practice.

   Includes bibliographical references and index.
   1. Social service—United States—Addresses,
essays, lectures.   2. Human ecology—Addresses, essays,
lectures.   3. Social adjustment—Addresses, essays,
lectures.   4. Environmental psychology—Addresses,
essays, lectures.   I. Germain, Carel B.
HV95.S62   362'.973   78-26351
ISBN 0-231-04332-5
ISBN 0-231-04333-3 pbk.

Columbia University Press
New York—Guildford, Surrey

Copyright © 1979 Columbia University Press
All rights reserved
Printed in the United States of America

Second cloth and third paperback printing.

DEDICATED TO THE MEMORY OF
LUCILLE N. AUSTIN
PROFESSOR EMERITA, THE COLUMBIA UNIVERSITY
SCHOOL OF SOCIAL WORK

63964

Contents

Contributors

CAREL B. GERMAIN, Professor, University of Connecticut School of Social Work, West Hartford

HARRY J. APONTE, Director, Philadelphia Child Guidance Clinic, Philadelphia, Pennsylvania

MARTIN BLOOM, Professor, Virginia Commonwealth University School of Social Work, Richmond

CHARLES CATALDO, Assistant Professor, Hunter College School of Social Work, New York

BARBARA JONES DRAPER, Lecturer, Columbia University School of Social Work, New York

DENA FISHER, Director, Social Work Department, Englewood Hospital, Englewood, New Jersey

EDA GOLDSTEIN, Supervisor of Research, Social Service Department, The New York Hospital–Cornell Medical Center, Westchester Division, White Plains, New York

CHARLES F. GROSSER, Professor, Columbia University School of Social Work, New York

L. ANN HARTMAN, Professor, University of Michigan School of Social Work, Ann Arbor

SISTER MARY PAUL JANCHILL, New York State Department of Mental Hygiene, New York, New York

JOAN LAIRD, Assistant Professor, Department of Social Work, Eastern Michigan University, Ypsilanti

ANTHONY N. MALUCCIO, Professor, University of Connecticut School of Social Work, West Hartford

IRVING MILLER, Professor, Columbia University School of Social Work, New York

RENEE SOLOMON, Associate Professor, Columbia University School of Social Work, New York

CAROL SWENSON, Assistant Professor, University of Maryland School of Social Work and Community Planning, Baltimore

Foreword

RENÉ DUBOS

THE MANUSCRIPT of *Social Work Practice: People and Environments* reached me as I was completing a review of several books dealing with modern trends in architectural design. Social work appears at first sight to be far removed from architecture, yet I found myself on familiar ground when I read in Dr. Germain's Introduction that the ecological perspective is becoming of increasing importance in psychiatry, nursing, education, social work, and other human service professions. As my book review mentioned above deals with certain ecological aspects of architecture, I shall extend its theme here with an example suggesting that the design of human settlements may have a bearing on social work practice.

I was born a few miles east of Paris in a small village called St. Brice, which was then separated from another small village, called Sarcelles, by a complex system of railroad tracks. Because of the housing shortage in the Paris area after World War II, Sarcelles was selected as the site for a huge "modern" housing development which was built in the early 1940s. This project consisted of tall anonymous apartment buildings, completely foreign to the traditional architecture and to the social habits of the region. The physical accommodations provided in the new housing project were better in many respects than those in most houses of the old village and of other similar Paris suburbs. Yet, within a short time after the occupation of the new Sarcelles, many of its inhabitants began to suffer from ill-defined organic and psychic disorders. In medical circles, this pattern of disease was facetiously referred to as an epidemic of "sarcellitis." Since disease incidence did not increase in the village of St. Brice, which had remained essentially unchanged across the railroad tracks, it was obvious that "sarcellitis" was a consequence of the social disorganization created by the new housing development. People found it difficult to live under conditions which appeared un-French to them, and to which they were not adapted.

I was recently told by a physician who practices in the Sarcelles– St. Brice region that "sarcellitis" has now almost disappeared. The inhabitants of Sarcelles have progressively recreated social structures and behavioral patterns very similar to those of the old village. Spontaneously, and with the guidance of social workers, they have introduced innumerable changes of detail in the grounds and the buildings of the housing development, and have recreated a human atmosphere rather typical of the Paris suburbs; it is probable furthermore that they themselves have undergone changes that make them better adapted to the new conditions. The emergence and spontaneous disappearance of "sarcellitis" illustrate that much of socio-medical pathology is due to adaptive failures which can be understood only in the light of ecological principles.

Changes in the health situation, very similar to those that occurred in Sarcelles, have been described for Harlow, the oldest of the English "new cities." Here again, a slow process of social adaptation progressively transformed a raw settlement, seemingly disease-prone, into a fairly successful urban agglomeration. There are other cities, however, in which this adaptive process has not yet been successful, or has completely failed. In Boston, for example, there is still doubt concerning the ultimate outcome of having moved people from the slums around the Massachusetts General Hospital to new settlements which are much more sanitary. The physical accommodations were poor in the slums but social life in them was well integrated, with human relationships much richer than in the new settlements. In St. Louis, the Pruitt-Igoe public housing project, which had been hailed as an enlightened scheme in the 1950s, had to be dynamited 20 years later because it had proved completely unsuited to the social patterns of the population for which it had been built.

The various chapters of this book describe and analyze many different situations in which human ecology is crucially relevant to physical and mental health. They provide evidence that experienced social workers can often intervene effectively in defective situations, and bring about in a relatively short time social improvements which would have required several decades if they had occurred through spontaneous adaptive processes—and which indeed might not have occurred at all. Each one of the chapters in the book can be read as the report of a social experiment from which practical lessons can be derived to help human beings adapt more rapidly and successfully to the ever-changing conditions of modern life.

Introduction:
Ecology and Social Work

Carel B. Germain

THIS IS A BOOK designed to bring before social work practitioners, administrators, and students a series of practice and programmatic applications of a developing perspective in social work. The perspective is derived from ecological ideas about the complex relations between living organisms, in this case people, and their environments. William Alanson White once observed, "A legitimate proof of the value of any new thinking in any particular field of human endeavor is the evidence that can be brought that that same way of thinking is growing up simultaneously in other fields." The ecological perspective is, indeed, emerging in many academic disciplines and in the human service professions of psychiatry, nursing, education, and psychology as well as in social work.

Sufficient experience in practicing and teaching from an ecological perspective is now available. Hence fourteen social work practitioners and educators whose thinking and work are rooted in ecological conceptions were invited to prepare papers presenting their ideas and their practice for inclusion in this volume. The book is, in a very real sense, the product of the personal and professional connections among the authors, the historical origins of their ideas, and the contemporary social, political, economic, and ideological context of practice itself.

The authors form a social network and, through their linkages, have reciprocally influenced the ideas of one another. The linkages

ST. PHILIPS COLLEGE LIBRARY

include shared experiences in teaching and learning, formal and informal encounters in schools, agencies, and professional conferences, and contributions to the professional literature. The authors' ideas have historical connections to earlier social work conceptions about people and environments. In particular, Professor Emerita Lucille N. Austin, to whom the book is dedicated, directly or indirectly influenced many of the authors to consider the usefulness of General Systems ideas for social work practice. In a similar fashion, the ideas of René Dubos, humanist and life scientist, exerted a powerful influence on most of the authors.

The turbulent environment in which social work exists has thrust up new social issues related to the growing perception of the salience of the environment in every aspect of human life. These, in turn, created professional dilemmas that have renewed the old debates between the "clinical" and the "social reform" segments of the profession, increasing the tensions among practitioners. The tensions led to efforts to redefine the profession's purpose and to reconceptualize its practice. This book is one such effort.

The sociology of knowledge suggests that the development of ideas and knowledge is influenced by the transactions between the professional interests and values of the individual advancing the ideas and the circle of others in the profession to whom he or she relates, and by the trends and conditions of the particular time and place.[1] An ecology of ideas might suggest that professional idea systems, like organic systems, evolve through transactions with their environment. In the process, they are subject to environmental selection for their survival and growth. Their usefulness to practitioners, teachers, students, and clients will ultimately determine their survival value. The authors hope, of course, that their ideas about the theory and practice of social work will possess sufficient interest and usefulness to influence further theoretical and practice developments by a wider and wider professional circle.

Clearly, then, the authors have collaborated at several levels. At one level there is a beginning quest to understand ecological concepts, to apply them to practice, and to suggest lines of further inquiry and development. At another level there is the search for a new professional commitment in response to rapidly changing social needs, values, and knowledge. All the authors use the same basic set of ideas, although they differ in the way they use them and in the particular practice areas they address. After a brief discussion of background issues, this chapter introduces some of those ideas as a frame of reference for the chapters that follow.

BACKGROUND ISSUES

Social work, historically, has been committed to a conception of its practice based upon a person-situation formulation. Through the years it has groped for ways to implement the dual commitment to helping people and changing environments, not altogether successfully. A salient reason for the difficulty lay in the absence of knowledge from which action principles could be derived for intervening in situations—principles that would match the richness of those available for working with people. By the 1950s the social sciences had developed more dynamic conceptions of social role, social class, ethnicity, family structure, deviance, and bureaucratic organizations. In the same period psychoanalytic theory consolidated its adaptive point of view, and new ideas about the ego and its relations with the environment rose to the fore. These developments were helpful to social work practitioners. Social functioning assumed importance as the object of professional concern, and the new focus was on the ego and its responses to the internal and external forces impinging upon it. The social environment seemed now to be more understandable, and diagnostic assessments were replete with references to social class factors, ethnicity, and family roles. Indeed, it was hoped that the concept of social role might become the link that would hold ego and environment together in the practitioner's formulations and actions.

Despite these theoretical developments there was little real change in many areas of practice, especially within the casework segment of practice. The new social science ideas contributed to diagnostic understanding but had little to offer for professional action. While diagnosis took environmental factors into account, intervention continued to be directed to changing behavior for the most part—to strengthening weak ego functioning, for example, or poor role performance. Role performance was not the link connecting ego and environment in the way that was anticipated. Useful for organizing multiple observations about social functioning, the concept of role contributed less to action principles for changing situations. This may have been due to the lack of social work knowledge about the environmental structures in which roles are embedded and which help shape role functioning.[2]

Since its beginning, direct practice had included an action concept, "environmental modification," as part of its framework of ideas. In general, this concept referred to very important forms of social provision: foster care and institutional care; discharge planning following hospitalization or institutionalization; financial and other "concrete" services; "manipulation" of relatives and others on the client's behalf; and—among group workers in particular—provision of experiences in the urban and natural environments such as excursions, camping, etc. Very often these forms of service were considered to be of a less than "professional" character. Acknowledged as important, they seemed to some to require less knowledge and skill than the forms of help directed to ego functioning and role performance at the psychological level. Environmental modification remained an undifferentiated and global concept and its procedures essentially unconnected to the complex structures which lay beneath the notion of "environment." Consequently, good intentions sometimes led to poor outcomes: children were sometimes removed from families unnecessarily, as Laird makes clear in her chapter in this volume; old people were institutionalized instead of natural support systems mobilized; "manipulated" relatives occasionally decompensated as the client's functioning improved, and "manipulated" teachers, physicians, or others complained that social workers did not understand organizational constraints on classroom or clinic activity.

Given the lack of knowledge for intervening in environmental forces, it is no surprise now, although it was then, that the revolutionary years of the 1960s produced criticism of social work's goals and methods. Casework, in particular, was accused of failing to serve the poor and other segments of the population whose problems were generated by environmental structures and processes. Although there was some truth in the criticism, there were also understandable reasons why social workers could do so little with respect to the environmental issues their clients or potential clients faced. First, with respect to problems on a massive scale such as structural poverty and racism, direct social practice per se can have little impact. Practitioners in social work policy and research can, perhaps, have some impact if they work collaboratively with other disciplines including law, economics, political science, and urban planning. While social work values call for efforts to eliminate all forms of social injustice, practice alone cannot solve these problems although some of the criticism in the 60s implied that indeed it could.

Second, with respect to environmental problems on a less-than-societal scale, no action principles were available from the environmental or behavioral sciences nor from social work's own lines of inquiry, except in two newly developed areas: milieu therapy and family therapy. Milieu therapy was designed for the environmental treatment of persons confined to mental hospitals and other total institutions. Family therapy proponents developed action principles with respect to that most intimate of environments—the family. It is curious that concepts and principles emerging out of the family therapy movement had little influence in social work practice until recent years except for a relatively small number of sophisticated practitioners often associated with psychiatrists or working in psychiatric settings. Even in the late 1970s some staff members in some family agencies continue to shun family treatment (and group services) in favor of work with individual members.

Outside of milieu therapy and family therapy—both limited in their application and influence—action principles for environmental intervention, beyond the global concept of "environmental modification," were simply not available to social workers in the 1960s. One example may suffice to demonstrate the significance of this void. Social science by the 1950s had already developed useful concepts about the functioning of complex organizations. Bureaucratic organizations are a dominant presence in the life space of social work clients and practitioners. Clients depend on educational, welfare, and health bureaucracies, sometimes for their very survival. Many, if not most practitioners work in bureaucratic structures and their practice is shaped by the nature of the organization's structure, policies, and procedures. Yet, until very recently, there were no action principles developed for intervening in organizations to change their structures, policies, or procedures on behalf of clients, or for achieving greater professional autonomy in meeting client need.

During the late 1960s and early 1970s a rapidly increasing and promising infusion of ideas from general systems theory took place in social work practice and theory-building.[3] Hope rose that these complex and abstract constructs would provide the action principles that social work practice was seeking. In a way they have. Many social workers will probably never again be comfortable with old concepts: linear causality, independent entities, separateness between systems, and notions of certainty. They will instead seek to understand feedback processes rather than simple causal chains, patterns and relations between entities rather than entities alone, boundaries and interfaces between systems rather than separateness, and their holistic thinking will be characterized by an emphasis on probability rather than certainty.

There are, I think, three shortcomings of general systems theory (which may only reflect the youthfulness of this system of thought), and they may be eliminated as conceptual development continues. The first is that, somewhat like ego theory and role theory before it, general systems theory provides rich insights into what is going on in the practitioner's domain of interest (the client's life space) but is not yet able to prescribe what to do about it. In fact, two practice questions we cannot answer are where, how, and when to intervene in a complex field of systems and what planned and unplanned consequences our interventions are likely to produce. Yet there are promising investigations by social workers and others into the notions of positive and negative feedback which may yield some action principles.[4] The notion of boundary work also seems fruitful.[5]

The second limitation in general systems theory for social work arises from a personal-professional bias among some practitioners, myself included. The language of systems is nonhuman. It is difficult to reconcile negentropy, heterostasis, equifinality, and deviation-amplifying mutual causal feedback processes with the endearing and infuriating qualities of human beings. The ideas beneath the terms are very important; the terms themselves have a certain mechanistic connotation that is not intended but is repugnant to some. Still, that's a personal matter and should not affect the incorporation of ideas important to practice if there's no way around the terminology.

The third limitation is closely related to the second. The constructs of general systems theory are at a very high level of abstraction in order to encompass a vast and exceedingly diverse range of phenomena from cells to societies. Hence it is difficult for the practitioner to apply the concepts to work, e.g., with an elderly woman grieving for the loss of her husband after 45 years of marriage. I think this may be why we hear the complaint from some social workers that general systems theory merely offers new and difficult words for the things we have always done in our practice. It's true that it offers new and difficult words, but I think the words refer to new and different elements that have heretofore escaped our professonal attention. The new terms permit an understanding of the complexity of transactions and present a different conception of causality, which affects how we view and handle phenomena in our practice domain.

These issues related to the person-situation commitment have led to the emerging interest in ecological ideas for social work. Moreover, within the societal context of the profession, ecological ideas are congruent with current scientific and humanistic themes and with practice trends in other human service professions.

THE ECOLOGICAL PERSPECTIVE

Ecology is a form of general systems theory: ecologists have always been systems thinkers concerned with the relations among living entities and between entities and other aspects of their environments. Ecology is cast in less abstract terms because of its biological rather than physical origins; for that reason it is closer to human phenomena. It rests on an evolutionary, adaptive view of human beings (and all organisms) in continuous transactions with the environment. As a metaphor for practice, the ecological perspective provides insights into the nature and consequences of such transactions both for human beings and for the physical and social environments in which they function. The perspective is concerned with the growth, development, and potentialities of human beings and with the properties of their environments that support or fail to support the expression of human potential. By clarifying the structure of the environment and the nature of its adaptive influence, the perspective appears to be admirably suited to the task of developing concepts and action principles for intervening in the environment.

A recent definition of social work is itself an ecological statement.[6] The professional purpose of social work arises from a dual, simultaneous concern for the adaptive potential of people and the "nutritive" qualities of their environments. In an ecological view, practice is directed toward improving the transactions between people and environments in order to enhance adaptive capacities *and* improve environments for all who function within them. To carry out the professional purpose requires a set of environmental interventions and a set of interventions into the transactions between people and environments to complement the sets available for intervening in coping patterns of people. The balance of this chapter represents a beginning effort to set forth some concepts from which such action principles may be derived.

ADAPTATION[7]

At the outset it is important to stress the meaning of adaptation as it is used throughout this volume since it is a central concept in the ecological perspective. Sometimes equated erroneously with passive adjustment to the status quo, the biological concept of adaptation refers to the *active* efforts of species over evolutionary time and of individuals over their life spans to reach a goodness-of-fit with their environments so they may survive, develop, and achieve reproductive success. In general, living organisms adapt to their environments by actively changing their environment so that it meets their needs, e.g., the nest-building of birds and the tilling of land by humans. Organisms also adapt to the environment by changing themselves biologically, including genetic change over evolutionary time through processes of mutation and environmental selection, and nongenetic change over the individual's life span through such passive physicochemical processes in human beings as adjustments in bodily temperature and blood pressure in reaction to environmental changes. Such nongenetic biological changes must remain within species-specific ranges, however, if the organism is to survive and develop. And, third, many species of life, including human beings, adapt to environmental changes and challenges by migrating to new environments. So human adaptation, while it includes passive or reactive changes in the self to conform to environmental pressures and demands, also includes active changes in the environment so that it will conform to human aims, needs, and aspirations.

Adaptation is a reciprocal process, however, and the environment is dynamically involved. The physical environment is constantly changing—not only as the result of the biotic action of all the forms of life, especially human life—but as the result of short- and long-term processes of climate, erosion, earthquakes, etc. Human beings and other organisms must respond to environmentally induced changes in addition to those they themselves have initiated. These reciprocal processes of adaptation result in a goodness-of-fit for both organism and environment when they "work," and undermine the fit-ness of either the organism or the environment or both when they don't "work." Thus organism and environment are regarded as a unitary system each part of which, while different, can only be understood in its interdependence with the other.

As stated earlier, adaptation is both an evolutionary process and a process that occurs over the individual life span. In human beings, the evolutionary aspect is now very different from what it once was. Until about 100,000 years ago, human beings adapted to changes in the environment through organic (biological) evolution just as all organisms do. Since then, however, their evolution has been more social than organic through the primary adaptive mechanism of culture. With the development of a large brain, language, and the capacity to symbolize, human beings' cultural adaptations superseded genetic change as the principal means of increasing the fit-ness of the species. Organic evolution became less and less necessary as humans became capable of effecting technological changes in their environments.

There are two problems in this for humankind. Environmental damage as energy use increased in intensity, particularly in the era since the Industrial Revolution, threatens our quality of life. The technological environments (both physical and social), which are very different from the environment in which humans' biological and psychological equipment evolved, threaten to exceed our adaptive limits biologically and psychologically. Dubos suggests we are paying for our high degree of biological plasticity—our ability to adapt to almost anything—with the diseases of civilization: physical illnesses that resist medical control, interpersonal discomforts, neurosis and psychosis, and alienation from other human beings and from the world of nature.[8]

Yet of all forms of life, humans are the least subject to either biological or environmental determinism. Humans have degrees of freedom from both biological and environmental limits to select and choose courses of action, and humans can be creative or destructive. Yet the relative freedom from determinism is the basis for optimism. Planning, choices, and action are possible to reduce technological pollution and the pollution of social injustice. With heightened public concern and growing knowledge, the consequences of intervention into physical and social environments can be anticipated and their destructive effects avoided or minimized. This is admittedly visionary, but there is comfort to be taken from efforts to develop new social designs and life styles and to improve rural and urban land use, from the spreading commitment to social values among scientists, and from the demand among people everywhere to have greater control over their lives and environments and greater diversity in their options.

Returning to the issue of determinism, an ecological perspective views humans as active, goal-seeking, purposive beings who make decisions and choices and take actions guided by the memory of past experiences and anticipation of future possibilities. This is in contrast to the tendencies toward psychic determinism in psychoanalytic theory, toward environmental determinism in behavioral theory, and toward genetic determinism in sociobiology. Humans are indeed programmed genetically, but for a range of possible lives and not just one fixed or predestined life. They are indeed conditioned by environmental circumstances so that the range of genetically based possibilities is narrowly or more fully expressed as the case may be. Human beings can, however, choose the environment in which they will function—within certain degrees of freedom—and which will then shape the expression of their genetic programs.[9] In this sense free will, willful action, "interferes" with both environmental and genetic determinism. A disturbing observation to be made is, of course, that large segments of the population here and in other parts of the world are deprived by other human beings (society) of the opportunity to make choices and to take action, thus making it more difficult or impossible for much of the potentiality of their genetic constitutions to be expressed. Again, though, an optimistic observation is that, with free will, the individual human being has diverse potentials for growth, provided environmental inputs release them. Similarly, environments have potential to support human diversity, provided humans use their capacities to bring out environmental possibilities.

Within contemporary psychoanalytic thought, ego psychology has moved away from the rigidities of psychic determinism and has developed ideas of the human's relative freedom from libidinal and aggressive drives, on the one hand, and relative freedom from environmental pressures on the other. Such autonomy is achieved and maintained by optimal inputs from both the internal and external worlds. The Eriksonian framework of developmental stages suggests how the autonomous ego develops.[10]

Personality theories tend to be culture-bound in some respects. Yet particular adaptive achievements such as identity formation, autonomy, competence, and relatedness to others seem to be universal, although their particular substance or content clearly shifts across cultures and historical eras. They are useful foci in considering adaptive capacities and patterns in an ecologically oriented practice although other human attributes might be useful instead of or in addition to these. Several of the chapters in this volume examine these particular attributes and their component qualities in detail, so only a few general observations about them will be made here.

Biologically, all organisms seek a degree of *autonomy* from the environment; human beings, with the vast amount and complexity of information contained in their DNA, have the greatest degree of such autonomy. As was mentioned earlier, human beings also have the greatest relative autonomy from their biological structure because of culture. Psychologically, human beings seek relative freedom from external control and inner pressures.

All organisms "seek" effective interaction with the environment for survival. Human beings strive toward *competence,* or the capacity to have an effect on the environment in spheres of life important to the individual and the cultural group. Competence refers to a wide range of abilities and skills with respect to the "inner life" of feeling, impulse, wish, and thought and the "outer life" of interaction with the environment. The content of those abilities and skills varies with age, sex, and culture.

Biologically most forms of life—except for lower organisms that reproduce asexually—need the cooperation of other members of their species for reproductive purposes and, among many higher animals, for cooperative efforts related to food, defense, and rearing of the young. In human being, *relatedness* is both a biological and a psychological imperative. The human infant cannot survive without the loving care of adults which must continue over a long period of socialization and integration into wider and wider circles of relatedness. Caring for and being cared for are deeply felt human needs as long as life lasts. Separation from or loss of an intimate attachment figure are excruciatingly painful experiences from infancy to old age. Loneliness, social isolation, and the self-hate of those who fear attachments are also painful states.[11]

The sense of *identity,* so important to human beings, may not be characteristic of other forms of life* since it seems related to consciousness of the self and its continuity as well as its inevitable death. It is related to the distinctive human capacity for culture and symbolization. In some societies, one's sense of identity is less an individual conception and more a tribal or a familial one, although all three elements are probably present to some degree, regardless of the society being considered. In our own society, sex, age, color, and other biological attributes have a profound impact on the sense of identity, arising as it does out of interaction with others and their perceptions and expectations.

Identity not only arises out of human relatedness, but influences the nature of relationships. It also arises from experiences of au-

---

* The possibility of some form of self-concept among the higher animals, especially the primates and cetaceans, is an emerging matter of conjecture.

tonomy and competence and, in turn, affects those attributes. Indeed, identity, competence, autonomy, and human relatedness are inter-dependent. Issues of autonomy are worked out in the contexts of human relatedness and experiences in the exercise of competence, and in the process of identity formation. Relatedness is the essence of identity, but it also reflects the kind of autonomy that permits one to be either dependent on others or independent as the situation requires. The fact that these human qualities—and all others—are the out-comes of interactions between the individual's genetic program and his or her environmental circumstances brings us to an examination of how the environment and the nature of its properties either support or stifle the development of human potentialities.

THE ENVIRONMENT

The idea of environment is complex in itself since it is not always easy—even conceptually—to distinguish between what is inner and what is outer. Leaving such philosophical and scientific issues aside, a conceptualization of the environment for social work practice must take into account physical aspects, social aspects, and the interplay between them and the culture. The *physical* environment comprises the natural world and the built world. The *social* environment com-prises the network of human relations at various levels of organiza-tion. Both the physical and social environments are affected by the cultural values, norms, knowledge, and beliefs that pattern social in-teraction and determine how we use and respond to the physical envi-ronment.

Cultural values, for example, shape the kinds of buildings we con-struct, and the buildings in turn shape the social interaction that takes place within them. Our views of the poor, the mentally ill, and other groups, for example, influence the location and design of such insti-tutions as mental hospitals, low-income housing projects, geriatric fa-cilities, and treatment cottages. Their location and design then influ-ence the self-image and self-esteem of those who reside in the facilities. They shape the relationships among the residents and be-tween them and staff, or between them and the surrounding commu-nity.

Both the natural and built worlds are important components of a sense of identity. Many persons, for example, have a deeply rooted sense of place, and their geographic origins are part of their sense of self. Others feel a kinship with the world of nature that is part of their sense of identity. Others have strong attachments to aspects of the built world such as a home or treasured objects, the loss of which is often experienced as an assault on identity. Both the natural and built aspects of the physical environment also provide opportunities and obstacles to the development of competence, relatedness, and autonomy.

The social environment became more differentiated for social workers by the introduction of the concepts of family structures and functions being influenced by cultural variations, the society, and physical settings. More recently, the concepts of social network and of bureaucratically organized service and work systems have further differentiated the social environment and expanded our understanding of its structure.

A social network is not simply the aggregate of an individual's social relations, but represents a set of communication paths and relational linkages such that the individual's behavior is influenced by the connections between individuals in the network, including those to whom he or she may not be directly linked. Included in the concept also are systems of mutual aid, self-help groups, and natural helpers. The concept leads to action principles for the practitioner.

Service and work organizations are salient features of the social environment which human beings have created to meet adaptive needs and goals and to which they must then adapt. Concepts pertaining to decision-making and authority structures, formal and informal systems, latent functions and goal displacement, statuses and roles established for the allocation of resources and tasks, and organizational relations with the political and economic environment contribute a clearer understanding of how organizations work, and lead to action principles regarding organizational interventions.

The social environment, interacting with the physical environment and the culture, affects the development of identity, competence, autonomy, and relatedness. Families, networks, and formal organizations may provide or withhold resources and opportunities for the development of competence and autonomy; they may contribute positive and/or negative components to the sense of identity, and they may provide for or inhibit the growth of human relatedness.

The natural, built, and social worlds are further characterized by textures of space and time. The anthropology of space highlights cultural variations in the way people respond to space and to the arrangement of objects in space, and how their spatial behaviors influence and are influenced by the physical and social environments.[12] Ward geography, for example, has been shown to affect the patterns of social interaction of patients and staff.[13] Transactional issues of crowding and isolation—psychosocial states—are more completely understood through recourse to spatial concepts borrowed from ethology, such as territoriality, home range, buffer zone, and personal distance.[14] Spatial behaviors—mediated by age, sex, culture, experience, emotion, and physical condition—are of import to the social worker since they bear directly on issues of identity formation, autonomy, competence, and relatedness. They also help clarify the nature of boundaries in the transactional area between person and environment.

Time, too, provides varying textures for the natural, built, and social worlds.[15] Biological rhythms pervade all forms of life, including human beings, through evolutionary processes of adaptation to diurnal, seasonal, and even cosmic rhythms of the physical environment. Certain social cycles of time created by human beings may violate these temporal aspects of our biological nature. Institutions for congregate living, hospitals, schools, social agencies and work sites, for example, have their own temporal structures which may or may not fit humans' biological rhythms. Orientations to time vary across cultures in the emphasis placed on' past, present, or future time and in the value accorded punctuality or the careful husbanding of temporal resources. There are also psychological differences in how people perceive pacing, tempo, and duration in life's activities. Thus time, like space, may be a resource, or a source of conflict and stress. Many issues of family life, for example, need to be understood in their temporal and spatial contexts. Hartman's chapter in this volume is, in part, concerned with the influence of figures and events from the past on current relationships as a family changes over time and moves across space.

This discussion has presented some transactions that occur between people and environments, some adaptive outcomes, and some observations about the structure of the environment itself. What remains to be examined are the negative human outcomes of people-environment transactions. These can be rather easily described since they are painfully apparent to all social workers. They are, however, more difficult to analyze since knowledge is still in its beginning stages. At the descriptive level, primate studies, observation of human infants in institutions, sensory deprivation experiments, and the experiences of persons in extreme situations (e.g., castaways, polar explorers, solitary prisoners) demonstrate apparent linkages between cognitive, emotional, biological, and social impairments and nonnutritive properties of the environment.[16]

Such observations and experiences suggest that perceptual, motor, and intellectual development and functioning can be undermined when the individual is deprived of sensory and cognitive input from the environment or of contact with other human beings. Our practice experience tells us that these environmental circumstances are also noxious to identity, autonomy, competence, and relatedness. Fisher's essay examines the consequences of such bland environments for hospital patients, particularly the terminally ill.

In the realm of public health, the effects of malnutrition before and after birth have been established, for example, and connections between substandard housing and disease are known. In the social-psychological realm, however, connections are far less clear. We know little about the optimal level, balance, and timing of nutritive environmental elements required for the expression of genetic potential. Little is known about how such inputs interact with individual factors of age, sex, culture, and experience to support psychosocial development, or even whether reversibility of damaging effects exerted by nonnutritive or missing elements is possible. In his essay, Bloom examines these issues in social prevention.

Theories of stress and coping are helpful in the absence of accurate knowledge of what constitutes a nutritive environment. Stress is conceptualized as an upset in the adaptive balance between person and environment[17] as a consequence of inadequate, noxious, or excessive stimuli or demands that are perceived to be beyond the usual adaptive patterns available to the person. Ambiguities and contradictions exist in the theory in its present stage of development but, in general, stress is conceived as a transactional phenomenon comprising internal and/or external stimuli and personal and environmental responses.[18] Coping is also a transactional phenomenon since the personal abilities involved in coping with stress are themselves dependent upon specific environmental inputs.[19] Ideas about stress and coping suggest action principles directed to the environment and to the transactional area between person and environment. Draper's essay in this volume uses ideas of stress and coping to examine the social functions of black language.

PRACTICE IMPLICATIONS

Returning to the definition of social work practice cited earlier, the professional purpose of social work arises from a dual, simultaneous concern for the adaptive potential of people and the nutritive qualities of their environments. In an ecological view, practice is directed toward improving the transactions between people and environments in order to enhance adaptive capacities *and* improve environments for all who function within them. Knowledge required to understand the complexities of people, environments, and the nature of their transactions draws upon evolutionary biology, environmental psychology, ethology, and organizational theory as well as disciplines more familiar to social workers. The value base of the practice refers to the kinds of transactions social work "prefers" for people and environments: those that express people's adaptive potential and environmental responsiveness and diversity. Both knowledge and values support the professional objectives of 1) releasing, developing, and strengthening people's innate capacity for growth and creative adaptation; 2) removing environmental blocks and obstacles to growth and adaptation; and 3) positively increasing the nutritive properties of the environment. Those transactions between people and environments are sought that will nourish both parts of the interdependent system.

The knowledge base and value position generate certain practice principles based upon life processes. Goldstein's chapter demonstrates how the knowledge base, value position, and practice principles combine to produce a practice form that differs in certain respects from other forms of practice. Differences are found especially in these areas: the definition of problems, needs, and objectives; the structure of the client-worker relationship; the nature of the action undertaken within an integrated method of service to individuals, families, and groups; and organizational arrangements that support the practice.

Because adaptation, stress and coping occur as transactional processes, human needs and problems are viewed as outcomes of those transactions. They are defined as problems in living arising from life transitions (developmental and social), interpersonal processes, and environmental issues.[20] Emphasis is placed on progressive rather than regressive forces, on health rather than on "sickness," and on the potential for growth.

The difference in the worker's relationship with clients—as individuals, families, and groups—arises from the interest in identity, autonomy, competence, and relatedness. Mutuality and reciprocity are built into the relationship as a way of promoting those attributes.[21] What is sought is not an egalitarian relationship since each participant brings different knowledge, skill, and experience to the activity, but rather a relationship that manifests openness, authenticity, honesty, naturalness, and human caring.

Professional action to achieve the objective of improved transactions may be directed to the person, the environment, or the interaction of the two. Action directed to the person will include procedures to increase self-esteem, reduce psychic discomfort, strengthen adaptive patterns, teach coping skills, provide information, etc.[22] Action directed to the environment includes providing opportunities for action, decision-making, and mastery, and restructuring situations for a better adaptive "fit." Analysis of these procedures and examples of their application are presented in the chapter by Maluccio. Environmental action also includes procedures to mobilize and support mutual aid systems within social networks, or to help clients extricate themselves from nonnutritive networks, or to connect isolated persons to existing or created networks. Swenson's chapter examines the concept of social network and applies these procedures. Environmental action also includes efforts to influence organizations, including the worker's own, to be more responsive to client needs. This involves the use of political skills of influencing, which include locating organizational barriers to service, identifying the forces likely to support or to resist change in policy or procedure, analyzing the power and decision-making structures, developing bases of influence, and devising strategies for introducing, implementing, and institutionalizing change.[23] Some of these skills are alluded to in Grosser's chapter along with his emphasis on worker and client participation in organizational processes.

Environmental action will continue to rely on the creative use of available resources and efforts to create them where absent. Traditionally, social workers, alone among the helping professions, have had the knowledge and skill required to connect people to resources. Despite the fact that social workers themselves have sometimes devalued this aspect of service, it is one that clients esteem and one that other professions (e.g., nursing) are beginning to emulate and even to take over in certain settings.

Action can be directed to the physical environment by helping clients to improve the quality of their lives with respect to spatial and temporal arrangements in schools, work sites, institutions and private dwellings, and agency settings.[24] The natural world may be used as a helping instrument in providing respite and growth experiences in rural or urban settings. Cataldo's essay highlights the use of a wilderness setting in the strengthening of identity, competence, autonomy, and relatedness.

Action directed to modifying maladaptive interpersonal processes includes helping families and groups recognize and change patterns of relationships and communications that interfere with the successful resolution of adaptive tasks faced by the collectivity and/or its individual members.[25] These skills are described and illustrated in the essay by Aponte and the essay by Miller and Solomon.

The fourth difference in an ecologically oriented practice refers to agency arrangements. Differential uses of space and time, for example, require greater organizational flexibility that will seek to be responsive to client need. Services and programs need to be situated in the life space of people when and where stress is experienced. They need to be structured in ways that are congruent with the life styles, interests, and tempos of the population, and they must provide for differential entry at individual, group, family, and organizational levels. Where possible, arrangements are needed for helping people before the stress generated by problems in living becomes intractable, recognizing that rapid social change results in the rapid obsolescence of people's usual adaptive patterns. Creativity is needed in working out arrangements that will take account of the unique skills, qualities, and the differential training and experience of varied levels of social work manpower so the many tasks can be achieved. Janchill's essay describes such ecologically oriented arrangements within an existing agency.

Calling ecology a subversive subject, the Cornell ecologist Paul B. Sears asks, ''Is ecology a phase of science of limited interest and utility? Or, if taken seriously as an instrument for the long-run welfare of mankind, would it endanger the assumptions and practices accepted by modern societies, whatever their doctrinal commitments?'' [26] The ecological perspective—a metaphor of ecology—may very well endanger some of the assumptions and practices of the social work profession. Ecological thinking challenges not only practice, but also the concepts that have structured social work service arrangements in the past. Whenever services have failed to meet need as it is experienced by users of the services, social work has sometimes responded by providing more of the same kinds of services.[27] This kind of change has usually not resulted in resolution of problems and has sometimes created additional ones. Totally new solutions are required, that go beyond present assumptions and practices to find creative adaptations and novel arrangements for providing services.[28] In the chapters that follow, the authors provide examples of such creative adaptations in social work practice and programs. They demonstrate that social work encourages growth and improves environments.

NOTES

1. Florian Znaniecki, *The Social Role of the Man of Knowledge* (New York: Columbia University Press, 1940).

2. The most recent work on action principles is George Brager and Stephen Holloway, *Changing Human Service Organizations: Politics and Practice* (New York: The Free Press, 1978).

3. The ideas had been the focus of interest for two prominent social work educators a decade earlier, but were not picked up until the 1960s. See Gordon Hearn, *Theory Building in Social Work* (Toronto: University of Toronto Press, 1958); and Werner A. Lutz, *Concepts and Principles Underlying Social Work Practice* (New York: National Association of Social Workers, 1956).

4. See, for example, Lynn Hoffman, "Deviation-Amplifying Processes in Natural Groups," in Jay Haley (ed.), *Changing Families* (New York: Grune and Stratton, 1971).

5. Gordon Hearn, "Social Work as Boundary Work," mimeographed paper presented at the Third Annual Institute on Services to Families and Children, School of Social Work, University of Iowa April 1970.

6. William E. Gordon, "Basic Constructs for an Integrative and Generative Conception of Social Work," in Gordon Hearn (ed.), *The General Systems Approach: Contributions Toward an Holistic Conception of Social Work* (New York: The Council on Social Work Education, 1969), pp. 5–11. I have taken some liberties with Gordon's formulation, including, for example, the substitution of "adaptive potential" and "adaptive capacities" for "coping patterns."

7. The material in this section draws upon the work of several scientists: René Dubos, *So Human an Animal* (New York: Charles Scribner's Sons, 1968) and *Beast or Angel?* (New York: Charles Scribner's Sons, 1974); George Gaylord Simpson, *The Meaning of Evolution* (New Haven: Yale University Press, 1949); Theodosius Dobzhansky, "The Myths of Genetic Predestination and Tabula Rasa," *Perspectives in Biology and Medicine* 19, no. 2 (Chicago: The University of Chicago Press, January 1976); and Jacques Monod, *Chance and Necessity* (New York: Alfred A. Knopf, 1971).

8. Dubos, *So Human,* p. 56.

9. Ibid., p. 49.

10. Erik H. Erikson, *Childhood and Society* (New York: W. W. Norton, 1963).

11. For excellent discussions of human relatedness, see Otto Will, "Human Relatedness and the Schizophrenic Reaction," *Psychiatry* 22, no. 3 (August 1959), pp. 1205–23; and Robert Weiss, *Loneliness, The Experience of Emotional and Social Isolation* (Cambridge: MIT Press 1973).

12. Edward T. Hall, *The Hidden Dimension* (New York: Doubleday Anchor, 1969).

13. Robert Sommer, *Personal Space* (Englewood Cliffs, New Jersey: Prentice-Hall, 1969)

14. For a helpful summary of these concepts and their usefulness in understanding interpersonal processes, see Irwin Altman, *The Environment and Social Behavior* (Monterey, California: Brooks/Cole, 1975).

15. Carel B. Germain, "Time, an Ecological Variable in Social Work Practice," *Social Casework* 57, no. 7 (July 1976), pp. 419–26.

16. See, for example, Jane Goodall, *In The Shadow of Man* (Boston: Houghton-Mifflin, 1971); Sally Provence and Rose Lipton, *Infants in Instititions* (New York: International Universities Press, 1962); Philip Solomon et al., *Sensory Deprivation* (Cambridge: Harvard University Press, 1965); Stuart Miller, "Ego Autonomy in Sensory Deprivation, Isolation, and Stress," *The International Journal of Psychoanalysis* 93, Part 1 (1962), pp. 1–20.

17. This adaptive balance is always a moving one. Human needs and goals change, and the environment itself changes. Change is continuous, although its rates may sometimes be imperceptible. Change itself is often the means for perserving stability.

18. David Mechanic, "Social Structure and Personal Adaptation: Some Neglected Dimensions," in George V. Coelho et al. (eds.), *Coping and Adaptation* (New York: Basic Books, 1974), pp. 32–44.

19. Ibid.

20. These ideas are developed in detail in Carel B. Germain and Alex Gitterman, *The Life Model of Social Work Practice* (New York: Columbia University Press [forthcoming]).

21. Ibid.

22. Ibid.

23. Ibid. See also Brager and Holloway, *Changing Human Service.*

24. Germain and Gitterman, *The Life Model.*

25. Ibid.

26. Paul B. Sears, "Ecology—A Subversive Subject," *Bioscience* 14, no. 7 (1964).

27. Philip Klein, *From Philanthropy to Social Welfare* (San Francisco: Jossey-Bass, 1968). Klein was referring to casework.

28. Paul Watzlawick et al., *Change: Principles of Problem Formulation and Problem Resolution* (New York: W. W. Norton, 1974), pp. 13–28.

1

PRACTICE
APPLICATIONS

1 The Hospitalized Terminally Ill Patient: An Ecological Perspective

DENA FISHER

Fisher is concerned with the hospital environment's potential power to advance or retard the efforts of patients and their families to cope with mutual tasks as the terminal patient faces death. Coping is an active process and, to be successful, requires environmental support of the patient's dignity, sense of worth, and competence.

Yet the very status of the patient is characterized by a high degree of passivity, some of which is necessary for treatment, but some of which often seems more related to the convenience of the staff. The patient is expected to cooperate with staff in an unquestioning way, to give up his autonomy and to endure physical discomfort without complaining, voicing his fears, or demanding too much. In return, he will be considered a "good" patient, deserving of staff attention to his needs. He is further expected to bend all his efforts to keeping his condition under control by following medical and nursing orders, even though he may not understand the reasons for them or they violate his cultural norms. He is expected to separate from his family, friends, and familiar surroundings, and to establish trusting relationships with a battery of strangers having immediate and very intimate access to his body and bodily functions. In some instances, he may be treated as an interesting medical curiosity rather than as a total person.

The professional function of the medical social worker is directed to strengthening the adaptive capacities of patients and their families, and helping to create nutritive environmental conditions that will support coping tasks. As Fisher indicates, providing a nutritive environment may involve protecting the patient from humiliating experiences that can weaken coping, affect the self-image, and undermine competence. It may involve creating opportunities for real and symbolic (cognitive) action on the part of even the very ill patient, so that coping is strengthened and adaptive functioning supported. If feasible (during remission phases, for instance) it may include the use of groups in which patients learn coping skills from one another, or the use of relatives' groups in which families help sustain each other through the exchange of information, experiences, and counsel. It always includes interprofessional collaboration and, sometimes, the use of organizational change strategies in order to increase the responsiveness of the service to patient needs.

While the current literature on thanatology supports staff openness in communication with the patient and family concerning diagnosis and prognosis, there are some patients and families who must rely on denial as protection against overwhelming anxiety and depression. In some of these cases, the social worker may gradually be able to relax the need for denial, to let in awareness of reality bit by bit. As more and more of the anxiety and depression is accepted, patients and families can begin their tasks of coping with manageable pieces of reality. For some, postponing full recognition at the beginning can lead to healthy adaptation later.

Fisher points the way to restructuring hospital social work services so they will support the coping efforts of the dying patient and his family, and help sustain the staff in their efforts to cope with reciprocal tasks and needs.

—C.B.G.

THE ATTEMPT to develop an all-encompassing theoretical framework for social work practice is gathering momentum as the effectiveness of practice is being questioned.[1] The turning toward general systems theory and the ecological perspective to meet this need has been widely considered as a way of providing that framework without discarding traditional social work skills, values, and knowledge.

In my view the ecological perspective is particularly useful in applying systems concepts to social work practice in hospitals. Thus my analysis will first consider the effects of the hospital setting on ego autonomy, competence, and adaptation for terminally ill patients and their families. I will then describe how these concepts were used by the social work department in one community hospital to develop a program aimed at achieving a better fit between person and environment. The intent of the discussion is to add "qualities of the impinging environment"[2] to the social work unit of attention, since much of the literature still presents coping behavior within the person as the important issue.[3] I believe the expanded unit of attention will help us provide a more nutritive environment for all individuals involved in the hospital system.

THE ECOLOGICAL PERSPECTIVE AND
THE LIFE MODEL

Erik Erikson defines integrity in the final stage of life as "an acceptance of the fact that one's life is one's own responsibility" and despair/disgust as ". . . the feeling that the time is' . . . too short . . . to try out alternative roads to integrity . . . [and] chronic contemptuous displeasure with particular institutions and particular people. . . ."[4] The ecological perspective suggests that one must look seriously at those institutions and people to see how they create despair and disgust through the destruction of ego autonomy. The life model ". . . may provide us with the necessary action concepts" particularly in "altering elements of the environment."[5] It offers social workers important tools to assist the terminally ill patients in the hospital environment.

In developing an ecologically oriented program for the terminally ill in a community hospital, it is important to consider the need to enhance the individual's competence in dealing with the environment. Since social competence has been defined as ". . . the ability of persons to participate effectively in the legitimate activities of their society,"[6] client participation in planning within the hospital environment must be legitimized.

One patient with whom I worked was a 54-year-old accountant, Mr. Smith, who set as his goal to live to celebrate his wife's birthday. When I spoke to him, rather than offering platitudes, I suggested we start planning the celebration. Mr. Smith looked at me most peculiarly, acknowledging that we knew both that "celebrating" was out of character for what he called the "cancer ward" and that he had been told that he might not live that long. Despite the fact that the celebration violated hospital protocol and that his prognosis was grave, from his hospital bed Mr. Smith organized a beautiful celebration which resulted in the staff institutionalizing similar activities for other patients at appropriate times. Mr. Smith's sense of social competence was remarkable as he stated that he did not think he had the physical strength (which he did not) to do anything else in his life. Had I offered to "do" anything beyond the verbal planning with him, his last statement of autonomy and competence would have been impaired. (He did die soon after the celebration.) He also helped the nursing staff to see the need of a terminally ill cancer patient to experience accomplishment at a time when everything else has been taken from him.

It is important in social work practice to consider with the client the appropriate size of the ecological unit. In the above-cited example much of the discussion involved defining this unit. As the worker, I was aware that Mr. Smith's plan to invite all the relatives from far-off Ohio, the entire staff of the hospital, and all his friends could mean failure of his plan. His decision to reduce the size of the unit of attention to his immediate family and close fellow employees resulted in a positive experience.

It is also important to look at the location of the ecological unit once the size is determined. The value of this view is that the worker can consider the possibility of change from within rather than auto-matically assuming that the hospital (substitute welfare system, prison, etc.) is totally unresponsive to the needs of the patient (recipi-ent, prisoner, etc.) Mr. Smith had originally planned to contact the administrator to demand that he be allowed to have a party. He revised his plan to involve only the nursing unit, as he rightly as-sessed that he could cause a "no" that might not be circumvented.

The value of the ecological perspective in social work practice is its emphasis on understanding the healthy adaptation of individuals. Without that understanding there is no explanation as to why Mr. Smith lived to celebrate his wife's birthday and no longer. The cancer had in fact metastasized to the brain. Following Mr. Smith's death four days after the party, the autopsy report seemed to indicate that he should have been delirious, yet that was not the case.

It appears, therefore, that the health of an individual cannot be explained by the state of his biological mechanism alone. A medical social worker and an internist at the same hospital collaborated closely in helping a depressed 94-year-old man, Mr. Jones, who needed to go from the hospital to a nursing home because his acute condition had subsided. He could not return to his apartment because round-the-clock home health services, which he would need in order to live alone, were unavailable in his community. Mr. Jones dreaded living in a nursing home, and his condition rapidly deteriorated after he entered. The autopsy failed to reveal the immediate cause of death, and the doctor felt that the patient had just stopped living one day. René Dubos in *Mirage of Health* discusses the phenomenon:

. . . health and happiness cannot be absolute and permanent values, however careful the social and medical planning. Biological success in all its manifestations is a measure of fitness, and fitness requires never-ending efforts of adaptation to the total environment, which is ever changing.[7]

This must be understood by the social worker who deals daily with life and death issues in the hospital environment.

Many medical social work departments assign discharge planning—particularly to nursing homes—to workers with a B.A. or lower training because of the view that such work is mostly concrete and dispositional.[8] I see this as a serious and possibly deadly mistake which fails to take seriously the importance of the "qualities of the impinging environment."

THE HOSPITAL ENVIRONMENT AND
THE INDIVIDUAL

In applying the ecological perspective to the acute-care hospital one is struck by the parallel to the literature on total institutions.[9] Most hospital personnel would be horrified if they read survivors' accounts of experiences in extreme situations and were shown how similar it can be to the terminally ill patients' experience in their "progressive" hospitals.[10]

The process of identity destruction can begin in the physician's office. Mr. Green, a patient whom I knew, reported overhearing his doctor call the Admitting Office, stating that he had "a possible brain tumor" for admission. Mr. Green had been told only that he was going to the hospital for routine tests for his headaches. Aside from the destructive nature of this manner of communicating such a possibly serious condition, Mr. Green suffered the added indignity of entering the hospital as a disease and not as Mr. John Green. In the Admitting Office to which he then went with overwhelming fear, he signed innumerable forms including permission for all kinds of possible surgery. He also indicated his next of kin and signed all his valuables and identification over to the hospital safe. (All this for routine tests.) He was given a wrist label which could not be removed easily.

Although Mr. Green drove to the hospital from his work as a top level business executive and walked into the hospital, he was not permitted to walk to his room. A "pink lady" cajoled him into a wheelchair with platitudes of reassurance—possibly as a mother might treat her child on the first day of school. He was rolled to a room and had his clothing removed. For security purposes, his family was told to take the clothes home. Mr. Green was given a gown which did not quite close in the back, making it embarrassing to leave his room. He was discouraged from wearing his own pajamas since it is harder for the busy physician to quickly examine his body.

In some cases, the patient is put to bed with the siderails up as an infant is kept in a crib for his own protection. Such patients must ask permission even to go to the bathroom. If the call bell is not answered, the patient may be labeled "incontinent." Eventually such behavior may necessitate having a catheter. As the days proceed there is a slow whittling away of independent functioning. A group of physicians may enter the room, remove the patient's sheet, examine his body, and talk over, about, and through him. Since patients may not always be told their diagnoses, language is guarded. Even charts are carefully worded since the patient has the legal right to his medical record. The patient does not question because at least there is attention to his problem. During an earlier experience in the hospital, he may remember, there were days when no one came to see him at all, his private physician being a busy man. David Rapaport describes "the lack of unobserved privacy coupled with the steady shower of information and orders, the lack of personal expression, the changing records . . ., the mortal fear of punishment . . .," [11] as robbing the ego of its autonomy so that the individual is totally subject to the whim of the environment. Actually, Rapaport's statement is about life in *1984,* but it also describes life in some modern, progressive, community hospitals.

The mortal fear of punishment, for example, cannot be minimized. I supervised a medical social worker who was working with the family of 16-year-old Susan Brown, a comatose patient with Hodgkin's disease. The Brown family reported to the social worker many complaints about the nursing care, all of which the social worker knew to be accurate. The social worker could not mobilize the family to discuss the complaints with their physician because of their fear of what they called "spite nursing." Miss Brown could not live four hours without nursing care, and the family could not afford private duty nurses. The family made the worker promise she would not pass the complaint on; they merely wanted her to see how totally dependent they were on people they felt did not care.

The effects of physical milieu observed in the psychiatric hospital also apply in the medical setting. Orientation to space and time are disrupted. "Orientation in space and time are such important ego functions that, in the extreme case, many normal people become disturbed and even hallucinated [sic] when all physical cues are removed."[12] The patient in his bed with the side rails up loses his physical orientation quickly. Even patients who have no history of mental disturbance and, in fact, do not seem otherwise disturbed have been known to ask what floor they are on or even where the hospital is.

Patients are also transported from room to operating room, to X-Ray department, etc., never even leaving their bed or stretcher. The image in Alexander Solzhenitsyn's *Cancer Ward* of the sound of the elevator which took bodies to the morgue is vivid;[13] the patients there demonstrated their need to know what had happened to whom. A nurse once reported to me how she had caused tremendous anxiety because she had told a patient he would soon be going "up" to the operating room as she gave him his pre-operative medication. It happened that she was new to the hospital and the operating rooms were "down," not up as had been the case where she had previously worked. When the patient was rolled into the elevator and the elevator went down, he—already quite groggy from the medication—was sure he was dying, surgery had been canceled and he was going to the morgue. The nurse relating the story realized how important the scheme of the physical setting was to the patient's orientation and identity.

The issue of time is important if the patient is to maintain any sense of personal future. Psychiatric consultants frequently write that the patient did not know what day it was on a routine mental status exam. I have often wondered how patients could possibly know the day, date, or time routinely. The patient is placed in an environment where every day is exactly the same. The terminally ill patient often receives intravenous feedings and cannot even gauge the time of day by meals. One patient reported to her social worker that she "enjoyed" cobalt therapy because she could tell when Saturday and Sunday came. (Cobalt was only available five days per week.)

I remember my own experience with hospitalization. Following the birth of my son late one Saturday night I was rolled to an empty room. I had missed several meals and reported to the attendant that I was quite hungry. I was told that breakfast would be served at 7 A.M. the next morning. I awakened at 7:30 A.M. (having secretly kept my watch) and could hear no signs of activity I knew to be appropriate for that time, such as change of shift, noise of meal trays, etc. Panic actually occurred before I learned that the clocks had been turned back due to Daylight Savings Time. Had I known it was only 6:30 A.M. my orientation would not have been disturbed. Elizabeth Kübler-Ross describes how the patient seeks to find out the rules, the system of rewards and punishments, timing, etc., in a system that does not even have an informal community of patients such as can exist in a mental hospital or prison.[14] I was alone and literally afraid of the consequences of ringing my call bell for such a trivial question as "what is the time?" The terminally ill patient cannot overuse the call bell because of the extreme dependence upon the nurse for all personal needs.

The destructive effects of time and space disorientation in the hospital setting include a loss of self-esteem and identity. If the patient cannot even figure out what day it is, it seems unlikely that ego-supportive psychotherapy related to past accomplishments will be meaningful. An emphasis, instead, on the immediate tasks and the integrative capacity of the ego suggests that, while a review of past accomplishments is important, the crucial element is immediate accomplishments of tasks within the hospital environment. Current experience of success is far more ego-supportive.[15]

One patient, Mr. Daniels, called the Social Work Department from his room with the plea: "I am dying and I need help." The social worker (who had never received such a referral) could not imagine what help he needed: she was tempted to suggest that the dying patient call his doctor. She was not, however, willing to ignore a direct patient request for social work services, a less than usual event for hospital social workers. She called Mr. Daniels' physician who stated that the patient knew his diagnosis and prognosis as well as the fact that there was no treatment for his advanced cancer. The physician did not know what the patient wanted. The social worker discovered that Mr. Daniels was a successful musician and, among other requests, wanted the right to bring electronic equipment to his room in order to listen to music. This was a violation of hospital electrical safety rules but the worker helped the patient get the necessary clearance. Mr. Daniels went on to plan with the worker his last days of life by creating—out of the sterile hospital environment—the environment in which he wanted to live. Mr. Daniels did not experience as helpful any attempt to discuss his successful musical career and clearly let the worker know how each day's musical accomplishments were far more important.

If we view the stage of life called dying as an opportunity to master the internal and external impact of a life event, much can be gained. The patient who develops a greater sense of mastery during this life process rather than feeling he must cope with the misery of death is able to both receive from and provide nutriments to the environment. The family of Mr. Smith, the patient described earlier, in their way spent the best year of their lives together. They talked to one another openly for the first time and shared many family "secrets" which had caused tension and unhappiness in the past. Mr. Smith spent many hours with his family reviewing financial management, insurance, and other matters which resulted in the teenage son's final statement to his father that he believed the family could survive their father's death. Mr. Smith mastered the tasks involved in living actively and purposefully through the time remaining to him, and helped his family master their reciprocal tasks. Before he died, he reported his sense of satisfaction to them.

EGO AUTONOMY, SOCIAL COMPETENCE, AND EFFECTIVE ADAPTATION

The concept of ego autonomy is well suited for work with the hospitalized terminally ill patient. The concept refers to the ego's relative freedom from undue bondage to the pressures of inner needs and environmental demands—as required for adaptive functioning. Yet too often the hospital setting undermines both aspects of autonomy. We have already described examples of isolation and stimulus deprivation which can cause regression, delusions, and loss of a sense of voluntary control. "Cataract delirium" describes what can happen to a relatively normal individual following a relatively minor operation when the patient is isolated from visual stimuli.[16] If such isolation is decreased the symptoms decrease as the ego regains its autonomy from the id. The problem, however, for the terminally ill patient is that there is no plan to create the conditions for increased autonomy.

Rapaport states that guarantees of relative autonomy from the id lie in cognitive, perceptual, language, and motor abilities and social relations, all of which provide connections to the environment. Guarantees of relative autonomy from the environment lie in the ability to remain attuned to one's inner biological and psychological needs.[17] Yet hospital environments often increase the patient's isolation from others—from family, friends, and even staff—and from familiar surroundings and belongings. And they often furnish inadequate, inappropriate, or even noxious cognitive and sensory inputs, such as blandness, excessive noise and smells, or information that negates the patient's own feeling-states. Moreover, autonomy appears also to depend upon opportunities for action, decision-making, and self-regulation. Yet few hospital environments provide such opportunities consonant with patient capacity. Thus we see that the patient begins to experience a greater dependence on an environment that is nonnutritive, in some respects, at the same time that his/her own internal and external resources are diminished.

In a similar manner, we can see the effect of hospitalization on the patient's sense of competence. Ego theory and socialization theory place special emphasis on being effective to achieve a sense of the competent self. One striking characteristic of the preretirement terminally ill patient is the attitude toward work. The 54-year-old accountant, Mr. Smith, described earlier, had originally been referred to the social worker by his employer because of his persistent refusal to apply for disability benefits. The employer wanted me to convince Mr. Smith to accept his illness (and let the company "off the hook"). The patient's belief that he would return to work was extremely important and his refusal to sign the form was his way of taking action toward that goal. His feeling of efficacy was enhanced as he shared with me his plan to eventually apply at no real financial loss to his family, since benefits would be retroactive. For now, however, the hope was more important than obtaining the funds. He also engaged in a positive interchange with his employer of twenty years through this action. The employer confided to me that he had not visited Mr. Smith before this issue arose because he did not know what he would say to a terminally ill man. The subject of benefits allowed them to share time together around a concrete issue which helped the patient mourn his lost employment and helped the employer work out his feelings about Mr. Smith's death.

There are many other areas of success which are denied the hospitalized patient. The failure to be socially competent is not necessarily the result of personal inadequacies. It can result ". . . from a system which poses tasks in an unduly difficult form."[18] I worked with a 30-year-old heroin-addicted patient, Mr. Short, whose addiction had masked symptoms of lung cancer. He had been in jail, and during the detoxification period, he developed severe pain. He was transferred to the hospital and when placed on methadone he again experienced no pain. Exploratory surgery revealed that this rather healthy-appearing individual had six to eight weeks to live, and the doctors agreed that he should remain in the hospital. Mr. Short tested the system each day until he died five weeks later. One day, for example, his girlfriend came to visit; they closed the door and proceeded to have sexual intercourse. The nurse who discovered them wanted that "god-damned drug addict" thrown out of the hospital, and I was actually called to arrange a discharge plan. The attending surgeon concurred with the nurse. At the time, I could not arrange for a methadone-maintained patient to be cared for in a terminal care facility but I did convince an internist that the patient really was a medical and not a surgical case any longer. Mr. Short was transferred to a medical floor where his behavior continued. He insisted on getting dressed each day, walking about the hospital with I.V. bottle in tow, and attending outpatient group therapy for methadone patients held across the street from the hospital. One day he even disappeared and went to a movie, carrying his I.V. bottle.

The denial of sexual activity pervades almost all hospital and chronic care facilities with which I am familiar. Yet the need to continue functioning in whatever areas of competence that have not been affected by actual physiological deterioration should be obvious. The nurse and surgeon could not imagine arranging to have sex under those circumstances. The staff, in general, could not accept this patient who remained active until his death. Discussions with them revealed that they felt comfortable with blaming Mr. Short for his drug addiction. Since he was responsible for his addiction and the acting out behavior associated with it they could be punitive without feeling that they were handling things poorly as professionals in health care delivery. Their anger toward Mr. Short was caused by their inability based on moral and professional codes to blame him for the acting out behavior associated with his terminal cancer condition. As a result, while they could not be supportive because of their feelings about drug addicts, they felt guilty about their feelings because he also had what they defined as a ''real'' medical problem: cancer. In addition, the patient was not compliant, cooperative, and receptive to the traditional hospital environment offered any terminally ill patient. The interesting aspect of Mr. Short's behavior was that in the drug treatment program he was a ''good'' patient but the difference was that the requirements of that environment fit his needs.

Dubos states that ''Many adaptive mechanisms are not permanent characters of the adapted individual but rather depend on temporary responses to the environment.''[19] Annette Garrett points out that ''Ego strength is not a static or fixed condition. . . .''[20] Yet traditional psychotherapy and ego psychology tend to view coping and adaptation as though they were solely matters of individual psychic choice in dealing with the environment. The result is a view of static ego strengths or ''the well-adjusted individual'' without looking at the ''goodness of fit'' with the environment.

David Mechanic's work on environmental components of adaptation addresses this issue.[21] First the person must have "coping capabilities," i.e., specific skills to deal with the demands of the environment. The hospitalized terminally ill patient who may be successful in all areas of life is in no way prepared for the demands of the hospital situation. He is a helpless recipient of stimuli in a system that demands passivity. Any attempt to influence or change the hospital routine, system, norms, roles, etc., is considered acting out behavior. Second, the individual must be motivated. The hospital system successfully reduces tension by lowering aspirations. The patient is made to feel grateful for an additional day of life and suffers disdain for wanting to improve the quality of that day. Third is the ability to maintain "psychological equilibrium" in order to improve mastery of the environment. The hospital environment tends to reinforce denial, avoidance, fear, panic, etc., and tends to keep the patient from becoming involved in his environment. If, for example, the patient is denied seeing his or her children until just before death, where are the supports to maintain equilibrium? The meaning of the child to the patient, his success at having raised him, and the sustenance and nurturing possible from the child are denied the patient. This does not even take into account what is denied the child who is about to lose the patient.

It is important also to recognize that there is a hierarchy of adaptive strategies. The current pressure to tell the patient the full extent of his illness as reflected by Kübler-Ross and others may not produce healthy adaptation for a particular patient. Enlightened social workers tend to see physicians who refuse to tell patients how ill they are as uncaring, playing God, and providing poor care in terms of total person issues. My first experience with the opposite view was when a graduate student, well-versed in the literature, presented for supervision her work with a dying man. The patient told her he was in the hospital for a minor procedure and would soon go home. The student wanted help with techniques for enabling the patient to move beyond denial. The student was a good student but the patient was not a "good" patient—he needed to deny and the student did not believe he should die without reaching the stage of acceptance. As I look back on the process now it is clear to me that in particularly frustrating reality situations postponing full recognition is often a healthy adaptation.[22]

The tasks for the social worker should include helping the terminally ill patient regulate the flow of information, at times increasing and at times decreasing the input. What was interesting in the above-cited example is that despite the student's motivation and skill, the patient maintained absolute control over his need not to know. He did not permit the student's need to be successful at her goal to interfere with his adaptation to the diagnosis of terminal cancer. What she hoped to do was focus on how the patient felt rather than on what he was doing to cope. She tended to view "the power of insight and the efficacy of a relationship,"[23] as the be all and end all of help. And since the patient died still rooted in his need to deny she saw herself as a failure rather than seeing the patient as a success—having lived every day of his life with the hope of a better tomorrow.

IMPLEMENTING A PROPOSAL FOR MEETING THE NEEDS OF THE HOSPITALIZED TERMINALLY ILL PATIENT

Ego theory stresses the important relationship between innate endowment and the nutriments in the social environment. Prisons and concentration camps exemplify the effects of arbitary power upon innate endowment. Their victims tend to lose hope, become apathetic, and accept their fate without a fight. This is strikingly true in the general hospital as well. According to Mechanic it is often through concerted group action that adaptation becomes possible. However, in most hospital settings patients are kept isolated, community is discouraged by frequent turnover and room rearrangements, and even staff teamwork may be discouraged. This suggests that social workers in hospitals should pay greater attention to this aspect of coping and should work to overcome the oppressive nature of the setting. A focus on tasks for ourselves, patients, families, and other staff, demonstrates that when there is nothing left to do, a sense of accomplishment and integrity has been achieved, rather than despair and disgust.

In my hospital, the social work department is working to increase interaction between the staff and the patient system, provide the nutriments necessary to die in as autonomous a way as feasible given the realistic physical limitations, and to develop competence in both patients and staff. An important step in implementing change in any setting is to take a serious look at the dehumanizing conditions for the recipients. "Hospitals often are not fit places to be sick in."[24] I think we tend to overlook this precisely because we feel as helpless as the patients do, in a bureaucracy upon which we depend for our own sustenance. Just as the community organizer needs to intervene in ". . . the social conditions which form the context in which behavior takes place,"[25] the hospital social worker should strive to make the hospital more nutritive to the maintenance of autonomy, mastery, and competence.

To achieve this kind of change, hospital social workers need to develop skills in implementing change from within organizations.[26] Using such organizing strategy, I first hoped to achieve the right to automatic social work intervention without physician referral. I sought out the forces that would favor such a change because it would be in their interests within the hospital. Such individuals included the public health nursing director who felt she was not getting referrals because patients remained in the hospital beyond the point where they could benefit from home care. Since terminal illness is a covered home care service and many patients would prefer to die at home if supportive services were provided, this was a positive force for change. Second, the chief of the utilization review committee found that the physicians justified hospital overstays by stating the social worker did not get involved until late in the patient's stay and this delayed discharge. He felt that with automatic social work intervention patients would leave the hospital earlier, and studies were produced to demonstrate this.

The change was presented as administrative, that is, it was a necessary tool of the hospital administration to keep beds available for acute patients and to assure payment since overstays are denied by third party insurance carriers. Statistical evidence was provided of inappropriate lengths of stay, financial losses, and failure in obtaining community resources to which patients were entitled. Since the department is mandated through legislation and accreditation standards to provide discharge planning services, it was eventually agreed by the Medical Board that the social work department could not accomplish its assignment without the right to early and automatic intervention, especially for terminally ill patients.

The department utilizes the availability of automatic involvement to improve life style within the hospital setting as well as to improve the quality of the discharge plan. This is achieved by interviewing as many patients and families as possible, as close to admission as possible. In addition to letting them know what resources are available, ongoing in-hospital services are organized as needs are identified by both patients and families. Special attention is paid to refraining from fitting the patient and family to the services of the department. Such activities have included groups for wives of cardiac patients when feelings were expressed that they were excluded from the network of hospital services. Another example is a group for discharged psychiatric patients who could not afford private outpatient psychiatric care but felt the need for continued contact with the hospital: "Making help available when and where it is needed in the life-space of people, represents a beginning commitment to the ecological point of view."[27]

In addition to traditional social work services such as groups, it is necessary to begin a program of improving the interactions of patient, family, and hospital by carefully assessing the interests and resources of all involved. Potential opponents of any change seen as beneficial to particular patients must be identified and the source and strength of their influence weighed. The neutrals and proponents for change must be involved but timing is important. Any plan must include utilizing the tension within the system prior to initiating the change effort. One example, in the case of the dying patient, is the fact that social workers are frequently called to get an irrational, angry, acting-out family member out of the hair of the staff. Psychiatric consultations are called when the patient exhibits such behavior. The psychiatrist then gives the problem to the social worker since he views the patient as a poor candidate for psychotherapy. All of this creates tension which can be utilized in an attempt to reorganize services.

Any proposal which changes hospital routine is more likely to meet with success if it is introduced by an influential physician. Since the change could be viewed as an attempt to impinge on the individual physician's care of his patient, it can best be handled by another physician. Brager suggests that calling a proposal a demonstration project tends also to lessen its threat.[28] We chose to work first with patients on the teaching service where there is greater flexibility in physicians' attitudes. At first we avoided service of any physician who had a reputation for resisting change. Eventually we made it clear that the patients of these resistant physicians were being denied services that other physicians could obtain for their patients. And finally, it became a valued service requested by even the more negative physicians.

Once the program is implemented, steps must be taken to insure its success. During this stage, social work, nursing, and physical therapy rounds which involve a review of all patients admitted to particular services of the hospital are very useful. As each patient is reviewed problems and goals are linked to who wants what kind of help and who is best able within the hospital environment to provide it. On rounds, for example, it was learned that a 35-year-old terminally ill cancer patient, Ms. Shore, was unusually depressed and angry about her stay in the hospital. The staff knew that she had worked as a fashion model both prior to and following her first mastectomy but had been forced to give up her career following her second mastectomy— although prosthetic devices could have permitted her to continue despite the prejudices against cancer victims. The physical therapy staff reported that she would not cooperate in physical therapy; the nurses found her generally despondent. The social worker who had been counseling both Ms. Shore and her immediate family reported that the patient felt that if she could only get dressed in street clothes she had modelled just once more in her life she would regain some hope. Rather than becoming heavily invested in the meaning of this request (since the consulting psychiatrist called it "unhealthy denial"), the nurse, physical therapist, and social worker planned their next step.

The social worker first discussed their idea with Ms. Shore who, while pleased, felt that she would find it physically difficult. She did however suggest that the social worker see her mother about it since she felt her mother would be very excited at the prospect. She suggested that her mother should select the outfit and that she would discuss the specific activities and tasks necessary with the nurse and physical therapist. The patient and her mother got rather involved with the staff in planning an elaborate presentation. Ms. Shore got excited about making a dramatic entrance onto the floor with family and staff present. She stepped out on the floor to their applause. Following this, the rapport among her, the staff, and her family improved dramatically and her depressed mood lifted. Her terminal illness progressed but she did not vegetate. She lived her final days in a healthier social environment.

Using rounds is an excellent way both to introduce steps toward implementation of change and to ensure that the period of implementation does not become the period of failure. Conflict and disequilibrium occur in this stage. Without a view toward institutionalization of the change as part of the care provided the program may lose its momentum. This period involves increasing the visibility of the program by offering the service routinely, creating procedures, and involving the patient and family in selecting an appropriate individual need that can be handled by changing the hospital environment. Ms. Shore was a good case in point since knowledge of what she did quickly spread throughout the hospital and made the hospital newspaper.

There is no limit to the creativity possible utilizing this perspective. Such activities take time but the change in the atmosphere and sense of community within the hospital environment especially for the terminally ill patient is well worth the investment.

CONCLUSION

There is surprisingly little in the literature specifically related to the destructive effects of the hospital experience on ego autonomy, competence, and adaptation. Even less is available on the subject as it relates to terminal illness. While it is beyond the scope of this article to review all the literature, it is worth citing a typical article to point out how researchers can fail to utilize the ecological perspective.

Andreasen, Noyes, and Hartford, in their research for a study they conducted, offer the following conclusion about three burn patients who died. They state:

Strictly speaking, of course, death cannot be considered a failure to adjust, but all the patients who died had already demonstrated an adaptive failure . . . , and for all of them death was the terminal event in a series of adaptive failures.[29]

They state that these individuals had not adapted successfully before the accident which had caused their burns and their admission to the hospital. By contrast, they report, successful "pre-morbid" patients adapted well to the hospital experience.

The ecological perspective, in its concern with improving the match between the patient and the hospital, may help us steer clear of blaming terminal patients for "failing" to live and of blaming hospitals for "failing" to keep them alive. Neither is accurate nor productive. It seems to me that "Maximum growth and development of the human organism *and* amelioration of the environment"[30] can be accomplished by designing and implementing programs directed at improving the interface transactions between the terminally ill patient and the hospital.

NOTES

1. Joel Fischer, "Is Casework Effective? A Review," *Social Work* 18, no. 1 (January 1973), pp. 5–20.

2. William E. Gordon, "Basic Constructs for an Integrative and Generative Conception of Social Work," in Gordon Hearn (ed.), *The General Systems Approach: Contributions Toward an Holistic Conception of Social Work* (New York: Council on Social Work Education, 1969), pp. 5–11.

3. For a review of the literature see Aileen Hung, "Coping Behavior of Patients and Their Families to a Life-Threatening Illness (Brain Tumor)," (D.S.W. diss., The Columbia University School of Social Work, 1976).

4. Erik H. Erikson. "Identity and the Life Cycle," *Psychological Issues, Monograph I* (New York: International Universities Press, 1959), p. 98.

5. Carel B. Germain, "An Ecological Perspective in Casework Practice," *Social Casework* 54, no. 6 (June 1973), pp. 323–31.

6. Thomas Gladwin, "Social Competence and Clinical Practice," *Psychiatry* 30, no. 1 (February 1967), pp. 30–38.

7. René Dubos, *Mirage of Health* (New York: Harper, 1959), p. 25.

8. See, for example, *Essentials of Social Work Programs in Hospitals* (Chicago: American Hospital Association, 1971).

9. See, for example, Morris S. Schwartz and Charlotte Green Schwartz, "Broadening the Conceptions of Health" in *Social Approaches to Mental Patient Care* (New York: Columbia University Press, 1964); John Cumming and Elaine Cumming, *Ego and Milieu* (New York: Atherton Press, 1962); and Erving Goffman, *Asylums* (New York: Anchor Books, 1961).

10. See, for example, Bruno Bettelheim, *The Informed Heart* (Glencoe, Ill.: The Free Press, 1960).

11. David Rapaport, "The Theory of Ego Autonomy: A Generalization," *Bulletin of the Menninger Clinic* 22, no. 1 (January 1958), pp. 13–35.

12. Cumming and Cumming, *Ego and Milieu* pp. 92–93.

13. Alexander Solzhenitsyn, *Cancer Ward* (New York: Bantam, 1969).

14. Elizabeth Kübler-Ross (ed.), *Death: The Final Stage of Growth* (Englewood Cliffs, New Jersey: Prentice-Hall, 1975), preface.

15. See, for example, Charlotte G. Babcock. "Inner Stress in Illness and Disability" in Howard J. Parad and Roger R. Miller (eds.), *Ego-Oriented Casework: Problems and Perspectives* (New York: Family Service Association of America, 1963), pp. 45–64.

16. Stuart Miller, "Ego Autonomy in Sensory Deprivation, Isolation and Stress," *The International Journal of Psychoanalysis* 43, Part 1 (January–February 1962), pp. 1–20.

17. Rapaport, "The Theory of Ego Autonomy," p. 16.

18. Gladwin, "Social Competence," p. 36.

19. Dubos, *Mirage,* p. 35.

20. Annette Garrett, "Modern Casework: The Contributions of Ego Psychology," in Howard J. Parad (ed.), *Ego Psychology and Dynamic Casework* (New York: Family Service Association of America, 1958), p. 45.

21. David Mechanic, "Social Structure and Personal Adaptation: Some Neglected Dimensions," in George V. Coelho, David A. Hamburg, and John E. Adams (eds.), *Coping and Adaptation* (New York: Basic Books, 1974), pp. 32–44.

22. Robert W. White, "Strategies of Adaptation: An Attempt at Systematic Description," in Coelho, *Coping,* p. 50.

23. Ibid, p. 66.

24. Irving Miller and Renee Solomon, this volume.

25. Francis P. Purcell and Harry Specht, "Selecting Methods and Points of Intervention in Dealing with Social Problems: The House on Sixth Street," in George A. Brager and Francis P. Purcell (eds.), *Community Action Against Poverty* (New Haven, Conn.: College and University Press, 1967), p. 239.

26. This discussion draws upon the work of George Brager.

27. Germain, "An Ecological Perspective." See also Lawrence E. Hinkle, "Ecological Observations of the Relation of Physical Illness, Mental Illness, and the Social Environment," *Psychosomatic Medicine* 23, no. 4 (July–August 1961), pp. 289–97.

28. George Brager, "Helping vs. Influencing: Some Political Elements of Organizational Change," Paper presented at The National Conference of Social Welfare, 1975 (mimeographed).

29. N. J. C. Andreasen, Russell Noyes, and C. E. Hartford, "Factors Influencing Adjustment of Burn Patients During Hospitalization," *Psychosomatic Medicine* 34, no. 6 (November–December 1972), pp. 517–25.

30. Gordon, "Basic Constructs," p. 9.

2 Wilderness Therapy: Modern Day Shamanism

CHARLES CATALDO

Cataldo describes the use of "wilderness therapy" with groups of severely disturbed, delinquent, inner-city youth from a public shelter.

Here is evidence that the world of nature is a dynamic, transactional feature of the life space that evokes and shapes human behavior as human beings respond to it and use it instrumentally. While all agree that human beings meet their needs and find a sense of personal meaning through their social ties, the psychiatrist Harold Searles would add that the human being has another task in relatedness. From an evolutionary or phylogenetic point of view, as well as from the standpoint of individual development, human beings must also achieve relatedness to the world of nature, conceived not in the sense of exploitation and subjection, but rather in the sense of appreciation for the connectedness of man to other elements of nature. Such a relatedness to nature is more similar to the world view of traditional Eastern cultures than that of the West. For Searles, as for poets and artists, the essence of man's being depends on both his human relatedness, and his sense of relatedness to the natural landscape and to other forms of life. [1]

Cataldo's group of young "outsiders" had endured lives of unrelatedness. Confined to their slum environments and later to society's most punitive institutions, they had few ties to other humans and none to the world of nature, which they had never experienced or even seen. Cataldo combined his social work knowledge and sensitivity with his skills for survival in the wilderness to restructure their situations. He constructed a nurturing environment that would provide opportunities for the boys to act upon it in ways that would assure their own survival and growth, enhance their own functioning, and increase the nurturing qualities of the environment. Here, environment refers not only to the wilderness world but to the environment that each member—boy and man—formed for every other member. Thus the boys learned to regulate primitive aspects of themselves as they responded to the beauty and the challenge of the primitive forest. They expanded the territoriality of their egos and realized more and more of their potential for social competence as survival tasks in the social and the physical environments were successfully met. They emerged from their experience with a heightened sense of identity, self-esteem, and a capacity for taking constructive action in their own behalf, either in their family or their institutional environments.

—C.B.G.

Surviving. That's what troubled kids have been doing for most of their lives, developing survival techniques to somehow deal with abuse, neglect, and most of all rejection. But these "street smarts" don't apply when you take the streets away—and that premise has been the cornerstone for a remarkable program at our Brooklyn shelter.[1]

HIRED TO DO something novel at the Jennings Hall Public Shelter of New York City, we set the stage for kids to do their own therapy. An outward bound club, we believed, might induce the curious to try the novel, make changes, and grow. The first group of violence-prone kids decided on a forest wilderness in northern New York. Their ordeal: to survive seven days without store-bought food; a month later, a five-day ordeal of rock and mountain climbing; and finally, a cross-country ski trip. Would they survive? Would the wilderness change them and their perceptions and behavior? Would it change us?

GETTING SET

A motley collection of city toughs getting set for an ordeal is an ordeal in itself. Each jostles for a position of power. Inevitably, there's the strong guy and his followers. Keto, 17 years old and of mixed German-Black parentage, qualified as the strong guy.[2] His social worker said he was unable to control his impulses. A history of brandishing knives and violent assaults gained him a reputation in a number of detention facilities. Flash, a 16-year-old Hispanic youth, needed regular dosages of thorazine to quell his rage. Despite medication, he had spent time at Rockland State Hospital for his sudden assaults. Spike, the 15-year-old unloved incubator baby, thrashed out in weekly epileptoid rages. Defacing walls, breaking windows, and stoning school principals were among his discredits. Kings County Hospital, Creedmoor State Hospital, and Spofford Detention Center had all tried to contain him. He seemed destined for an institutional existence. Leon's speciality was killing squirrels, cats, and frogs. He found his mother strangled by a paramour. Earlier, his father had slipped accidentally to his death from the roof of a local tenement. Leon was also known for his outbursts of rage, homosexual assaults on younger peers, and threats of arson. There were six other followers with histories of equal horrors.

As they organized their new gang, they "conned" us for advantages and tested our psychic limits. They were to choose an adult advisor for every crew of three youths. Choose they did: self-assured yet warmly accepting adult workers representative of their ethnic and cultural groupings. Clearly, they wanted self-assured adults. A sureness of self could be contagious: it could temper their fears and their excessive bravado.

Just how were we three adults to be self-assured with this cast of characters? If this were to be our ordeal as well, then we should have a say. Hence, we proposed the pledge, the admonition, the simulation, and then the journey. These were to be the rites of separation from their accustomed physical setting to a strange habitat. In effect, we became tribal shamans showing the initiates a passageway over and around hazards.[3] The passage would involve physical exercise and mental concentration. There would be the ecstasy of stretching the limits of physical prowess, while meeting the maturational crises of the next life stage. The uncovering of hidden talents and wellsprings of strength could lead each youth to a new consciousness. Were we shaman mystics involved in magic for the unholy goal of control? We thought not.

RITES OF SEPARATION

The Pledge. The ordeal refers to a sequence of activities used to challenge one's character or endurance. For our purpose, it was de-

on a hierarchy of power. In the simulations, we begin to practice the new morality. Later, its efficacy will be essential to survival.

In the simulations, we test the point schedule. Every member will self-reward his own efforts. This meets the craving for approval without causing dependency. As the pains of perseverance toward a goal increase, the instant points buoy up flagging self-esteem. Points are never deducted or allowed to be irrevocably lost, because the swing back to feelings of worthlessness leads to rage, avoidance, and further failure when one's predictions of success are not fulfilled.[10]

The Journey. The youths are literally transported by ferrymen to the distant and strange habitat, the Adirondack mountain wilderness. "That's not upstate, man, that looks like Africa," one youth declared. At some point there comes the uncomfortable realization that there's no turning back. This realization is essential for change. To stay with the tribe, or risk injury, starvation, and possible death, provides motivation to face one's self. Keto couldn't go AWOL in the forest for long when his bossy ways lost him his followers.

In contrast to the old habitat, the wilderness demands a new perception of reality that conflicts with stereotyped projections. To trust your life to a line held by a "sniveling weakling" (projection) while rappelling off (descending) a hundred foot cliff is counterproductive and downright dangerous. Teamwork required for survival helps break up such projections. Each man is essential and necessary to the survival of all.[11]

The break from the familiar turf to strange new places elicits one's assertiveness and creativity. In Spofford, Flash was constantly pushed around by stronger kids like Keto who, in Flash's own perception, sought to enslave him. His unpredictable assaults occurred at such times. By contrast, life in the forest favors self-direction.[12] So instead of taking drugs to contain his rage, Flash asserted himself against dangers. Being a crew leader kept him busy making cogent decisions about thirst, starvation, cold nights, biting insects, and getting lost.[13]

RITES OF TRANSITION

The rites of transition enable the initiates not only to assume new identities appropriate to adulthood, but, more importantly, to transcend their damaged selves.[14] For Spike, it was freedom from ungovernable rages. For Flash, it was freedom from the power of smothering sensations that terrorized him. For Keto, it was freedom from the defense of omnipotence.[15]

While different for each candidate, all the covenants of transition proceed through four phases we have called competence induction, perceptual hitching, bisociation, and transcendence.[16]

In the *competence induction* phase all initiates develop a courage born of success in overcoming physical obstacles. As elder shamans, we sought not to have them imitate our instructions, but rather to discover for themselves ways to overcome the physical obstacles. In contrast to the tribal shamans of hunter-gatherer tribes, we, as modern day shamans prefer to accent the nonmagical forces within individuals. These include curiosity about novelty and movement, the urge to complete the unfinished, the reward of activity for its own sake, and the desire to be a tribe member. In place of mana needed to do superhuman heroic feats, there is the nonmagical sense of competence achieved through mastering a sequence of challenges.[17] Our youngsters' growth was inhibited by magical components in their perceptions and affects.

In the second phase, most candidates go through a struggle within themselves. It is the struggle between two incompatible perceptions of one's self. In the phase of *perceptual hitching* the candidates unwittingly move themselves into a psychic crisis of their own making.

This struggle can be followed by *bisociation,* or the transposition of a new perspective to replace the old maladaptive one. Concentration followed by sudden insight often occurs and leads to a state of peak performance. A psychic dilemma is resolved by achieving a new level of consciousness. As in the tribal initiations, the present identity is supplanted by a new one. In the first phase, the rites of transition promote *transcendence* from a magical consciousness of self to a reality-oriented sense of self. No longer will the youth perceive the world animistically as peopled by threatening objects. Spike, Flash, and Keto, for example, tended to contaminate reality with past memories, given a triggering context. We hypothesize that such replay represents the retrieval of past images, and accompanying affects.[18]

Our aim was not to prevent the seizures, hallucinations, and projections from occurring in the candidates. It was, instead, to strengthen the ego's ability to retrieve those images or ego sets which could promote survival.[19] With individually designed experiences, we planned to help each candidate summon up those positive images, reflexes, and affects of his past in order to solve present puzzles presented by the physical environment.[20] Our intent was also to help each youth's ego incorporate new memories and images through mastering new obstacles set within different situations.

To achieve these aims means choosing pathways that are within the margins of tolerable stress, thus promoting exploration instead of apathy. To stay within those margins of tolerance means the experiences must be synchronized with body cycles for exercise, food, talk, and rest. There must also be sufficient pleasure to promote overcoming a challenge that has multisensory impact.[21] An example will indicate the importance of this requirement.

During the first three days the hours from 4:00 to 7:00 P.M. were marked by fighting and inability to complete tasks. We finally realized that we were eating much later than the accustomed 5:30 P.M., and were consuming far more calories in the hiking than were consumed in city activities in a similar period. The depleted glycogen level plus the sharp drop in body temperature were probably sufficient to mark this time span as beyond the margins of tolerance. The need to stress ourselves physically in *demanding* environments had to be balanced with the need for nutritive intake in a sustaining habitat. The candidates needed to become sensitive to the low and high points of several major body cycles.[22]

After a group discussion, the crew leaders took a new interest in choosing routes of travel that would intersect by late afternoon with the territorial paths of game birds and animals. We sought forest clearings by streams and flowing swamps. Edible berries would replace the city's midafternoon coke and sustain the youths as they fished for trout or set snares for hares.

Three sets of experiences were developed around natural interests in exploration. Survival would require ability to traverse new landscapes that presented 1) rivers and swamps to cross, 2) caves and overhangs to go beneath, and 3) heights to climb up and descend. The first set of experiences included finding a safe route and using safety belays (roping up), and using safe techniques to get across, down, under, and up. Survival also would depend on the ability to satisfy hunger and thirst while traversing various terrains. This second set of experiences starts with locating an area with sufficient plants and animals to allow some depletion. It includes identifying them, making them edible through skinning and cooking, sharing the catch, and recycling waste.

In the final analysis, survival depends on extending one's ability to maintain body homeostasis despite sleeping on hard cold ground, being drenched in thundershowers, or being exposed to windchill above the timberline. This third set of experiences includes making decisions on footwear and clothing needed for the journey, on how to protect limbs from undue exposure, how to treat sores and skin breaks, search for natural shelters, and make bough beds.

Competence was induced by the successful completion of five to seven steps, beginning with simulations and ending with tests of skill. In rock climbing, for example:

On the way to the Adirondacks we stopped at the "Gunks." The cliffs of basalt rock are considered the finest for climbing in the East. The place was dotted with novice and experienced rock climbers. The boys noted the activity with interest. Spike asked Mr. Cruz why he was chalking his hands and was told that this permits gripping the smooth surfaces of rock. Each boy now had the opportunity to try to climb the smooth rock using finger holds and crevices for the feet. Spike started up and was surprised to see how high he had climbed. He was commended for his effort and urged to consider learning rock climbing. It was the first time I had ever seen him smile. He felt good for something; and he obviously enjoyed the praise given by Mr. Cruz and the climbers. Cruz was the elder Spike had chosen to seek out when he needed advice. Cruz may have reminded him of his West Indian uncle who played with him as a toddler. Using his point book Spike credited himself and his crew nine points for his success.

In finding and using edibles, for example:

Keto caught a garter snake for the supper meal. Spike caught a Red Newt (salamander). These acts required adeptness rehearsed to the point of reacting almost automatically. Such reactions are common to youths who are unpredictably aggressive toward others. It is as though such aggressions are awaiting the appropriate situation to enact an intention. The task of catching snakes, etc., fitted these already acquired motor responses.[23] This, we said, was a valuable use for such adept action and promoted the tribe's survival. The main course that evening was snake, skinned and fried with some seasonings. The boys were fascinated by moving muscles. We all ate the snake meat and found it to be stringy. Frogs' legs and salamanders, together with edible greens, were then cooked and appeared to be enjoyed more. Caloric content of this meal was well below 4,000 per person. Hunger and what to do about it was the topic of discussion at the evening council fire. "Only animals we did see out here are them little frogs [and the snake and salamanders]. All you see is bird wings," "we saw a deer. Yeah, that was good, a serious deer. We chased him but we couldn't catch him. This m—— f—— was flying, man. And we couldn't even get bow and arrows made in time, 'cause we was still walking the trail. But we wish we could." By the end of the first day the group begins to realize the animals will not come forward like food in a cafeteria. Passive responses to events, even if novel and striking, will not assuage hunger. Scarcity of prey, hunger pangs, and the desire to explore provided the motivation to devise strategies to overcome hunger.[24]

One sign that competence was developing was the decision of the tribe to become nomads again, trekking upward to a new elevation, with a colder, wetter climate.[25] A task that was simple at a lower elevation now became progressively more complex. The tribe altered the point system to reflect the new cognitive demands and the required refinement of skills.[26]

As we approached an elevation of 2,800 feet, according to the hand altimeter I carried, the flora changed to Paper Birch, Balsam, and Red Spruce. Plants such as Labrador Tea and Wood Sorrel became common. The undergrowth became thicker. It was hard to find clearings through which to ascend, so we climbed along the stream bed. The view of Mount Dix across the gorge was impressive. The streams and running water diminished. At about 3,200 feet Mr. Cabrera and I surveyed ahead and picked a spot amidst spruce trees for a bivouac. Instructions on how to make bough beds and to rig tarps were given. It was obvious that showers would continue through the night. Clouds of mist began to soften the hillocks and ridges about us. The crews got fires going despite the wetness of everything. It was tough going for about an hour until they learned that Paper Birch bark in large quantities made an intense enough heat to burn wet twigs. Once lighted, the spruce wood burned too fiercely to fry birds' eggs; but they warmed the toes of the chilly, sleepy-eyed kids. Boiling tea water can take forever in the lowered air pressure, and blueberry biscuits remained gushy in coals that died out in minutes. The crews had challenges aplenty in contending with new obstacles and new opportunities in this new terrain.

The tasks were to find wood, start and keep a fire going, cook for four people, and clean up the campsite, so a crew of three plus a shaman guest was barely adequate. The skills needed to be successful in this environment made the behavioral setting seem clearly under-manned,[27] and meant increased responsibility for each crew member. No one could be left out. Interdependence was crucial to sustaining one's life. Knowing ''how to'' mattered more than ''who could bully whom.''

As one would suspect, our kids became aggressive toward others when the stresses of this set of tasks required adaptations beyond tolerance limits. Often it was only after resolution of the conflicts that the youths could go on to deal with the next set of stresses. But by now the group was ready to complete routines without coaching. When crew members begin to coach their elders in how to do new twists on old skills, the time has come for the next step. The crew selected a 24-hour ordeal, traveled to a new location on their own, remained overnight, and returned. They decided to climb and camp out atop 5,000-foot Mt. Haystack, carrying out all steps on their own.

The climbing continued steep. At one point we reached the last known spring. Water would be rationed from this point on. Two climbers descending the mountain told of the bugs ahead and the difficult going. At one spot we had to edge around a cliff face on slippery soil. The grousing began as we reached timberline. Increasingly, we were bitten by black flies. The breeze was slight, not enough to scatter the clouds of following bugs. Handkerchiefs, etc. had long been tied around the heads and ears. The exertion seemed more tiring above 4,000 feet than at sea level. It was difficult to climb more than a dozen steps without panting. How much farther? was a constant query. Though the top looked so near the mirage effect was considerable. The toil went on and on. Trees became dwarfed and, finally, just low-lying ground mats. Sodden, wet grass gave rise to black flies just as in tundra locations farther north. Mats of yellow Diapensia, found mainly in the Arctic, carpeted the depressions.

Spike and Flash were the first to climb the final cone. Beneath us in the setting sun, a hundred mountain tops settled. Above us circled some red-shouldered hawks. They announced to all that new predators had arrived. But this starkly beautiful biome was also the most dangerous. Before the night would end there would be near-freezing temperatures, the wind-chill of rapidly passing clouds of mists, the danger of being lost in the fog, the ever-present fear of falling, and the added presence of thirst and unfilled bellies. In this biome man could be the endangered species. The risks, however, were lessened by feelings of earlier accomplishments, knowledge of how to tackle the constraints, and a readiness to enjoy the opportunities of this dramatic setting.

Help in competence induction rests on perceptually oriented techniques:[28]

1. Making the goal to be reached vivid (foresight).
2. Visually recalling earlier successes, for example, how Spike made goals in basketball (hindsight).
3. Foreseeing how to reach the goal—by visually moving self along toward a goal (foresight as extrapolation).
4. Foreseeing how placement of a piton could make the difference in goal achievement (foresight as interpolation).
5. If the route up the cliff is hidden in places, moving to a stance from which to view it differently (recentering).

Perceptual Hitch. The image of being an accomplished hunter posed a stern test for Keto when he was asked to share his booty—several good-sized trout—with peers who wouldn't be submissive. He could not perceive the current reality that survival of the group depended on the efforts of each. Instead he misperceived the situation as being like one in his past, where submission to others meant submitting to brutality. By sharing the trout he would lose face and feel himself a weakling. By not sharing the trout he would fail to obtain the award attesting to his being the best hunter. Keto was in a *perceptual "how-to-do-it" hitch.*[29] How was he to obtain their cooperation yet keep them submissive? The hitch arose when he sought to realize two goals at once, both of which seemed compatible, yet were not.

Keto had expected cooperation because he had kept his crew in line before. As tough guy at the public shelter, he had status. His physical prowess brought acceptance from peers and even some respect from adults, although he couldn't be a "lone hunter" at a shelter where watching T.V. was the primary occupation. In the wilderness, however, he could show his abilities in surviving, yet being tough no longer won him respect. He couldn't get the crew to do things for him as they did at the shelter. He found himself having to fight the crew members in turn to get them to find wood to keep the fire going so he could cook. Eating time was fraught with fights. Even the food Keto caught wasn't enough for the whole crew. So why should he help them? He would go it alone. But to be alone was to be abandoned, and this he couldn't bear for long. He needed the others in order to feel strong. A crisis had occurred: all his usual techniques had failed. It was then that he became vulnerable to either a breakdown or to new emotional growth.

It was Flash, however, who finally brought the crisis to its end point. He was given to outbursts of rage against those perceived as suffocating aggressors. With increasing confidence as a crew leader, he began to perceive Keto as suffocating his new-found independence. Flash feared he was going to go berserk. He too had reached a perceptual hitch. He sought to be a competent, decision-making crew leader while keeping allegiance to the dominion of uncontrollable forces threatening to suffocate or maim him. He had let his perception become contaminated with past ego sets based on a symbiotic tie to mother.[30] If he could free himself from such hitches he could separate his growing ego from that of his mother. Keto, a symbol of the symbiosis, provided him the chance. Would he be maimed or suffocate if he gave in to his rage? Or would external and internal forces be within his control? The latter required him to reevaluate his own perceptions.

Excerpt from Diary, Day Three, Wednesday, July 24—1st Survival Trip:

Flash opens up. Dawn broke with a hazy sun. Before breakfast Flash came and said he was under too much pressure and could no longer take Keto's bossing him. He said he could go berserk. It happened before when he was hospitalized at Rockland State Hospital for jamming a pencil into a kid. He had lost control of himself in a flash. He thought he was rapidly reaching that point now. I told him that there was no reason why Keto should boss him. He was a crew leader too, and he could begin to operate as a crew leader, with cooking done by crews. Returning to the campfire, I told a sullen Keto that Flash had asked to cook by crews. Whichever crew starts the fire, should keep it going for the second crew. The second crew then cleans up. Was that fair? Both agreed. Keto did say that he thought he was the President. Yes, I said, but a president has certain prerogatives and responsibilities aside from those of crew leader. He wanted to know what these were. The crisis for the moment was averted. I knew it was far from resolved. It was important that Flash deepen the perception of himself as self-responsible.

Excerpt from Diary, Day Four, 7:00 P.M., Thursday, July 25—1st Survival Trip:

Keto caught three brook trout. Flash was empty-handed despite an hour of fishing. Keto, the victor, said he would cook for all who would help him. As Keto started to cook, Flash suddenly became tense and motionless (he looked white-faced). I sensed that something was about to happen. All at once Flash started for Keto. Caught off guard, Keto backed off and brandished a knife from his pocket. (Where he got it, we didn't know.) At that, Flash rushed to pick up a nearby stone. In a moment he had it raised above his head. Somehow Mr. Cabrera, the crew's adult advisor, managed to move Keto back. Mr. Cruz and I blocked Flash's advance. We ordered both to put their weapons down. Flash began to pant hysterically and then dropped the stone. Mr. Cabrera took the knife from an unresisting Keto. I stated loudly that if they both wanted to fight, they could fight fairly and right now. Flash directly challenged Keto to a fair fight. He said he was sick of his bossing people around. There was a minute's pause. Keto said he wasn't going to fight; he turned around and walked down the trail. Within five minutes he returned, came to the fireplace, and declared that everyone must cook for themselves.

"What-for" hitches are more serious. They occur when surviving is not in keeping with one's self-image. Jay, for example, went on the survival trip because his friends were going, not because he wished to prove himself able. Jay knew he felt at ease as long as he was with his friends. Perceptually, he failed to see that his playing the "bad-ass nigger" (male) role was but a mask that covered the frightened child. His perceptions became contaminated by seeing threat in all that was novel in the wilderness. He found himself unable to integrate the new contexts with any of his existing ego sets.

The forest darkness, the yawning depths beneath his feet, endless toil uphill, thirst and hunger, the fear of never getting out of the primitive forest—all these trials created threats to his being. To quell his panic, Jay seized opportunities to fight with peers on whom he could displace his anxiety. Perceptually, these fights lessened the anxieties of the unknown and permitted him some fit to an earlier learned ego set.

Jay also cursed the elders for getting him into something he hadn't bargained for. For what should he have to endure these stresses? Everyone was failing to take care of him. He couldn't perceive accurately that his survival demanded purposive acts to keep up. Like the "how-to-do-it" hitch, the "what-for" hitch marks the youth's vulnerability to breakdown or to new emotional growth. It presents a more serious hazard on survival trips because it interferes with developing a sense of pride in mastering an obstacle. The steps in competence induction and the chance for achievement had not motivated Jay, and so he had no new memories of achievement with which to meet challenges. The trip will be remembered as an agony rather than an immense satisfaction. Nevertheless, Jay did overcome the hitch and demonstrated his ability to tolerate stresses he couldn't have coped with earlier.

Perceptual hitches occurred more frequently during the late afternoon when body cycles are at low ebb. The irritability caused by hunger, the conscious thought and effort needed to catch edibles, the teamwork required to maintain a fire and to cook, and having to share the meager bounty presented sufficient stresses to precipitate perceptual hitches.

Bisociation. In bisociation, the youth synthesizes his new information about himself with the old and transposes his new perception over the maladaptive one.[31] Keto, faced with a "how-to-do-it" perceptual hitch, had to fashion a new perception of himself to permit him to share and thus to obtain the needed cooperation of peers. What he did was to reinstate an old ego set of caring for his step sisters. He began to care for his crew members as he had once cared for his step sisters. This transposition of perception served him adaptively. It was no longer necessary to alter his peers' actions by force: he changed himself to meet the realistic needs. The positive responses of his peers further reinforced the new perception and the new actions contingent upon it.

Excerpt from Diary, Day Four, 7:15 P.M., Thursday, July 25—1st Survival Trip:

Within five minutes Keto returned, came to the fireplace, and declared that everyone must cook for themselves. Angrily, he began to clean and cook the trout he had caught. He softened his stand after a while to say he would cook with his crew. A few minutes later he asked if I was going to punish him. I told him that he'd been punished too much in the past. I heard him mutter "that was the truth." He asked if he would lose points because of this incident. I told him no, because points are always earned, never taken away. After eating, Keto said he was going to sleep out that night deep in the forest and build his own fire. Would he receive points? I answered this affirmatively.

Thirty minutes later, while Keto was building a fire:

I asked him why he was trying so hard to get me to abandon him, too. He said that is his life. He has been moved around so much. There was a pause, and then he asked, "maybe there is a bad part of me; that is why nobody stays with me." "Maybe," I said, "it is rather you feel nobody can ever keep you, be with you again and so you keep them away? . . . Do you really want these guys to fear you?" He said he can't help it. It's the way he is. I told him that he had a real battle ahead—how to keep from losing friends. He was smart enough and had enough courage to win the battle. "I've been alone all my life," he said. There was another pause, and I said, "Why don't you try it like I do with the guys, thank them for whatever they do? It may help, or maybe you can think of something better. Good luck." I stood up and began to leave. I remember turning and saying quite emotionally and spontaneously, "Keto, do you want your epitaph to read when you die: an able leader but a bully unloved?" Later in the evening, two of the youths complained that the zippers to their sleeping bags were broken. To my surprise, Keto said he'll exchange his bag with the boy in his crew provided he would receive three points for the act of service. It was agreed. The remaining three days were without incidents.

On the fifth day of the ordeal Keto substituted actions conducive to a new perspective in place of bossing his peers. He helped them when they requested it, and quietly asked for their help when needed. He was heard to thank them for their help.

Flash had to reorganize the perception of himself after his fight with Keto. First, he was surprised that he had been able to control his anger without medication, and that he felt more confidence in his role as leader. Nevertheless, we counseled him to talk out his angers with a friend rather than passively to allow his body to tense up. Second, he was surprised that Keto, who he feared would maim him, turned out to be less of a threat than he had perceived. We suggested that unless he tests out the reality of his perceptions they will continue to distort ordinary things, by making them appear gigantic. On the sixth day, Flash found it difficult to talk and felt he was choking. As mentor I counseled him to visualize his throat opening up and to talk out his anger at his mother and others for trying to suffocate him. He did and within thirty minutes was in renewed control of himself.

In similar sequences, Spike learned to go to Mr. Cruz for a walk or a brief but firm embrace as ways to head off an impending epileptoid seizure. Spike felt relief at controlling himself. He said maybe he was no longer crazy.

With all three youths, restorative regimens inserted at critical times during the day were paradoxical to the original actions.[32] To express thanks to the other instead of beating him, to talk out instead of tensing one's body, to be embraced instead of venting rage were the prescriptions. The new action-chains were linked to the new perceptions of self. Concern for others replaced a "beaten child" image in Keto. Ability to control one's self replaced a "berserk parasite" image in Flash. Worthy of being loved replaced a "crazy retardate" image in Spike.

On Leon's third trek he was able to depose the fear of some "spirit" crippling him, and began to trust. During the first trek a perceptual hitch became evident when he refused to jump into a dark pool of water. He felt ashamed of his inability since he was beginning to perceive that he had strong legs and could outwalk anyone. Confronted with a jump, however, he feared his legs would be broken as he had seen his father's legs broken in a fatal fall. Looking to me as a new father, he gradually fashioned a new self from new perceptions. By the third trek he began to trust me, put aside his usual bad-mouthing, and led his crew through deep snow that covered a large pond. Leon went through several such "how-to-do-it" hitches before the new sense of relatedness led to a firm new perception of himself. The image of "apprehensive bad-mouthing child" gave way to the image of a trusting adolescent able to act and achieve. The change was dramatic and lasting. In bisociation, timing is crucial. The mentor must intuitively know the moment when the candidate is exhausted from his struggle to correct dissonance between the desired results and what he obtained.[33] Often that moment is signaled by the candidate's going off alone in self-pity.

In addition to timing, the context must support transposing a new perspective. First, there must be no place where the candidate can go to avoid the task. Second, there must be no one in the group to use as an ally in maintaining his old self-image. Third, the setting must favor the new behavior over the desired behavior. There should be no way, for example, by which the best surviving crew is also the one in which members work by bullying each other. This is the most crucial of the requirements. *The behavioral setting must coercively favor the prosocial alternative.* To wrest a living from the forest requires each member to attain the level of skill needed for survival. This is what makes each indispensable to the others. And it is this social bond that prevents each from abusing the other beyond tolerance levels.

Fourth, the candidate should have gained a sense of competence in solving the puzzles that the physical environment presents. Fifth, the urgency of the situation should demand a resolution. Incipient hunger or another unmet need should be present. Sixth, the candidate should have an ego set from his past that can be linked to a newly fashioned perspective.

The adults acted as mentors to help the youths recognize the distorted perceptions, their history, and their likely consequences. The actual techniques of bisociation used by the mentor are similar to those used in competence induction:

1. Making vivid the goal to be reached, for example, to be the best surviving crew (foresight).
2. Noting achievements and skills on the trip to date, for example, asking the youth to think about how he applied his skills before and to visually recall his helping others (hindsight).
3. Envisioning the use of trial and error methods to reach the goal. Noting the discrepancy between the point of desire and where one is likely to reach. For example, suggesting that since the Tiger crew members fight among themselves they won't make the points the Sharks will. They will end up hungry and in sec-

ond place. Similarly, noting the long-range personal consequences for Keto if his bullying continues (foresight as extrapolation).

4. Asking the youth to consider the duration and origin of the past
   pattern. At this point, he may open up with a flood of words
   reflecting a release of feelings (insight).

5. Asking the youth to look at the differences between the past
   context and current context. Linking the way he perceived the
   past to how he is contaminating his current perception (foresight as interpolation).

6. Helping him recenter his view of the situation by asking him to
   choose a different way (preferably opposite to his usual way of
   coping), and to visualize his doing it (recentering).

7. Urging the youth to test the new perception at least three times.
   Saying thank you for all help given, for example, should provide gratifying and reinforcing feedback (enactment).

The techniques are designed to help the youth correct distorted perceptions, utilizing his actual experiences in a new and challenging environment. Within a favorable environment including positive relationships he is helped to dissolve magical projections and distortions
that impede growth. Some emotional insight in circumscribed areas
accrues. For example, Keto came to realize that his beating others
was an attempt to get himself rejected by others, to relive his initial
abandonment by his mother, and to prove to himself over and over
that he couldn't be loved, that he couldn't belong to anyone or to any
group, and that he was making himself a loner for life.

Transcendence. This refers to the ecstasy, serenity, or peak performance experienced after resolving an acute psychic dilemma through
bisociation.[34] The emotional depression of the long struggle gives
way to elation when the conflict is resolved. The elation, however,
has special meaning in that one has found himself—his identity. A
new consciousness of self creates a division between his person and
the rest of reality. He has moved from the dominance of stereotyped
projections and hallucinations to a hyperaroused state of experiencing
his intimacy with the cosmos.[35] There is an absorption of self in per-
ceiving, doing, enjoying, or creating. The search for excitement for
the sake of novelty is replaced by the heightened excitement of mov-

ing toward the goal of one's own growth. The youths have a term to symbolize the change. It's a simple, "He broke," meaning he broke with an old way. He surpassed what he thought were his own limits.

RITES OF INCORPORATION

Having developed a new consciousness of self, the youth incorporates his new self-images and perceptions in his everyday relationships. The rites of incorporation that seem to occur in some of the youths can be described as processes of Communitas, Reincorporation, Backslide, and the Search.

Communitas. This refers to the bond of friendship that develops among those who "broke," those who transcended an old level of consciousness. There is an altruistic concern for each other, and a commitment to helping each maintain his self-actualization. Toward the end of the second survival trip in August 1974, it wasn't uncommon to hear a youth declare that he had already talked out his problem with another member. This communitas or brotherhood is ritualized by a clasp of hands while sitting in a circle. It is at such times that we affirm our relatedness in seeking growth of consciousness: that is, each person can accomplish his own tasks only by taking account of the life force of every other person in the group.

Communitas is also experienced in our interdependence with all the other species of the wilderness. It is because of this sense of interdependence that we meet our hunger needs from only those species needing depletion in order to conserve the balance of nature. The concept of coexistence among species, each with its own processes, is explained as it applies to the final landscapes we trek through.[36] Our own place within the web of nature is examined. Only then is the tribe ready to test communitas and coexistence with other forms of nature in the last ordeal: a journey through an environment where the tribe itself is the disadvantaged species. The group thus completes the last step in competence induction.

Reincorporation. Return to the old habits that triggered former behavior was often vigorously protested by those who had changed. Keto wanted to go to an upstate facility quickly because he feared he might be pushed by others at Jennings Hall to fight. Vehemently,

Spike protested returning to school, for he feared being forced to sit in class without an opportunity for time out when agitated.

Backslide. The obstinacy with which the newly learned patterns persisted a year later in situations quite different from the wilderness setting was remarkable. Of the six youths who had modified their perceptions and their associated behavior, two showed a temporary backslide to the original behavior within a few weeks of the ordeal. With our stressing how able they really were despite their actions, both were quick to reassert the new pattern. Upon returning to the shelter after the first survival trip, Keto involved himself in a fight, and was jailed. After his release, he asked to go on the second survival trip.

Here is an excerpt from a report of a volunteer counselor, Peter Seiford, 2nd Survival Trip, August 24, 1974:

> Keto was determined to make this trip without physical violence or other acting out. On the last day of the trip we were trying to decide whether to leave for New York City in the day or evening, or even the next morning. Keto was verbally abusive and demanded we leave immediately. We called a meeting of all the men; there was no consensus to leave that quickly. Keto would not accept this and stormed off alone. We watched and were hoping he had the strength to hold to his determination. Keto returned in a short while, and Flash went to talk to him—to help him. They both went off, and then returned together. Keto said nothing, but Flash said Keto was fine.

The Search. This process was represented in efforts by the six youths who had modified their perceptions to find habitats that would support their gains.[37] Flash found an upstate facility that accepted him as a crew leader of other youths. Keto found an upstate farm where reality therapy was practiced. Spike found a group home that arranged with the school to allow him time out during periods of agitation. The three others returned to live with parents or relatives, all of whom had now changed their minds about wanting them home.

SHAMANISM AND
THE ECOLOGICAL PERSPECTIVE
Our concern was with the transition of adolescents into the society of young adults. In hunter-gatherer tribes that transition was often

marked by a sequence of formal rites (initiations). The aim was to invest youths with the rights of maturity—a divestment of the ties to kin and an investiture into the adult society of young hunters.

In today's fast-paced world, the elders can no longer prescribe the future life of their adolescents. Though not formally recognized in today's society, the neighborhood gang accomplishes some of what was once done by tribal elders. It loosens the youth's ties to kin; but may also prepare him for a life of criminal adventure. The tragedy is that the creative potential of many youths is stifled by harsh environments.

As modern day shamans we intervened to provide new experiences in a physical and social setting that would promote growth at the critical juncture in the adolescence of these youths.[38] The ordeals represented a medium in which people of different generations and different cultures interacted to find common meaning. To be able to identify oneself as distinct from one's parents, and yet be able to relate realistically to adults, is to overcome the major transitional crisis of adolescence. The mentor often provided the supportive firmness of a father figure the youth never had and had never before acknowledged needing. The capacity to invest energies in youths and gain empathy with them may be the rite of passage for the adult. For Mr. Cruz, it culminated in the decision to seek a social work career. He had found himself effective in bolstering Spike's self-image and sense of identity. The change in Mr. Cruz was in sharp contrast to his initial attitude of controlling youths by playful and not so playful force.

The cogwheeling of the needs of youth and elders occurs more prominently at certain times than others in the tribe's history.[39] The pledge represents a time for both adults and youths to deepen their commitment to a common endeavor. The admonition tells of the temperament all will need in order to pass through their elected ordeal. The journey separates us from all that is familiar and takes us to a new environment with new opportunities and constraints. Competence induction focuses on exercises to develop ability to solve the puzzles presented by physical obstacles. These interventions fall within the realm of experiential education, but unlike the educational role of the shamans of old, we partake of the ordeals with the youth. Thus, we learn together how to educate each other.

The life model of practice depicts the person maturing developmentally as he transacts with changing environments.[40] As we mature and as we learn more about ourselves, we seek out new habitats more fitting to our needs. We search for social and physical environments that present puzzles and challenges to promote further actualization. Communitas symbolizes finding in each other challenges to promote each other's growth further. By extension it applies not only to each other, but to other species in the landscapes we traverse. To find one's growth even in an environment of many potential stresses represents the final step of competence induction. Finding a challenging environment when the tribe disbands is represented by the phase we titled simply as the Search.

Like our tribal forebears we, as modern day shamans, sought to restore the youth's harmony with himself, with his other tribal members, and with the surrounding ecosystem. Like shamans we utilized rites or exercises to restore balance with the environment. Spike's period of firm embrace, Keto's pattern of obtaining help, and Flash's deliberate pacing of impulses all represented restorative regimes cycled into the activities of the day whenever each youth was subject to specific distress. The feelings of distress may themselves relate to out-of-phase biorhythms within the body. In what has come to be defined as an ecological approach to health, well-being is conceived as the consequence of the interplay of a host of somatic, psychosomatic, and sociocultural factors.[41]

In place of the animistic notions of our shaman forebears, we employed conscious thought as a means of unraveling the history of emotional and perceptual distortions. This is not to say that this method of helping is more effective than any other. It represents, rather, our own reflection that full participation in American urban life requires a vastly expanded conscious use of self to meet the complex and conflicting demands and opportunities it presents.[42]

In another time or another culture, distress might be attributed to demon possession or a soul that has strayed and must be recovered. As modern-day shamans, we assume instead that affectual images have taken dominance over one so that he can no longer perceive the current situation correctly.[43] The youth experiences a perceptual hitch when what he expects, based on his past perceptions, does not happen. New habitats, devoid of the usual encounters, demand action based on accurate perception. Any deviation in actions away from those necessary for the group's survival stand out for all to witness. Since all are affected by one another, the challenge is both a cause for alarm and a call for harmonic restoration. In the bisociation phase perceptual dissonance is resolved by recentering one's way of seeing a distressing situation. The working through of perceptual distortions has some kinship to experiential therapy as described by Lucille Austin.[44] In our case, however, the shaman mentor to the youth in distress may often be a nonprofessional. And the therapy may take place in a setting that is psychologically supportive to recall and recentering (e.g., a nearby cave).[45]

In place of purification rites for the return of a strayed soul, we together fashioned restorative regimens paradoxical to the action spurred by old images. The regimen was sometimes an exercise, a ritual, or a transaction with others. Whether a dyadic, triadic, or a group transaction, it was fashioned to restore intrapersonal harmony and interpersonal coexistence.

NOTES

1. Harold Searles, *The Nonhuman Environment* (New York: International Universities Press, 1960).

---

1. David Fleishman, "Outward Bound for Inner Survival," *Vibrations* (Staff Newsletter, NYC Department of Social Services, June 1975).

2. The names of youths mentioned in this article have been altered for reasons of confidentiality.

3. The term shaman originated in Siberia. It has been used to denote all tribal personages who are endowed with supernatural potential and abilities. As medicine men, they are often regarded as sick men who have succeeded in curing themselves. Shamanism presents a theory of illness relevant to the group's culture and life that is conveyed to others needing a cure. For elaboration see Mircea Eliade, *Shamanism:*

Archaic Techniques of Ecstasy (Princeton, N.J.: Princeton University Press, 1972), pp. 4–6.

4. Veteran parachutists are calm at the point of jump but suffer their highest stress in the hours just before the event. The reverse seems true for new jumpers. The implication is that training and experience makes the difference. For a review of studies see Ogden Tanner, *Human Behavior Stress* (New York: Time-Life Books, 1976), pp. 18–23.

5. Urban ecology workshops for inner city youths are on the increase. Youths gain a new perspective by viewing the city as an ecosystem composed of consumers, producers, and reducers. This approach is detailed by John Burk and Marjorie Sachett in "Nature and the City," *Appalachia Bulletin* 43, no. 1 (February 1977), pp. 24–26.

6. Working with clients exhibiting mirror and idealizing transferences is detailed in a number of recent articles. See, for example, Arnold H. Modell, "The Holding Environment and the Therapeutic Action of Psychoanalysis," *Journal of the American Psychoanalytic Association* 24, no. 2 (1976), pp. 285–308.

7. For further information on the roles of a naturalist and those of a mystic consult Joseph Luft, *On Human Interaction* (Palo Alto, California: National Press Books, 1969), pp. 101–4, 108–11.

8. The youths should be helped to create their own rituals. For a rationale behind this approach consult Margaret Mead, "Social Change and Cultural Surrogates," in Kluckholn and Murray (eds.), *Personality in Nations, Society, and Culture* (New York: Alfred A. Knopf, 1953); Ralph H. Turner, "The Real Self from Institution to Impulse," *American Journal of Sociology* 81, no. 5 (March 1976), pp. 989–1016.

9. Robert H. McKim, *Experiences in Visual Thinking* (Monterey, California: Brooks/Cole, 1972), pp. 40, 43–46, 88–91.

10. Behavioral reactions are thought to occur when a lack of correspondence develops between what we predict and what we encounter. This seems especially so for our youths. See William H. Ittelson and Hadley Cantril, *Perception: A Transactional Approach* (Garden City, N.Y.: Doubleday Papers in Psychology, 1954), pp. 28–30; Samuel Yochelson and Staton E. Somenow, *The Criminal Personality, Vol. I: A Profile For Change* (New York: Jason Aronson, 1976), pp. 265–71.

11. The relationship between a harsh environment and mutuality is discussed in Ashley Montagu, *On Being Human* (New York: Hawthorn Books, 1966), pp. 25, 80–82.

12. Nomadic life is contrasted with a sedentary existence in Walter Goldschmidt's "Ethology, Ecology, and Ethnological Realities," in George V. Coelho, David A. Hamburg, John E. Adams (eds.), *Coping and Adaptation* (New York: Basic Books, 1974), pp. 13–31.

13. There is some evidence that constructive creative work tends to occur in explorative behavior. Play behavior, on the other hand, is more suitable for the symbolic acting out of fantasies. See Ann Weisler and Robert B. McCall, "Exploration and Play, Resume and Redirection," *American Psychology* 31, no. 7 (July 1976), pp. 502, 503.

14. Mircea Eliade, *Rites and Symbols of Initiation: The Mysteries of Birth and Rebirth,* trans. Willard R. Trask (New York: Harper & Row, 1965), pp. xii–xiii, 122; Eliade, *Shamanism,* pp. 64–65, 182.

15. The problem of dominance in hallucinations is discussed by Paul H. Hoch, *Differential Diagnosis in Clinical Psychiatry* (New York: Aronson, Jason, 1972), pp. 92–93.

16. A rite of spatial passage can become a rite of spiritual passage as well, see Arnold Van Bennep, *The Rites of Passage* (Chicago: University of Chicago Press, 1960), p. 22.

17. Mana is a Polynesian term denoting transmissible magic that endows the person with supernatural qualities. This can be represented by a totem, a memento, a keepsake, a favorite knife, or a gun.

18. Wilder Penfield, *The Mystery of the Mind* (Princeton, New Jersey: Princeton University Press, 1975), pp. 18–27, 51–54. The concept of affect images refers to specific emotions represented in images. See John Perry, *Roots of Renewal in Myth and Madness* (San Francisco: Jossey-Bass, 1976), pp. 18–19.

19. John Cumming and Elaine Cumming, *Ego and Milieu* (New York: Atherton Press, 1962), pp. 32–43. Ego is defined as the internal representation of a sequence of events experienced as part of an environment, coupled with a specific affect.

20. Jerome Bruner, *Beyond the Information Given* (New York: W. W. Norton, 1973), pp. 406–40. Bruner discusses tailoring knowledge to fit the retrieval of memories.

21. Hans Selye, *Stress Without Distress* (New York: Lippincott, 1974). Selye calls feelings of pleasure in reaction to the stressor "U stress." Margins of tolerance are approached when a specific stressor impacts on a susceptible body system. See pp. 14, 20, 34–36.

22. Gay Luce, *Body Time* (New York: Bantam Books, 1971), pp. 287–95.

23. Bruner, *Information Given.* The enactive mode of retrieving memories refers to the retrieval of motor responses. The symbolic mode refers to the retrieval of words and concepts. The iconic mode refers to the retrieval of images and spatial orientations.

24. Robert White, "Competence and the Psychosexual Stages of Development," *The Nebraska Symposium on Motivation* (Lincoln, Nebraska: University of Nebraska Press, 1960), pp. 97–140. Effectance is the motivation to explore the properties of the environment. It can operate independently as an appetitive drive in itself until the novelty wears off, or in double harness with other drives such as orality and aggression.

25. Kurt Lewin, "The Psychology of Success and Failure," *Occupations,* no. 14 (1936), pp. 926–30. Competence once achieved leads one to seek situations where self-esteem can be enhanced. The achievement might not be a psychological success unless the goal fits the person's self-concept. Selye, *Stress,* chapter 1. Heterostasis is a new steady state induced by a treatment to stimulate physiological adaptive mechanisms. Physical and intellectual training can be such a treatment.

26. The notion of environmental demands and supplies as it relates to the person

was developed by John French, Willard Rogers, Sidney Cobb, "Adjustment as Person-Environment Fit," in Coelho et al. (eds.), *Coping and Adaptation,* pp. 316–33.

27. Roger Barker, "Ecology and Motivation," in Stephen Friedman and Joseph B. Johasz (eds.), *Environments: Notes and Selections on Objects, Spaces, and Behavior* (Monterey, California: Brooks/Cole Publishers, 1974), pp. 50–69.

28. These techniques are discussed in McKim, *Visual Thinking,* pp. 43–46, 109–12, and in Arthur Koestler, *The Act of Creation* (New York: Macmillan, 1969), p. 59. Bridging the logical gap by inserting the missing links is called interpolation. Extrapolation is the extension of the series.

29. William H. Ittelson and Hadley Cantril, *Perception,* pp. 28–29; F. P. Kilpatrick, "Some Suggestions for Experimentation Stemming from a Transactional Point of View," Appendix A, *Explorations in Transactional Psychology,* ed. F. P. Kilpatrick (New York: New York University Press, 1961), p. 379. Hitches are defined and Kilpatrick distinguishes "how-to-do-it" from "what-for" hitches.

30. See Perry, *Roots,* p. 48. Perry presents the Jungian viewpoint on initiations. He also indicates the special difficulties that reactively schizophrenic youths go through. Flash's fight for selfhood came with the symbolic slaying of his "regnant" mother. Flash, the young hero, finds in Keto the semblance of the terrible Mother monster.

31. Koestler, *Creation,* pp. 35–44; Paul Watzlowick, John Weakland, Richard Fisch, *Change: Principles of Problem Formation and Problem Resolution* (New York: W. W. Norton, 1974), chapter 7, "Second-Order Change," pp. 77–91. Bisociation represents a second-order change.

32. Gerald Mozdziez, Frank Macchitelli, and Joseph Lisiecki, "The Paradox in Psychotherapy: An Adlerian Perspective," *Journal of Individual Psychology* 32, no. 2 (November 1976), pp. 169–84. Watzlawick, et al., *Change,* chapter 6, "Paradoxes," pp. 62–76.

33. Leon Festinger, "Cognitive Dissonance," *Scientific American* 207 no. 4 (October 1962), pp. 93–102.

34. Abraham H. Maslow, *Toward A Psychology of Being* (New York: D. Van Nostrand Co., 1968), pp. 73–94, 103.

35. Roland Fischer, "On Creative, Psychotic, and Ecstatic States," in John White (ed.), *The Highest State of Consciousness* (New York: Doubleday Anchor, 1972), p. 86. The intimacy approaches the meditative. Hyperarousal is the state of tranquility and ease. At the same time, there is inner excitement of self-discovery.

36. Judith and Herbert Kohl, *The View From the Oak* (New York: Charles Scribner's Sons, 1977).

37. Heinz Hartmann, *Ego Psychology and the Problem of Adaptation* (New York: International Universities Press, 1958), p. 27.

38. Piaget, *The Origins of Intelligence in Children* (New York: International Universities Press, 1952). The idea of intervention at the critical junctions in life comes from Piaget in his discussion of stimulus nutriment ("aliment").

39. Erik H. Erikson, *Insight and Responsibility* (New York: W. W. Norton,

1964), p. 115; William C. Menninger, "Mental Hygiene Aspects of the Boy Scout Movement," *Mental Hygiene* 13, no. 3 (July 1929), pp. 501–2.

40. Alex Gitterman and Carel B. Germain, "Social Work Practice: A Life Model," *Social Service Review* 50, no. 4 (December 1976), pp. 601–10.

41. René Dubos, *Man, Medicine, and Environment* (New York: Mentor Books, New American Library, 1969), p. 43.

42. Edward T. Hall, *Beyond Culture* (Garden City, New York: Doubleday Anchor, 1977), p. 54.

43. Perry, *Roots,* p. 27.

44. Experiential therapy was first advocated by Lucille N. Austin in 1948 as a way to alter specific nonadaptive behaviors and attitudes. Lucille N. Austin, "Trends in Differential Treatment in Social Casework," *Journal of Social Casework* 29, no. 6 (June 1948), pp. 203–11.

45. Chris Argyris, "Conditions for Competence Acquisition and Therapy," *Journal of Applied Behavioral Science* 4, no. 2 (April/May/June 1968), pp. 147–77.

3 The Development of Group Services for the Elderly

IRVING MILLER AND RENEE SOLOMON

An ecological view of services to the aging may provide additional clarity about the complex relations between the aged person and the environment as each seeks to adapt to changes in the other.

The authors take the position that aging is not a disease process imposed upon a particular stage of the life cycle, but is a social process that is inherent in the life cycle as it is lived out in a particular historical and cultural context. It is the social processes that lead to the problematic aspects, since disease processes occur anywhere along the life line. The societal environment in which the elderly are located offers opportunities for, as well as obstacles to, successful adaptation to our shared human fate of growing old. Societal values and attitudes toward and within the family, demographic trends, geographic migration, the postindustrial economy and work force, housing patterns and changing neighborhoods are major influences that bear for good or ill on the quality of life for all elderly people. They pose new adaptive tasks at every turn, yet institutionalized solutions, even to the more expectable adaptive tasks, are not always available. In large measure, one's location in the social structure governs not only the availability but also the quality and quantity of socially provided coping resources. Thus aged minority persons and the aged poor, the isolated and the frail elderly, all carry an awesome adaptive burden. The plight of these segments of the aging population requires the social worker's special efforts to locate them and to proffer services geared to their particular needs, interests, capacities, and life styles.

In general, however, social workers may be less aware of the physical en-

vironment's impact on the functioning of the aged person. The nature of the sensory-perceptual stimuli provided by the physical setting of institutional or familial or community life is particularly important for the aged person whose sensory-perceptual acuity is declining. Bland environments that fail to provide a variety of textural, olfactory, thermal, visual, and auditory cues and experiences may precipitate a pseudo senile state. Maintaining an orientation to the environment, a sense of self, and the treasured sense of dignity and autonomy depend, in part, upon sufficient sensory-perceptual input, as well as on the social structure. Social work services can be useful in providing such experiences preventively and remedially, but the responsibility for working at the organizational level to bring about a more stimulating environment must not be overlooked. Social workers can also help other staff to understand the spatial behaviors of their aged residents and patients. The aged person with diminished sensory acuity often compensates by seeking physical nearness and touch in his or her relations with others. These behaviors may be experienced as intrusive by young staff who then attempt to keep the aged person at arm's length. Similarly, family members may be helped to understand that the old person's "clutter" is not willful messiness but a means of coping with declining sensory powers. Having familiar objects within close view and within easy reach is reassuring, as transactions with the physical environment become more difficult.[1]

Like space, time is a component in all adaptation, and is therefore a critical variable in services to the aged. Miller and Solomon consider the salience of past time in the context of reminiscence. Present and future time may also have age-related meanings. In one sense, time passes very quickly for the aged person as "time remaining" dwindles. In another sense, however, adaptation to changes in the environment and in the self take time to develop—perhaps more time than the elderly person wishes to spend from his precious hoard of days. A shorter lifetime in one's familiar environment may be more preferable than the promise of a longer lifetime in a changed environment. The future may be of less importance to the elderly person than to the family or staff members concerned about him or her—for the present is here to be cherished and the future may not come. Changing biological rhythms and cultural tempos of the elderly are sometimes violated by the rhythms and tempos of institutional life and even by the life styles of families caring for their aged members.[2] *By maintaining sensitivity to spatial and temporal disjunctions between the individual and the institution or the family, the practitioner will be prepared to work at organizational, familial, and group levels to reduce such sources of stress.*

Miller and Solomon emphasize the need for freedom of choice among services, programs, and modalities in order to enhance the aged person's self-esteem, competence, and autonomy to the fullest degree possible. They show that the ecological view underscores the developmental aspects of aging, the adaptive strengths of the elderly person, and the kinds of environmental sup-

ports required for successful adaptation and mastery of the pertinent life tasks. Little knowledge is so far available for specifying the changing life tasks across the lengthened span of old age. Erikson's single issue of integrity versus despair, helpful as it is, may not take sufficient account of sex, cultural and environmental differences, or the differing tasks confronting the young-old and the old-old. There are fruitful research questions to pursue in this area for the ecologically oriented social work researcher.

—C.B.G.

THE AGING are the most rapidly growing group within our total population and are increasing at a faster rate than the population as a whole. They also are, by socioeconomic and general health criteria, the most deprived and disadvantaged part of our population. The apparent popular concern for the aging in our society is not usually matched by a corresponding allocation of resources nor a professional commitment to practice with and to develop services for that group. This situation has profound significance for all: for the elderly themselves, for their families, for the economy, for our politics, and finally and more particularly, for the development and delivery of health, educational, and social services. The 22 million people who comprise the over-65 or aged population, while an enormously diverse group, are generally subject to a multiplicity of personal and environmental stresses often occurring concurrently. While people of all ages suffer from stress and loss, it is the occurrence of simultaneous or closely clustered loss which justifies characterizing the aged as a population at high risk.[1] Consequently they are becoming heavy users of social and medical services—services which employ significant numbers of social workers. Although political and historical considerations will inevitably intrude upon the symmetries of program planning and design, we have found it important to identify some demographic data which have implications for the development and delivery of services to the elderly. Following this we have offered some theoretical perspectives relevant to the development of social services generally and specifically group services for the aged.

SOME DEMOGRAPHIC DATA

Never before in our history have we had more people over 65 in America, numerically or as a proportion of the total population. In

1900 there were 3 million people over 65, or 4 percent of the total population. The 1970 census counted about 20 million Americans over 65 in a total population of 203 million (about one out of ten). Although the present population under 65 is 2½ times as large as it was in 1900, the group over 65 is 6½ times as large.[2] Explanations for this dramatic increase are familiar and are attributable to medical, social, and economic advances. The significant change and increase since 1900 is in the number of Americans who achieve age 65. Once that status-defining milestone is reached, life expectancy thereafter is only a few years more than it was at the beginning of the century. Population projections which do not assume major medical breakthroughs in the illnesses of old age, still show that the older population is likely in this and the early part of the next century to constitute between 11 and 18 percent of the total population.[3] Should medical breakthroughs occur in major cardiovascular-renal diseases, the number one killer of old persons, as well as in cancer and heart disease, this figure could increase sharply.

Thus the older population represents a huge group, equaling the total population of our 21 smallest states. There is tremendous variation and diversity within this group in health, housing, and socio-economic status, though to be sure they have more health problems, poorer living arrangements, and are over-represented in the poverty group. The population of aged persons is itself "aging" as the oldest part grows fastest. The median age is 73; four out of every ten old people are over 75, while 1 million are over 85 years of age.* The rate of increase of those 75 and over has escalated to three times as great as that of the group 65 to 74 years old. In other words, of the 3.5 million increase in the total older population between 1960 and 1970, only 1.4 million of the increase was in the 65 to 74 age group, while 2.1 million were in the 75 plus group.[4] These data are very pertinent to social policy perspectives on the social functions of, and long-range needs for total institutions for the elderly, as well as to the limits on a currently laudable trend towards keeping the elderly in their communities and out of institutions. Most authorities agree that although much needs to be known about old age and aging, much more is known than is applied in practice. There is much to know and

---

* The Social Security Administration has reported that in 1969 there were 3,200 Americans over 100 years of age receiving benefits; in January 1971, 5,253 were receiving benefits.

show before we can begin to overcome the myths and half-truths concerning the aging in our society.

The aging are a diverse, changing population not easily amenable to quick and ready generalization. Each day about 4,000 Americans achieve age 65 and, at least statistically, join the 65 and over cohort; each day about 3,000 people over 65 die.[5] Crucial here is that the 4,000 65-year-olds joining the group daily are quite different particularly in educational and physical status from those who have just died and left the group. It is enormously diverse by income, health, domicile, educational level, i.e., virtually in every socially significant consideration.

The 1976 census report shows that as America's elderly population continues to grow, women continue to outlive men by an average of almost 8 years—that as of 1974, women could expect to live 75.9 years and men 68.2 years. Today, there are 100 females for every 69 males over age 65; 40 years ago, the proportion was about even. By the year 2000, the projection is about 65 males for every 100 females in the age group. Further, the sex ratio disparity within this group increases with progressive age: at present there are 124 women to 100 men at age 65–69, 146 to 100 at 75–79 and 179 women to 100 men at age 85 and over. These figures provide at least one important explanation for why we work with so many more older women than we do with older men.

The middle-aged woman with a husband 5 years *younger* than herself, not the usual pattern, has a fifty-fifty chance of being a widow before her death. If the husband is about the same age as the wife, the chances of widowhood increase to two out of three. If the husband is five years older than the wife, a more common pattern, the chances for widowhood jump to three out of four.[6]

Living arrangements of the older population reflect such obvious factors as marital status, income position, and availability of housing choices; also such potent psychological considerations as intensity of family ties, desire for independence, and attitude toward being a burden on adult children or other family members.[7]

Estimates for the beginning of 1970 show that most older people live in a family setting of some kind but mostly in their own households; the trend away from living with children continues to grow. This continues despite the financial sacrifices involved in maintaining independent domiciles, and is probably made possible by increased social security benefits and the increase in home health care services.

Of every 100 older persons, 67 live in a family setting and more than 28 (21 of whom are women) live alone or with nonrelatives; 5 percent or one in 20 older persons live in institutions. These figures conceal such important variations associated with advancing age as the fact that 10 percent of those over 75 years of age live in institutions and two-thirds of all those in institutions are widows.

Income. Whatever may be its importance as major sources of status and role satisfaction, work is, of course, the best single source of income for most people. Retirement brings a reduction of between half and two-thirds in money incomes as retirement benefits replace earnings as the principal source of income.

Median income for older families has consistently been less than half of that for younger families: $6,426 compared to $12,935 in 1973. Older persons living alone or with nonrelatives fare even worse: their median income is well under half of that of their younger counterparts, $2,725 as compared to $5,547 in 1973. In essence, the older population is a low income group. Shelter and health costs must be paid first. What remains leaves little for food and clothing and even less for such "luxuries" as transportation and recreation.

There is much that we know and much more to know and to do in work with the aging. The demography, some of which has been put forward above, can provide the base and be linked to some theoretical formulations relevant to social work practice with the aging.

THEORETICAL PERSPECTIVES
FOR SERVICE

Current conceptions view aging as a normal developmental phase in the life cycle. Just as all stages in human life require the successful management of certain tasks, so is it also required in the aging phase of life.

A tendency to treat and define our aging citizens in stereotyped and negative ways persists despite experience and research indicating that old age can be a time for growth, new learning, creativity, and productivity. Such a view and corresponding program emphasis provides a frame of reference which has considerable utility for social work. The developmental perspective is an antidote to the often pessimistic attitudes and perceptions brought by service providers to work with the aging. It permits us to make use of and adapt to our work what we have learned from providing services to other age groups. This view is conducive to seeing the variety and diversity of normal and special needs among the aging, and to developing services accordingly. Finally, a developmental view enables us to understand that many of the most significant difficulties of older people are related to their social situation and social definition, rather than being intrinsic to aging itself.

To most readers it will become immediately apparent that we are talking about the life cycle and life stages concepts formulated so heuristically by Erik Erikson.[8] Essentially the life cycle idea suggests that every person, if he is to survive, moves through various stages of development—infancy, childhood, young adulthood, maturity, and old age. To function effectively, there must be means provided by which a person can move into and from one status or position to another. Every phase of the life cycle is marked by important changes which are related to those which occurred earlier. The ability to cope successfully in the present depends upon mastery or competence in preceding stages. The older age period of life brings changes in physical and psychological capacities as well as changes in social circumstances which impose the requirement to make substitutions and to reorganize behavior, much the same as is required in earlier life stages.

The life cycle concept offers a model for studying a wide range of phenomena associated with aging. Like all other phases of life old age is filled with challenges which must be negotiated and can be a time of growth and realization of one's potential. The life cycle concept allows for analysis of the interrelatedness of physical, psychological, and social forces and includes, therefore, a social change component. This is more useful (and more hopeful) than the traditional medical model with its emphasis upon pathology and adjustment to institutional requirements.

What Erikson called the resolution of "integrity vs. despair" as the central concern of old age, is beginning to be specified by gerontologists in the differential tasks, roles, problems, and sources of gratification associated with the last stage of the life cycle. Moreover, the wide age range of the aged group has caused Ethel Shanas and others[9] to suggest that we view the aged in two categories, the young/aged, from 65 to 74, and the middle and old/aged who are 75 and over. Life crises and their associated developmental tasks differ markedly at these stages, and the development of services to old people needs to reflect an understanding of these differences.

To illustrate: The widow with children, who becomes 65 today, was married during her 21st year, had her first child when she was 23. She was 52 years old when her last child married, and she and her husband had 11 years together without their children before his death when she was 63. She and her husband had more middle and later years together and fewer child-centered years than did women in previous generations, and if the present trend continues, today's middle-aged woman will have even more of these years in her lifetime.

The new 65-year-old widow had fewer children than did either her mother or her daughters, and typically she became a grandmother when she was in her late 40s. At age 65, it is likely that she will have spent a portion of her adult life working outside her home, that she was housewife and mother during her 20s and 30s, entering and returning to the labor force either when her children were all well established in school, or if not then, in her late 40s or early 50s when her children were grown.

As a recent widow, she is coping with the developmental tasks of mourning while she continues to function and to develop new relationships. She may be struggling with loneliness, being alone and with increased financial burdens.

It is not unusual for our newly 65-year-old woman to be a daughter, as well as a mother, a grandmother, a wife or widow, and a sister. The more than one million people over 85 are the parents of many of the younger members of our over-65 group.

Clearly we cannot view this enormous age group of 65 and over as if all members were at the same point in the life cycle. The 85-year-old is not newly widowed, but may in fact have spent as much as one-third of her life in this status. She has been a grandmother for more than a third of her life; her grandchildren may now be parents. She is one of a million who are older than almost everyone around and one of the last survivors of her family and her generation. Few people remember her as a bride; fewer still remember her as a child. She is faced with the tasks of developing relationships of greater dependence with her children and other younger family members, of coping with increasing physical disabilities, of conserving her remaining physical, emotional, and financial resources. She may also be struggling with a decision about a move from independent living to institutional care. She has, in short, lived and coped for 20 years with the tasks our present 65-year-old is now facing. Though socially and statistically defined as members of the same group, their respective life tasks are significantly different.

From an historical perspective, the 65- and 85-year-olds may have lived on the same earth together for the past 65 years, but they have experienced it differently. For the 85-year-old, World War I was his war; his peak earning years were blighted by the depression; most of his life occurred before the Social Security System became fully operational, so that his benefits are at or near the minimum. Compared with other age groups he benefited little from the affluence of the 1950s and 1960s. He remembers a world without automobiles, airplanes, radio, telephones, refrigerators, and Freud.

Our 65-year-old was in grade school during World War I; he grew up during the '20s, entered the labor market at the start of the depression, and with his generation bears its scars in the deepest psychological sense. His is the generation of materialists against whom the young people of the '60s and early '70s were in revolt. World War II was his war, and the patriotism which he developed at that time leaves him puzzled and angered with what he perceives as a lack of patriotism of young people today. He enjoyed at least 30 years of coverage under Social Security; his benefit is substantially higher than the 85-year-old's; he took this retirement income for granted, knowing that he earned it. He benefited from technological advances and had the time to develop some leisure time interests.[10]

To conclude and summarize our effort to put forward some general characteristics of this age group and the differences among them: the over 65 population is not a stable, homogeneous group. Its composition changes daily. Life cycle tasks associated with the younger aged are much different from those associated with the older aged. Though the 65-year-old and the 85-year-old have inhabited the earth together for 65 years, they have experienced it differently. They come into their old age with different life histories and having developed differing sets of norms, attitudes, and values. In work with the aged as with any age group one must keep in mind and simultaneously attend to both their universal characteristics as a group as well as the specific attributes and life situations of the specific individual in that group.

THE DEVELOPMENT OF SERVICES
FOR OLD PEOPLE

Old people must be treated with the same regard for differential life tasks as are other age groups, for life crises and their associated developmental tasks continue throughout life. Often, the variety and complexity of these tasks remain unexplored because the physical, psychological, and social assaults endured by old people are seen as endemic to the aging process, and therefore irreversible. We in the social services have failed to make available the array of resources which can help the aged client to cope. We do not assume this stance in relation to other population groups; there is no good reason to do so with old people.

Choice from among services or choice within a service is the linch pin of dignity and mutuality. Its absence degrades and confirms one's disadvantaged status. Old people are particularly vulnerable to this moral calamity because age itself is a stigma. It is a stigma which is elaborated and sustained because their options have become severely limited by role depletion and loss. In the organization of social services for the elderly, we must avoid, however easy it is to do otherwise, professional judgments about what is best for them. Instead our creativity and innovation should be expressed in the construction of service situations in which the client can decide what is in his best interest. Decent and respectful services for the elderly rest on the mutual interrelation and interdependence of choice and individualization, each to its optimal extent. Taking this into account in organizing services for the elderly means services which reflect differences as well as shared interests and concerns among the elderly.

Age-homogeneous services are those which reflect similarities within each of the cohorts (i.e., the younger or newly aged group and the older aged group). These services help people cope with developmental tasks associated with the specific life crises of aging. Such services distinguish the younger elderly from the older elderly, and diminish or prevent conflict around leadership and turf. This distinction within the large group of elderly reflects both the constantly changing composition of the aged group and some real differences between the newly old and the oldtimers.

Age-heterogeneous services are those which reflect similarities within the entire cohort or group and afford each old person opportunities to participate in areas of interest, and to work on shared concerns of the entire group. The simultaneous organization of age-homogeneous and age-heterogeneous services is congruent with demographic data viewed within a life-cycle, historical perspective.[11]

THE ECO-SYSTEMS PERSPECTIVE
IN SOCIAL WORK PRACTICE
WITH THE AGED

The potential relevance of the eco-systems approach to practice lies in its notion of causality as opposed to the conception of causality inherent in a traditional treament model. Derived from the latter is the general notion of behavior as symptomatic and the assumption that if you get at the cause you will be able to move toward the cure or know the cure. Social workers have always held that human problems are "psychosocial" and cannot be understood except as "person-in-situation." There has been, however, little systematic approach to the analysis of situation, and consequently much in our present approach largely focuses on the person with the problem in such a way that the problem in effect is considered to be located in the person. Within the the eco-systems approach, human interactional phenomena are not viewed or explained in the context of pathology or a taxonomically appropriate label; the "reason for" a particular behavior can be seen not just by tracing its etiology, but by examining its function for another system.

This approach may help us refine some of our more simplistic notions, e.g., that self-awareness is a prime determinant or precondition of change. It not only attends to system goals but to mechanisms that enable the system to revise and alter goals, bringing them into better relation with a changing environment, etc.

One obvious implication for work with the elderly is that we cannot indulge in the resigned and shrugging attitude which says: "What can you expect from a person 65 or 75 or 85 years old?" Their problems need to be taken seriously—as if crises can be overcome and better coping achieved—as if environmental supports are there and need to be searched. Merely being old cannot justify prolonging the problem. Social workers have not been immune from the societal stereotype of old age as a time of natural and irreversible losses, losses which the client must be helped to accept. That losses do occur and must be accepted is real; that many losses can be minimized through the provision of needed resources, along with the mobilization of the clients' coping capacities, is equally real and demonstrable.

The ecological perspective is especially relevant in work with the aged insofar as it focuses on strengths rather than deficits. Because the social, physical, and emotional assaults of old age are often calamitous for the individual, we have tended to become occupied exclusively with the deficits and lose sight of individuals' demonstrated capacities to cope with such changes as a move to a new neighborhood, a move to a child's domicile, survival on a small, fixed income, loss (of spouse, friends, and family members), replacing these with new relationships (with grandchildren and great grandchildren, with young neighbors and older neighbors). To build on the strengths—the determination, the humor, the assertiveness, the capacity for enjoyment, the gratification of work, and the satisfaction in accomplishment—is the task. Social work interventions must seek the support of meaningful personal relationships and the provision of opportunities for continuity of social roles.

The essential characteristic of the social work function is to provide and sustain access for the older person to needed resources; to connect the individual or group with those people and institutional and community systems which are needed to maintain decent and dignified social living. The particulars of the needed resources may come from the client, or be mutually defined by the client and social worker, or by the client and family. The activities of the social worker with the elderly strongly emphasize helping the individual (or group) negotiate and achieve greater control than otherwise over some system or systems with which the older person is interacting and in which the "problem(s)" may be located—family, neighbors, human service agencies, housing, etc. The activity may be directly with the older person or with a system on his behalf. (When the unit of attention is the family, the family itself becomes the system the older person needs to negotiate.)

The difficulties elderly clients bring to most of the agencies in which we practice may be usefully "explained" as being caused by deficiencies in the very service systems developed to help them. Many service systems intensify the misery they are intended to mitigate. Many nursing homes institutionalize despair; hospitals are not fit places to be sick in, etc. Institutions, including those for the elderly, seem to move inevitably and ineluctably towards greater concern with their own maintenance than with their intended purpose. And all the disappointments and inadequacies to which all service systems are heir are presided over by decent professional people (like our readers and ourselves), not by easy-to-despise villains. It's the unwitting bad done by the "good" people that really complicates things for the elderly, not the intended evil of the "bad" people.

To work effectively with the elderly, social workers must become experts in understanding how these systems work so that they can pay informed attention to influencing them to work for the client and to develop service delivery systems whose style and substance is congenial and relevant to the lives of old people.

If social work practice with the older person is to be distinctive and capable of increasing social relevance, it must operationalize the eco-systems approach into a corresponding role model for the social worker. This we believe is in large part accomplished by defining the social worker as a "mediator" in the arena of service systems, "intervening" to bring the client and the community's institutions and services into a more congenial and beneficial juxtaposition than would otherwise be the case. This implies attention to both the concrete needs of the client and ways in which the structure of social services may be changed to meet those needs. This idea is by no means a new one; it has been within the purview and practice of the social worker. However, the ways in which social services have been organized and supporting ideologies conceptualized have rendered the mediating function secondary. Other ways of defining problems and services have carried more prestige and have been more congenial to agency style, and to the type of client that the agency and staff preferred. The effective implementation of the eco-systems approach requires that the mediating role which is included in prevailing theory and permitted in practice, become primary to theory and prescribed for practice.

For most clients and older clients particularly this approach to practice is more attuned to social realities than alternative approaches. Social workers have always asserted the importance of the environment and have tried to develop its application to practice. However, we have not always been effective in doing so. To be sure, this is a difficult task. We ought to avoid at least one source of difficulty and that is a tendency to act as if the social environment were self-evident, as if recognizing its existence were equivalent to understanding it, taking it into account and making use of it in practice.

GROUP SERVICES FOR THE ELDERLY

Group work with the aged has traditionally consisted of activity, recreation, and entertainment. Institutional and community center people have tended to utilize groups as the principal means of filling leisure hours. Spending leisure time pleasurably, participating in enjoyable activities are indeed very good things, needing little justification, especially when days without them are long, tedious, and lonely.

To help old people pass the time is only one good reason for group services. Other, perhaps more important reasons (at least for social workers) are to help old people to develop new and caring relationships, to maintain and enhance feelings of self-worth through the continuity of social roles and the development of new ones, and to exert control over their lives through confronting and engaging some of the problems of living in the institutions or in the community. Further, because they are mutual aid systems, groups enable members to give and receive help from each other around common concerns and interests and in general carry out tasks which could not be carried out without the help of others similarly situated. Professional groups, political groups, tenant groups, consciousness raising groups, PTA's, and special interest groups all share similar purposes: to exercise greater control over our own lives, to find a reference group which sees things as we do, to develop mastery in new areas and so feel better about ourselves, to make new friends, etc. For most old people resources and opportunities to meet their needs have been thwarted. To see the development of group services for old people as meeting those thwarted needs is to understand the basic case for the importance of such services.

Our discussion, though limited to the development of group services for the elderly, will attempt to identify some of the differences between group work with the elderly and group work with other population groups.[12] Groups have been defined as "a collection of people who need each other to work together on a common task, in an agency which is hospitable to the execution of that task."[13] "Common task" becomes group purpose, "people who need each other" is translated into mutual aid. The third component, agency sanction, will be dealt with later.

The purposes for which groups are formed, fall generally into four categories:[14]

1. *Formal and informal educational groups,* where purpose is to help people develop or maintain mastery and competence in areas of common interest. Examples of such groups are music listening, arts and crafts, newspaper writing, cooking, reading and discussion, movement, poetry, horticulture, etc. The development of formal educational groups for old people has been a rather recent development. Such groups have been developed and sponsored either in an agency or school setting. Although an entire range of courses from art to zoology may be available, courses of special interest to old people have

included general psychology, the psychology of aging, the physical aspects of aging, budgeting and financing, the changing American family, ethnicity and American society.

This category of groups are age-heterogeneous since these interests cut across the entire aged group. If interaction between members is deemed desirable, optimal size of group would be between 15 and 20.

2. *Life task, or problem-solving groups,* the purpose of which is to help people who share similar concerns work together and overcome feelings of being alone and hopeless. Included here are groups that deal with life crises and their associated developmental tasks. For example, groups for recent retirees, for couples where one or both are recent retirees, for recent widows and widowers, for people who have recently become disabled, for people living in foster care or adult home settings, and for people who are contemplating a move from independent to institutional living.

While some of these groups are as relevant to an institutional as a community based setting, there are problem-solving groups which are specific to an institutional setting. These include: (a) Applicant groups for people awaiting admission to the institution, where purpose is to ease the strain of admission, share information about the institution, and express fears and anticipatory anxieties. (b) New resident groups where newcomers to the resident facility meet on a planned short-term basis to discuss what life is like for them, the good things and the bad things, and how they manage them. A group for new residents brings together persons with common fears and shared needs for information and new relationships. The activity of the worker is guided by these purposes, and the content of the group meeting is related to such matters as giving information, sharing past and present experiences, and engaging in mutual aid. (c) Men's clubs where the male minority can meet as men to discuss their concerns as men, and can plan activities of special interest to them. (Sexuality, marriage, the absence of institutional sanction for heterosexual activity are a few of the content areas generally covered in such groups.) (d) Groups where couples can meet to share their concerns and to plan activities of special interest. (e) Volunteer groups of healthier residents organized to offer various services to the institution and, where possible, to the community. (f) Short-term family groups comprised of key family members of newly admitted residents to deal with common concerns of placement, sharing of information about institutional policies and services, and delineation of institutional tasks and family tasks. The family group can be the means by which the institution encourages the maintenance of ties with the elderly resident.

These groups are age-homogeneous since they are designed to help people with specific life transition crises. Because these groups provide people with opportunities to work and develop relationships with people similar to themselves, it is desirable for them to consist of 8 to 10 members with specific common interests among members clearly defined.

3. *Self-government groups,* the purpose of which is to help people maintain some control over what happens to them in the senior center or in the residential institution. Such groups deal with concerns related to agency or institutional policies, procedures, and services. Though their latent purpose may be to create an image of democracy for the organization, they do in fact also deal with schedules, food, program, interpersonal problems, staff problems, and efforts to enhance access to necessary resources and services. Specialized committees usually spin off from the larger executive or resident council groups. Committees to plan programs for the overall organization, religious committees to plan services and holiday celebrations, dietary committees to advise on menus, committees for special celebrations are some examples.

Two problems tend to arise in the development of self-government groups under the aegis of an organization which fundamentally controls the resources, i.e., goods and services of the organization. The tendency is for self-governing groups to serve the purpose of the organization rather than its own formal presumed constituency. In the popular jargon they tend to become coopted by the administration and/or become an elitist, self-serving group of people.

The second problem concerns the nature of its own leadership. Self-government groups tend to be led by the most articulate and resourceful members or residents who struggle among themselves as an elite group for power and authority about who owns and runs the group. Social workers assigned to work with such groups can mitigate such tendencies by helping the group pay attention to its tasks and to each other. The social worker also offers technical assistance concerning problems of accountability to its own constituency and mediates efforts of administration to control and coopt.

4. *Social action groups* provide opportunities for people to continue to exert control over their lives by affecting political and social issues of concern to old people (as well as issues of general concern), e.g., a change in the mandatory retirement age, problems of housing, transportation, public amenities, traffic lights, increased police protection, increase in Medicare and Medicaid benefits, etc. Social action groups are age-heterogeneous. Feelings of strength are often associated with large numbers, i.e., large membership.

For reasons already described, age-homogeneous services are generally problem-solving or socialization groups, while age-heterogeneous services include self-government, social action, and educational groups. Group services organized along the range suggested provide older people with opportunities for choice: groups to develop new, caring relationships, to maintain some control over their lives, to assume new roles and responsibilities, and to gain access to needed resources.

OBTAINING SANCTION FOR GROUP SERVICES

There is much more to obtaining sanction for and institutionalizing group services than achieving professional understanding and conviction about its value. Group services disrupt existing organizational arrangements for service delivery; they require a new stance towards clients and a shift from the familiar and comfortable one-to-one style of work and service modality; group services create a subtle redistribution of power and control between client and worker requiring the worker to "hang" looser and be prepared for the unexpected. It makes service more visible and less "manageable"—but the rewards in better service for clients and greater professional virtuosity for the practitioner more than make up for these "difficulties." To be effective, group services in the institution must be supported by all significant parts of the institution. For example, creating a group in a long-term care facility cannot be accomplished by calling a meeting of certain individuals and getting on with it. Other people and systems need to be carefully considered: schedules of other services, nursing shifts and schedules, transportation to and from meetings, rooms in which to meet, conflicting perceptions and priorities about service needs mandate that we operate within the reality of departmental interdependence.[15] The nature of the organizational adjustments required by group services also require ever renewed and reinforced administrative sanction. Anyone who has worked in institutions where a range of group services exists knows that the group worker is quickly identified as the "trouble maker," especially when groups express concern about meal service, the long wait to see the eye doctor and podiatrist, the need for comfortable chairs in the lounge, and the need for closets which lock, etc. These can be perceived as (and perhaps are) undermining of other staff. Yet the worker cannot be effective in helping the group negotiate these concerns without causing some tension and irritation. This is why continuing administrative sanction is so important. Such support goes along with the acceptance of the risks inherent in almost every worthwhile effort. The worker cannot, for example, control the group process, and administration may not share the group's perception of problems. The administration must, however, engage and negotiate with the clients' view of his own needs. This approach works; it helps to maintain a dynamic tension within the institution, capable of resisting and mediating the institution's own stultifying organizational inevitabilities.

The importance of agency sanction in the institutional setting obtains similarly for the community based setting. Here, too, the role played by the intake worker in helping to connect new clients to needed agency resources is pivotal. In most agencies the intake worker gets the initial picture of the aged applicants' interests and problems. Often, this information remains on application forms and with the intake worker. Agency sanction for group services must be an intrinsic part of intake, expressed in the sharing of information about existing groups with the applicant, and information about the applicant with the group service workers, and then following through by connecting the applicant with desired group service.

LEVELS OF GROUP DEMAND

Each of the four types of groups already described makes different demands upon group members. The amount of interdependence and mutual aid which is required of group members varies depending on the type of group. On a continuum, formal and informal educational groups may be defined as low-level demand groups, while life task or problem-solving groups may be defined as high-level demand groups. This specification or classification has important implications for the organization of group services and for worker role. These distinctions are illustrated by two examples from practice:

A number of residents on an infirmary floor in a new long-term care facility individually spoke with the worker about the problems of living in the institution. The food came up cold; no condiments were served with meals; there were no locks on their closets or dressers; things were disappearing; and tipping was depleting their meager funds. All residents on the floor suffered from some degree of physical disability but most were mentally alert. Some were able to move off the floor for activities; most spent the day on the floor. The worker, in talking with residents, sensed overwhelming feelings of helplessness about being able to effect change, and hopelessness that things could change. "Sure we live in a beautiful place, but there's more to living than nice furniture and drapes. They have to care about you, and who's going to listen to a crippled old lady?"

The suggestion that a group be formed to discuss these issues was made to several residents, who agreed to consider the idea. After sanction was obtained for the formation of a floor group to discuss and deal with concerns of living on that floor, all 35 residents were invited individually to attend a first group meeting. Reminders about time and place were provided; nurse aides were properly authorized to bring people who needed help to the meeting. To the social worker's delight, 15 people actually attended the first meeting.

For one month, the worker attempted to develop mutual understanding about group purpose and ways of working together. The worker also conveyed her tested conviction that they could do things together to better the situation even if it was hard and sometimes frustrating work. Despite administrative sanction for the group, the residents spoke of not wanting to complain, "things weren't so bad," "everybody did the best they could," "it takes time." As it became apparent that no one person was willing to risk sharing her/his feelings and perceptions, it also became apparent to the worker that although the members lived together on the same floor, few of them knew each other. The needed more time to get to know and trust each other before they could risk the kind of exposure demanded by such a group.

The worker shared her understanding and acceptance of their reluctance to become involved in the group and much relief was expressed as the decision to disband the group was made. Three special interest groups were then formed on the floor: a music listening group, a newspaper discussion group, and a cooking group. Through twice-weekly participation in these low-level demand groups, residents got to know each other better and shared some of their past with each other, and some new friendships and some trust began to develop. Two months later, the floor group was reorganized because group members felt better able to be open about their concerns. Although still fearful about "making waves" and recriminations from staff, they began to work first on the food issue, which seemed safest, and then gradually on other issues.

A second, somewhat shorter example comes from work in the outpatient geriatric psychiatric clinic of a large urban hospital. The chief psychiatrist approached the worker about organizing a group for eight patients, all of whom were seen in the clinic on the same morning. These men and women, ranging in age from 62 to 83, were in varying stages of isolation and depression associated with retirement, the death of a child, or a probable move to institutional life. Again, the group was organized as a problem-solving group to work on similar life struggles. Although group participation had not been part of the lifestyle of any of them, eight people came to meetings for two weeks and during these meetings spoke of the weather, of transportation to the clinic, etc., but not of their troubles. At the end of the second meeting, the worker suggested they might like to try some simple crafts at the next meeting (the worker could only help with simple crafts) and suggested that if they brought some lunch, they could eat together. This was readily agreed to. In the process of helping each other with tile craft and copper enameling, members began to see each other as unique individuals. There was some talk about their children and later about their loneliness. Lunch became the time for sharing deeper concerns and this happened as they got to know each other and felt enhanced competence in the activities preceding lunch.

Participation in low-level demand groups is not necessarily a prerequisite for participation in high-level demand groups. We need to develop clarity about different demands which different kinds of groups make upon their members and plan group services accordingly.

THE HELPING PROCESS IN GROUPS

The Initial Phase (Preparation)

In developing group services, several critical factors require attention. First, many old people are reluctant to join groups because group participation has not been part of their lifestyle. This is the case more often for the older cohort than it is for the younger cohort of the aged. Where it has been present it has been, for the most part, instrumentally rather than affectively oriented. In both community and institutional settings, the pattern seems to be for some people to participate while most find it difficult to become engaged in group activity, particularly in problem-solving groups. This reluctance demands a great deal of ''outreach'' efforts which are specific and clear about group purpose and connected empathically to the needs and interests of the specific individual. The announcement of a new group on the agency bulletin board or over the loudspeaker may be heard by many but listened to by few and does not replace personal contact with prospective members.

The physical effort involved in getting to group meetings, availability of transportation, and the physical arrangement of the meeting room all significantly influence whether or not the group service itself can become a reality. What may seem to be ''a stone's throw'' from home for a younger person, may be dragging a stone for the older person. Ramps, short flights of stairs, accessible toilets, elevators, physical arrangements (e.g., a round table) that accommodate visual and hearing impairments, or a pleasant room in a quiet spot in the building express and convey interest, respect, and caring far more eloquently than words ever can.

Beginnings

The focus of work with all groups in the beginning phase is the establishment of mutual understandings between members, and between members and workers (agency), about group purpose and about how that purpose will be accomplished, i.e., the division of labor between members and worker. Specific delineation of purpose provides focus for the work throughout ensuing phases; it provides structure safeguarding members and workers alike from unnecessary intrusions into other aspects of their lives. The achievement of mutual understandings (which we call contracting) establishes a frame of reference about what is relevant to the work of this group, and serves as an accountability tool for both worker and group members. The steps in this process include a statement by the worker about why the agency is offering this service which in form and content demonstrates to group members the worker's (agency's) understanding of their situation. The worker then needs to reach for feedback to enable members' differing interests in the new service to emerge. Worker and members then negotiate around the range of interests or stakes, and if the service being sought or offered is seen as one which the agency can provide, purpose becomes mutually defined and the direction of work is set.

This process, so briefly outlined, applies to work with all groups, and is critical because how one begins will profoundly affect what follows. Particular difficulties in work with old people arise from their tendency to view the worker as the expert, the authority on whom they can depend for need fulfillment. While the dependence-independence struggle is present in all groups, its resolution can take longer with groups of old people, and unless the worker is sensitive to this issue, it may appear to be resolved when in fact it is not. The societal view that others, and particularly younger others, know what is best for old people, has been incorporated by many of the elderly, particularly the older cohort. This takes two forms. First, a tendency to accept, to acquiesce to the worker's perception of purpose, particularly where purpose is stated empathically. Acquiescence does not result in mutuality but in a facade of mutuality wherein the group becomes the worker's creation. A worker who is sensitive to the group process may realize in several weeks that she is working exceptionally hard to help group members maintain focus on group purpose, and/or that attendance is falling off. This may well be the signal to reopen the issue of purpose, to reach for and explicitly identify possible negatives—in short, to seek feedback. The older, more dependent person finds it extremely difficult to express the negatives, to disagree, and the worker who is aware of this at the outset has an edge in contract renegotiation.

A second manifestation of the independence-dependence issue is in how the group will accomplish its purpose, i.e., what is to be the division of labor between worker and members. Group members particularly in the older cohort tend to see the worker as more powerful than they, having more immediate access to needed resources, and as more articulate (especially in the initial phase of work), and they expect that the worker will assume responsibility for follow-through in group decisions which involve contact with almost all external systems. The worker, on the other hand, reluctant to validate the self-perceptions of members as powerless, helpless, and useless, tends to press them to assume responsibility for follow-through. The worker's unassailable but unshared perception of division of labor is to help members of the group arrive at their own solutions, help them with planning and, if needed, with follow-through, but not do it for them. The consequence may well be a stalemate in which work on the environmental problem stops, group members feel not understood, and the worker becomes even more convinced of the virtues of helping members become more independent.

The worker's private question, "How can I help the members of this group accomplish the task for which they have come together?" is replaced with, "How will they function without me when I leave at the end of the year, if I don't help them act for themselves now?" In turn the group members might reply, if indeed they did verbalize such things: "If she does these things for us that would really be helpful and we will know that she respects our wishes, and cares about us. It takes so much to do these things; we don't have the energy and she does. Besides, she'll do it better than we could." The undesirability of being dependent is so ingrained in our culture and professional values that workers' reluctance to provide certain help and assistance lest they encourage dependency is understandable. It is so much better after all to do for oneself! To indulge or yield to such reluctance may however be securing one's own higher principles at the expense of the legitimate needs of others. This dilemma, which is at least partly real, may be resolved by viewing the older client's "dependency" as similar to the needs of clients in other circumstances who are considered able to help themselves yet whose needs for concrete services are readily met by the worker. Helping the older person on his own terms may be, at least initially, paying proper homage to "starting with people where they are" and demonstrates to members that the worker has heard them, respects them, and cares for them.

Often what is defined as dependency is a reaction to the actual absence of needed supports, and when these are in fact provided, dependency decreases rather than increases. Therefore, when defining the division of labor with groups of old people (and this is true for other dependent and stigmatized groups) the stalemate over who does what can be eliminated, or at least attenuated, by the worker's sharing with members of the group her perception of what tasks they can in fact perform. The worker can also offer to accompany and help group members with task performance, or invite them to join her as she performs the tasks. Finally, all else failing, the worker can carry out the necessary tasks without their help, out of respect for their wishes, notwithstanding their competence to do the work. What matters most is an approach which avoids the stalemate or power struggle. When these continue over time, a residue of ill feeling between member and worker develops which hampers positive group experience.

Throughout the work, the older group member must be accorded full adult status, not that of an aged child.

The Ongoing Phase

The central concern in the ongoing phase of work with all groups is sustaining the problem-solving process. To do this, the activities of the group members must be focused on the purposes which brought them together and on members being able to help each other to develop their own solutions to problems. The worker facilitates these processes by guarding the focus of work as established in the contracting process, breaking down larger problems into more manageable pieces, identifying and pointing to the obstacles to their work, providing technical help and information relevant to the social reality impinging on the group, and finally conveying his/her own faith that the members' common efforts and mutual aid arrangement will pay off.

A distinctive feature of work with older people in this phase is their greater tendency than most groups to view themselves as powerless to control their lives and effect changes in their environment. This strains the worker's ability to maintain a working balance between a tendency to either overidentify with members' fears (and sink into a joint despair) or to make unrealistic demands for work (and court stalemate and struggle).

A second difficulty in this phase of the work lies in the worker's reaction to "undesirable" behaviors of some group members. Many workers, new to work with the aged, come with an idealized image and unrealistic expectations of old people. They expect them to be kind, caring, and wise. There may also be a fear of generating or intensifying conflict among people whose emotional and physical resources are already limited. This may result in wanting to smooth over tensions and taking over the group's problems.

Issues of scapegoating, the authoritarian member, the acting-out group member, are obstacles which prevent all groups from working on their developmental and environmental concerns. The worker's task with groups of old people, as it is with all groups, is to help group members confront these isues. To do this, the worker needs to become aware of countertransference issues which with older people include a need to protect or infantilize. A too quick move by the worker to protect the member who is different may only result in moving the conflict underground.[16] Whatever ambiguities and uncertainties there may be in working with older groups, or any groups, we are fairly confident that they can confront, cope with, and survive the human relations issues and conflicts we may wish to spare them.

The Termination Phase

The central concern of the termination phase with groups is to preserve the integrity and reality of the group experience. Endings are difficult because they reawaken past separations (many of which may not have been resolved).[17] Because they are difficult, group members and workers alike may wish to avoid the process. Throughout this phase, as in other phases of work, affective as well as cognitive components need to be present in discussion. The principal tasks for workers in termination include: calling attention early enough to the fact of termination to allow sufficient time for the evasion, anger, acceptance, and finally the actual goodbyes so characteristic of the process. Of overriding importance is that worker and members not deny or intellectualize the experience. How one ends with groups will influence how well the group will continue to function as an ongoing group, or how well members will be able to risk themselves in a new group experience.

For many workers, endings with old people are extremely difficult. They see themselves as inflicting still another loss on people who already suffer from so much loss. Some workers maintain distance from clients throughout the encounter because they feel the loss of an intimate relationship will do great harm to the old person. This is often rationalized as a desire not to create dependency on the worker. Some workers delay and unduly condense or telescope the process. Still others avoid termination by a "farewell party," permitting only positive sentiments to prevail. Since these strategies are rooted in worker need rather than client need, they deny elderly clients adult status. Older people are experienced victims or survivors of loss. To say that the loss of the worker will inflict great harm is to negate the strengths of old people and to indulge in subtle but unseemly feelings of professional omnipotence. If the worker can get past guilt about "abandoning" group members, and focus on the required tasks, the termination phase can become one which will preserve the integrity and reality of the group experience.

One closing point about gift-giving may be in order because it is peculiarly pertinent to the situation of aged clients. There are differences among professionals in the field about the appropriateness and desirability of the exchange of gifts between members and workers; more specifically from members to workers at termination. If the gift is viewed by the worker as an expression of thanks as well as a way of saying, "We can do for you, as you have done for us," it also becomes an important symbol whose purpose is to momentarily equalize an essentially unequal relationship. It represents for group members an attempt to redefine the relationship in more equal and symmetrical terms.[18] The worker who refuses the gift out of regard for agency policy or his/her own values communicates a "put-down" and a wish to maintain the status distinctions implicit in the benefactor-beneficiary relationship. In view of what already has been said there is hardly or rarely an aceptable alternative to the gracious acceptance of such proferred gifts. Balanced consideration of this issue requires mentioning that it emerges from an institutional context in which gift-giving represents the purchase of services and entitlements already paid for and established and thus becomes a bribe. The bureaucratic preference for rules without exceptions or distinctions is consequently part of the problem.

REMINISCENCE IN AGING

No discussion of social work practice with the aged should overlook the process of reminiscence. It is theoretically and practically important to understand and appreciate it. While people of all ages reminisce, it is particularly associated with and has a distinctive function for the aging process.

Reminiscence is defined as: (1) the act or process of recalling past experiences, events, etc.; (2) a mental impression retained and revived; (3) a recollection narrated or told.

Erikson, in his monumental work on ego identity and the developmental tasks associated with mastery of psychosocial crises, formulates the final crisis in the life cycle as the crisis of integrity vs. despair. "It is the acceptance of one's one and only life cycle as something that had to be, and that, by necessity, permitted of no substitutions."[19] What was, was, and now there is time for reflection, but not time to go back and live a different and better life. In this formulation the acceptance of the historical inevitability of one's life and death is a major developmental task of the aged. Reminiscence, the act of recalling and narrating past experiences, becomes an important vehicle for mastery of this task. In remembering his past life, the old person is engaged in ordering his life, of accepting what has been, sometimes reworking aspects of the past to make them more acceptable to him.[20] Recalling painful struggles, the joyous times, the manifold relationships, also helps to rekindle feelings of mastery and power, feelings which are all too frequently absent from the aged person's current existence. Reminiscence is a vehicle whereby the wholeness of one's life, the integrity of one's self is preserved. To remember coming to America alone at age 17 to avoid the draft in Czarist Russia, the ensuing struggles to survive, to marry and to raise a family; to remember trade union struggles or the building of a business; to remember mothering a family, struggling to make ends meet; to remember the accolades of an achievement is, at least during the moments of remembering, to once again count as a contributing human being.

Communication theorists assert that all communication consists of two levels of messages, the explicit or content level and the implicit or relationship level.[21] Examination of the implicit messages sent to the social worker by the old person who is reminiscing reveals how he wishes to be perceived in the relationship. First he is saying that he has not always been as he may now be: "I was once more like you are now." This may be seen as an attempt to establish greater symmetry or equality in a relationship which is largely complementary, or one-up, one-down. Second, in giving of himself by sharing aspects of his past, the old person communicates that he cares about the other and wishes to be cared about. Through the act of reminiscence, he is thus reaching for appreciation and acceptance from the other. There is an implicit invitation to become part of the older person's life through the past as well as in the here and now—to come closer together, perhaps even to replace a lost loved person.

Social workers have sometimes been frightened of two specific aspects of reminiscence. First, its repetitive nature is often taken to denote the presence of organic mental syndrome, and second, the invitation to replace a lost loved one is seen as developing into dependency and manipulation of the relationship. While in some situations this may indeed be the case, this assessment in no way diminishes the importance of reminiscence to the aged person. It is crucial, therefore, that we not "tune out" through head nodding and mind wandering, but rather in these situations offer the acceptance and appreciation being sought, while at the same time we present the reality of the present situation.

Old people who are mentally intact often repeat the same event as they reminisce. Butler believes that the life review is a process that exposes unconscious material with particular concentration upon former unresolved conflicts.[22] If the repetitive stories are viewed as reflecting these unresolved conflicts and as an attempt to work them through, then the worker's use of reminiscence as a therapeutic tool becomes clear. Within the repeated story which may recall an unhappy or a happy event, may lie guilt about acts performed or not performed, or stresses which were life-threatening in nature. These feelings will not become conscious until the worker helps the client probe the situation. In this way, the old person is given the opportunity—a second chance—to resolve his problem.[23]

When a worker participates in the process of reminiscence with an old person, he is giving that person the opportunity to be valued in his entirety. Each person's wholeness includes his past and his present; each person has the right to present his strengths as well as his weaknesses and dependencies. The worker, on the other hand, is given the opportunity to understand the totality of that person's life experiences which have made him what he is today. Also, in these times of rapid change, reminiscence helps to preserve the struggles of the past, so that old and young can learn from them. To encourage and participate with the aged client in the process of reminiscence enhances the client-worker relationship in that it brings the two closer together and denotes an appreciation and acceptance of the total aged person by the social worker.

NOTES

1. See, for example, M. Powell Lawton, "Ecology and Aging," in Leon A. Pastalan and Daniel H. Carson (eds.), *Spatial Behavior of Older People* (Ann Arbor:

The University of Michigan–Wayne State University Institute of Gerontology, 1970), pp. 40–67.

2. Carel B. Germain, "Time: an Ecological Variable in Social Work Practice," *Social Casework* 57, no. 7 (July 1976), pp. 419–26.

---

1. Elaine Brody, "Aging," *Encyclopedia of Social Work* (New York: National Association of Social Workers, 1971), p. 51.

2. Most of the data in this section were derived from Herman B. Brotman, *Useful Facts Series Nos. 1–42, Memoranda,* Administration on Aging, U.S. Department of Health, Education, and Welfare; and Herman Brotman, "Who Are the Aged," paper delivered at the New York State Association of Gerontological Educators, November 1974.

3. United States Census Bureau Report, June 1976.

4. Brotman papers.

5. Ibid.

6. Rose Dobrof, "Serving Older Men and Women in Senior Centers and Vacation Programs," unpublished paper delivered at Vacations for the Aging and Senior Center Association, 225 Park Ave. So., New York, N.Y.

7. Brotman papers.

8. Erik Erikson, *Childhood and Society* (New York: W.W. Norton, 1963).

9. Ethel Shanas, Peter Townsend, et al., *Old People in Three Industrial Societies* (New York: Atherton Press, 1968); John Clausen, "The Life Course of Individuals," in Matilda Riley, Marilyn Johnson, and Anne Foner, *Aging and Society, Vol. III* (New York: Russell Sage Foundation, 1972), p. 457; Allen Pincus, "Toward A Developmental View of Aging," *Social Work* 12, no. 3 (July 1967), pp. 33–41.

10. Dobrof, "Serving."

11. Ibid.

12. Our own orientation (expressed as "social work with groups") is derived in large part from the reciprocal or interactionist model as developed by William Schwartz. See, for example, William Schwartz, "Social Group Work: Interactionist Approaches," *Encyclopedia of Social Work* (New York: National Association of Social Workers, 1971); "The Social Worker in the Group," *The Social Welfare Forum* (New York: Columbia University Press, 1961); Schwartz and Zalba (eds.), *The Practice of Group Work* (New York: Columbia University Press, 1971).

13. Schwartz and Zalba, ibid., p. 7.

14. Gerald Euster, "A System of Groups in Institutions for the Aged," *Social Casework* 52, no. 8 (October 1971), pp. 523–29.

15. Cohen and Hammerman, "Social Work with Groups" in Elaine Brody, *A Social Work Guide for Long Term Care Facilities* (Rockville, Md.: National Institute of Mental Health, Department of Health, Education and Welfare, 1974).

16. Mark Foreman, "Conflict, Controversy, and Confrontation in Group Work with Older Adults," *Social Work* 12, no. 1 (January 1967), p. 80.

17. Fox, Nelson, and Bolman, "The Termination Process: A Neglected Dimension in Social Work," *Social Work* 14, no. 4 (October 1969), pp. 53–63.

18. Watzlawick, Beaven, and Jackson, *Pragmatics of Human Communication* (New York: W.W. Norton, 1967).
19. Erikson, pp. 268–69.
20. Robert Butler, "The Life Review: An Interpretation of Reminiscence in the Aged," in Robert Kastenbaum (ed.), *New Thoughts on Old Age* (New York: Springer, 1964), and in *Psychiatry* 26, no. 1 (February 1963), pp. 65–76.
21. Watzlawick, Beaven, and Jackson.
22. Butler.
23. We would like to thank Barbara Levi for this formulation.

ADDITIONAL SOURCES ON GROUP SERVICES FOR THE ELDERLY

Allen, Ruth. "A Study of Subjects Discussed by Elderly Patients in Group Counseling." *Social Casework* 43, no. 7 (July 1962), p. 360.

Berger, Lynne, and Berger, Milton. "A Holistic Approach to Psychogeriatric Patients." *International Journal of Group Psychotherapy* 23, no. 1 (October 1973), pp. 432–64.

Cartletti, June. "Group Treatment of Chronic Regressed Psychiatric Patients." *Social Casework* 44, no. 2 (February 1963), pp. 68–73.

Euster, Gerald. "A System of Groups in Institutions for the Aged." *Social Casework* 52, no. 8 (October 1971), pp. 523–29.

Kastenbaum Robert, and Slater, Philip E. "Effects of Wine on the Interpersonal Behavior of Geriatric Patients." In Robert Kastenbaum (ed.), *New Thoughts on Old Age*. New York: Springer, 1964, pp. 191–204.

Klein, Wilma; LeShan, Eda; and Furman Sylvan. *Promoting Mental Health of Older People Through Group Methods*. New York: H. Wolff, 1965.

Kubie, Susan, and Landau, Gertrude. *Group Work With the Aged*. New York: International Universities Press, 1953.

Lowy, Louis. "The Group in Social Work with the Aged." *Social Work* 7, no. 4 (October 1962), pp. 43–50.

—— "Roadblocks in Social Work Practice with Older People." *The Gerontologist,* 7, no. 2 (June 1967), pp. 109–13.

Oberleder, Muriel. "Restoring the Mentally Ill Through Reality Orientation." *Informational Outline #4*, February 1969, New York Federation of Protestant Welfare Agencies.

Ross, Mathew. "A Review of Some Recent Group Psychotherapy Methods for Elderly Patients." In Max Rosenbaum and Milton Berger (eds.), *Group Psychotherapy and Group Function.* New York: Basic Books, 1963. See pp. 487–509.

Salmon, Robert. "Creative Programming in Vacation Settings for the Aged." Paper presented at Vacations for the Aging and Senior Center Association, May 1973.

Shere, Eugenia. "Group Therapy with the Very Old." In Kastenbaum, *New Thoughts,* pp. 146–60.

Unger, Joyce, and Kramer, Elaine. "Applying Frames of Reference in Group Work with the Aged." *The Gerontologist,* Part 1, Spring 1968, p. 51–3.

Vickery, Florence E. *Creative Programming for Older Adults: A Leadership Training Guide.* New York: Association Press, 1972.

Weiner, Hyman. "Group Content Issues in Work with the Aged." In *The Social Worker's Use of Group Approaches in Work with the Aged.* New York: Central Bureau for the Jewish Aged, 1966.

4 *Diagnosis in Family Therapy*

HARRY J. APONTE

A continuing emphasis in professional social work practice from its begin-nings has been on diagnosis and its connections to treatment. For Mary Richmond, social diagnosis was the basis for social treatment. It was con-ceived as the gathering of the greatest possible number of facts concerning the client's situation as the base for determining what needed to be done.[1] Gordon Hamilton's psychosocial formulation of diagnosis broadened the unit of attention to include biological and emotional factors along with the social and cultural but she restricted data-gathering to those with relevance to the problem.[2] Treatment was to be directed to changing the dysfunctional personal or social aspects in the client's situation. But Richmond's and Hamilton's conceptions of diagnosis and treatment were based on a disease or medical metaphor, and social workers influenced by the metaphor con-tinued to seek the causes of dysfunction chiefly within the person. Similarly, the goals of treatment were often conceived as cure or improvement of an internal state.

With the advent of general systems theory, attempts were made to broaden the notions of diagnosis and treatment to encompass the totality of person and environment.[3] The terms assessment and intervention were in-troduced as semantic tools to help social workers move away from the limi-tations of the medical idiom.[4] Efforts to help were to be based on under-standing not only the person and the situation, but the complexities of their interaction.[5]

Writing within the family therapy tradition, Aponte uses the terms diag-nosis and treatment. Clearly, however, he uses them holistically with the ecological context as the frame of reference. The problem is located in the interface or boundary area between child and family, or child and school, or child and other aspects of the environment, rather than in the child. Help seeks to improve the transactions at that interface.[6] Thus treatment proce-

dures may be directed to the individual, the environment, or to the transactions themselves. In the single consultative session reported here, Aponte shows how ecological diagnosis and treatment focuses on the transactions between the identified patient and his family and on the transactions among all family members since these affect all members. The parents had themselves selected their problem with Aldo for discussion with the consultant. Aponte indicates that in future sessions, the cotherapists may very well focus on the family's or patient's transactions with the school, the peer network, the physical setting of home and neighborhood, or other interface areas as needed. But for now, the consultant is concerned with the structure and functions of the family system itself, as a set of interacting parts. Neither the individual personalities nor the family system are viewed as pathological. Rather the position is taken that relations and communications among members of subsystems, and between subsystems, are awry.

Aponte takes full account of this Chicano family's minority status, and of how cultural aspects may affect familial roles, perceptions and expectations.[7] The importance of the consultant's own Hispanic background and his sex and age is underscored as Aponte discusses his entrance into the family organization. These consultant-variables are skillfully used in supporting the father's masculinity and bolstering his faltering leadership within the family. The consultant helps father understand his sons and his role in their development; he helps the brothers relate supportively to one another, and he helps mother to recognize and support father's strengths. His moves are designed to change the structure of the family system so that transactions among the parts change in a positive direction. This can be expected to enhance individual coping and to improve the family organization as the intimate environment in which all are functioning.

The effectiveness with which this restructuring is done rests upon diagnosis as a continuous moment-to-moment process. Aponte specifies certain hypotheses he entertained as they arose out of his transactions with the family during the consultation. These are continually tested out, and extended or discarded on the basis of further transactions. Thus diagnosis is continuous, fluid, and changing to keep in touch with the fluid and changing life processes that are being observed and experienced moment-to-moment by the therapist and family together. It is this notion of diagnosis (or assessment) as process rather than as product that characterizes the ecological perspective. The conception is quite different from structured, formalized diagnoses or assessments that frequently rely on psychiatric labels and tend to take on a static or fixed character despite their avowed tentativeness.

The reader may note in this single session many points of theoretical and practical import. Prominent among these is Aponte's use of task. Family members are actively engaged in the therapeutic process. Father, for example, is asked to speak directly with Aldo so that he may ascertain if Aldo is afraid to disagree with him. Father, mother, and the sons are given tasks to work on at home. Such tasks are designed to enhance functioning, within the cultural life-style, by continuing the restructuring of the family organization begun in the consultation session. The emotional and social impact of the tasks derives from the diagnostic understanding mutually reached by the therapist and the family—especially the father—during the session.

—C.B.G.

T HE A PPROAC H to the diagnostic process in family therapy is as essential to the therapy as are the change-inducing techniques that are employed. Yet, the diagnostic aspect of family therapy is either underplayed or overlooked.

The standard we have for diagnosis is the medical model for the investigation of bodily disease. It is the study of the individual. This model focusses on the individual organism with all its biological systems—their current functioning along with their developmental and medical histories. Interest in persons other than the patient is based on concern about genetic history and infectious contamination.

Psychological diagnosis calls for a radical departure. The individual psyche is uniquely dependent upon its relationship to others for its formation as well as for its functioning. This is not only a developmental dependence but a continuing dynamic one. The intrinsic social dependency of the psychological person is the reason for family therapy and other social systems approaches to psychotherapy. It is the basis of the need for an approach to diagnosis that differs from the medical model.

The diagnostic approach to physical illness can serve as a useful analogy for the conceptualization of models for the study and investigation of emotional problems as long as the analogous nature of the comparison is not lost sight of. One of the limitations of the diagnostic models of individually oriented therapies has been the effort to extend diagnostic methodology and nomenclature of physical illness into the psychological sphere. With the emergence of the systems therapies there is need for a methodical approach to the diagnosis of emotional-social problems with its own vocabulary that takes into account the nature of the ecological context in which human problems are generated and solved. To diagnose in family therapy is to understand a module of human behavior the ecological context of which this behavior is a product. It is to see how all the forces in that context converge to produce a specific action at a particular moment in time. In this consideration the physical-biological dimension would need to be accounted for along with dynamics ranging from the broadest social considerations to the psychological structure of the individual personality. Obviously the complexity of this ecosystem prohibits complete comprehension, but some of the proximate, overriding determinants are within the grasp of our perception.

In the social and psychological sphere of the ecosystem, the component systems are functionally organized or structured in patterns that form the basis for operations of the systems. And these structural patterns are as dynamically interdependent as are the systems to which they belong. A political entity or system has its own structure of patterns, its institutions and laws, which distinguish it from other political entities which influence the lives of the citizens who compose it. A family has its own unique traditional internal and external relationships and ways of doing things that give it a certain predictability and that colors everything done by the family. Each individual has his or her own psychological structure which is a uniquely complex world of its own, but a world which continually evolves its identity and its operational ability through its interactional dependence on the other social systems in its ecological context. An action of any unit in this ecosystem whether by a single individual or by an entire family is produced out of the convergence of all the above patterns of the various systems at a moment in time. Repetitions of this action, the repeated convergence of all these dynamics form another pattern in itself. It is upon these concepts of dynamic interdependence of social systems that our approach to diagnosis is based.

The structural family therapist utilizes the ecological context as the framework for his or her diagnostic efforts. The technical problem for the therapist is how to approach the complex ecosystem of an individual, a couple, or a family in a way that will not overwhelm the therapist with data, but which will provide the information most relevant to understanding the problem or problems the clients present.

The first determinant of the diagnostic approach is that the primary goal of the understanding is to solve a problem. This means that the therapist will seek to obtain only the information needed to solve the problem and will not make the quest of understanding a personality or a family a study for its own sake. It is likely that the diagnostic effort will stop far short of a comprehensive psychological or sociological study, which is one reason why many have underestimated the importance of diagnosis in family therapy. The therapist searches for diagnostic data that is relevant to solving a problem and nothing more.

A corollary to the pursuit of information related to solutions is that the method of searching for the information is intrinsic but subservient to the interventions employed to solve the problem. Every problem has its structural underpinning in the ecological context of the people presenting the problem, and this is the ecostructure. From the very first transaction between the therapist and the family members, every action of the therapist is directed towards modifying this structural underpinning. The therapist continually experiments with the effectiveness of change-inducing techniques, developing hypotheses about the relative value of different therapeutic approaches. The diagnostic probes are thus incorporated into these therapeutic efforts so that both are clearly intrinsic to any one intervention.

The second major determinant of the ecostructural diagnostic approach is the premise that the forces that are creating the problem are all active in current behavior and transactions. For the structural family therapist every transaction in a session among the family members and with him or her is a product and representation of the structural patterns that underpin the lives of those in the session, including the therapist. The therapist attempts to create a context in the session in which some of the same principal dynamic structures will be reexperienced and reenacted among family members and with the therapist. The therapist must become so connected with the family in the sessions and consequently in the treatment that he becomes a dynamic factor in the structural patterning of the family and its members. The control that the therapist is able to exert over his or her actions in the sessions becomes the variable against which the family's behavior is measured and understood. The therapist becomes the factor which is grafted onto the structures that are being lived out in the session and which can shape and influence them. On this basis, behavioral and transactional patterns tied to certain problems are observed and changed in a session in ways that will carry over outside the therapy.

The third determinant of the ecostructural diagnostic approach is that each intervention in a session as well as the entire course of treatment flow out of a progressive series of diagnostic hypotheses. With this backdrop to the approach to diagnosis, the therapist concerned with the structures of the ecological context, or ecostructure, views each session as analogous to an experimental laboratory. The therapist determines what problems are to be addressed. The therapist develops his or her hypotheses about their ecostructural girding and proceeds to intervene in ways that at one and the same time test the hypotheses and move the systems towards the changes thought necessary at the moment. The hypotheses include considerations about what aspects of the structural make-ups of the individual personalities and the various relationships that exist within and outside the family affect the problem in question. Hypotheses will be discarded or confirmed, and if confirmed will need to be elaborated upon throughout the course of therapy.

Diagnosis is essential to family treatment as to every other form of treatment. Out of each transaction in a session the therapist draws hypotheses about its meaning in the context of the interview and about what it might imply about the family and individual structural patterns that underpin the problems being presented outside the session. Every action of the therapist is meant to test out these hypotheses at the same time that it is geared towards the personal and family changes that are the therapeutic goals.

The basic steps reflecting the ecostructural approach to diagnosis are:

1. Identify issues or problems to be addressed.
2. Collect relevant data, reported and experiential.
3. Develop diagnostic hypotheses.
4. Determine tentative therapeutic goals, immediate and longer range.
5. On the basis of all the above, decide on immediate intervention that will lead toward therapeutic goals.
6. Observe effect of intervention to confirm or discount hypothe-

ses about effectiveness of intervention and accuracy of diagnostic hypotheses.

With the last step the cycle begins all over again.

The detailed intricacy of this diagnostic process can only be communicated through clinical material. Parts of a session conducted as a consultation will be used here for illustration. Obviously all of the consultant's assumptions cannot be brought into consideration here, but we hope to convey something of the unifying fabric which the structural family theory provided through the diagnostic and therapeutic moves made by the therapist.

The family is of Mexican ethnic background and the consultant is Puerto Rican. The nuclear family is composed of the parents, who are in their early forties, about the same age as the therapist, and five children, three boys and two girls: Fred, 16, Aida, 14, Esteban, 13, Aldo, 11 and Elena, 4. The family has been in treatment for some months. The consultant has been told that the family has so many problems that it was difficult for the two therapists working with them to attend to any. There is considerable conflict between the parents. The mother was described as active and involved in the therapy and the father peripheral both to therapy and his family. Although there are problems with the other boys, the original problem was Aldo's inattentiveness in school and "childish" behavior.

On the basis of this brief description, the consultant hypothesized the following ecostructural picture on the bases of the structure of force, boundary, and alignment in the systems involved. Speaking first to the dynamic of force in the family systems, the consultant conjectured that in the operation related to the management of the children the mother had greater influence than the father. The therapists spoke of much conflict between the parents, which also suggested to the consultant a conflict for control, possibly over the children as over other areas of their lives. Considering the problem of the identified patient but even more so the confusing array of problems alluded to by the therapists, the consultant also considered that the mother's sway over the children might not be effective, which could be related to the counterresponses of the father. This also raised the possibility that the identified patient was caught in the crossfire of the parents' struggle and was not able to exert influence or personal force in his family appropriate to his stage of personal development.

With respect to boundaries in the family structure, the father was described as an outsider in his own family. Yet he was apparently not resigned to the position since he was engaged in fighting back against his wife. His continuous participation in the therapy certainly suggested that he had not elected to surrender his place at home and his position in relation to his children around whom most of the problem revolved. His participation in the therapy and his struggle with his wife, added to the tradition of male dominance in his Latin heritage, also suggested the possibility of there existing for him as well as for the other family members the expectation that he would provide a model and a distinctive leadership role for the boys in the family. However, considering the conflicting claim of the parents on the children and the possible lack of appropriate influence of the identified patient in his family, the boy's own personal boundaries within his family could have been diminished. His own sense of self, the boundaries of his self image, could be relatively undefined for his age, leading to "childish behavior."

In terms of the alignments in the family, the supposed assumption of the management of the children by the mother suggested an alignment of the children with her. Yet the information about the father's conflicting claims also compelled the consideration of conflicting loyalties of the children between the parents. This certainly had to be thought of as a factor with the identified patient. That this child was singled out as the problem child also brought with it the thought the boy might be scapegoated, blamed by other members in his family, being therefore in a negative alignment in relation to other family members.

It was this kind of hypothetical thinking that determined the consultant's first action. As the family came into the room and selected seats, the consultant requested the father to switch chairs with Aldo so that he, the father, would be sitting next to the consultant. The consultant would thereby offer himself as an ally to the father, drawing him into the center of the happenings in the session and giving the father the opportunity to assume more active control over what would take place with his family in the session. Implicitly the consultant wanted to see how each family member would behave if the father had the opportunity to assume a central role in the proceedings. The therapist followed up the seating plan with a request to the father, Mr. Gonzaga, to introduce the family to him, again further centralizing the father and linking him with the consultant. (The group sat in a semicircle. From right to left there sat the consultant, the father, Aldo, Esteban, the mother, Elena, Aida and Fred.)

CONSULTANT:	Why don't you switch chairs so you will be next to me (*Aldo and Mr. Gonzaga switch chairs*) . . . okay. Introduce your family to me.
MR. GONZAGA:	(*pointing to boy next to him*) Aldo . . .
CONSULTANT:	Aldo . . . how old is Aldo?
ALDO:	Eleven.
CONSULTANT:	And him? (*pointing to next boy*)
MR. GONZAGA:	Esteban . . . (*skipping over his wife*) Elena . . .
MRS. GONZAGA:	(*interjecting spontaneously*) Elena is four.
MR. GONZAGA:	(*continuing*) Aida. Fred . . .
CONSULTANT:	(*to Mr. Gonzaga*) You've been coming for a couple of months, right?
MR. GONZAGA:	Six, seven months.
MRS. GONZAGA:	Three months.

Mrs. Gonzaga's two remarks thus far helped to reinforce the consultant's hypothesis that she was a more aggressive figure than the father in the context of their domestic life, particularly as it involved the children. Mrs. Gonzaga remembered the consultant's interest in ages, which the father forgot, and she was, as the consultant learned later, correct about the length of treatment. Both moves on the mother's part tended to draw the consultant to attend to her and give less weight to the father. The consultant risks not gaining the mother's alliance by not responding to her in both these sequences. The consultant chose to stay with father for the present to push further his effort to centralize him in the family and to test out the significance of the hypotheses about the father's position in the family. Mrs. Gonzaga's gratuitous comment on Elena also hinted at a positive alignment between two of them.

CONSULTANT: (*addressing Mr. Gonzaga*) I listened to the two of them
                (*the cotherapists with the family, who were sitting a short
                distance away*) describe a little bit about what's been
                going on. It was so complicated that I couldn't keep up
                with it . . .
MR. GONZAGA: That's right. (*laughing*)
CONSULTANT: . . . but there seemed to be so many things that you fight
                about and so many things that you are worried about . . .
                you two have got problems, and Aldo has problems, and I
                don't know, Esteban or somebody else has problems.
                Anyway, it just seemed like so many things, that I already
                got confused. (*to Esteban*) Do you want to take your
                jacket off? (*he gestures no*) Are you cold? (*gestures affir-
                matively*) Okay . . . ah, so I was sitting here waiting,
                and I figured I don't want to go through what you have
                been going through for two months and go over every
                problem. We only have about an hour, and I would like
                this time to be for your benefit . . . so, if you could pick
                just one thing, just one problem, that we could concen-
                trate on during this hour out of all the things that you have
                talked about . . . then we could try to do something
                about it and change that . . . even if we don't change
                anything else . . . if we could just pick one.

The consultant wanted to get some control over the situation from the
beginning by choosing to focus on one issue. Only by doing so could
he structure the session in a way that would allow him to follow his
own line of inquiry. He was also working on the hypothesis that,
among other things the confusion of problems was used as a defensive measure by family members to avoid dealing with any problems.
He asked the father first to point to a direction for all of them in the
session, attempting to strengthen the father's position in the family.

MR. GONZAGA: What would you like to talk about?
CONSULTANT: This is your family . . . I don't really care . . . it could
                be for one of you, and it could be for all of you . . . you
                just pick one thing out and we'll work on that.
MRS. GONZAGA: Well, we came here for Aldo . . . that's why we came
                . . . everything else was discussed along with Aldo . . .

but we still haven't solved Aldo's problem, why he be-
haves the way he does at times . . . why he gets behind
schedule in his work . . . why he hasn't been keeping up
. . . why he acts babyish . . .

CONSULTANT: Among all the problems that you have, you would rather
talk about Aldo?

MRS. GONZAGA: Well, the other children are fine, and (*inaudible*)

CONSULTANT: What?

MRS. GONZAGA: . . . we just keep going round and round . . . my husband and I . . . he thinks one way and I think another
way . . . but we are getting to understand each other better now because we know it will never change . . . you
know, it will be that way all the time. (*laughs*)

CONSULTANT: That's one way to solve a problem (*laughs*) . . . alright.

MRS. GONZAGA: He thinks one way and I think another way . . . we can't
change that.

CONSULTANT: Yeah . . . okay . . . alright . . . so if you are blind
then you learn how to use a stick, right . . . or a seeing-
eye dog . . . you don't try to cure the blindness.

MRS. GONZAGA: We work to understand each other but we respect each
other . . . like he thinks he's boss and I let him think he
is boss. (*laughing*)

Mrs. Gonzaga has taken over defining the problems for the family,
adding further confirmation to the hypothesis about her dominance.
Mr. Gonzaga, in the face of his wife's articulateness, withdraws to
silence, which also says something about him. Mrs. Gonzaga could
be an effective channel through which to help Aldo and perhaps even
to try to amplify her husband's status at home and to solve their
power struggle. But the consultant had chosen to work through the
husband and has intervened accordingly, which provides the baseline
from which to measure the mother's assertiveness and the father's
reticence. At the moment Mrs. Gonzaga is not only upstaging her
husband but is taking over the directing of the session from the consultant. She is replicating with the consultant some of her power
struggle with her husband. The consultant has thus far attempted to
methodically create a structure in the session that would centralize the
husband. The constancy of this effort offers a standard from which to
test the reactions of the family members both as to the structural rela-

tionships to which they tend to rebound and as to their ability to change. The latter also has to be part of a diagnostic assessment.

The consultant then turns to Mr. Gonzaga to reinclude him in the discussion and reintroduces the question of what is to be discussed. It gives Mr. Gonzaga another opportunity to influence the choice of problem for discussion.

CONSULTANT: *(to Mr. Gonzaga)* Which means you're not *(boss)*? *(laughs)* But, you know, of all these things, which one do you want to talk about during this hour . . . we won't talk about anything else but that.

MRS. GONZAGA: I always talked so let him talk *(motions to Mr.)*.

CONSULTANT: *(laughing)* Well, you're the boss so you want to let him talk, right? Okay, she's allowing you *(Mr.)* to talk.

MR. GONZAGA: Well . . . whatever you want to talk about . . . I don't have too much of a big problem . . . I know what I am supposed to do . . . her problem or Aldo's I guess . . . we worried about Aldo because he was behind too much in school.

CONSULTANT: Uh-huh.

MR. GONZAGA: I don't think there's is too much else of a problem.

CONSULTANT: That's fine, now, I don't want to give you a problem . . . I just want you to tell me what it is and that's what we'll talk about.

MR. GONZAGA: Aldo.

CONSULTANT: Aldo . . . so you've both decided that it's Aldo? Okay . . . and you *(Mrs. Gonzaga)* have already described what you've thought was going on with Aldo. I think you said that he was acting immature, like a baby, and he wasn't keeping up in class . . . I don't remember what else you said.

MRS. GONZAGA: He hasn't kept up all these years and I have always been after the teachers because they ignore it and say, "he's just going through a stage" . . . they always say that but that's been going on every year now . . . I keep on going back and I said I am not trying to be pesty . . . I just want to know why is he staying behind and I come and ask the teachers . . . they always say he is okay and then we get the report card . . . it's not okay because he's on a very low level and his grades didn't show results . . .

	well, this first card he got . . . a few weeks ago, the last marking period, that was the best card he ever had since kindergarten.
CONSULTANT:	Is the problem over?
MRS. GONZAGA:	I think it's getting to be over . . . it's on the way but we still need to work with him on the way he behaves.
CONSULTANT:	Meaning what? Be very specific with me.
MRS. GONZAGA:	Aldo will try to attract attention one way or another . . like make a lot of faces or make a lot of noise.
CONSULTANT:	Uh-huh.
MRS. GONZAGA:	Or just act silly . . . he think's somebody is looking at him, but it's not funny. Marie and Joan (*the family's co-therapists*) said, "time him . . . time him and see how long he'll take . . . one minute, two minutes or seconds or whatever . . . then the next day keep on timing him." Well, we keep on doing that and it still doesn't work.

Mrs. Gonzaga also solicits the consultant's support against the teachers and against her current therapists as she has against her husband. It was not long before Mrs. Gonzaga again took control over what was happening in the session. If she obtains the childrens' alliance against her husband and diminishes his stature at home the way she does in the interview, his leverage with the children cannot be much. Not only are the original diagnostic hypotheses about Mrs. Gonzaga's dominance and Mr. Gonzaga's peripheral role in the family being confirmed, but they are also being fleshed out. It is up to the therapist to begin to restructure in the session. The consultant reincludes Mr. Gonzaga and Mrs. Gonzaga responds to the attention by striking back out at his wife.

CONSULTANT:	Uh-huh . . . alright . . . do you (*to Mr. Gonzaga*) see it exactly the way your wife's describing it, or do you have another . . . something else that you can add to that?
MR. GONZAGA:	No, I see it the same way, it's just like she says . . . he acts up more when she's there . . . when I'm around, he doesn't act like that.
CONSULTANT:	He doesn't.
MR. GONZAGA:	I think it is probably like I told her . . . you let him slide too much or something.
CONSULTANT:	She's too easy with him.

MR. GONZAGA:	All she does is holler and holler but she don't do nothing.
CONSULTANT:	So that's easy . . . never mind timing him . . . if she were just a little tougher with him then you wouldn't have a problem.
MR. GONZAGA:	That's the way I look at it.
CONSULTANT:	That's simple.
MRS. GONZAGA:	That's his view, not mine.
CONSULTANT:	*(to Mrs. Gonzaga)* Oh, that's not yours . . . *(back to Mr. Gonzaga)* but he doesn't do it when you're around.
MRS. GONZAGA:	No, no . . . he doesn't . . . but then . . .
CONSULTANT:	*(to Mrs. Gonzaga)* So how can you argue with success?
MRS. GONZAGA:	He's been very strict with him all the time . . . so, strict is okay, okay, but not when you scare him.
CONSULTANT:	You think he's too strict with Aldo?
MRS. GONZAGA:	He's strict with all of them. ·
CONSULTANT:	Remember, we just want to talk about one problem . . . he's too strict with Aldo, that's what you're saying.
MRS. GONZAGA:	Yeah.
CONSULTANT:	So, he's saying I succeed with him . . . he doesn't act like a fool with me . . . you *(Mr. Gonzaga)* are saying he doesn't act like a fool with me and *(Mrs. Gonzaga)* you're saying that's because he's scared of him . . . that's not a solution . . . right?
MRS. GONZAGA:	Yes.
CONSULTANT:	Okay . . . *(to Mr. Gonzaga)* find out from Aldo if he's scared of you.

Diagnostically, how more direct an approach to explore Aldo's relationship with his father than to have them interact? But the diagnostic inquiry is conducted within one of the structural goals at that moment in the session, which is to strengthen the father's position in the family. Related to this goal is the aim of bringing father and son closer together. The mother's critique of her husband in the boy's presence placed her between them. So the consultant asks the father to approach his son directly about the fear issue.

MR. GONZAGA:	Are you scared of me?
ALDO:	No.
MR. GONZAGA:	Are you afraid of me? *(in a threatening sounding tone)*
ALDO:	No.
CONSULTANT:	*(joking to Aldo)* You better give the right anser or he'll

	punch you in the mouth. (*Mr. Gonzaga and consultant both laugh*)
MR. GONZAGA:	You're not afraid of me? Is there anything that you're supposed to be afraid of?
ALDO:	Of hitting.
MR. GONZAGA:	That's part of it, right . . . when you don't do things that are supposed to be done . . . that's why you don't do well?
ALDO:	No.
MR. GONZAGA:	That's your problem . . . and your mother . . . she don't hit you. (*Aldo shakes head no*) That's what I think it is.
CONSULTANT:	Uh-huh.
MRS. GONZAGA:	They never get . . .
CONSULTANT:	Wait . . . wait . . . (*to Mrs. Gonzaga*) this is between them.
MR. GONZAGA:	She keeps on telling him, don't do this . . . don't do this . . . and he keeps on going and going but not really doing anything about it . . . he just keeps on doing it.
CONSULTANT:	You believed him though, when he said that he wasn't scared of you?
MR. GONZAGA:	In a way I do and in a way . . . he's not really scared of me . . . it's just a problem that he has, respect in a way that if he don't do things the way he's supposed . . . if I tell him more than three or four times, I'm going to . . .
CONSULTANT:	He's going to get it.
MR. GONZAGA:	That's right.
CONSULTANT:	Yeah.
MR. GONZAGA:	And if he does it, it's alright, he doesn't have to get spanked.
CONSULTANT:	Uh-huh.
MR. GONZAGA:	And I explain to him why you don't have to get spanked because he's old enough . . . he doesn't have to be spanked . . . he does the things that are supposed to be done.
CONSULTANT:	Alright . . .
MR. GONZAGA:	That's all.
CONSULTANT:	. . . but do you think he's said enough now that you believe what he's said to you just now . . . that he doesn't live in fear of you all the time?
MR. GONZAGA:	I don't think he's in fear of me at all . . . cause I . . .

Mr. Gonzaga did not really engage with his son around the issue of the boy's fear. Here we see our questions about what is happening between father and son taking added dimensions. Father and son appear not to be close. Mother seems to stand between them. Father is relatively uninfluential in relation to his son. The consultant further hypothesizes that the father may be trying to compensate for the distance between them by sternness. The therapist wants to see how the father will handle the boy without the mother; how sensitive he can be to the boy; how close he can get to him. He stays with the same intervention attempting to refocus the father's attention on his son's behavior with him.

CONSULTANT:	He said so little . . . it's hard for me to understand . . . I don't know what your relationship is.
MR. GONZAGA:	He plays with me, you know . . . we joke with each other and I don't see that makes him afraid of me . . . because if he can joke with me then he, he shouldn't be afraid of me . . . only when I tell him seriously that . . .
CONSULTANT:	Check it out with him.
MR. GONZAGA:	Check what out with him?
CONSULTANT:	See if he agrees with you.
MR. GONZAGA:	Do you agree with me or don't you . . . what I just got through saying?
ALDO:	Yes.
CONSULTANT:	Did he understand you?
MR. GONZAGA:	Do you understand me?
ALDO:	Yeah.
MR. GONZAGA:	What did I say?
ALDO:	You said that if I don't do the thing right and you tell me about five times, then you'll hit me.
MR. GONZAGA:	What else?
ALDO:	That I ain't afraid of you because I always joke with you . . . sometimes.
CONSULTANT:	You know what the real test is whether a kid is afraid of you or not?
MR. GONZAGA:	What is it?
CONSULTANT:	Whether he can disagree with you.
MR. GONZAGA:	On his own?

CONSULTANT: That's right . . . whether he can ever have an opinion that is different from yours and say hey dad, you know, I see it this way.

MR. GONZAGA: Yeah.

CONSULTANT: Whether he can speak up.

MR. GONZAGA: For themselves.

CONSULTANT: That's right.

MR. GONZAGA: Well, they do.

CONSULTANT: I mean him. (*Aldo*)

MR. GONZAGA: Oh, I don't know.

CONSULTANT: That's the test.

MR. GONZAGA: He doesn't have too much to say . . . he never disagrees with me . . . he goes along with whatever I say.

CONSULTANT: Well, find out . . . see if there's one area that he disagrees with you on . . . cause see, if he never disagrees with you, he's scared . . . it's not human to never disagree with somebody.

MR. GONZAGA: What do you disagree with me against?

ALDO: I don't know.

MR. GONZAGA: Is there anything that you can disagree with me . . . you think I am wrong?

ALDO: No.

MR. GONZAGA: That you don't agree with me . . . then anything I say is right . . . it's okay?

ALDO: Not anything.

MR. GONZAGA: Okay . . . what is it that you don't like or . . .

ALDO: When you force me.

MR. GONZAGA: Oh . . . how do I force you?

ALDO: Like you say, "go, go read" even after I did it.

MR. GONZAGA: Then what?

ALDO: I don't know.

MR. GONZAGA: Well something . . .

ALDO: Then I just go do it.

MR. GONZAGA: Oh, you don't want to go read . . . is that it or what is it?

ALDO: No, cause I already did it.

MR. GONZAGA: Oh, it's when I send you again to go read . . . you read when I am not home, right? Then I tell you to go read again.

ALDO: Sometimes.

MR. GONZAGA: That's when you don't agree with me . . . how come you

	didn't say anything? You just proved to me *(silence)* . . . I guess because you are afraid of me *(everyone laughs)* . . . is that right?
ALDO:	I'd *(pause)* . . .
MR. GONZAGA:	And then you *(to consultant)* were right about me . . . he goes along with me whether he likes it or not.
CONSULTANT:	Uh-huh.
MR. GONZAGA:	Well, he can't say no.
CONSULTANT:	And you are going to have trouble with him if he can't disagree with you . . . cause then he won't learn how to disagree with teachers, and . . . you know, if you are going to grow up, you have to know how to disagree with people without causing trouble and when a kid doesn't know how to diagree without being disrespectful, that's when they cause trouble . . . they can't say no, so, what they do . . . they don't do it or they do it slow or they do it wrong on purpose because that's the only way they know how to disagree.
MR. GONZAGA:	That's the only way they can say no.
CONSULTANT:	They have to learn how to be able to say . . . like, you know, I'm sure . . . what kind of work do you do?
MR. GONZAGA:	I'm a packer.
CONSULTANT:	I'm sure you have somebody over you, a foreman or somebody . . . you disagree with the person . . . you know how to say, hey that's not the way to do it or this isn't the time, without it becoming a big problem . . . you probably don't even think about it . . . you know, it comes kind of natural . . . you have to be able to do that . . . if he doesn't learn how to do that, he won't grow up.
MRS. GONZAGA:	May I say something? Fred's about the same like Aldo but Fred's older. He grew up the same way as Esteban. He's almost like Aldo but thank God, at a different point he snapped out of it . . . he said he was being picked on by children in his class, uh, by the teachers along with everybody and I'm not like that so I used to tell him to fight back, argue back, ask questions, uh, talk back to them . . . don't always be . . .

The consultant has gotten the father to really talk to his son and find out how he is affecting him. The father's ability to persist in a personal way with Aldo is diagnostically revealing. It demonstrates the father's openness to hear his son and Aldo's readiness to respond to him. The consultant takes the issue a little closer to the father's own attitude towards authority, attempting to get him to view himself as a model to his son. Mrs. Gonzaga can hold back no longer and stacks another son on the pile of those whom the father intimidates. The father is ready to accept the blame and retreat. The therapist aggressively takes the issue back to the father and momentum away from the mother and pushes the father towards Aldo again.

CONSULTANT: (*to Mr. Gonzaga*) Want me to tell you what I think is going on in your family? It's that he or they may learn how to respect you, but you are not teaching them how to disagree with you in a respectful way . . . she then tries to teach them how to disagree, Mrs. Gonzaga, and that doesn't work . . . that doesn't work . . . it can't be her teaching them to fight back and you teaching them to obey . . . they've got to learn from you how to obey and how to disagree, without being disrespectful . . . they've got to get the same thing from both parents . . . cause otherwise, the two of you are like lawyers on two sides of the same case . . . so, teach them how to disagree with you now. (*Mr. Gonzaga is silent groping for what to say*) There must be something that's coming up that you have to take care of today . . . tomorrow . . . something that you suspect he may have a different point of view on than you have.

MR. GONZAGA: I don't know what to say to make him disagree with me.

CONSULTANT: Well, ask him . . . maybe he knows and he can help you figure out an area where he might want to disagree with you on something that's coming up . . . homework or going out or something like that that you have been discussing with him.

MR. GONZAGA: It's best to get into reading, I guess.

CONSULTANT: Ask him . . . don't try to do it all yourself . . . see if he can help you.

MR. GONZAGA: Would you like to read for three hours straight?

ALDO: No.

MR. GONZAGA: Why not?

ALDO: I get very bored.

MR. GONZAGA:	How are your time tables?
ALDO:	I know them already.
MR. GONZAGA:	You know them already? That's fine. (*silence*)
CONSULTANT:	It's hard isn't it?
MR. GONZAGA:	What else can I ask him?
CONSULTANT:	I don't know . . . but that's the one you've got to solve.
MR. GONZAGA:	Got to solve . . .
CONSULTANT:	Uh-huh . . . see, and I don't want her (*Mrs. Gonzaga*) to help . . . so, then you are back to the same old thing . . . I want you to solve that one with him.

The consultant hypothesizes that this has been part of the pattern. Father gets frustrated and discouraged and Mrs. Gonzaga takes over. The consultant does not want to reinforce the pattern. He still does not know how much the father is capable of doing and tests him further by continuing to make the expectation that he talk with Aldo and help him to disagree.

MR. GONZAGA:	(*to Aldo*) Is there anything else that you don't want to do that I say . . . that I ask you to do besides reading?
ALDO:	No.
MR. GONZAGA:	Nothing else? (*silence*) That's the only thing you disagree with me . . . reading and what . . . anything else besides that . . . that you don't like to do that I ask you to do or something? (*silence*) Tell me what else. (*laughs*)
ALDO:	I don't got nothing else.
MR. GONZAGA:	It's the same I guess (*silence*) That's all I guess . . . what am I supposed to say?
CONSULTANT:	You're both stuck . . . you haven't solved it man! You're both stuck.
MR. GONZAGA:	We need help Esteban.

The consultant is still expecting father to do something with Aldo. Interestingly, he turns to another of his children, Esteban, who is sitting on the other side of Aldo. The father is not so proud that he cannot solicit assistance from another son. Esteban will respond. He will become a resource for father. Structurally father will not be isolated with all children lined up behind mother's protective shield. The consultant will support this alliance with Esteban at this moment looking to see how it affects the father in his task with Aldo.

ESTEBAN:	(*to Aldo*) My father, what he means is, do you like it when he tells you to do stuff like . . . like, this morning, he told you to look for your shoes . . . you couldn't find them . . . you looked in the same place two times, three times . . . did you get mad?
ALDO:	No.
ESTEBAN:	You felt like . . . just not looking for it.
ALDO:	No . . . it's because my pants . . . the cuff broke off.
ESTEBAN:	No, but you didn't want to look for your shoes.
ALDO:	I was looking around.
ESTEBAN:	Yeah. (*incredulously*)
CONSULTANT:	I think, Esteban, you know something about Aldo that Aldo doesn't know about himself.
ESTEBAN:	He gets upset easy . . . like, if they tell him to do something he gets mad because he goes . . . (*demonstrates gesture of annoyance*) like that.
ALDO:	How about when you got mad at me and you threw the ashes on the floor?
MR. GONZAGA:	(*to Aldo*) That's something between you and him.
CONSULTANT:	Esteban, I think you've picked it up alright . . . (*to Mr. Gonzaga*) He just showed you how Aldo does get mad . . . but Aldo doesn't even know that he is mad . . . he still doesn't know he was mad this morning about the shoes.
MR. GONZAGA:	He makes a face . . . I guess that makes him angry . . . because you can tell . . . they change their expression.
CONSULTANT:	But if he had been able to say to you something like . . .
MR. GONZAGA:	He would have said it right there.
CONSULTANT:	. . . said something . . .
MR. GONZAGA:	Yeah, that's right.
ESTEBAN:	Aldo doesn't talk out like us . . . we, like, if something is wrong, we tell him (*Mr. Gonzaga*) but Aldo, he just doesn't say anything.
MR. GONZAGA:	He never wants to talk too much.
CONSULTANT:	Uh-huh . . . so, Aldo's problem isn't that he fights you . . . his problem is that he doesn't fight you. (*laughs*)
MR. GONZAGA:	He keeps his mouth closed . . . that's all.
CONSULTANT:	Yeah, that's it. (*silence*) And he didn't even understand his brother at all just now.
ALDO:	I did.

CONSULTANT: You did?

ESTEBAN: What did I mean?

ALDO: You said that I . . .

ESTEBAN: No I didn't say what did I say . . . what did I mean?

ALDO: You meant . . . (*everybody laughs; Mr. Gonzaga, laughing, gestures to quiet Esteban*)

CONSULTANT: (*to Mr. Gonzaga*) Don't be embarrassed . . . we'll sit him over here (*in consultant's chair*) later on.

ALDO: He means that I get mad without knowing it.

ESTEBAN: He just listened to what we said.

ALDO: Uh uh . . .

MR. GONZAGA: Whatever is it, what is it? Like you said he don't like to . . .

CONSULTANT: I don't know whether he is afraid or what . . . he's not able to disagree . . . he gets mad, he gets frustrated.

MR. GONZAGA: He holds it inside.

CONSULTANT: Holds it inside . . . right? And he probably just fights in another way without even realizing it . . . I don't know why but I mean it's such a simple thing . . . his brother is saying to him, look, your father was telling you to go look for your shoes, you look in the same place over and over again. It bothered you . . . it was all over your face and Aldo says, no, "it was alright I didn't mind" . . . and I believe Esteban. Who do you believe?

MR. GONZAGA: I believe Esteban cause I was there myself . . . I was seeing it.

CONSULTANT: Uh-huh, okay.

MR. GONZAGA: I told him where . . . he still looked in the same place . . . I told him where to look after that.

CONSULTANT: Yeah.

MR. GONZAGA: I say, go look on the porch for them.

CONSULTANT: And it bothered him . . . could you tell?

MR. GONZAGA: I told him.

CONSULTANT: Yeah, but could you tell that it bothered him . . . you telling him?

MR. GONZAGA: Well at the time I didn't see him . . . I was yelling at him . . . I told him look in the porch.

CONSULTANT: Esteban was saying it bothered him . . . Aldo said, "it didn't bother me."

ESTEBAN: Cause I see him, when he was going in the kitchen, going

	back into the room when my father tell him to go look for them again . . . I seen him and he was mad.
ALDO:	Uh uh . . . I just jumped on the bed and then Freddie goes, "get off the bed."
ESTEBAN:	I don't know anything about that . . . I'm talking about you went into the kitchen and he made you go back to look for them.
ALDO:	I went all round and then I looked under the bed.
ESTEBAN:	No. When he told you that he said, "go look, go look again, look until you find them" . . . then you walked with your hands down.
ALDO:	I was just walking.
ESTEBAN:	You were mad . . . I could tell.
ALDO:	You couldn't even see my face.
ESTEBAN:	Yeah . . . when you were turning inside the room, I seen you look like that . . . you looked like you were crying.
CONSULTANT:	Who do you believe?
MR. GONZAGA:	Esteban . . . I know Aldo . . . I know the way he is.
CONSULTANT:	Can you help him now to realize that he was bothered by that? For some reason he thinks he can't say he was.
ESTEBAN:	I think he can't talk in front of everybody because he's too bashful.
CONSULTANT:	He doesn't tell his father other times, right?
MR. GONZAGA:	Were you really upset?
ALDO:	Uh uh.
MR. GONZAGA:	Tell me . . . you don't have to be afraid . . . you can disagree with me.
ALDO:	No. (*wasn't upset*)
MR. GONZAGA:	Then you were happy?
ALDO:	No.
MR. GONZAGA:	You weren't happy? You must have been upset . . . it had to be one of the two.
ESTEBAN:	What were you then?
ALDO:	I don't know . . . mad.
MR. GONZAGA:	That's the same thing . . . were you mad? (*Aldo shakes head no*) You wasn't mad?
ESTEBAN:	Aldo, then how come when . . .
ALDO:	I was just going . . .
ESTEBAN:	How come when I teach you something . . . like the time tables, you take a break and then he tells you to do it

	again each time . . . you tell me, "see, he makes me do everything."
ALDO:	I didn't say that . . . I didn't say he makes me do everything.
ESTEBAN:	Wait until you are . . .
ALDO:	I just go and then I just start all over, and then I get mad at you the other day because you were mixing me up.
ESTEBAN:	Like what?

Father is not isolated in this transaction now that Esteban has joined him. Would Esteban have felt so free to do so had the consultant not been acting as a barrier to the mother's activity all through the session? Esteban serves as a bridge for the father to Aldo. The consultant then wanted to see how father would do without Esteban. The consultant, who is himself of Latin background, is sensitive to the cultural expectations of manhood and fatherhood. He works towards his structural goals through them, calling on the father to teach his son to disagree in order to help him be a man in his own image. Later in the interview a qualification to the ability to disagree, the quality of respect, is added to this theme. That the therapist was also male and of similar age allowed him to approach the father with a feeling of camaraderie. A therapist with a different personality, sex, or background would, of course, have had to find avenues towards the same goals that were congruent with his or her circumstances.

CONSULTANT:	See if you (*Mr. Gonzaga*) can find one time that he's really gotten mad at you but didn't tell you . . . maybe you can think of something that happened yesterday, I don't know.
MR. GONZAGA:	What was the time that you really got mad at me?
ALDO:	Time tables.
MR. GONZAGA:	That really got you mad . . . how come you didn't say those things . . . you were afraid of me . . . huh?
ALDO:	Guess so.
MR. GONZAGA:	When was that? (*silence*) . . .
ALDO:	Ah, before I was starting on my nines and tens . . . I mean my nines and my eights.
MR. GONZAGA:	(*laughs*) After that you never got mad at me anymore or did you?

ALDO:	No.
MR. GONZAGA:	This morning you got angry at me.
ALDO:	No . . . I was just . . .
MR. GONZAGA:	You were pretty quiet, weren't you?
ALDO:	I was looking . . . I looked in the drawers. (*silence*)
CONSULTANT:	He is never going to grow up to be a man if he doesn't know how to disagree.
MR. GONZAGA:	What will make you real angry that I do to you that will make you really upset? (*silence*) . . . You have to say or otherwise you will never grow up . . . like he said, "you will never grow up." (*laughs*)
CONSULTANT:	He'll never be a man.
MR. GONZAGA:	He'll be afraid all the time.
ALDO:	Ah, when we're in the middle of a movie looking at it, you come in and turn it off.
MR. GONZAGA:	I turn it off and that makes you really angry?
ALDO:	No.
MR. GONZAGA:	What happens? (*laughs*)
ALDO:	And then when you go . . . "did you do any work today?" Then I go, no, and then you go, "go do it!"
MR. GONZAGA:	That makes you angry?
ALDO:	Yes.
MR. GONZAGA:	You don't want to do it anymore . . . it's not alright to tell you to go do your homework?
ALDO:	No.
MR. GONZAGA:	Do I have to keep you happy all the time?
ALDO:	No.
MR. GONZAGA:	Why?
ALDO:	Because the others don't . . .
MR. GONZAGA:	Don't do it.
ALDO:	No.
MR. GONZAGA:	The others don't have to do it why? They do it, they . . . (*inaudible*)
ALDO:	Not Esteban and Freddie.
MR. GONZAGA:	Esteban does what he has to do . . . Elena does homework, too.
CONSULTANT:	No, the point isn't that you have to keep him happy . . . the point is that if he's unhappy, he should be able to tell you . . . he may still have to do the homework but he should at least be able to say to you . . . you know, I

	don't really feel like doing it tonight . . . why do I have to do it tonight? It gives you a chance to explain things.
MR. GONZAGA:	Give something . . .
CONSULTANT:	So that for once he can open his mouth.
MR. GONZAGA:	(*to Aldo*) Okay, I guess we'll have to work on that.
ALDO:	Yeah.
CONSULTANT:	You know, you're the only one in this family who can solve that problem for him . . . cause, if he's going to learn to be a man he should learn how to be a man from you . . . and, if he can't open up his mouth to you, he's never going to learn from you . . . maybe he will learn from some other man, but he won't learn from you . . . So this is one your wife can't help with unless you want him to learn how to be a man from her . . . okay? (*silence*) . . . Well, we didn't solve that problem but at least we know it's your problem . . . right?

The fact was that the father achieved a good deal with Aldo. Father talked with him for a good long while, becoming increasingly more focused on him and Aldo responded. Father also had Esteban with him. Mother was able to stay out after several attempts to take over. Finally, the father saw for himself the problem he had with his son and made a commitment to change, a far cry from the unchangeable person whom the mother had hinted about in the beginning of the session. The father seems disposed to taking on more responsibility. He is demonstrating the ability to develop within his own family.

MR. GONZAGA:	I thought it was his problem but it's my problem. (*laughs*)
CONSULTANT:	It's your problem . . . absolutely.
MR. GONZAGA:	Okay, Aldo . . . it's my problem . . . I guess you're right about that . . . I have to start someplace . . . it better be me, I guess.
CONSULTANT:	He's got to learn how to disagree with you and still be respectful so he can open up his mouth and learn to be a man . . . you wouldn't respect him as a man if he didn't know how to disagree with people . . . right?
MR. GONZAGA:	Yeah . . . right . . . it's my turn . . . (*pats Aldo on the shoulder*) we'll work it out.
CONSULTANT:	Okay . . . so we did as much as we could with that one . . . let's have another one.

ESTEBAN AND	
ALDO:	Freddie. (*everyone laughs*)
CONSULTANT:	It's up to the two adults . . . okay now . . . Aldo and Esteban want to talk about Freddie but it's got to have your okay . . . the two of you have to okay that if we're going to talk about that . . . is it alright with you? (*Mr. and Mrs. Gonzaga both say yes*)
ESTEBAN:	Freddie . . . when we're seeing a movie . . . Freddie comes . . . a commercial comes on and he starts messing around.
CONSULTANT:	I don't think anybody can hear you . . . it's you two guys who want to talk about Freddie. (*Aldo and Esteban agree*)

Esteban and Aldo join together to point the finger at Fred. The effect is that they are drawing Fred into dealing not only with them, but also with their father with whom in this session they themselves have become actively involved. Structurally, the stage is being set for the father to be reincluded into the family by the boys. They are aligning themselves with him and augmenting his power in relation to them by their deference to his position. The girls are not jumping in. They are staying with their mother, who has for the moment opted to stay out. The consultant had hypothesized that the father's position had a special significance to the boys and this is being demonstrated in the way the boys are responding to him once the mother does not insert herself between them and the father. The hypothesis is being confirmed and elaborated. Esteban and Aldo are also helping to answer questions about Fred and his relationship to the father as well as the rest of the family.

ESTEBAN:	Ah, like when we're seeing TV and come a commercial, he starts beating me up and then Aldo jumps in with him but . . .
CONSULTANT:	Aldo does what?
ESTEBAN:	Jumps in.
CONSULTANT:	On who's side?
ESTEBAN:	On my side.
CONSULTANT:	Okay . . . on your side.
ESTEBAN:	Then when it gets . . . when the TV comes back on, the program . . . then we stop. If we hit him too hard, he'll

really hit us . . . that's when I get mad and I try to protect Elena . . . she's not doing nothing . . . Freddie messes around, you know, he knocks down the blocks or do something like that . . . so, I say, "go leave her alone, Freddie" . . . then he keeps on doing that . . . I say, "you're 16 and you act like a two-year-old," and then he gets mad and beats me up again . . . then Aldo helps me, and keeps on going like that.

CONSULTANT: Aldo, you speak up now.

ALDO: I think he does it because he's mad, he gets mad at my mother or something, and then he takes it out on us.

ESTEBAN: Because my father tells him to do something . . . like when he has to do his work and when I'm in the room with him he goes, "see, see, it's all because of you" . . . he hits us and he goes, "I'm going to get back at you" . . . then when he hits us, "that's for telling on me . . . that's for doing something."

ALDO: He holds grudges.

CONSULTANT: So you're both saying that when he gets mad at both your parents . . . right? . . . then he takes it out on the rest of you?

ALDO: Like he starts on Esteban and me and then Elena.

CONSULTANT: Uh-huh . . . alright.

ESTEBAN: Or else . . .

CONSULTANT: Wait a minute . . . let's give the man a chance to speak for himself.

FRED: Well, I do get kind of upset sometimes when my father and mother says anything to me but . . . okay, I'll be upset at my brother in the room . . . he'll look at me like I'm stupid or something . . . he'll go like that . . . and I say don't look at me like that Aldo . . . or else sometimes I'll just hit him or you know I'll say, cut it out, and you know I'll . . . I ask Aida a question or something and she says, "I got homework to do." Okay, I can understand that but then she says it that way . . . she just shout at you, "I got homework."

CONSULTANT: Uh-huh.

FRED: So then . . . "you (*Aida*) don't have to scream at me," you know . . . so, in other words I hit her back for screaming at me, you know . . . and then Esteban comes out with something that he thinks. He knows too much, you know, he thinks he's older than me I guess, you know . . . cause he says, "I'm better than you" and different things, you know.

CONSULTANT: Uh-huh.

FRED: And I go, "I've been around here longer than you have, you know." (*everyone laughs*) So, we start arguing once in a while and I'll hit him, you know, and I'll say, cut it out, or we'll fight and fight.

ESTEBAN: Then Aldo jumps in.

FRED: Then my brother jumps in . . . well it really starts getting into play fighting, and then pretty soon it gets serious, you know.

CONSULTANT: So why do you knock her (*Elena's*) blocks down?

FRED: (*laughs*) Things will pop up in my head like . . . okay, I've been sitting down looking at my brothers and sister doing something and I'll go, man I don't have nothing to do . . . then I come out with something like . . . and I wonder how my sister will look if I pulled her hair (*laughs*) . . . you know, like mess around, you know.

CONSULTANT: Uh-huh.

FRED: See, Elena, you know, she just came around you know . . . so she's playing there by herself and I think about the same way with all of them, you know . . . an idea comes in my head . . . Elena, I knock over her blocks and she'll start arguing with me, you know . . . she'll come up to me and she starts hitting me, biting and everything, you know.

CONSULTANT: She gives you a little entertainment.

FRED: That's what I like.

CONSULTANT: Okay.

ESTEBAN: When we had a dog he used to take it out on him . . . he used to go fight with the dog and I used to come over and say, "leave him alone, Freddie, that's how come he never likes you . . ." the dog used to like me the most . . . Freddie would still like fighting and the dog was barking and everything . . . then I say, sick-em, and then the dog gets on Freddie and Freddie hits him with the broom like if he scratches on the door . . . like at night . . . Freddie goes, "shut up" and then he still scratches on the door and he gets a broom and he hits the dog . . . he goes like that and I go, Freddie, don't be so rough on him.

In this sequence Esteban and Aldo are challenging Fred. The consultant helps keep the struggle among them with both parents out— structurally this becomes another approach to assisting the boys to deal with their problems without depending on mother, who increasingly looks like the mediator in the family. Drawing the boys together will also serve to augment the father's position, because earlier in the session Aldo and Esteban had already been tied to him around Aldo's disagreeing with father. Including Fred in this issue will eventually also link him to the father. The sequence is also revealing of Fred, who looks to be lonely and to feel quite inadequate. He provokes others to get attention and to even the score when he feels demeaned. There is also the suggestion that he cannot stand up to either of his parents and that that contributes to his frustration and feeling of inadequacy. This kind of interchange can be quite revealing. It formed the basis for a series of diagnostic hypotheses about Fred. The consultant can then focus more pointedly on Fred as an intermediary step before getting back to the father, who is the key figure at this stage of the therapeutic effort. The consultant's dialogue with Fred will also separate him from the younger boys, giving him a place of his own in the discussion and in that way building up his position in relation to his siblings.

CONSULTANT: Okay . . . let me check something out, when your mother and father get mad at you Freddie, why do you take it out on them (*the siblings*)?
FRED: Ah . . . I don't really take it out on them . . . but see, when I come in the room like I said, the first thing I will see was Aldo's face or Esteban, you know, and, okay, I'll go back to work or something, and then Esteban comes to me . . . "hey Freddie, what's this," you know, and I'll say, I got a lot of homework, Esteban, you know . . . I'll shout at him, then he comes to me and says, "I only asked you a question," and then . . .
CONSULTANT: But you're all boiling up inside.
FRED: Yeah.

CONSULTANT: Because of what happened with your mother and father, right?

ESTEBAN: I didn't . . .

CONSULTANT: *(to Esteban)* Wait, wait . . . why didn't you *(Freddie)* settle this first with these two *(the parents)* before you got back into the room?

FRED: Ah, it's that I'm lazy just once in a while . . . they'll tell me something and then that's when I really get mad . . . I go, I got so much to do, I got homework, you know, I'm trying to schedule this whole thing out . . . so, then I still got time for myself, you know, like for TV and stuff, you know.

CONSULTANT: Yeah?

FRED: I really like TV, you know.

CONSULTANT: Right?

FRED: See, and ah, if there is something that I like to see on TV . . . I don't care . . . I'll kill to see it.

CONSULTANT: Yeah . . . okay. *(laughs)*

FRED: It's true because when Aida wants to see something and I see something, we'll fight over the TV, you know . . . I'm changing it another way . . . I'm changing it back and, you know, it ends up like that all the time, you know.

CONSULTANT: But wait, you still haven't answered my question . . . if you're lazy and you haven't done what you should be doing, and your mother or father tell you something, and it bothers you right? . . that gets you up tight?

FRED: It does . . . and then . . .

CONSULTANT: Why don't you settle it with them before you go back into the room where these people are so you don't take it out on them?

FRED: Well, okay . . . the first thing is when I am arguing I don't like to talk back to my mother and father . . . my mother once in a while, we get into some pretty heavy arguments.

CONSULTANT: Yeah.

FRED: And I say, forget it . . . I just . . . right there I start throwing things or I'll go to my brother and I'll punch the wall or something, you know, and then . . .

CONSULTANT:	What about with your father?
FRED:	Oh, my father, I can't say nothing to him . . . if I do, you know, right across my face and that's what I'm thinking, you know.
CONSULTANT:	Yeah.
FRED:	See . . .
CONSULTANT:	You can't say anything at all?
FRED:	I can say a couple of things but then, right there and then my mother will jump in or else she'll say, "don't talk to him" and I'll say, "okay" I'll just go in the other room.
CONSULTANT:	You mean she tried to protect you from your father?
FRED:	No, no . . . she just tries to put her point across . . . you know, like my father sometimes don't listen to what I'm already saying, you know, like I'll come out with something and showing off, you know, I think I know so much and then I'll say . . .
CONSULTANT:	Yeah?
FRED:	. . . you know that people like to do certain things like this and that and then he says, "don't worry about other people" . . . and I go, I'm just telling you what they do . . . and that's what I'm trying to tell him . . . and then she says, "your father don't want to listen to that, okay . . . so go in the other room."
CONSULTANT:	She does that to protect you?
FRED:	Yeah, that's right.
CONSULTANT:	Why can't you settle it with your father? Why can't you talk with him without her getting in the middle of it and treating your father like he's some kind of wild ape who she's got to protect you against?
FRED:	He's no wild ape . . . I don't know, I guess . . .
CONSULTANT:	(to Mr. Gonzaga) Now you come off looking awful.
FRED:	I guess I don't really like to fight with him.
CONSULTANT:	I didn't say fighting . . . I said talking back.
FRED:	Oh . . . (silence) I talk back to people but . . .
CONSULTANT:	I'm talking about talking back to people the right way, not talking back in a way that gets you in trouble.
FRED:	Yeah.
CONSULTANT:	You don't know how to talk back.
FRED:	I can talk back.
CONSULTANT:	You don't know how to talk back right . . . cause what

you just described was that you get mad and you start arguing with your mother, and you end up throwing things around and you go back in there and you beat them up . . . what kind of talking is that? Or you yell back at your mother . . . you know, that's not talking back.

FRED: I guess anger gets in my head before I can even say anything . . . see, and then sometimes I'm like Aldo, I won't say nothing about my father, you know . . . see, I go . . . I think he is right and that's where I start going wrong . . . see, because I know what I'm . . . I think I know what I am doing there you see by telling him this, you know, then he says a certain word that I don't like, you, you know, he'll say, "it's a lie."

CONSULTANT: Uh-huh.

FRED: "Where's the proof?" . . . he wants facts, you know, not fiction or theories or nothing like that . . . he wants the proof.

CONSULTANT: Uh-huh.

FRED: See, and then I go, "What do you want me to do, go get you . . . go get you this and this and this?"

CONSULTANT: And as soon as you say that you are in trouble.

FRED: No . . . no, that's what's going through my mind.

CONSULTANT: I see.

FRED: So, then I go, "Well I don't got no proof, you know" . . . so then I shut up and or else maybe I'll get mad at him, and I'll go wow I can't even say nothing to him . . . that's what gets me mad, you know . . . right there, that one word, "lie."

CONSULTANT: Then you don't know how to get around that?

FRED: No . . . (*silence*) . . . unless I pull out a fact or something, you know.

CONSULTANT:: Don't you think he cares for you?

FRED: Yeah . . . I think he cares for me . . . he brings home certain things that I want and certain things I know . . . he even told me that he loved me and everything, you know . . . he says, "all of us are different" and he talks with us and jokes around.

CONSULTANT: So, if he uses the word "lie" . . . why can't you go back and try to get at him through another side instead of going back at that word . . . one word, "lie" . . . cause you can't get over that fence . . . that's impossible . . . you can go back to him another way and say, hey you know Dad, we're not talking . . . I'm not getting my point across and I'm making you call me a liar . . . and I don't want you to call me a liar . . . I really want you to understand me. If he's not out to get you, he'll want to listen to you, right?

FRED: *(silence)* I don't know. *(Aldo tries to speak)*

CONSULTANT: No, not yet . . . I haven't forgotten you two guys *(Aldo and Esteban)*. I want to get back to the old man over here because he looks so mean and bad after these kids talked about him, I've got to just find out what's going on . . . we got the same problem right back.

MR. GONZAGA: Same problem we had already.

CONSULTANT: Same problem.

MR. GONZAGA: My fault?

CONSULTANT: That's right.

FRED: It could be memories, too.

MR. GONZAGA: It's my fault all the way.

FRED: It could be memories, too, of the past . . . see, when I was a kid I couldn't even open my mouth . . . see, he used to tackle me harder than Aldo . . . he would have me study, and study and study, the same thing every day, and then I'll say, "I'm tired of this, you know . . . you know, I see my friends, they're probably outside, you know . . . I'm right here stuck inside doing this" . . . ah, then he said, "this is going to pay for you later," and I said, "okay" . . . I'm always studying my heart out and then I get pretty good grades . . . then, what do I get for a prize, you know . . . this isn't the way and then if I even said anything, he'd slap me in the face.

CONSULTANT: *(to Mr. Gonzaga)* You're lucky you're not in jail after all these descriptions.

FRED: It's just that I don't like to get hit, hit in particular from him . . . I don't like it! I don't want him calling me a liar or hitting me or . . . any of these things, you know.

Fred continues to add to the picture of a boy who is afraid of his father but is also yearning for his approval. The father appears to be limited in what personal options are available to him to reach out and influence his son—possibly related to a restriction in his personality as well as to the problem with his wife who seems to have preempted him with the kids. One can certainly speculate about whether the father's minority status in alien culture may have made him experience himself as less effective than in his own homeland. Could this have led him to put even greater pressure on his oldest son to achieve? These considerations will certainly need to be in the therapists' minds as they look ahead in treatment and deal with the schools and the neighborhood of these children. But at the moment the consultant addressed what was immediately before him, a father and son who wanted to reach each other but could not.

CONSULTANT: *(to Mr. Gonzaga)* I want these kids to talk to you . . . I am serious . . . I don't want them to talk this way . . . I don't want them to feel this way about you . . . because you wouldn't be talking to them the way you talk to them if you didn't care about them, right?

MR. GONZAGA: Yeah . . . I think you're right.

CONSULTANT: Yeah, so I want them to, to be able to be close to you. I want them to respect you, you know, but I also want them to be close to you. That means they have to learn from you, not from me, and not from their Mom.

Here the consultant links himself up with the mother as a person who must stand by and give father room to handle the boys in his own way. This move hopefully serves to help mother not feel completely excluded as the consultant attempts to centralize father vis-à-vis his boys. At this point, however, the consultant moves from disengaging Fred from the misdirected fights with his siblings to linking him directly to his father.

CONSULTANT: They have to learn from you how they can disagree with you in a respectful way that will make you want to listen to them . . . 'cause there's a way to disagree, and there's a way to disagree . . . some ways you can disagree . . . you don't get somebody angry . . . another way you can disagree and they want to hear you . . . the person wants to listen to you and say, hey, you know, I missed the point and tell me, I didn't understand you. Still, it may have to come out your way and they still may have to do

	what you tell them to do . . . they still have to tell you . . . am I coming down too hard on you?
MR. GONZAGA:	No, no . . . you're coming on pretty good.
CONSULTANT:	Okay.
MR. GONZAGA:	I understand . . . that's true.
CONSULTANT:	That's true . . . it's the same thing.
MR. GONZAGA:	It's the same problem.
CONSULTANT:	Yeah . . . that's . . . you talked with Aldo before. (*to Aldo who was about to talk*) I don't want you to talk right now, Aldo, I want your father to talk to Fred . . . cause Fred is a little low right now (*to Mr. Gonzaga*) . . . he doesn't have much time left at home . . . there are a couple of things he didn't learn . . . cause if he, I mean at his age, if after he talks to you, he's mad and he's going to pick on his little sister, you know, and his brothers and everybody, I mean, that's childish . . . he should have been able to settle it with you in a way that it's between the two of you . . . you two settle it . . . you have a disagreement . . . he does what he has to do . . . he talks with you in a way he has to talk with you . . . it's settled . . . it's over between you two, and he doesn't go around picking on little kids, right? (*Mr. Gonzaga nods head yes*) Okay . . . and, he doesn't have much time to learn this before he leaves home . . he's looking at you . . . he's waiting for you to say something to him.
MR. GONZAGA:	What can I say? (*laughs*)
CONSULTANT:	I don't know.
FRED:	You want me to disagree with you?
MR. GONZAGA:	Yeah, go ahead . . . say whatever is on your mind.
FRED:	That's it.
MR. GONZAGA:	Huh, that's all?
CONSULTANT:	Tell your father how, what he can do . . . your father's . . .
MR. GONZAGA:	(*interrupting*) You don't want me to say to you . . .
FRED:	(*to consultant*) I can't produce the facts right there and then.
CONSULTANT:	Don't look at me . . . look at him . . . your father really does want to know how to deal with you.
FRED:	(*to his father*) Well, see like certain things . . . ah, like

	when you say, "I want the facts now" . . . well, there's certain facts that I can get in awhile . . . it doesn't come like that you know (*he snaps his fingers*). Well, what I am saying is it's like when you put me down, when you say I'm a liar . . . and then, I look at Aldo, it gets me mad because he looks so funny at me sometimes.
CONSULTANT:	Now, now wait a minute . . . don't get off on Aldo . . . you just said when your father calls you a liar, he puts you down . . . he makes you feel like nothing . . . right?
FRED:	Yeah.
CONSULTANT:	Okay, so in a way, you don't mind him telling you what to do but you want him to respect you . . . you don't want him to put you down?
MR. GONZAGA:	Well, I guess I'm going to have to start all over again.
CONSULTANT:	Yeah, you got to have the responsibility of . . .
MR. GONZAGA:	Start a different way . . . well, you (*to Fred*) have to improve yourself too . . . not only me.
CONSULTANT:	Yeah . . . he needs you to help him improve himself . . . but you're so important to him that he needs to feel that you love him and that you respect him . . . cause you're that important to him . . . and, when you put him down, it hurts him more than when anybody else puts him down.
MR. GONZAGA:	Yes.
CONSULTANT:	I mean it just crushes him . . . so you're absolutely right . . . he needs to improve himself but he needs to feel that you have respect for him too, and that you care . . . he has to feel your love . . . he has to feel your respect . . . he has to think that in my father's eyes I'm somebody, somebody who's worth listening to . . . somebody who's worth caring for . . . because if he doesn't feel that you respect him, then what does he know . . . does anybody respect him if his own father can't respect him?
MR. GONZAGA:	Yeah, you're right . . . I got a father too . . .
CONSULTANT:	Yeah . . . right . . . he wouldn't be this upset if he didn't care for your opinion . . . you're a very important man . . . you're the most important man in the world to these kids. (*silence*) . . .
MRS. GONZAGA:	Ah, does it help like now he's going around to see the,

	the . . . what do you call it . . . where you have the sparring, the matches? Every Saturday he goes to see them . . . like before he didn't go, I mean he took him fishing and a lot of things.
CONSULTANT:	Yeah?
MRS. GONZAGA:	But now he's more interested in all of them . . . so, he's seeing them sparring . . . I think that's important and I think that's fun.

Mrs. Gonzaga had held back as so much took place between the boys and father. The consultant had just been busy trying to build a unique position in the family for the father. The mother comes in and starts by sounding as if she were acknowledging a good effort on father's part, but in a few words ends up reminding everyone how he has neglected his kids in the past. Old patterns die hard. The consultant begins to negatively qualify her statement but father finishes it, demonstrating that he has taken in the meaning of his transactions with his sons. He is as articulate at this moment as his wife.

CONSULTANT:	But that's not quite it.
MR. GONZAGA:	The word though . . . what he's really saying is when you put him down . . . like a few minutes ago, when he said I put him down by saying he's a liar . . . that is the important thing to communicate between him and me . . . talk it out and get it out.
CONSULTANT:	Let me help you with your wife . . . (to Mrs. Gonzaga) see, your husband has to do something with his kids that nobody else in the world can do.
MRS. GONZAGA:	Like I can't step in and help?
CONSULTANT:	You can't help, because all you can do if you step in is you can protect the kids from him . . . you might even want to tell them something that he thinks cause you think you might be able to help communicate for him . . . it doesn't help . . . he is their only father and he is the only man in the world who can get across to them respect and love and closeness . . . nobody else can do that for him . . . I could talk here until I am blue in the face . . . you can talk you know . . . everybody else can give all kinds of advice . . . only he can make Freddie feel, "my father respects me . . . I got to respect my father . . . I got to

listen to him and my father respects me, and my father thinks I am worth something" . . . nobody can do that for him.

MRS. GONZAGA: Let's see, how come they're more sensitive, right? I mean they're more sensitive than the others or . . .

CONSULTANT: Who's more sensitive?

MRS. GONZAGA: These two! (*pointing to Freddie and Aldo*)

CONSULTANT: I don't know.

MRS. GONZAGA: Ah, well Esteban . . . he can communicate with his father . . . so can Elena.

MR. GONZAGA: Yeah, because . . . because I give more of myself to them (*Esteban, Aida, and Elena*) than I do to the others because with these ones I agree with them in a lot of ways because they were more ahead of their work in school and everything . . . which, with these ones (*Freddie and Aldo*), they were behind and instead of helping them, I put them down . . . that's it.

CONSULTANT: Yeah.

MR. GONZAGA: Because Esteban and Aida they were more smart in school or whatever.

CONSULTANT: It's hard, it's hard to treat . . .

MR. GONZAGA: I put him (*Aldo*) down like I put Freddie down, well, you know, "you're not as smart as Esteban and Esteban is smarter than you" . . . things like that instead of coming across with each other trying to solve the problem between me and him instead of the other way as I understand it.

CONSULTANT: (*to Mrs. Gonzaga*) He understands it.

MRS. GONZAGA: Well, ah . . .

MR. GONZAGA: That's why in a way with Aldo, instead of helping him, I put him down and that ain't helping us by putting him down . . . the others, I don't tell them nothing because they're smarter in a way, and in this way I talk to them more and they talk to me more . . . and they communicate with each other . . . same as I do with Aldo and Freddie . . . Freddie . . . what I do is put him down, "You didn't do this . . . how come you got bad grades" . . . you know? It's a mess . . . instead of our helping, just keep putting him down, and down and down.

MRS. GONZAGA: I just tried to tell him to take them fishing . . .

CONSULTANT: I really want you to stay out of it, and I'm not doing it just because I think you should . . .

MRS. GONZAGA: Yeah.

CONSULTANT: I just think you can't help . . . you cannot help your husband . . . you're living in the house and it's going to upset you because you're going to see things that bother you . . . but you cannot help him in what he has to do with these two boys . . . I'm sorry . . . (*silence*) and it's a tough one.

MRS. GONZAGA: It is hard because with some people I can talk and make a lot of sense. (*referring to how difficult it is to talk with her husband*)

CONSULTANT: He knows why . . . (*pause; then to Mr. Gonzaga*) hey you know, I think that it's all heavy enough, right?

MR. GONZAGA: Yeah . . . it was very good.

CONSULTANT: We did enough here.

MR. GONZAGA: I was gonna tell him (*Freddie*) it's your fault . . . it's my fault . . . now (*laughs*) all the time I thought it was your fault . . . I'll make good if I can help you.

CONSULTANT: Okay, that's it.

MR. GONZAGA: Okay (*silence*) . . . okay.

At the end, Mrs. Gonzaga speaks up more. She was pent up the entire session with no opportunity to talk. The consultant had kept her out seeing his interventions in the context of the ongoing treatment. The therapists who had been working with the family were identified with the mother, not the father. She had their support and will continue to have it after the consultant left. The consultant felt that at this stage he must establish the father in a position of effectiveness with his sons.

SUMMARY

In the session here discussed a series of hypotheses arose dealing with the father, the mother, their marriage, Aldo (the identified patient), Fred, and the other children. The consultant worked with a complex of premises that revolved around the question of the father's centrality in the family. He tested them by trying to organize the beginning of the session around the father. He subsequently dealt directly with Mr. Gonzaga's relationship to his son Aldo as he structured the interview to encourage them to talk together. They did so with difficulty and the father eventually requested an older son's (Esteban's) assistance, which was readily given. This drew father, Aldo, and Esteban together, strengthening the boundaries around this subsystem and consequently drawing the father into a more active and responsible involvement in his sons' lives. Eventually the discussion led to the oldest boy, Fred, who was also drawn into this father/son grouping. However, the consultant dealt first with Fred and his brothers, then Fred alone, and finally Fred and his father, with which he completed the circle. The mother at various points attempted to regain her status of centrality with the children but was moved back by the consultant and ultimately by the father himself who saw and experienced more clearly what his role could be with his children.

The end of the interview was an elaboration of the beginning. It was of one and the same fabric. What made this possible was that the entire session was based on the original working hypotheses. These did not have to prove right to allow for this continuity. They only needed to be tested, expanded, and worked with in a consistent manner throughout. The diagnostic process, which is after all no more than the exploration of hypotheses based on a cohesive theory, was the underlying cohesive foundation of the session.

CONCLUSION

Each sequence of transactions in a session must be seen in the context of the process of the session itself, which is only a phase of the entire treatment. The treatment not only reflects the lives of the individuals and the family itself, but is itself interwoven with their lives. The problems and concerns of the family and its members are brought into the therapy session. The therapist, trying to allow for the distortions that his or her presence creates, abstracts from the actions and interactions of the family members to speculate about the structure of their lives outside therapy, and specifically about the dynamics of the ecostructural girding underpinning the problems they present. The therapist becomes a powerful dynamic in those personal and family patterns to change them. The therapist views every word and action of his or her own as the material upon which a new pattern will be built within and among these lives. But purposeful action is enlightened and guided by diagnostic understanding.

The therapist is always in the process of hypothesizing about what he sees. Thus the therapist does so whether he or she wants to or not. We cannot stifle our speculations. Our responses to others are always at least implicitly based on these hypothetical premises. By making these speculations conscious and by controlling the contextual format of the session the therapist can create an experimental situation in which these speculations can be examined as the therapist actively proceeds to bring solutions to problems.

The effort in this detailed analysis of a session was to show how such speculations are based on the transactions in the session, how attempts to restructure inherently carry diagnostic questions, and how each intervention is determined by the answers to these questions as they develop in the session. This focus evolves in the interview in a way that allows the therapist to build and elaborate hypotheses from one intervention to the next, from one stage of the session to another, and from session to session.

NOTES

1. Mary Richmond, *Social Diagnosis* (New York: Russell Sage Foundation, 1917).

2. Gordon Hamilton, *Theory and Practice of Social Casework,* 2d ed. (New York: Columbia University Press, 1951).

3. For example, see Carel Germain, "Social Study: Past and Future," *Social Casework* 49, no. 7 (July 1968), pp. 403–9, reprinted in Beulah Compton and Burt Galaway (eds.), *Social Work Processes* (Homewood, Illinois: The Dorsey Press, 1975), pp. 263–74.

4. For a discussion of metaphor and idiom, see Carel Germain, "Social Casework," in Harleigh B. Trecker (ed.), *Goals for Social Welfare, 1973–1993* (New York: Association Press, 1973), pp. 125–37.

5. An historical analysis of this extension in the scope of diagnosis is provided in Mildred Mailick, "Situational Theory in Social Work," *Social Casework* 58, no. 7, (July 1977), pp. 401–11.

6. For a description of intervention at the child-school interface and the family-school interface, see Harry J. Aponte, "The Family-School Interview: An Eco-Structural Approach," *Family Process* 15, no. 3 (September 1976), pp. 303–12.

7. Useful content and additional references can be found in Grace Burruel and Nelba Chavez, "Mental Health Outpatient Centers: Relevant or Irrelevant to Mexican Americans?" in Alan B. Tulipan, Carolyn L. Attneave, and Edward Kingstone (eds.), *Beyond Clinic Walls* (University of Alabama: The University of Alabama Press, 1974).

REFERENCES

Aponte, H. "Underorganization in the Poor Family." *Family Therapy: Theory and Practice*. New York: Gardner Press, 1976. Chapter 25.

Aponte, H. "Organizing Treatment around the Family's Problems and Their Structural Bases." *The Psychiatric Quarterly* 48, no. 2 (1974).

Minuchin, S.; Montalvo, B.; Gurney, B. G., Jr.; Rosman, B.; and Schumer, F. *Families of the Slums: An Exploration of Their Structure and Treatment*. New York: Basic Books, 1967.

Minuchin, S. *Families and Family Therapy*. Cambridge: Harvard University Press, 1974.

Aponte, H. "An Eco-Structural Approach to Systems Change: A Brief Discussion." *Mental Health in Children*, Vol. 1 (of 3), ed. D. V. Silva Sankar. Westbury, N.Y.: PJD Publications Ltd., 1975. See pp. 229–36.

5 Mothers of Psychiatric Patients Revisited: An Ecological Perspective

EDA G. GOLDSTEIN

Goldstein reexamines traditional clinical views toward women in general and toward the mothers of psychiatric patients in particular. For this large group of social work clients, she suggests new directions for service based on an ecological perspective that takes specific account of the problems of women in American society.

In an interesting perspective on psychopathology, Arieti has suggested that psychopathological structures are open systems, because if they were closed systems they would follow psychological entropy and soon disappear. Because they are open systems, however, they are maintained by negative psychological entropy coming from outside the system.[1] Thus it seems reasonable for social work to reconceptualize psychopathology (including the so-called pathologies in mothering) as life-space transactions and to intervene at points where dyadic role relationships, family processes, organizational processes, and societal attitudes and constraints interact to maintain the psychopathological structure. The aim is to shift the system from a state of entropy to negentropy, or from disorganization to more adaptive interchange with the environment. Such a view in no way denies the importance of personality in social functioning, nor fails to consider and to help with the pain in the person and in the environment. It does, however, relocate the social work point of entry to the transactional area between person and environment, and suggests that the emphasis in social work intervention should be on the forces interacting in the complex transactional field. Goldstein, in her essay, examines some of the value issues and therapeutic concerns posed by such a change in emphasis.

One of the contributions of ego psychology to social work is its recognition that the developmental crises of adulthood, like those of childhood and adolescence, involve ego and role tasks. Their successful resolution depends on how well the environment meets its reciprocal tasks of supplying appropriate biological, psychological, and social stimuli and nutriments. Where this mutual "fit" is poor, task mastery becomes difficult, the ego may lose some of the autonomy it has gained, and tensions between the individual and elements of the environment are likely to increase, at severe cost to both.

Thus the case of women in a sexist society emphasizes the futility of considering adaptation, or failures in adaptation, without viewing them contextually. Recognition of the socialization processes in learning gender roles, and awareness of the depriving aspects of the social and cultural environment in which women are situated, impels social work toward an understanding of stress and coping as transactional processes, neither one of which is to be located solely within the personality or within the environment. This understanding, in turn, demands a redefinition of the objectives of help and of the helping procedures themselves so that both have a better fit with complex life processes. This is the professional task which Goldstein accomplishes in the essay that follows.

—C.B.G.

DIFFERING THEORIES of personality; psychopathology, and intervention strategy have been utilized in understanding and modifying the relationship between maternal characteristics and psychiatric dysfunctioning in children and adults. While each theory highlights at least in part the centrality of the mother in producing abnormality, there is virtually no attention given to the stresses that impinge on the maternal role stemming from the complexities of women's psychosocial existence in our society. These theories and their consequent practice implications embody a disparaging and dehumanizing view of women that neglects consideration of the impact of their phase-specific needs and available environmental supports, and of those societal obstacles that limit productive personal and social functioning. These views must be modified in order to formulate a contemporary approach to social work intervention with women.

An approach that encompasses these issues with implications for social work intervention draws on what Carel Germain has termed an "ecological perspective"—a view highlighting the creative capacities of man and woman, the process of growth and adaptation, the therapeutic potential of life events, and an individualizing role for social work services with an emphasis on understanding all of the transacting forces in a person's total life space and on intervening in ways that promote growth.[1]

As it relates to women, such a perspective must take account of the problems of all women in American society. It must recognize the stress women undergo when the traditional view of what constitutes their happiness as well as the means for achieving it are challenged by a depriving and conflicting psychosocial reality. It must be based on an understanding of the shared and unique dilemmas faced by women of varying class, ethnic and racial backgrounds. An enlightened social work practice, wherever it is located, must identify and commit itself to a way of using its "interface" function in helping women "to match" their "coping" patterns with "qualities of impinging environment" in order both to induce growth in the person and to ameliorate those aspects of the environment that limit that growth.[2]

This paper will explore first how the relationship between mothers and psychiatric disorder in children and adults has been described. Then it will illustrate how an ecological perspective offers an alternative conceptualization more in keeping with a contemporary approach to the concerns of women as it relates to mothers of psychiatric patients.

One prevalent perspective dealing with the relationship between mothers and psychiatric disorder is a by-product of interpretations of psychoanalytic theory. It emphasizes the impact of maternal qualities in causing emotional disorder in children. The mother of the emotionally disturbed child, adolescent, or young adult has been called abusive, cold, controlling, and rejecting on the one hand, and passive, dependent, overprotective, and submissive on the other. She can be masochistic, narcissistic, or sadistic. She can be schizophrenogenic—overtly rejecting, covertly rejecting, or double binding. She can fall into any diagnostic category. The adjectives cited to describe her are endless. Whatever her characteristics she is always to blame. Yet in the studies reviewed by John Spiegel and Norman Bell,[3] and by John Baxter,[4] none of the traits or relationship qualities can be correlated with a distinct or predictable pathological outcome.

The practice implications of this approach suggest a two-fold emphasis on teaching mothers how to raise their children better and "treating" the individual personality of the mother in order to modify the psychopathology-inducing characteristics. If the parental personality is to blame, then certainly intervention must be geared to affecting it.

A major limitation of this view is that it does not seek to understand the specific ways in which mothers are supported or abandoned by their environments in fulfilling their maternal functions, nor does it identify the specific needs they have according to the particular phase of child-rearing. It does not address the mutual impact of mother-child relationships. It is possible that disturbed children cause disturbed mothers. Since the approach does not identify the context in which the "negative" maternal traits exist, it focuses the helping efforts on modifying the mother's intrapsychic conflicts rather than on bridging her needs with the support systems around her.

Moreover, this perspective, in taking as its model of intervention psychoanalytically oriented therapy, reflects the classical psychoanalytic view of women. Joy Rice and David Rice[5] have pointed out that women were described by Freud as "less ethical, with less of a sense of justice, more envious, weaker in social interest, more vain, narcissistic, secretive, insincere, masochistic, passive, childlike and incomplete." It is ironic that the characteristics that Freud thought were attributes of normal women are couched in abnormal terms and are similar to many of the characteristics cited above as inducing pathology in children. Paradoxically, it seems that in orthodox psychoanalytic theory, for women to be normal is to be pathological. On the other hand, for women to show traits such as aggressiveness, strength, resourcefulness, or other characteristics which are equated with mental health in adult males is for women to be pathological also.[6]

The disparaging view of women in this model reflects the sex role biases of our society and contributes to the undermining of women's self-esteem. It blames them for defects in their personalities and in child-rearing capacities that are at the same time felt to be inherent in their personalities. Similarly, insofar as psychotherapy and social work attempt to help individuals achieve a more comfortable fit into society, it seems likely that they have been prone to label what may well be role conflict in women as psychopathology, interpreting it in intrapsychic terms, and not appreciating the social context in which it emerges.[7]

This irony is not moderated by the fact that social work intervention stemming from this model is carried out in psychiatric settings largely by females. Not only are such workers a product of these theoretical and cultural biases but they tend to be supervised by male psychiatrists toward whom they bear a subordinate position in the medical hierarchy that reinforces the same biases. While it is true that a number of adherents to psychoanalytic theory have pressed for revisions of its feminine psychology and that the actual practice of dynamically oriented therapists undoubtedly reflects greater awareness of the limitations of the traditional model vis-à-vis women, a revised theory of women's development has not been forthcoming nor has an intervention approach been articulated that stems from such a revision.

One alternative explanation to viewing maternal characteristics as causal in producing emotional disorder in offspring is to define the relationship problems existing between mother and child as a function of a discontinuity existing between this mother-child system and their surrounding support system. This could be described as a lack of fit between the mother's and child's phase-specific needs and their environmental supports. Intervention would not overlook the personality characteristics and conflicts of the mother nor the constitutional predispositions to physical and emotional problems that the child may bring to the relationship. However, the focus would be on understanding the combination of multiple factors in the personalities of the mother and child and in the intrafamilial and extrafamilial support systems that may be contributing to the stress and which may become part of the solution.

A second prevalent perspective that relates to the mothers of psychiatric patients does not focus on the mother per se as causal in producing psychiatric disorder, but on the structure and process of family life as it produces and sustains emotional symptoms in its members. Rather than the mother being the sole causal force, the marital dyad, the triad consisting of parents and psychiatrically ill son or daughter, or the family unit itself are seen as causal in producing and sustaining emotional disorder. While an offshoot of psychoanalytic theory, this approach's theoretical base was broadened by contributions from the social sciences. Its clinical impetus came from work with children, adolescents, and young adults who were treatment failures in the more traditional psychoanalytic model.

This perspective describes each family as a well-regulated homeostatic unit, unique in the way it organizes to meet the needs of its members and in the conscious and unconscious rules it lives by. Symptoms in an individual family member serve to balance forces within the family as well as to balance the individual's internal needs. In this view, a focus on maternal (and paternal) traits and relationship qualities is superseded by a focus on family role expectations, modes of decision-making and problem-solving, communication processes, and unconscious collusions among family members. Thus, the focus shifts from the schizophrenogenic or double-binding parent to the schismatic or skewed family,[8] the family composed of an undifferentiated ego mass,[9] the one characterized by pseudomutuality,[10] or the one expert at scapegoating.[11] There is no unified family systems theory and each has a different assumption about what produces pathology. In some ways they have rescued the mother from her central blameworthy position as well as offered a challenge to the orthodox psychoanalytic concept that present illness is determined solely by past behavior.

This theory's practice implication also shifts the goal of intervention from intrapsychic change to a change in the current balance of forces in the family that sustains the pathology. The social worker, who formerly took the role of individual psychotherapist as a model, becomes a family therapist (still generally supervised by male psychiatrists). It is no longer the mother's "failure" alone but her "family's failure" to provide a healthy environment for each of its members.

As with the first approach, there are no studies that confirm that the family characteristics described predictably lead to or sustain a pathological outcome, nor are there studies that support this approach's efficacy over the traditional model of individual treatment. The approach also has several serious problems associated with it. First, while shifting its focus from parental traits to familial processes it merely shifts the burden from intrapsychic forces alone to intrafamilial processes alone. It does not connect the individual needs of the family members, the phase-specific needs of the family over time and those aspects in the social environment that support or thwart the family's level of functioning. Secondly, its view of family life is based on a traditional view of the nuclear family, replete with sexual role stereotyping, as well as other prescriptions reflecting society's biases concerning "normal" behavior. As such, social workers and psychiatrists practicing this approach cannot help but reinforce these biases regardless of whether this is beneficial for an individual family member.

In addition, by focussing on the family in isolation from its network it ignores the strains on the family stemming from our increasingly urbanized, transient, and mechanized society and risks forcing more of a burden on the family than it can tolerate.[12] A closely related criticism is that the family model has derived from practice and research largely with white, middle-class, intact families and does not reflect an integration of knowledge about the shared and unique values, family structure and communication processes, environmental supports, and special problems of other groups in our diverse culture. Each subgroup within our society has its own prescriptions for women's roles and has functions both inside and outside the family that may vary both in kind and degree from that of the dominant culture.

An alternative to viewing emotional disorder as the result of family systems pathology is to see the dysfunction as located between the individual, the family, and the society. Because of a lack of external support systems or a mismatching between a family's needs and available resources, too much need gratification or conflict emanating from the family's relationship to society may be focused within the family, increasing the burden on all of its members. Family members may need help in finding external support systems, having more resources made available, and matching resources with their needs. The "family treatment" perspective focuses on the inner workings of the family alone and does not relate the family to its surrounding environmental supports or to ameliorating environmental obstacles to family functioning.

Supports not only refer to environmental resources but to the role expectations that govern people's concepts of themselves as effective individuals. Thus a lack of fit can occur when the expectations people have of what constitutes happiness, normality, the good life, being a wife, mother, career person, etc., do not fit the reality of one's daily existence.

Women seem particularly vulnerable in this regard. They experience increased stress and diminished gratification in their roles as wives and mothers while simultaneously being bound to house and family by tradition, ethnic and historical expectations, and lack of meaningful participation and power in the political-economic system. The stress on mothers or on family life that in turn produces dysfunctional behavior in children may be related to societal expectations of the mother that she cannot possibly meet given the breakdown of traditional supports as well as increasing environmental pressures. Leaving aside for the moment considerations such as poverty, unemployment, racism, etc., even "middle-class" expectations of marriage and parenthood are showing themselves to be mostly mythical in our society. Rhona Rappoport's article [13] on the intrapersonal and interpersonal tasks of marriage as well as Edgar LeMaster's study [14] of parenthood as crisis suggest the complexities inherent in assuming these roles particularly in terms of the gap between people's expectations and the actuality of their lives. "Just Mollie and me and Baby makes three; we're happy in my blue heaven," may possibly have described the lives of people thirty years ago but it does not tell the whole story in this decade. For many women the isolation they feel in caring for their children sets in very soon after the birth of their children, as does the challenge of their expectation that they should know how to take care of their children automatically. If a woman is uncomfortable or uncertain in her maternal role, it seems to her the result of a defect in her personality.

It is no wonder that many women experience depression, anxiety, anger, disappointment, and guilt that they are not meeting their own or others' expectations of them. These emotional reactions may not be easy to understand, let alone to deal with effectively, creating additional strain for the mother in her care-taking functions. This is not to suggest that the mother's level of personal maturity does not have any bearing on her relationships with her children or on the way she deals with certain stress factors, but rather that the problem is much more complicated than the individual personality of the mother.

Women seeking psychiatric help can be viewed better in this light. The statistics cited by Sol Levine et al.[15] that indicate the tremendous upsurge in both the amount of emotional disorder in women and in their help-seeking, compared to men, have been interpreted as due to women having more permission than men to seek help. This increase may be due to the multiple stresses on women coupled with an increasing "consciousness" about the widespread nature of their shared problems. Rice and Rice[16] have cited some of these:

1. The traditional role for a woman is maternal and sexual. She is a child's mother or a husband's wife. She has no identity apart from these relationships. She exists for other people and when her children grow up or she is widowed her identity is lost. This has been poignantly described in terms of the "empty nest syndrome";

2. The feminine housewife role as portrayed in the media is a hoax while the futility, repetitiveness, and goallessness of the tasks of wife and mother that weigh her down are seldom recognized;

3. Men's roles are more esteemed despite the spoken sanctity of the maternal role. There is little formal preparation for child rearing, child caring work such as teaching has low professional status, and there are virtually no public child-care facilities;

4. Our consumer society advocates a predominantly erotic role for women, and turns her into an object rather than a person; and

5. A woman's self-image is deeply affected by contradictory expectations of her. She should be intelligent enough to get a man but not too intelligent if she wants to keep him. She should be strong and weak. She is overtly told to value herself, yet covertly taught to hate herself.

These points are made with regard to white, middle-class women and do not address the additional dilemmas faced by women living in poverty or in subcultures that differ with respect to the flexibility of women's roles, the availability of environmental resources, and access to the labor market.

These considerations have seldom been taken into account in trying to understand and deal with women, let alone with the mothers of psychiatric patients who are even less prone to be individualized in this way. They become consumers of therapeutic or social services not because of their own presenting problems but because of their children's problems. In addition, traditional psychotherapy supports the notion that the child's problem is the mother's problem or the family's problem and thus reinforces the negative identity problems of mothers and of the family as a whole. Moreover, if the goals of the traditional psychoanalytic model are to alter the woman's character structure or help her come to terms with its past devastating effects, it is difficult to see how this can enhance her self-concept. A family approach on the other hand may not individualize sufficiently the mother who may need to be freed from the narrow confines of family life as the main source of her gratifications and sphere of activity, nor will it easily be applicable to the multiple family forms currently extant in our clients' circumstances.

A reformulation of the nature of causality seems a first step necessary to a new approach to this topic. This change is an important aspect of an ecological perspective. In contrast to the linear view of causality inherent in orthodox psychoanalytic theory, as well as to the broader but still restricted family systems view of causality, a multicausal or systems perspective seems crucial. When applied to this content area it focuses on the caretaker-child relationship (in our society the mother-child relationship) and all the forces that impinge on this system stemming from the biological and intrapersonal capabilities and attributes of each of the members, as well as from the existing network of interpersonal, intrafamilial, extrafamilial, and societal influences. In this view neither the mother-child relationship nor the family system exists in a vacuum.

This multicausal perspective suggests that in assessing what is "causing a particular problem" one must address the total field of transacting forces that operate at any given point in time and intervene in ways that set in motion curative forces as well as remove those which are obstructive. Max Siporin[17] has described the nature of this broader based assessment in his work on situational diagnosis. The therapeutic task has been suggested by Bernard Bandler:[18] "First we must identify and help remove the blocks and obstacles . . . . second we must mobilize the progressive forces with which we can

ally ourselves and which, at the appropriate time, we can mobilize.''
These progressive forces are not confined to the individual on the one
hand nor the environment on the other. Rather there is a fit between
the environment and the person that can be strengthened in the service of ''producing growth-inducing and environment-ameliorating
transactions.''[19]

This perspective suggests that there are optimal combinations of
factors which support emotional well-being and that the provision of
resources as well as alternative roles and life styles for people might
be conducive to mental health. Regarding women in particular, one
possible mode of preventive intervention might be to affect the way
in which women view themselves and provide alternatives for them.
Not all women should have children and not all women who have
children should be caretakers in the way that our society defines the
maternal role. Yet the view that these are requirements for women in
our society prevails, with those who cannot meet societal as well as
their own expectations feeling that they have either failed or are
deviant.

In applying an ecological perspective specifically to the mothers of
older children who are psychiatrically ill, e.g., adolescents or young
adults, there are other changes in focus that are important for social
work. The mothers of these patients come to psychiatric settings
when they are in mid-life. Their children have, according to psychoanalytic theory, passed the critical phases of their development. According to family systems theory, the mother (and father) may be actively sustaining the adolescent's or young adult's pathology. What is
to be done, if anything, for these women? Let us suppose that they
have been in some even indirect way ''causal'' in their children's
problems in the past as well as sustaining the problems in the present.
Could a change in them benefit their children? Could a change in
them be beneficial irrespective of their children? Are these two issues
related in any way? Can women change at all in mid-life? What
should their lives be like in the future? To whom and to what is their
responsibility?

Reconceptualizing an approach to these women requires a change
in values. In contrast to a deterministic theory that sees man and
woman bound in the present by unconscious conflicts rooted in the

distant past, an ecological perspective sees life as infinitely more complex and dynamic. Not all of a person's energy need be bound up in conflict. Growth, successful adaptation, and coping do not stop at a prescribed age but continue all through life. While personality is dependent on the past, the relationship is not a simple or a deterministic one. The interplay of contemporary events and needs are crucial, and at any given critical phase when the personality is more fluid and environments are supportive, an individual may resolve previous difficulties in mastering current tasks. This view does not suggest an abandonment of Freud's ideas concerning the role of intrapsychic conflict in "freezing" certain personality characteristics, conflicts, and capacities for change. It emphasizes, however, that even if certain structures within the personality are stable, certain behaviors and aspects of personality are more fluid and malleable. Moreover, personality change comes not only through resolution of past conflict but through mastery of present life tasks.

In this view, treatment is not the only vehicle for change in adults. The natural processes of life can themselves produce change and growth.[20] The "crisis theorists"[21] have described not only the traumatic crises that individuals face but also the "normal" crises of development (Erikson's Eight Stages) and of role transitions (e.g., marriage and parenthood). They have described the potential for adaptive change available to people at these critical points throughout life. Germain[22] has pointed out that when one views the demands on coping resulting from what Toffler has described as "the transience, novelty, and diversity" of our contemporary existence, it should be clear that critical points abound in our lives. Perlman,[23] Meyer,[24] and others have emphasized that since clients seek social work assistance during such crucial moments in their lives, we as social workers are optimally positioned to be catalysts of growth.

Mothers of psychiatrically ill adolescents and young adults usually face two different but simultaneous crises in their lives that upset their coping mechanisms. The crises are: the developmental stage of middle age and the trauma of having a psychiatrically ill son or daughter. These two different types of crises can be related in the following ways:

1. The loss of a primary meaningful role for women in middle age

is especially acute when children grow up and become more autonomous as well as geographically distant. This may result over a period of years in parental attempts to rely on children as a means of dealing with the awareness of the imminent loss of one's roles and the inability to find new ones. This may precipitate symptomatic behavior in the adolescents and young adults, who experience tremendous pressure to remain emmeshed in the family or who experience guilt in separating from the family;

2. The increasing awareness that one is about to lose meaningful roles may precipitate changes such as divorce, employment, etc., that disturb the family equilibrium and the ways of relating in the family. This may in turn produce symptomatic behavior in an adolescent or young adult who has been involved in a pathological closeness in the family and who experiences the change as a rejection. Guilt in the parent may be intense;

3. With the process of aging the marriage itself may be threatened. Children may have been holding a marriage together by gratifying some of the needs of both of the partners. When the adolescent or young adult leaves the home in reality, or symbolically through growing up, the threat of emptiness, divorce, or other marital abandonment may be intense. This may put additional pressure on adolescent or young adult members to maintain the balance;

4. Aging may make the couple aware that time is marching on and may lead to an increased desire not to have the responsibilities of dependent children. This may lead to rejection of the children prematurely, which may in turn precipitate symptomatology. The illness of the child may exert more pressure on the parents to continue their caretaking functions;

5. Death, separation, or divorce may cut off meaningful roles and relationships and put too much burden on the relationships remaining in the family;

6. Families who are burdened by socioeconomic deprivation may not be able to care for the needs of members, who as a result of psychiatric symptomatology cannot contribute to the financial betterment of the household. This may induce further family burden or dissolution; and

7. The emotional disturbance of an adolescent or young adult off-

spring usually leads the parent to feel that she or he is "to blame" and is a failure at a particularly vulnerable time in life, or it may add to the general feeling of deprivation and low self-esteem of a family that does not see itself as effectively participating in the rewards of the society. This is true despite whatever denial the parents may have regarding the seriousness of their children's problems and their role in causing them. This denial is generally accompanied by intense self-recriminations, externalization of blame or depression, or other symptomatic behavioral expressions of distress, e.g., physical illness, alcoholism, etc.

These examples are not meant to be exhaustive nor are they specific to one type of personality diagnosis of the mother or to one type of family systems pathology. Predisposing factors in the personalities of each of the participants are important but are influenced greatly by restriction of roles, external pressures, and lack of environmental resources. If there were more alternatives open to women and more supports available in carrying roles many of the predisposing factors might be eliminated. Similarly, if there were more ways available for dealing with the middle-age crisis the intensification of forces which affect the adolescent or young adult might not occur.

The question becomes how to help these women and whether helping them can accrue to the benefit of their children. The following case example illustrates the process of social work intervention with an "ecological perspective" in mind.

Mrs. R., a white, Jewish, recently separated clerical worker was 49 when her 17-year-old daughter D. was admitted to the hospital following mild drug abuse, depression, and serious suicidal behavior. D.'s problems seemed to escalate when her father, age 55, left the family at her mother's request one year earlier and moved to another state, where he set up residence and was living on a Civil Service Pension. D., Mrs. R., and her youngest child, an 11-year-old son, E., lived in a 1-bedroom middle-income housing project in a deteriorating section of the city. Mrs. R.'s bedroom was the living room. Except for receiving a small amount of child support she supported herself. Mrs. R. married when she was 25. She had two sons and then D., her only daughter, in quick succession. She gave birth to a fourth child, another boy, E., six years later. Both Mr. and Mrs. R.

came from economically poor immigrant families and in the early years of their marriage Mr. R. earned very little but was never without employment. They always paid their bills through Mr. R.'s careful budgeting and there were never "any extras".

Mr. R., unfaithful since early in the marriage, was gone for weeks at a time on "business trips." When the boys were children, Mrs. R. did not know her husband was unfaithful to her and she felt she had no reason to complain about his frequent absences. Yet she felt lonely and depressed much of the time. When D., was small, Mrs. R. learned of her husband's adventures but felt helpless to do anything about them. She felt grateful that he came back to her even though they were in chronic conflict. She thought of leaving him but was frightened about being on her own and having no way to earn a living. The desire to leave and the fear of being alone both intensified when Mr. R. had turbulent encounters with the children. Mrs. R. had wanted to work part-time to supplement her income but allowed her husband's protestations to keep her at home. Aside from one married male sibling with whom she felt close and who lived nearby, she had no other family in the city. Her mother died when she was two years old, and she spent many years in an orphan asylum before joining her father and stepmother. Her father died when she was in her early thirties. She had poor relationships with her older siblings who were very much older than she and who lived in another state.

Mrs. R.'s main activities all through her married life centered on her children, partly due to her own wishes and partly due to her husband's jealousy of outside relationships. She sought comfort in her children's presence while resenting the burden of responsibility for them. She alternated between feeling gypped that marriage and parenthood were so different from what she had hoped for and feeling critical of herself for being unhappy. She always felt particularly close to D., whom she felt was more sensitive to her needs because she was female. Shortly after Mrs. R's 40th birthday, her oldest son left home for the army. Against her husband's wishes she took a part-time job. She began to look forward to getting out of the house but felt guilty about this. Nevertheless she continued to work and began to pay more attention to how she looked. Her husband accused her of being unfaithful and seemed to use this as an excuse to be absent from home for longer periods of time. When the oldest son returned he moved to his own apartment in New York City and began working while the second son left home "to bum around the country."

Mrs. R. began to feel increasingly dissatisfied with her life and after an incident in which the husband flaunted an expensive present for his woman friend, Mrs. R. asked the husband to leave. She then began working full time. Mr. R. contributed a small amount of child support and despite his relentless attempts to reconcile, Mrs. R. remained adamant about their separation. D. became increasingly upset and was admitted to the hospital. At this point it was thought that Mrs. R. had an infantile personality with narcissistic and depressive features. She was described as having a strong symbiotic attachment to her daughter. In addition to D.'s symptoms being interpreted in terms of her own personality functioning, they were also viewed as both an expression of her symbiotic attachment to her mother as well as an attempt to separate from her when the closeness of their relationship intensified with the father's absence. Individual treatment of the mother was supposed to be geared to helping her gain insight into and alter her destructive attempt to hold on to her daughter.

When Mrs. R. began casework treatment she was intensely self-critical for her failure. She said she wanted her daughter to be independent. She, herself, felt she had been weak all of her life and that when, in an act of strength, she dissolved her marriage and tried to make something more of her life, she wrecked her daughter's life. Her life felt empty. She had some acquaintances, no close friends, and relied on her brother and oldest son, both of whom she saw infrequently but spoke to regularly as sources of emotional support. The second oldest son was in regular contact with his mother but lived in an art colony in another state. The youngest son was in junior high and had been doing poorly academically since a year prior to his father's departure, when he became moody and a bit of a loner. In addition to her concern about D., Mrs. R. was fearful that she had harmed her son through depriving him of his father, though in fact the father himself chose not to visit.

The social work assessment of Mrs. R. did not ignore her personality diagnosis and its possible origins in her deprived childhood. It was cognizant also of her "symbiotic" relationship with D., and its possible relationship to Mrs. R.'s attempt to cast D. in the role of a maternal substitute for her own mother who died in her early childhood. However, neither of these considerations seemed sufficient to understand Mrs. R.'s life story and current situation and to establish meaningful goals.

In reviewing Mrs. R.'s life history it was impressive that she functioned so well, given the nature of her early experiences. In terms of both personal and societal expectations she obtained for herself, on the surface, a "normal" existence with a stable, albeit problematic marriage. Despite the lack of a supportive marital relationship, family, and friends, she conscientiously tried to "do the right thing" with her children. She was overburdened and did not know how to deal with her situation in different ways. She felt that devotion to family was critical and had few expectations for herself that would have provided her with more gratifications outside of her family life. She did not know people who could serve as alternative models for her. Those people she had established relationships with she lost contact with through her husband's urging.

It can be said that the nature of her dependent strivings and low self-esteem were critical factors in her adult life but the realities of her existence presented few sources of gratification other than her children. It is true that some women in the same circumstances would have done more to lift themselves out of their situation, but the fact that so many women in similar plights do not suggests that more is involved than pathological personality development, unless most women who find themselves in situations which trap them are, by definition, pathological.

While one could argue that the strength of Mrs. R.'s masochistic needs kept her locked in her marriage and that conflicts surrounding her own deprivation functioned to keep her tied in a pathological closeness with her daughter, nevertheless Mrs. R. began to break both ties herself. This occurred when she was faced with her 40th birthday, her sons leaving home, and her daughter getting older. Whatever role her personality dynamics played, she entered a different phase in her personal and family life at this time—one that brought with it changes in her needs as well as possible alternatives for gratifying them. She did not have to be tied to the house and children so much. It was more acceptable to her that mothers of older children work to supplement income. While one could argue also that her feeling of having done the wrong thing was a function solely of her "need" to continue to be dependent and to be punished, this neglects the impact on her of having a daughter emerge as psychiatrically ill with all of its resultant guilt and self-blame, two feelings that society as well as the psychiatric hospital reinforce.

Though her statement that she wanted her daughter to be independent, as she had never been, could be viewed as embodying the opposite wish to keep her dependent, there was no real reason to think this. She had more acquaintances and a close friend or two at one time but her husband had discouraged these relationships through threatening abandonment. It seemed that were Mrs. R. able to feel comfortable in getting her needs met outside of her family, she would support her daughter's independent strivings, allowing her to separate. While her relationship with her oldest son and brother were important to her she was herself concerned about overtaxing their relationship, and while wanting to branch out felt she had to be both mother and father to her son, E. Thus the casework task became: 1) allying with and mobilizing that part of Mrs. R. that had attempted to get more for herself; 2) trying to alleviate those aspects of her definition of herself past, present, and future, that were obstacles to her continued growth; 3) connecting her with available resources and alternatives, 4) helping her to use these resources and alternatives; 5) helping her to identify and separate out herself from her youngest son and daughter and restructuring her relationship with both of them; 6) supporting those elements in her relationships with her oldest son and brother that were beneficial; 7) promoting new relationships.

The process began with exploration of Mrs. R.'s view of herself as dependent, weak, and worthy of blame for being a failure as a wife and mother. This view was questioned by the social worker in the light of her having taken effective action in separating from her husband and seeking employment. Mrs. R., too, had felt for a time that she was stronger but when her daughter became ill she became confused again. On the one hand she thought she should have been more assertive all though marriage, and on the other, she worried that her assertiveness later in life was destructive. She felt she couldn't have been different earlier because she did not know how to be. Her step-mother had always told her that a woman's lot was to suffer and that all one should expect from a man was that he be "a good provider and not bother her too much sexually." She used to feel there was something wrong with her because she liked her husband to "bother her." She didn't question her own unhappiness in her marriage except at times when she wondered what life was all about, since she had always hoped there would be more than she seemed to have. When asked what made her able to separate from her husband she said she just felt more able to do things for herself because her children were getting older. She felt she wouldn't be hurting them but she guessed it was wrong. When asked why doing things for herself and being a good wife and mother were contradictory, she said: "Well they are, aren't they?"

Mrs. R. was helped to talk more about the contradictions in her life between what she thought she should do as opposed to what she wanted to do, as well as about her expectations and hopes for herself. It was difficult for her initially to express and even be aware of her hopes. She had suppressed them, feeling she did not have the power to make them happen. She was helped also to talk about the difficulties she experienced in raising her children. It never had occurred to her that she had so few supports to help her. She had always assumed she should be able to take care of her children just because she was their mother. She had the following insight: "I guess I felt so needy I looked to D. to meet some of my needs. But maybe that was the only way it could have been. There was no one else."

However, the major activity of the client and worker had little to do with the promotion of insight. In addition to exploration, there was an active questioning of Mrs. R.'s one-sided view of herself and of the "proper" role of a wife and mother. There was active encouragement and reinforcement for the "'selfish" strivings Mrs. R. had—all those things that were associated with her enjoyment rather than the enjoyment of others. Thus the first phase of the casework process involved helping Mrs. R. to question, probe, and recognize the social context in which she had lived her life and some of the historical, personal, and social antecedents for her view of herself. Her self-criticism lessened and her resolve to be more "independent" strengthened. However, she felt she did not know how to be. Interestingly, her daughter began to improve markedly shortly after this phase in her mother's social work activity.

The second aspect of the social work process involved helping Mrs. R. identify the areas in which she would like to effect some change but felt quite unable to do so: 1) being a better mother to her youngest son; 2) obtaining a bigger apartment in the same project so that all three of them, Mrs. R., E., and D., would have more privacy; 3) obtaining a new job with a better salary; 4) obtaining a divorce, and 5) meeting new people. When Mrs. R. discussed this she was asked why she couldn't put things for herself first even though the bulk of her time and energy went into her anxiety about her employer, financial problems, and her husband. While acknowledging this was true she felt selfish for wanting in reality to devote some time to looking for a new job, even if it meant not being home with her son as much over her vacation. She also felt grateful to her employer for having given her a job when she needed it so that she ''should'' stay and work for him despite the way he currently exploited her in terms of hours, demands, and salary. When she was helped to focus on her realistic needs as well as the service she provided she began asking people about salaries and learned that in fact she could be earning a lot more. Within two weeks of her decision to seek other employment she found an excellent job. This success was accompanied by a decrease in her hopelessness and helplessness about her housing situation, which was more complex and which she also tackled to her satisfaction within the next few months. It is of note that while her relationship with her son was not discussed directly during this period of many months, Mrs. R. reported that his grades improved dramatically and in talking with his teacher she learned that he was more extroverted in school than he had been and was part of a group of boys who were scientifically inclined and working together on special projects. This pleased Mrs. R. and she quipped that she should ignore him more since he seemed to benefit from it. In subsequent sessions during the remainder of the case contact, Mrs. R. increasingly brought up her son less resentfully than initially. Mrs. R. found herself yelling at him less and reported on ''the good talks'' they were beginning to have. She spoke with growing

sensitivity to his needs as different from hers. His school performance continued to improve and he began inviting boys home with
him to do school work, something he had never done before.

The third aspect of the social work process involved discussions of
Mrs. R's ongoing relationships. She had few friends, was dominated
by a male boss in a nonfulfilling job (much the same as her marriage)
and while interested in men felt that she should not date until she was
divorced. The social worker took an active role in helping Mrs. R.
restructure some of these relationships by advocating new behaviors
and attitudes in regard to them as well as encouraging her to reach
out to old friends. Mrs. R. did not recognize the anger and helplessness she experienced when being her usual indirect, subservient, and
compliant self and the possible gratification that would come from a
more direct and assertive stance with people. She felt more comfortable with her old self. Rather than explore the antecedents for this in
her upbringing the worker questioned the stereotype Mrs. R. had of a
woman being a slave and the problems she had in adopting a different
view of herself. As her "experiments" in relating succeeded in getting a better job, more money, and a new apartment, she began feeling more comfortable in her new ways and her self-esteem was
enhanced. This phase was accompanied by some interviews with
Mrs. R., her daughter, and the daughter's psychiatrist. These were
used by both mother and daughter to restructure their ways of dealing
with each other rather than to dwell on their "pathological" relationship. The interviews provided a testing ground where both could
see that doing "selfish" things would not be destructive to either
mother or daughter. D. continued to improve.

Another aspect of the social work process was ushered in by what
began as the social worker's problem. Mrs. R. wished to obtain a
divorce and get out of the house more but said she couldn't afford
legal fees and didn't know where to go to meet new people. The
worker attempted to explore the client's "ambivalence" and, when
this led nowhere, shifted her tactics. In trying to locate resources for
Mrs. R., the worker discovered how difficult it is for women to obtain divorces as well as for middle-aged women to meet people.
When a women's legal association and a discussion group were located the client was most gratified and contacted them. She started

proceedings for her divorce and attended the group's meetings regularly. For the first time she felt she was in charge of her own life and at the same time like other people. One of the women in the group arranged a "date" for Mrs. R., and while the relationship was short-lived it increased Mrs. R's desire to find other relationships.

Despite the "therapeutic" nature of the self-help discussion group, Mrs. R. continued to see the social worker for a brief time as she still had feelings of guilt in enjoying herself and fears about being self-directing. She continued until her daughter left the hospital, after a two-year stay, very much improved. Mrs. R. felt she should be "discharged" too, as she now had a busy full life.

There are many traditional elements in this case. It was an individual process performed by a professional social worker and included a period of family work in collaboration with a psychiatrist. It relied on a helping relationship that supported the client's ability to grow and to identify new ways of thinking and acting. It should be noted that the focus was on the client's autonomy rather than on the social worker's magical power, and on connecting the client with opportunities in the here and now of her life situation. This approach presented the client with choices as to how she might live her life. Women have suffered due to the absence of alternatives for them and the lack of challenges to society's stereotyping of them. Suggesting alternatives for clients is not the same as directing the client. It can help them choose for the first time those behaviors and roles which are positive for them.

In summary, important elements in this approach are: 1) a different view of the nature of causality—a multicausal perspective; 2) an appreciation of the conflict-free sphere of the ego and of the capacity for growth all through the life cycle; 3) an awareness of the mutuality between an individual's phase specific needs and environmental supports; 4) an appreciation of natural life events in promoting change and growth; 5) an assessment based on an understanding of all the transacting forces in a client's life space; 6) interventions geared to promote growth and remove obstacles to growth in the client through encouraging autonomous ego functioning as well as creating and mobilizing positive resources in the environment.

The social worker is in a unique position. He or she is generally ''at the crossroads of life . . . at the location in the scene of the natural life event [that makes] help available and more possible.''[25] A social worker using this perspective has to redefine the nature of the social work task with the mothers of psychiatric patients, calling forth the best in them rather than expecting the worst. This redefinition can lead not only to enhanced personal and social functioning for the mothers but to growth and improvement in their children as well.

NOTES

1. Silvano Arieti, ''Designated Discussion,'' of ''General Systems and Psychiatry—An Overview,'' by Ludwig von Bertalanffy, in *General Systems Theory and Psychiatry,* ed. William Gray, Frederick J. Duhl, Nicholas D. Rizzo (Boston: Little, Brown, and Co., 1969).

1. Carel B. Germain, ''Social Casework,'' in *Goals for Social Welfare 1973–1993: An Overview of the Next Two Decades,* ed. Harleigh B. Trecker (New York: Association Press, 1973).
2. William E. Gordon, ''Basic Constructs for an Integrative and Generative Conception of Social Work,'' in *The General Systems Approach: Contributions Toward a Holistic Conception of Social Work,* ed. Gordon Hearn (New York: Council on Social Work Education, 1969).
3. John Spiegel and Norman Bell, ''The Family of the Psychiatric Patient,'' in *American Handbook of Psychiatry,* Vol. I, ed. by S. Arieti (New York: Basic Books, 1959).
4. John Baxter, ''Family Relationship Variables in Schizophrenia,'' *Acta Psychiatria Scandinavica* 42 (1966).
5. Joy K. Rice and David G. Rice, ''Implications of the Women's Liberation Movement for Psychotherapy,'' *American Journal of Psychiatry* 130, no. 2 (February 1973), pp. 191–95.
6. Ibid.
7. Ibid.
8. Theodore Lidz et al., ''Schism and Skew in the Families of Schizophrenics'' in *Modern Introduction to the Family,* ed. N. Bell and E. Vogel (Glencoe: The Free Press, 1960).

9. Murray Bowen, "A Family Concept of Schizophrenia," in *The Etiology of Schizophrenia,* ed. D. Jackson (New York: Basic Books, 1960).

10. Lyman Wynne et al., "Pseudomutuality in the Family Relationships of Schizophrenics," *Psychiatry* 21, no. 2 (1958), pp. 205–20.

11. Nathan Ackerman, "Prejudicial Scapegoating and Neutralizing Forces in the Family Group, with Special Reference to the Role of 'Family Healer,' " in *Theory and Practice of Family Psychiatry,* ed. John Howells (New York: Brunner/Mazel, 1971).

12. Talcott Parsons and Renee Fox, "Illness, Therapy, and the Modern Urban American Family," in Bell and Vogel.

13. Rhona Rapoport, "Normal Crises, Family Structure, and Mental Health," in *Crisis Intervention: Selected Readings,* ed. Howard J. Parad (New York: Family Service Association of America, 1965).

14. Edgar E. Le Masters, "Parenthood as Crisis," in *Crisis Intervention: Selected Readings,* ibid.

15. Sol V. Levine, Louisa E. Kamin, and Eleanor Lee Levine, "Sexism and Psychiatry," *American Journal of Orthopsychiatry* 44, no. 3 (April 1974), pp. 1327–36.

16. Rice and Rice.

17. Max Siporin, "Situational Assessment and Intervention," *Social Casework 53, no. 2 (February 1972), pp. 91–109.*

18. Bernard Bandler, "The Concept of Ego-Supportive Therapy," in *Ego-Oriented Casework,* ed. Howard J. Parad and Roger R. Miller (New York: Family Service Association of America, 1963).

19. Gordon.

20. For an application of these ideas to social casework with a dying woman see Eda G. Goldstein, "Social Casework and the Dying Person," *Social Casework* 54, no. 10 (December 1973), pp. 601–8.

21. For example, see Howard J. Parad (ed.), *Crisis Intervention; Selected Readings;* Lydia Rapaport, "Crisis Intervention as a Mode of Brief Treatment," in *Theories of Social Casework,* ed. Robert W. Roberts and Robert H. Nee (Chicago: University of Chicago Press, 1970); and Erik Erikson, *Childhood and Society* (New York: W. W. Norton, 1950) and "Identity and the Life Cycle," in *Psychological Issues* 1, no. 1 (1959).

22. Carel B. Germain, "An Ecological Perspective in Casework Practice," *Social Casework* 54, no. 6 (1973), pp. 323–31.

23. Helen Harris Perlman, *Persona* (Chicago: University of Chicago Press, 1968).

24. Carol H. Meyer, *Social Work Practice: A Response to the Urban Crisis* (New York: The Free Press, 1970).

25. As quoted by Meyer, ibid.

6 An Ecological Approach to Child Welfare: Issues of Family Identity and Continuity

JOAN LAIRD

Child welfare is one of the oldest fields of practice in social work, and it is also a field that has remained uniquely social work's own. In child welfare, the profession is not subordinated to another as social work in health care is subordinate to medicine. It is not a guest in a host setting as social work is in the schools. Social work has been sanctioned by society as the primary profession responsible for the provision of services to children in need of substitute care. The sanction for services to the families of such children, however, has been less clear, creating tension between the profession and other segments of society.

Like other public services, but increasingly in private child welfare agencies as well, child welfare services are provided by large numbers of social workers without professional education. Yet the demands for knowledge, skill, and commitment are great. Indeed, child welfare is considered by many to be the most difficult of all fields of practice. This is not only because of the built-in conflicts of its triangular structure (substitute caregiver; child's natural family; and agency-worker), but because of the unrelenting emotional demands placed on the worker by the life and death issues of separation, loss, abuse, and neglect. These issues are not always recognized as referring to parents as well as to children. Nonetheless, parental loss and grief, and society's neglect of the natural parents, also form part of the emotional freight carried by child welfare workers.[1]

Laird asserts that an inescapable consequence of an ecological perspec-

tive in child welfare is a newly articulated imperative for sustaining connectedness to the natural family. Many more children could remain with their own families if support services were available to help with the tasks of parenting. Many more inadequate parents, who nevertheless love their children, could be helped to provide more adequate care to their children. Such help can, and occasionally is, provided by skilled social workers with reasonable case loads in agencies with a primary commitment to natural families rather than to placement as the first response. In those instances where substitute care is unavoidable because of crisis or danger, many more children could remain with extended kin and even neighbors.

Nowhere in social work practice have we sufficiently recognized the extent and the strengths of natural support systems among diverse cultural groups. Blacks have a long tradition of giving care to related children.[2] Recent research has revealed the presence of strong social networks and systems of mutual aid in ghetto life.[3] Even if not married to the child's mother, the father and his family are often important emotional and material resources to the black child. They have been largely overlooked by child welfare services and, as a resource, all but destroyed by AFDC policies.[4] Similarly, Hispanic groups have a natural child welfare system of godparents (compadres and patrinos) who assume nurturing and caregiving functions. Such real-life supports must be utilized as a way of sustaining the child's connectedness to his family.

The use of neighbors as foster parents is related to the important sense of place that is also part of one's identity and sense of continuity—one's own neighborhood, one's own block, and all the nurturing aspects that the familiar physical environment represents, along with the associated social environment of peers, school, church, and other neighborhood ties. Wherever and however substitute care is provided, there are many ways to sustain the child's connectedness to the biological family, as Laird clearly shows.[5]

Recent research emerging from an evolutionary view of human parenting,[6] ethological research on mammals (especially nonhuman primates),[7] and anthropological studies of contemporary hunter-gatherer societies[8] lend support to the idea of a biological (whether genetic or congenital) base in attachment behaviors of both mother and child from conception through infancy. Therefore, in addition to the familiar psychosocial components of identity and self-image we must consider the likelihood of a biological component as a fundamental layer of the sense of self. Such research raises serious questions about present obstetrical and hospital practices and the violation of innate needs of mothers and infants for connectedness. But the research findings also raise new and pressing questions about child welfare practices that interfere with the child's deepest sense of self.

The child who must be placed in substitute care at any age, and regardless of the reason, is torn from the biological and symbolic context of his identity. No matter how nurturing the substitute care, the child's ongoing

task will always be to reweave the jagged tear in the fabric of his identity, to make himself whole again. Laird addresses this quintessential need with compassion for the children and the adults involved, and with courage to confront the revolutionary changes required in child welfare practice.
                                                                —C.B.G.

CHANGE in today's world occurs at such rapid rates that human beings' adaptive abilities are strained to their very limits. On the other hand, in some areas change or progress seems painfully slow. On a societal level we have only recently become alarmed enough about the destruction of our natural environment to seriously examine the impact of social, economic, and political planning and decision-making on the systems upon which we must depend for future survival.

Social workers, in spite of their historical focus on human beings in relation to their social environments, have also often been slow to recognize the far-reaching destructive effects that policies, programs, and service delivery approaches may have on delicate but vital human systems. A case in point is the undermining effect some kinds of practice have had on that most important natural human system, the family. Perhaps nowhere has resistance to change, resistance to take account of, support, and protect natural systems been more troublesome or more paradoxical than in the field of family and childrens' services, that area of practice known, interestingly enough, as ''child welfare.''

The metaphorical use of principles from ecology focusses attention on the extent to which people are dependent upon and immersed in their social, physical, cultural, and emotional environments.

What are the implications of an ecological orientation for practice in child welfare? In this chapter we will describe what current child welfare practice seems to look like and how an ecological perspective would alter it. We will explore some of the resistances and obstacles that may stand in the way of change. Finally, we will describe some applications of ecological practice principles in specific practice situations.

THE BIOLOGICAL FAMILY

This presentation takes as its starting point the conviction that human beings are profoundly affected by the family system of which they are a part. Kin ties are powerful and compelling and the individual's sense of identity and continuity is formed not only by the significant attachments in his intimate environment but also is deeply rooted in the biological family—in the genetic link that reaches back into the past and ahead into the future.

This view of the significance of kin ties runs deep in American culture and is expressed by such sayings as "blood is thicker than water." Whether this deep sense of kinship connection is biologically based [1] or is a cultural "artifact" [2] is hotly disputed. No matter which explanation one favors, the felt experience of the importance of kin ties does exist, whether it is a part of our genetic heritage or a part of our cultural heritage. And although there are many other sources of identity, continuity, and attachment, the importance of the biological family cannot be ignored.

Ecologically oriented child welfare practice attends to, nurtures, and supports the biological family. Further, when it is necessary to substitute for the biological family, such practice dictates that every effort be made to preserve and protect important kinship ties. Intervening in families must be done with great care to avoid actions which could weaken the natural family system, sap its vitality and strength, or force it to make difficult, costly adjustments.

Although this position is based on the importance of individuals' connection with their family systems, there are other considerations which lead to such a conception of ecological child welfare practice. The most important of these is the demonstrated fact that it is difficult, expensive, and wasteful of valuable resources to locate and support substitute forms of care. Consider the cost in human and material resources of maintaining a single child in institutional care. Consider the cost of foster home care in terms of professional services and financial support, to say nothing of the psychological cost to children and foster parents of the frequent replacements which continue to typify the foster care experience.

CURRENT CHILD WELFARE PRACTICE

Although one should be careful of generalizing, and certainly we can point to many outstanding exceptions to general trends, our largest social, economic, and professional investment continues to lie in obtaining and maintaining substitute care arrangements for children, and in the treatment of emotionally damaged children. As Salvador Minuchin so bluntly phrases it, even though we have conceptual knowledge which enables us to understand family difficulties in an ecological framework, as products of transactions between the family and its surrounding life space,

Our armamentarium of interventions has failed to change in response to our broadening conceptualizations. . . .[3] [The] response of social agencies in general is still to break up the family. The records of improvement in foster care and residential treatment are not encouraging, and the costs of these approaches is discouraging, but there still has not been an organized, overall conceptualization of the delivery of services to families in this country. The family is studied and respected as a viable socialization unit when it is working; when trouble arises, the response is to split it.[4]

The typical child welfare case looks something like this:

Janet Roberts calls the police, reporting that her sister-in-law Denise Jackson is at the local bar with a boyfriend, having left her four children ranging in age from 3 to 11 alone. The oldest daughter, age 14, is in a foster home. The police remove the children to an emergency "temporary" foster home. The following day a Protective Services worker visits Mrs. Jackson, finding her alternately angry and tearful, worrying whether the children have enough clothing, and accusing her sister-in-law of "trying to get my children." The worker learns that Mr. Jackson is in jail, having stolen from his employer. The house is disorderly. From the case record, the worker is already familiar with a family history reflecting several years of multiple problems, unemployment and underemployment, marital stress, and conflict with both maternal and paternal extended families. The protective worker, hoping to reunite the family, spends considerable time with Mrs. Jackson, counseling, cajoling, advising, insisting that she clean up the house, supervise and discipline the children more consistently, and initiate therapy at the local mental health clinic. Mrs. Jackson, although she makes many promises and some ineffectual attempts, does not follow through, and a petition of neglect is adjudicated. The case is then transferred from the Protective Services Unit to Foster Care. The foster care worker's efforts center on helping the children with separation difficulties and adjustment to a new environment, and working with the foster family around a variety of parenting issues and related concerns. The visiting of the natural parent(s) often becomes the most potentially flammable issue, the one requiring the most sensitive work. Mrs.

Jackson begins to fade as a central part of the case, her visits taper off, she seems disinterested. . . .

What was visualized originally as a temporary foster placement, a stop on a circular path to the reunion and rehabilitation of the natural family, has instead become a straight and narrow road toward substitute care. This can mean permanent placement or, as is often the case, a dismal succession of repeated separations and placements in foster homes and institutions sometimes interspersed, when resources are exhausted, with temporary and unsuccessful trips home.

Some of the more blatant examples of current policy and/or practice which belie our publicly stated goal of supporting and strengthening natural family systems should be mentioned:

1. Native American and other concerned professionals are descrying what they describe as the destruction of the American Indian family, as it is alleged that some 25 to 35 percent of Indian children are being placed in foster or adoptive care. Surely widespread removal out of race, culture, and family heritage is an illogical and destructive approach to the enhancement of healthy development for Indian children![5]

2. Public agency protective and other family service units continue to be plagued with high caseloads, inadequate human and financial resources, and heavy paper and reporting responsibilities which may be needed but which interfere with direct service potential.[6]

3. While funds for services to families are limited, we seem willing to invest $10,000 to $20,000 per year to care for one child in a residential treatment center.

4. We seem to believe, in this society, that an AFDC mother deserves less and can support her child on less income than can a foster mother.

The most ironic note is the troubling question of whether our investments are successful, whether, in our public and professional roles as substitute parents we are doing a better job than natural families might have done if left to their own devices, let alone given similar time and investment. How do we explain the statistics on the numbers of repeated, unsuccessful placements, the number of children in limbo, without permanent planning? How do we continue to justify the return of children who were removed because of neglect to families who are no more economically, physically, socially, or emotionally equipped to give adequate care than they were when their children were placed? How often are these decisions made on the basis of lack of agency and community resources but described as appropriate treatment plans?

How do we explain the return home of children from residential treatment facilities to families who have not been involved in the treatment effort? How can we expect the returning child to shoulder the burden of adjusting to or even changing a stressful family system which itself has perhaps accommodated to the child's absence? How long will it be before the child has been recast into his or her traditional role, whether it be scapegoat, delinquent, or some other type of family symptom bearer?

Such practices are not only "unecological" but paradoxically "antifamily" in their effects. If an ecological approach to child welfare means the preservation of the natural family wherever possible, we clearly need to scrutinize our seeming inability to shift direction.

OBSTACLES TO
AN ECOLOGICAL APPROACH

Why have we not put our stated beliefs about family life into practice? This is an exceedingly complex question which defies any simple "cause and effect" answer. Economic, political, cultural, and professional forces combine to inhibit change in child welfare, thus the emphasis on substitute care and the failure to "think" or "act" family persist.

Perhaps the most striking obstacle is the lack of consistent philosophical agreement in the United States as to the role of government in relation to the family. We have no "family policy" as such, for example, one which supports or guarantees universal basic income or service levels for all families. Only recently has interest developed in the notion of examining the "impact" on the family of political and economic planning and decision-making. Our national ambivalence is surfaced as we promote policies and programs which pressure AFDC mothers of young children to seek employment, yet fail to provide an adequate day care system for fear of usurping the traditional family role of child-rearing.

Not only do we lack commitment to a uniform family policy, but we also continue to struggle with the sometimes conflicting interests of parents and children and to debate the issue of whose rights take precedence. Clear definitions of "minimal standards of child care" and "neglect" continue to elude us, as social, moral, economic, and racial factors influence our thinking. Some social critics state that in our society, abuse and neglect are inevitable in an economic environment in which children continue to be viewed as commodities or property and thus exploited.[7] The abuse and neglect of children in public and private institutions continues and confusion about the nature of abuse is expressed in the Supreme Court's refusal to rule against corporal punishment in the schools.[8] Cynical and uncomfortably provocative questions are raised concerning the latent role of child welfare programs. One prominent analyst recently attacked the myth that "child care facilities and agencies are sanctioned and supported by the community primarily out of concern for children and what is best for the child," suggesting that our real function may be that of removing "embarrassing debris from visibility," the "social control" role social workers have often unwittingly performed.[9] Even more challenging is the suggestion that social workers not only perform social control functions but are acting as brokers of a very valuable and increasingly scarce commodity, young children. The practice of transracial and transcultural adoption, for example, has been under angry attack as professionals are accused of exploiting poor and minority families in meeting the "demand" for babies in a market whose character has changed drastically as a result of increased birth control, legality and availability of abortion, and fewer surrenders on the parts of unmarried parents. Are we indeed guilty, in the name of "child-saving," of brokering children from poor to rich families just as we found poor city children to act as farm labor in the 19th century? Such questions are frightening and challenging, but exceedingly necessary.

At the program level child welfare suffers from lack of clarity concerning program objectives. Even when overall objectives are clearly defined, successful coordination of a variety of services and interests is difficult.[10] And finally, child welfare is plagued by the same criticisms all human services face, a dearth of tested methods for evaluating the outcome of our efforts, the achievement of objectives.[11]

In addition to these political, social, and economic variables, there are other powerful forces which influence current child welfare practice. One major handicap is our lack of understanding of family systems. Historically, our knowledge and training was shaped by psychoanalytic and child development theories, and was largely confined to the understanding of individuals. We have been trained, albeit often inadequately, to monitor child development, to construct models for healthy physical, social, and emotional development, and to attempt to understand and diagnose a variety of adult and child pathologies. The bulk of the child abuse literature, for example, centers on the psychological profile of the abusing parent.[12] Understandably then, the choice of intervention often leads us to removal of children and referral to mental health facilities, and to treatment of individual family members. Child welfare workers are often frustrated as parents seem "uncooperative," "unmotivated," do not follow through with treatment plans, and the treatment of the emotionally damaged child becomes a long expensive process with what often seem limited gains.

This is not to suggest that knowledge of individual psychological development and functioning is not valuable or essential, but only to say that new ways of understanding family systems in space, in relation to their complex environments, and as they develop over time are now available as well and should be used by child welfare workers. Concepts from family system theorists, from ecological and general systems theory, and from communication theory, are aids to understanding and assessing the transactional relationships among family members and between the family and its environment.

Ironically, social work can be proud of the fact it was the first profession to "think" and "act" family, and has a tradition of being the profession concerned with the total person-situation complex. Other disciplines have only recently discovered, for example, the assessment and intervention potentials of home visits! In the last 25 years, however, while child welfare has largely clung to older "medical model" approaches, the family therapy field, dominated by psychologists and psychiatrists, has been characterized by an exciting development of new frameworks or models for understanding and intervening in complex family relationships.[13] It is time now for child welfare to examine and integrate new thinking about families in their world.

All workers must deal with the impact of their own personal and familial experiences on their professional development. Young workers, called upon to make decisions affecting the future lives of families, parents, and children alike, are often themselves in the height of their own efforts to separate and differentiate from their families of origin. It may well be that this conflict strengthens their wish to rescue children from their families.

Issues of adulthood, of identity consolidation, never totally resolved for anyone, profoundly affect how we view and work with client families. A group of child welfare trainees, presented with a living family sculpture which demonstrated the family emotional system, were asked to resculpt the family as they would like it to be, or as they would want it to change with family intervention. The trainees were surprised and amused to discover that each had his own ideas on the subject. These ideas, which were argued enthusiastically, seemed to reflect either their real or idealized images of their own families.

In another family sculpture experience, a child welfare worker in her 40s, herself a parent, found she was the only person in the room feeling empathetic with the parents in the presented family, while most of the younger workers were more identified with the children. How much conviction, how much hope we have about the family, is deeply related to our own family relationships and experiences. Some workers, perhaps having had painful experiences with their own parents, view their roles as obtaining "better" parents for children. Young workers, testing out and not yet acclimated to their own new roles as adults with power and authority may find it easier to identify with and to work with children than to plunge with conviction into family work with adults who may be angry, attacking, and involved in a seemingly hopeless, tangled procession of psychological, marital, social, economic, and other difficulties.

The preceding attempt to search out some explanations for our reluctance to move toward a clear family emphasis in child welfare is intended to raise questions which need to be addressed. There may be no easy solutions, but the first step surely must be to critically examine the issues, dilemmas, and myths which shape our practice.

ISSUES OF PARENTING AND IDENTITY

A particularly profound, persistent, and troubling challenge in child placement is to understand and ameliorate the traumatic effects on children of both temporary and permanent separations from their families of origin or other primary caretakers. The child welfare worker is also faced with the task of helping children cope with threats to healthy identity formation and consolidation provoked by physical and emotional cut-offs from their biological roots.[14]

Although we share a common knowledge base,[15] social workers in general seem vulnerable to dichotomies which, in their extreme form, tend to retard progress. Just as we have in the past separated ourselves into the caseworkers and the social changemakers arguing about which is best and which is the "real" social work, so today we find ourselves debating with renewed vigor an enduring controversy in the child welfare arena. We might call this the "case of the biological parent vs. the psychological parent," as if one had to rule finally that one or the other were the "real" parent!

The family itself, variously described in recent years as outmoded, overwhelmed, functionless, or breaking down, is making a comeback. Whatever the reasons, people seem to be fighting to preserve the family as a meaningful and viable institution. There is, for example, a new surge of interest in geneology and in family reunions, predating but also stimulated by Alex Haley's *Roots*.[16] In the mental health field, the interdisciplinary family therapy movement, now some 25 years old, attracts increasing numbers of trainees, as new ways of thinking about and working with families are generated.

At the same time that we are experiencing the renewed interest in the family and particularly the biological family, Anna Freud, Albert J. Solnit, and Joseph Goldstein take a strong position in defense of the concept of the psychological parent.[17] Few would argue against their efforts to better define that nebulous term, the "best interests of

the child,'' or would contest their basic premise that the guideline of
"continuity," of "the need of every child for unbroken continuity of
affectionate and stimulating relationships with an adult" is paramount
in child welfare.[18]

It is the next step the authors take which this writer finds illogical
if not potentially damaging to progress in child welfare. The position,
never explicitly clarified, is most dramatically implied in the following excerpt concerning parental visitation and custody issues in divorce situations:

Children have difficulty in relating positively to, profiting from, and maintaining the contact with two psychological parents who are not in positive
contact with each other. Loyalty conflicts are common and normal under
such conditions and may have devastating consequences by destroying the
child's positive relationships to both parents. A ''visiting'' or ''visited''
parent has little chance to serve as a true object for love, trust, and identification, since this role is based on his being available on an uninterrupted
day-to-day basis.

Once it is determined who will be the custodial parent, it is that parent,
not the court, who must decide under what conditions he or she wishes to
raise the child. Thus, the noncustodial parent should have no legally enforceable right to visit the child, and the custodial parent should have the
right to decide whether it is desirable for the child to have such visits.[19]

To argue that a child's psychological parent, and thus the source of
his own psychological identity, is determined solely from his nurturing, caretaking experiences seems an oversimplification of a very
complex human situation. Children identify both positively and negatively with many real and fantasy figures other than their full-time
caretakers, from the loving weekend and summer vacation daddy to
the deserting father "who kicked my mother in the stomach when she
was pregnant with me"[20] Most child welfare workers have experienced the pain, frustration, and feeling of failure when, in spite of
dedicated efforts to provide a supportive environment for a child, a
foster child acts out destructively in a way which reflects the few
facts he may have about his hidden or lost parents, or even worse, on
the basis of his fantasies about the lost object. Family systems therapists understand that family secrets, physical and emotional cut-offs

from family, and family myths can contribute as powerfully if not more powerfully to individual dysfunction as those family conflicts and crises which can be openly identified and thus tackled.

In recent years we have witnessed a growing interest on the part of adult adoptees in searching out their origins and in some cases in meeting their natural parents or extended biological families. Accounts of these difficult and often emotionally draining adventures have portrayed human beings' deep psychological needs for rootedness. The following comments are illustrative of the experiences many of them share.

One writer, a psychologist and family therapist who was raised in foster care and as an adult embarked on an "identity trip," tells of the impact on him of seeing for the first time a picture of his deceased mother. The experience of seeing oneself reflected in another human being is described as "a stunning experience!"[21]

A foster child, David, was recently reintroduced to his long lost extended family through the determined efforts of his worker, who traced his family while she was on a vacation to the east coast. He expressed his relief this way:

I told my caseworker . . . after seeing my grandparents and aunts, uncles, cousins, etc. and knowing now that I have them . . . before I never felt that I belonged anywhere or if for that matter, [it] mattered if I had anyone. The reason I say belonged anywhere is because of my other grandparents dying when I was 13, and then going through a number of different foster homes. . . . After seeing my grandparents, I feel as though I belong now, and that I am somebody and that is the best feeling anyone could have in this situation.[22]

Many adoptees are not necessarily interested in reunion, but in knowing their biological histories.[23] Such information "provides a frame for their lives, and a continuity with their pasts. It confirms and solidifies their images of themselves" in a search to achieve a unity and persistence of personality.[24]

This need for "rootedness," has at times been characterized by professionals as neurotic or is said to exist only in those unhappy, unfulfilled persons who have had inadequate alternate family experiences. Psychiatrist Robert Jay Lifton, in contrast to the view developed by Freud and her colleagues describes "the duality of all involvement—*immediate* psychological struggles around connection and separation, integrity and disintegration, and movement and stasis; and *ultimate* struggles with forces beyond the self, with meanings around historical and biological continuity."[25] Lifton stresses that identity formation is not simply a matter of one's immediate life experiences and relationships but is also strongly influenced by one's larger sense of heritage.[26] The adopted child and the foster child, however reluctant we may be to admit it, each has two families. It is a major life task to understand and integrate the meanings and experiences from both families, to incorporate his or her historical and biological heritage into the foster or other family experience. It is our responsibility to help the child achieve this bio-psycho-social integration.

We have often encouraged children to estrange themselves from and to repress painful family experiences. In doing so, we robbed them of their rights to their own histories and of opportunities to gain freedom from the emotional "stucktogetherness" which can inhibit functioning. We have recognized that adults need the opportunity to experience and master the developmental and situational crises of death, of separation, and divorce. Cannot we offer the same opportunity to children?

The second implication of the view expressed by Freud and her colleagues is that loyalty conflicts, whether between divorced parents or between biological and foster parents, are more harmful to a child than what amounts to a possible repudiation of a major part of self. One writer points out that the authors' view lacks any basis in empirical research, and in fact cites several studies which support the belief that those children who fare best after divorce are those who are free to develop relationships with both parents. "Children are not only deeply pained by . . . [a parent's] . . . absence but they interpret it as abandonment; as a consequence they feel devalued and guilty, and yet they find they have few ways to express their anger and confusion."[27]

Just as we cannot decide that one biological parent is to own the psychological parent role, we cannot separate biological and psychological identity as if they were two opposing and isolated parts of human personality. Nor should we ask that children make such choices. Instead we need to help children come to terms with and maintain their biological realities in whatever ways may be possible. Certainly the integration of potentially competing and conflicting forces, whether maternal and paternal, biological or adoptive family, fostering or visiting parent, are difficult for everyone concerned—for the child, the adults, and the professional. The solution, however, lies not in obliterating one side of the competition but in reexamining our biases and enhancing our knowledge and skills so that we may better help our clients master these life challenges.

AN ECOLOGICAL APPROACH
TO CHILD WELFARE

The most effective way to preserve natural family ties is to strengthen and preserve the family itself. While it is beyond the parameters of this chapter to discuss working with natural families in any depth, a few comments should be made.

The first step in moving toward ecological practice mandates a serious reexamination and clarification of our goals and priorities, coupled with a willingness not only to advocate for new programs and funding but to shift a large portion of our energies and funds from a placement to a natural family focus.

We have the conceptual framework which enables us to better understand the complex relationships between families and their ecological environments, to identify those interfaces where there is stress, conflict, or insufficient exchange across family-environment boundaries, and to plan interventions which can most quickly and economically promote major improvement in family functioning. Such practice models encourage both workers and families to mobilize and utilize potentially enriching natural support networks.[28] This knowledge is seeping into child welfare practice, but a model of ecological family-centered practice must be developed and refined for child welfare, and all workers must have training in work with families.

Family-centered practice is an empty concept, however, if we are unable to provide families with the institutional supports and services needed to prevent family dysfunction and enrich family life. For example, on a larger scale, this country has yet to commit itself to an adequate family income program, equal educational opportunities for all children, meaningful employment opportunities for all who are able to work, or universally available health and medical care. In the last fifteen years the introduction of homemaker and day care services has provided an important resource in the preserving of family life, but often even these services are extremely limited and the eligibility requirements narrow and prohibitive for many families. We need to broaden the availability of such programs and services and to expand opportunities for family education and self-fulfillment.

Where priorities have been reexamined and efforts made to sanction and support work with natural families through provision of special training and expansion or reallocation of resources, results are encouraging. Recently, in a New York State demonstration project, worker caseloads were limited to ten families, and project agencies were required to meet client needs for homemaker, day care, vocational, and educational services.[29] It was found that fewer children in the experimental group, who received "intensive" services, entered placement than in the control group, who received "usual" service. Additionally, those children who did enter placement remained for shorter periods of time, and a larger percentage of them had been returned home by the end of the evaluation period.

In Michigan, the Temporary Foster Care Project is designed to encourage foster care workers to widen the unit of attention to include intensive work with natural families. Workers are given several days of training in family assessment and intervention, they are introduced to newly developed family intervention tools and provided with follow-up consultation. The training emphasizes assessment and intervention in the interface between family and ecological environment, although workers are also introduced to family systems frameworks for assessing the internal family system. Workers are asked to identify specific goals and tasks and taught to develop time-limited contracts between family and worker. The project's stated goal is to "move children from the uncertain and temporary status of foster care to a more permanent and hopefully stable situation, preferably a return to the biological family."[30] At the end of the first project year, the percentage of placed children returned to their biological families within six months of placement more than doubled over the previous year in all four of the pilot counties.[31] Workers are also better able to move confidently toward permanent planning and termination of parental rights in those cases where families will not be able to resume care of their children. Project leaders hope to spread the family orientation and training opportunities to other counties and service units through the use of peer trainers.

PRESERVING FAMILY TIES IN PLACEMENT

Even if a major shift toward family-centered practice is accomplished, there will continue to be some children who will need temporary or permanent substitute care. Family assessment and intervention knowledge and techniques backed by careful court review and monitoring are not only helpful in making more intelligent decisions about placement and termination of parental rights but in helping families and children master the separation and relinquishment process. Further, a family systems perspective is extremely valuable in improving our potential for making more accurate, dynamic, predictive assessments of potential foster and adoptive families.

An ecological approach in child welfare suggests that those placement systems closest to the natural system promise the least disruption for child and family and should be explored first. This maxim has been accepted as we have preferred foster care over institutional placement in order to approximate the natural family relationships. The obvious implication here is that every effort should be made to utilize the extended family as a placement resource.

This implication is frequently given short shrift. For one thing, many workers assume that if one member of a family has abused or neglected a child, other members will do the same. This point of view is given considerable support in the child welfare literature. Blair and Rita Justice state:

Breaking the multigenerational cycle of child abuse, then, is of paramount importance. Accomplishing this often means that children must be kept out of the hands of their grandparents and the abusing parents must be helped to break away from their families of origin.[32]

I believe this position is based on a serious misinterpretation of Bowen family theory. The authors confuse the concepts of "differentiation" and "separation" as used by Bowen and other family theorists. Those individuals who are poorly differentiated, according to family systems theory, have more intense unresolved emotional attachments to their parents than most, they are more fused or emotionally "stuck together." [33] Some practitioners assume that dysfunctional family relationships are best handled by withdrawing, putting physical distance between individuals and their families. Thus they view abusing families as families from which children should be encouraged to physically and emotionally separate. However, in the family therapy field there is widespread conviction that physical and emotional distancing promotes rather than weakens psychological dependency. In situations where the physical and emotional cut-offs become intense, as in prolonged placements, the child may be even more prone to duplicate destructive family patterns in his or her own adult interpersonal and family relationships.

Certainly we see evidence of this phenomenon, as many emotionally damaged children repeat the dysfunctional marital and parenting patterns of their parents in spite of adequate placement experiences and supportive service. We need to help children instead come to terms with their families, to renegotiate their family relationships, whether they remain in their own families or, for protective reasons, are placed.

A child may represent different meanings for grandparents or other relatives than he does for his parents. And relatives themselves may not relate to him in the same way they do to the child's parents. We know that particular children are selected out for scapegoating in order to maintain family homeostasis. Similarly, in Bowen's theory, the "triangled" child refers to the child who is the main focus of the family projection process. [34] Which child is selected depends on many factors such as personal characteristics, sex, or sibling position. Another issue to consider is that the abusing parent, who may have been the abused, scapegoated, or triangled child in his or her generation of siblings, may be functioning at a lower level of differentiation than either grandparents or other relatives. Negative assumptions about the child-caring potential of relatives must therefore be carefully questioned, and family dynamics assessed on an individual basis, in order to make intelligent decisions about the potential of particular relatives for assuming care of children.

Practitioners are further influenced toward placement outside of the family by a welfare structure which is reluctant to provide relatives with the same financial resources available to strangers. This bias, which in effect results in shifting children from poor to more economically secure environments, reflects the idea that "if they really cared, they would make the necessary sacrifices." The fact is, there are many families who might want to care for a sister's or a nephew's child but cannot absorb the financial burdens presented by the addition of another child.[35]

A third reason workers sometimes avoid placement with relatives has to do with their own anxieties about and inadequate preparation for helping families deal with emotionally charged issues of possessiveness, competitiveness, and loyalty which may arise. It is somewhat easier to avoid these particular conflicts if children are placed with strangers. Yet, from the child's point of view, the separation may be far less painful, the physical and emotional cutoffs less severe or psychologically damaging if the child remains with relatives. The child's sense of belonging, of biological identity, is more easily maintained. The following example illustrates one worker's approach:

Jeffrey Marino, aged 6 months, was soon to be released from the hospital after surviving severe burns from scalding at the age of 4 months. Although Mrs. Marino claimed the baby had accidentally turned hot tap water on himself while left alone in his bath for a moment, the worker, supervisor, and doctor believed the mother, under extreme stress as a result of her husband leaving her for another woman the week before Jeffrey's birth, and lacking family or other environmental supports, had displaced her hurt and anger onto the child. Jeffrey would need extensive physical therapy at home and frequent doctor visits. It was felt that Mrs. Marino could not cope with these demands nor was she emotionally ready to resume care of her child without extensive psychological and environmental intervention.

In exploring potential resources for Jeffrey's care, the worker felt that the paternal grandparents were in the best position to meet this child's need for intensive, loving, physical and emotional care. The supervisor recommended against placement with relatives since she feared the worker and the agency would become involved in heated family rivalries and conflicts. Agency concerns and potential sources of conflict and difficulty were discussed with the mother, both sets of in-laws, and with Jeffrey's father, who had returned to the area. Ultimately, Mrs. Marino chose to place Jeffrey with her in-laws.

In assessing the results, the worker and agency believed the decision to keep Jeffrey in the family had been justified. Family rivalries, jealousies, and open conflicts occurred frequently throughout the placement, straining the worker's mediating skills and agency patience. Jeffrey's progress, however, surpassed everyone's expectations. It had originally been feared he might not walk, but by his first birthday he was taking his first steps. The placement had unanticipated consequences for Mrs. Marino's adaptation to the dissolution of the marriage and her own emotional adjustment. Neglected and emotionally deprived in her own disturbed family of origin, her relationship with her in-laws had been extremely important during her marriage, and she saw the elder Mrs. Marino as a positive maternal figure. The abandonment by her husband represented a double loss, as she felt betrayed again by parental figures.

A key element in the placement was the younger Mrs. Marino's right to visit, and the understanding that if possible she would resume care of Jeffrey over a period of time. This process was not without its crises and conflicts, but its positive results were significant. Much of Mrs. Marino's bitterness dissipated as she was able, on somewhat changed terms, to establish a workable relationship with her in-laws, and to take a more adult stance in relation to her own parents, who kept threatening her with isolation if she had any contact with the in-laws. She was gradually able to understand her own role in the marital conflict and family triangles. She could accept Jeffrey's need to have a connection with his father.

It is important to mention that, in addition to and simultaneously with intensive work with the extended family system many other interventions were made in the family life space. They were designed to build an ongoing supportive network for the mother in order to decrease her social isolation.

If placement with relatives is not feasible, the next system closest to the natural family system is that of neighborhood. Often a neglected resource, temporary placement of children with neighborhood families has obvious advantages. Children are not forced to adjust to separation from family *and* social milieu and thus can maintain family, peer, neighborhood, and school relationships more easily. Some agencies are developing group home placements for troubled youths located in their own neighborhoods.[36] The following vignette is more typical of child welfare practice:

The protective worker received an emergency call at 7 P.M., learning that a Mrs. Ramirez had died in the hospital that day, following complications after surgery, leaving a family of 11 children. The supervisor had already lined up emergency placement homes. The small ghetto house was dirty and chaotic, and the neighbors who had gathered were like the Ramirez family, Puerto Rican and Spanish-speaking. The worker, well-intentioned but overwhelmed by the crisis and the confusion, lacked familiarity with the community. Unable to provide a homemaker she spent the night placing all 11 children in four agency foster homes ranging from five to sixty miles from the community. The following day the worker learned that several neighbors were willing to take in the children at least until permanent plans could be made, there were two aunts living in the neighborhood who might, with financial help, care for the children, and further, Mrs. Ramirez's common-law husband, father to the three youngest children, might have managed to keep the family together.

In the above example, the children need not have been so abruptly severed from family, neighborhood, and culture. Social workers in general are members of urban, individualistic, middle-class nuclear families that are usually small, independent, and "semi-closed." Thus a worker may overlook the possibility that certain client families have the kind of "openness" and deep ties to extended family and neighborhood which are more characteristic of folk societies.[37]

The Ramirez vignette exposes another possibility often ignored, the potential of the male single parent for maintaining the family. If he receives adequate services as needed, including financial assistance, homemaker-teacher aid, chore service, day care, counseling and family life education, placement can often be prevented altogether or children in placement returned to their natural environments.

If none of the alternatives is feasible, temporary foster care or small group home placement may become necessary. It still may be possible to place in the same neighborhood, parish, or school district. The tragedy of child welfare, however, is that the intended "revolving door" between foster home care and natural family all too often becomes a door that is closed, locking the child into an uncertain future as a foster child. This unintended consequence is understandable, given the inherent difficulties and financial costs of rehabilitation compared to prevention. Not only must workers possess the knowledge and skills necessary to effect change in a complicated, expanded client system which now includes natural family, foster parents, and foster child, but they must also have available the organizational supports and resources necessary to promote the rehabilitation and reuniting of natural families. The latter is frequently lacking as most child welfare structures support the maintenance of children in foster care.

As mentioned earlier, in those projects where permanent planning for children was stressed and supported with financial and service resources, the numbers of children returned annually to their own families greatly increased. In another approach—court monitoring—Festinger found that periodic court review of all cases of children in voluntary placement served as a catalyst in stimulating agencies to make "permanent" decisions—to return children to their biological families, to continue foster care, or to free them for adoptive placement. When the court slackened its monitoring function, agencies tended to drift again and delayed decision-making.[38]

While children are in substitute care, whether temporary or permanent, the issues of biological family identity and maintenance of family ties can be crucial to the emotional growth of the child. However, we are usually more protective of foster parents' feelings and privacy than of the natural parents' rights, feelings, and concerns about their children, or of the child's right to family contacts and his need to "belong."

Several factors may support this tendency. Just as the triangle is seen as the basic building block of the family emotional system, so the socio-emotional system of natural family, foster family, and foster child may be viewed as a triangular relationship. As tension mounts between two corners of the triangle, for example, between natural and foster parent, efforts are made by one or both to triangulate the third member, the child, into an emotional alliance. The child and foster family, for example, may achieve some feeling of togetherness and comfort by pushing the natural parent to the "outsider" position. Similarly, the worker may be pulled into interlocking triangular relationships, frequently occupying the same corner as the child, caught in the middle of the tension between the two sets of parents. The worker's increasing discomfort can lead to an attempt to detriangulate by extruding one member, usually the natural parent.

Another reason the natural parents may be shut out arises from an understandable need on the part of the worker to avoid pain, the worker's own and that of the child. Just as parents were sometimes discouraged from visiting their hospitalized children because the children would cry when they left, making it more difficult for staff physically and emotionally, parental visits are said to upset children and to make foster home adjustment more difficult. In this instance the avoidance of emotional pain becomes more important than the opportunity to master the separation and conflict.

Lack of natural parent involvement is also influenced by the workers' anxiety around preserving tenuous foster home placements, particularly in urban areas where foster home resources may be seriously limited. Foster home placements, even if less than desirable, are sometimes maintained at the expense of parent-child contact in order to mollify burdened and critical foster parents.

Foster parents themselves are in a difficult and paradoxical position. They have been asked to love and care for a child as if he were their own, but at the same time they must be ready to relinquish him at short notice for return home or adoption. Additionally they are expected to show tolerance for parents who may seem neglectful, hostile, repulsive, or deviant to them. Insecure, fragile, conditional relationships between foster parent and child are frequently the result of trying to balance these difficult involvements, as foster parents dare not risk the deep emotional hurts which accompany separating from a loved child.

One difficulty in managing productive visiting is related to confusion about and lack of preparation for the foster parent role. The gradual professionalization (in the positive sense) of the foster parent role through foster parent training, more adequate remuneration, and redefinition and clarification of the place of the natural family in the child's life may enable foster parents with worker help to reconceptualize their role as that of serving child *and* family.

There are many ways in which workers with a family orientation and a conviction about biological connectedness not only can help a child integrate his biological and psychological identities, but help insure that the foster home is generally used for temporary substitute care. The most important prerequisite for both connectedness and potential return home is personal contact and sharing of life experiences between biological parents and children. Many parents of children in placement, after early efforts to maintain contact, tend to drift away, to terminate visitation, and are finally accused of lacking interest in their children. The visiting rights of others are reduced or terminated as a result of intense conflict between foster and natural parent or because it is concluded that visiting has deleterious effects on the child.

While some parents will not be able to maintain personal contact, very often the lack of sensitivity to the difficult position of the parent in the life of the child are crucial elements in discouraging visitation. Phyllis McAdams writes of her shattered self-esteem and of feeling excluded from the lives of her children as she painfully tried to maintain a relationship with her children in foster care. She questions the fact that neither workers nor foster parents seem to feel that parents can or should participate in such seemingly minor but emotionally important considerations as whether a child should have a new hair style, whether she should have swimming lessons, needs a winter coat this year, or how she can get along better with a particular teacher.[39] Couldn't children be allowed to telephone their parents or relatives more frequently to share their happy and sad experiences? Must even temporary foster care often result in an almost total termination of parental involvement in the child's life? Unfortunately these emotional cutoffs lead to alienation and loss on the part of both family and child which militate against eventual reuniting.

We need to consider and test new approaches to shared parenting, to support and encourage parental visiting with both emotional and concrete help. The child's extended family can also often serve as a positive resource for nourishment of family identity, in addition to or in place of the parents. Where parents are judged to be too destructive or are deceased, as in the case of David cited earlier, workers should carefully explore the possibility that other relatives might provide a meaningful family connection for a foster child, and sustain his/her sense of belonging.

In addition to or in lieu of visitation, natural family ties can be enriched and connectedness preserved through the use of family history, pictures, mementos, and possessions. The genogram is another tool used by more and more protective, foster care, and adoptive workers. This creative device, used as an assessment and intervention framework in family treatment, is described in chapter 8. Some child welfare workers who use the genogram report feeling far less critical of abusing and neglecting parents. The genogram helps them develop a dynamic understanding of the parents' family environments and family history. The genogram also helps preserve family and biological history for children who are separated from their families. In a sense it is a road map of one's family heritage and biological rootedness. Its usefulness in exposing powerful intergenerational family patterns, strong identifications, losses, and so on may prove valuable not only in helping the placed child understand and differentiate from dysfunctional family patterns but in connecting him with strengths and sources of pride.[40]

As workers became more sensitive to the importance of preserving family ties, they themselves develop creative techniques. Some child welfare workers report they are actively engaged in convincing foster parents to allow children to bring in other cherished possessions. One group of workers created an ecological pictorial map of the foster child's life space, including own family, foster family, and other significant systems which the child could color and talk about with the worker. This helps the child master the placement experience.[41] The worker-child-family construction of "life books" or family scrapbooks, which include genealogical information and accounts of significant experiences in the life of child and family are of increasing interest.

These techniques, simple to learn and use, are valuable in helping parents and children master the placement experience, and in helping to alleviate the deep feelings of loss and rootlessness.

The same issues exist and the same techniques can be employed for emotionally disturbed, physically handicapped, delinquent, or other children whose special needs require placement in institutional settings for brief to extended periods of time. Some institutions, primarily custodial and/or disciplinary, offer little or no treatment to either child or family. Those institutions or residential centers which are treatment oriented, focus chiefly on psychological or social-psychological treatment of the child. Often highly identified with the child, practitioners become, if not angry with parents, discouraged by what seem regressions in the child's adjustment after weekend and vacation visits home. Families are sometimes seen for diagnostic purposes and progress-reporting sessions, but relatively few centers involve the family in the total treatment plan.

The lack of family participation can have serious repercussions. First of all, the more the child is emotionally and physically distanced, the family system forms a new homeostatic balance without his presence. If and when the child returns, he may find the family has adapted to his absence in a variety of ways which may be experienced as further rejection and isolation. Whittaker assumes that success in treating childhood disorders varies according to the ability of the helping person to involve parents "as full and equal participants in the helping process." [42] He suggests ways for agencies to help parents maintain contact and meaningful involvement with their institutionalized children.

Before turning to identity issues and family ties in adoption practice, it is important to consider briefly the changing status of the single parent. Harsh attitudes toward illegitimacy are slowly easing and more unmarried parents are opting to raise their children. Agencies must be ready with a variety of supports for single parents who make this decision. One adoptive agency, in shifting its priority from obtaining and placing children to supporting "familiness," established a residence for unmarried mothers and their infants. It provides a supportive environment where young mothers learn parenting skills and are provided with a variety of concrete services and employment and educational opportunities to help parent and child prepare for community living. Putative fathers, whom agencies have traditionally disregarded or avoided except for issues of child support and legitimacy, are encouraged to visit the residence.[43] Such a setting encourages the involvement of both biological parents in the life of the child, laying the groundwork for the preservation of biological family ties in whatever ways may be possible.

Finally, no matter how extended our resource system or how skillful our interventive measures, there are and will continue to be children for whom a permanent family must be found, through adoption.

Adoption practice is currently undergoing reevaluation and change. Two major developments are having a far-reaching impact on the field of adoption and are presenting new challenges and shaping new models of practice. These are open adoption and the changed character of the "adoption market." Growing concern for continuity of identity and family ties has led to a questioning of closed adoption files and secrecy about origins, and has pointed to the consideration of other kinds of adoption models, "open adoption," and a range of forms of shared parenting.

While advocates of these models recognize that sensitive issues need to be confronted which carry the potential for rejection, hurt, and disappointment to all three parties in the adoption triangle, nevertheless conviction is growing that children have the right and should have the opportunity to know who they are, that "it is time to reconsider the strange legal policy of the sealing of records and the equally strange role of adoptive agencies in perpetuating the whole constellation of deception and illusion."[44] While thinking historically and from a cross-cultural perspective, others maintain we need "a wider range of options for parents who can neither raise their own children nor face the finality of the traditional relinquishment and adoptive placement process."[45]

Early adoption practices in the United States permitted adoptive records to be open to all who wished to examine them and diligent efforts were made to preserve biological and historical information for adoptive parents to impart later to their adoptive children. But in more recent times adoptive practice placed more emphasis on secrecy.[46] Betty Jean Lifton suggests that secrecy has been rationalized as a way of protecting the child from the shame of illegitimacy while, in actuality, secrecy sanctions the adoptive family's "emotional need to live *as if* they had produced offspring of their own."[47] Agency efforts to "match physical characteristics and religious background perpetuate the delusion."[48] Lifton sums up the adoption dilemma:

The adoption experience cannot be free of dislocated human arrangements. For the most part our society handles the dislocation by offering a substitute family, but at a price. That price is the suppression of the adoptee's life story—the psychological and practical exclusion of his or her personal history and biological connectedness. What has been excised is replaced by fantasy—the adoptee's, the adoptive parents', and society's. The fantasy . . . begins with the falsification of the birth certificate and extends indefinitely around most of the adoptee's life process.[49]

In other societies and cultures, the importance of one's original family membership and the continuity of the genealogical line is stressed.[50] In our own country, our ambivalence in relation to the preservation of natural family identity or contacts means that adoptive parents have often received little or no help in helping children come to terms with troubling identity issues nor in resolving the disappointment of their own infertility.

New thinking about adoption calls into question old practices which allowed only two acceptable but extreme options for a parent: surrender or keep. For parents who may not have the desire or the psychological resources to raise a child themselves, there is a pressing need for "a new kind of adoptive placement in which they can actively participate."[51] In this arrangement parents who have previously been reluctant to surrender their children for adoption but may not be in a position to raise them can have the security of knowing they have provided their child with opportunities for a healthy loving environment, without giving up the possibility of knowing their child's fate and without abandoning the hope of maintaining some ties. An "open adoption" is defined as "one in which the birth parents participate in the separation and placement process, relinquish all legal, moral, and nurturing rights to the child, but retain the right to continuing contact and a knowledge of the child's whereabouts and welfare."[52] Natural parents, as their part of the contract, provide as complete a family history as possible and agree to keep the agency informed of their whereabouts. Before surrendering they are prepared for and agree that the child may someday choose to know about them or may even wish to meet them.

The advantages to the child are obvious, as he or she can have the opportunity to come to terms with fantiasies and those uncompleted, unknown parts of identity. Adoptive parents can be educated to understand the child's psychological needs, indeed his right, to know his roots from the beginning of the adoptive relationship.

The "open adoption" contract thus leads to a self-selection process in the sense that those adoptive parents who cannot relinquish the "as if" fantasy and who are unwilling or unable to accept the child's need for knowledge about and perhaps even eventual contact with his biological family will choose not to adopt.

Still, several difficult questions are raised. Most families with adopted children have been assured that birth records will remain sealed and parents who relinquished their children have been assured of anonymity. Is it fair to those adults to change the rules? While this writer believes the evils we know and have opportunity to exorcize are usually less destructive than those which are hidden or repressed, some children enter adoption from extremely troubled situations. Examples include children born of incestuous relationships or children severely and sadistically abused as infants. What if the natural parent is psychotic, a criminal, an addict? Would it not be better for the child to cling to his fantasies, whatever they are, than to know the hurtful reality? What information would be given? What withheld? At what age are children able to assimilate genealogical information? What is the role of the adoptive parent here? Of the agency? What if the natural parent turns away from or rejects the child? Should older adopted children be encouraged to forget and repress earlier experiences which may have been painful and unhappy? Lifton, who searches for, finds, and finally meets her natural mother, and must abandon any hope of nurturing the relationship because of her mother's need for secrecy and inability to acknowledge her existence in her current life, suggests that "just as one must have the courage to find one's natural parents, one must have the courage to say goodbye, if necessary. To let go."[53]

As child welfare administrators and adoption workers reconsider and redefine their practice goals, new roles and new techniques emerge. Some workers and some agencies have already begun to help individual adoptees and self-help organizations such as ALMA in their searches. Others tackle the role of mediator among all three parties to the adoption triangle where one or more seek information or even reunion. Many adoptees have taken matters into their own hands, initiating searches, petitioning courts, cajoling agencies to produce records, and forming self-help organizations to assist other searchers. One agency at least, as part of its research efforts, has held adoptee, adoptive parent, and natural parent forums to air attitudes and feelings.[54]

The need for such help emphasizes the importance of developing and helping families make use of postadoption services. The lack of such services again illustrates denial on the part of families and professionals that adoption is different from biological parenting and that parents and children have special tasks to perform and may need some expert help in dealing with these special tasks. Post adoption services should not only be available, they should be offered as developmental and educational rather than remedial services. Adoptive families should be able to find consultation around their special tasks without being defined as problematic.

As we move to more open forms of adoption, adoptive families and their children may well need to use consultation at various crucial points in the child's life. This can help them help the child deal with his or her special status, with identity issues, and with information about or contact with their biological families. These issues emerge differently at different points in the child's development, particularly in latency when the concept of being an adopted child begins to have meaning, in adolescence when issues of identity and differentiation surface with such intensity, and again at marriage as the adopted person moves toward becoming a parent.

A second major factor altering adoptive practice is the rapidly changing nature of the "adoption market." The availability and legality of abortion, widespread knowledge about and use of effective birth control devices, and the increasing number of single parents who elect to keep their babies have led to a marked decrease in the number of infants available for adoption, especially white infants who once constituted a major portion of those adopted.

An early response to the growing shortage was the move to transracial and international adoption. This practice generated concern and criticism as well as efforts to defend and justify it.[55] American blacks and other racial minority groups and the governments of many poor countries question both the morality and the effects on children of such adoptions. Particular concern is focussed upon just the issue addressed in this discussion, namely the issue of identity formation and consolidation. "In a system of gross economic inequality, they say, is it right that weaker groups should be systematically deprived, first of their ability to make a living and then of the children they are unable to support?"[56] But are we to abandon children who are victims of war, poverty, and abuse while we wait for society-wide solutions to massive social problems? On the other hand, how much will it postpone needed social and economic changes if we continue to temporize with second best or ad hoc solutions?

A second response to the changing adoption market, reinforced by the child advocacy movement, is a major redefinition of the adoptable child. Gone are the days of the study home where infants and children stayed until the agency was able to assure a potential adoptive couple that a child was healthy and "normal" in every way. Every child is now considered potentially adoptable, including the physically or mentally handicapped, the older child, the child who has suffered emotional damage, and the child of mixed or uncertain heritage, many of whom once grew up in foster care or in institutions. The adoption field has redefined its major task from finding babies for childless couples to finding families for children in need of permanent homes. Many of these children are older and remember biological family members and experiences. Many have been removed from their biological families because of irreversible patterns of abuse and neglect and remember those experiences. There has been a tendency to help such children deal with painful pasts by totally cutting them off from their biological families. Such cutoffs do not really sever the emotional bonds. Recently, one public child-caring agency discovered that many of the older children whose parents' rights had been terminated years earlier had, on their own and unbeknownst to the agency, kept up regular contact with their parents or other members of their biological families.

In the case of older children, the concept of "closed adoption" is a fiction. In fact, concern around potential adoptive families being troubled by members of the older child's biological family has sometimes led to such children being defined as unadoptable. As we move such children into adoptive homes, the need for postadoptive services to help families and children deal with the complexities inherent in the adoption of an older child is once again highlighted.

SUMMARY
An ecological perspective in child welfare takes as its starting point the importance of the biological family. In considering a range of practice from supportive through substitutive care services, this conviction remains central.

Every effort is thus made to support the family, to enhance its functioning, and to avoid separation and placement. When separation is necessary, the importance of the family continues to be recognized through active efforts to maintain family ties, to support shared parenting by biological and foster parents, and to work, wherever possible, toward reuniting the family. In adoption practice, this perspective suggests a consideration of open adoption and a range of pre- and postadoption services which help all of the parties in this complex human situation accept rather than deny the fact that an adopted person has two families.

NOTES

1. Shirley Jenkins and Elaine Norman, *Filial Deprivation* (New York: Columbia University Press, 1972).

2. Herbert G. Gutman, *The Black Family in Slavery and Freedom* (New York:

Pantheon Books, 1976). See chapter 5, "Aunts and Uncles and Swap-Dog Kin," pp. 185–229.

3. Carol B. Stack, *All Our Kin: Strategies for Survival in a Black Community* (New York: Harper, 1974).

4. Colin C. Blaydon and Carol B. Stack, "Income Support Policies and the Family," in *Daedalus,* "The Family" (Spring 1977), pp. 147–61.

5. The importance of supporting ties to the natural family has recently been validated in the Columbia University study of foster care, which shows that high parental visitation during periods of foster care is significantly associated with the child's return home. See David Fanshel, "Parental Visiting of Children in Foster Care: Key to Discharge?" *Social Service Review* 49, no. 4 (December 1975), pp. 493–514.

6. See, for example, Marshall H. Klaus et al., "Maternal Attachment," *The New England Journal of Medicine* 286, no. 9 (March 2, 1972), pp. 460–63; Marshall H. Klaus et al., "Human Maternal Behavior at the First Contact With Her Young," *Pediatrics* 46, no. 2 (August 1970), pp. 187–92; Lee Salk, "Thoughts on the Concept of Imprinting and its Place in Early Human Development," *Canadian Psychiatric Association Journal* 11 (1966), pp. S295–S305; Aidan Macfarlane, *The Psychology of Childbirth* (Cambridge: Harvard University Press, 1977), pp. 5–13, 81–83; Daniel G. Freedman, "Infancy, Biology, and Culture," in Lewis P. Lipsitt (ed.), *Developmental Psychobiology* (Hillsdale, New Jersey: Lawrence Erlbaum Associates [distributed by Halsted Press Division of John Wiley & Sons], 1976).

7. See, for example, John Alcock, *Animal Behavior* (Sunderland, Mass.: Sinauer, 1975); R. A. Hinde, *Biological Bases of Human Social Behavior* (New York: McGraw-Hill, 1974).

8. Mary D. Ainsworth, "The Development of Infant-Mother Interaction Among the Ganda," in B.M. Foss (ed.), *Determinants of Infant Behavior,* Vol. 2 (New York: Methuen, 1964); R. B. Lee and I. DeVore (eds.), *Kalahari Hunter-Gatherers* (Cambridge: Harvard University Press, 1976).

---

1. Richard Dawkins, *The Selfish Gene* (New York: Oxford University Press, 1976) and Edward O. Wilson, *Sociobiology* (Cambridge, Mass.: Harvard University Press, 1975), pp. 106–29.

2. David Schneider, *American Kinship: A Cultural Account* (Englewood Cliffs, N.J.: Prentice-Hall, 1968), p. 116.

3. Salvador Minuchin, "The Plight of the Poverty-Stricken Family in the United States," *Child Welfare* 49, no. 3 (March 1970), p. 125.

4. Ibid., p. 129.

5. Editorial Notes, "Destruction of American Indian Families," *Social Casework* 58, no. 5 (May 1977) pp. 312–14. Also see Charles E. Farris and Lorene S. Farris, "Indian Children: The Struggle for Survival," *Social Work* 21, no. 5 (September 1976) pp. 386–94.

6. Douglas J. Besharov, "Putting Central Registers to Work," *Children Today* 6, no. 5 (September–October 1977) pp. 9–13.

7. David G. Gil, "Unraveling Child Abuse," *American Journal of Orthopsychiatry* 45, no. 3 (April 1975) pp. 346–56.

8. Karen Schaar, "Corporal Punishment Foes Strike Out," *Children Today* 6, no. 5 (September–October 1977), pp. 16–23.

9. Alfred Kadushin, "Myths and Dilemmas in Child Welfare," *Child Welfare* 56, no. 3 (March 1977), p. 143.

10. Marvin Rosenberg and Ralph Brody, *Systems Serving People: A Breakthrough in Service Delivery* (Cleveland, Ohio: School of Applied Social Sciences, Case Western Reserve University, 1974).

11. Ann W. Shyne, "Evaluation in Child Welfare," *Child Welfare* 55, no. 1 (January 1976), pp. 5–18.

12. Srinika Jayaratne, "Psychological Characteristics of Parents Who Abuse Their Children" (unpublished paper presented at the 1977 Annual Program Meeting, Council on Social Work Education, Phoenix, Ariz., March 2, 1977).

13. For an excellent compilation of the approaches of leading family theorists, see Philip J. Guerin (ed.), *Family Therapy: Theory and Practice* (New York: Gardner Press, 1976).

14. These dilemmas have periodically been explored in the mental health literature, and some of the earlier classics from the child welfare field may still provide us with the most sensitive descriptions available of the meaning of separation and the importance of the natural family to children's sense of identity. See, in particular, Alameda R. Jolowicz, "The Hidden Parent: Some Effects of the Concealment of the Parent's Life Upon the Child's Use of a Foster Home" (unpublished paper presented at the New York State Conference of Social Welfare, New York, November 1946); and Ner Littner, *Some Traumatic Effects of Separation and Placement* (New York: Child Welfare League of America, October 1956).

15. Most child welfare workers are familiar with the work of Erikson on identity and on the interaction of biological, social, and psychological factors in human growth and development. See, for example, Erik H. Erikson, "Identity and the Life Cycle," *Psychological Issues*, Monograph 1 (New York: International Universities Press, 1959), and *Identity: Youth, and Crisis* (New York: W. W. Norton, 1968). The work of Bowlby and others on attachment, separation, and loss and on the need for continuity of nurturing is also familiar to most child welfare workers. See, for example, John Bowlby, *Attachment and Loss (Vol. I: Attachment; Vol. II: Separation)* (New York: Basic Books, 1973). R. A. Spitz, "Anaclitic Depression," *Psychoanalytic Study of the Child* 2 (1946), pp. 313–42.

16. Alex Haley, *Roots* (Garden City, N.Y.: Doubleday & Co., 1976).

17. Joseph Goldstein, Anna Freud, and Albert J. Solnit, *Beyond the Best Interests of the Child* (New York: The Free Press, 1973).

18. Ibid., p. 6.

19. Ibid., p. 38.

20. The writer was told this by a 16-year-old young man in residential care whose goal, as soon as he was discharged, was to find the father who had abandoned the family before he was born.

21. Fernando Colon, "In Search of One's Past: An Identity Trip," *Family Pro-

cess 12, no. 4 (December 1973), p. 433. Adoptee Florence Fisher describes a similar feeling when she met her natural mother for the first time—a sense of wonderment and joy at discovering one's genetic reality. See Florence Fisher, *The Search for Anna Fisher* (Greenwich, Conn.: Fawcett Publications, 1973).

22. Quoted from a letter from David to his social worker.

23. For a discussion of the Scottish experience, see Rita Dukette, "Perspectives for Agency Response to the Adoption-Record Controversy," *Child Welfare* 54, no. 8 (September–October 1975), pp. 545–54.

24. Florence Fisher, p. 10.

25. Robert Jay Lifton, "Foreword: On the Adoption Experience," in Mary Kathleen Benet, *The Politics of Adoption* (New York: The Free Press, 1976).

26. Ibid., p. 3.

27. Melvin Roman, "The Disposable Parent" (unpublished paper presented at the Association of Family Conciliation Courts, Minneapolis, Minn., May 1977), p. 14.

28. For ecological or systems approaches to social work practice, see Alice H. Collins and Diane L. Pancoast, *Natural Helping Networks: A Strategy for Prevention* (Washington, D.C.: National Association of Social Workers, 1976); Beulah Compton and Burt Galaway, *Social Work Processes* (Homewood, Ill.: The Dorsey Press, 1975); Alex Gitterman and Carel B. Germain, "Social Work Practice: A Life Model," *Social Service Review* 50, no. 4 (December 1976), pp. 601–10; Ann Hartman, "The Generic Stance and the Family Agency," *Social Casework* 56, no. 4 (April 1975), pp. 199–208; and Carol H. Meyer, *Social Work Practice: The Changing Landscape,* 2d ed. (New York: The Free Press, 1976).

29. Mary Ann Jones, Renee Neumann, and Ann W. Shyne, *A Second Chance for Families: Evaluation of a Program to Reduce Foster Care* (New York: Child Welfare League of America, 1976).

30. Gloria Thomas, "Temporary Foster Care Project: The First Year (Michigan State Department of Social Services, November 1977), p. 2. Report of a research project, mimeographed.

31. Ibid., p. 6.

32. Blair and Rita Justice, *The Abusing Family* (New York: Human Sciences Press, 1976), p. 68. Other authorities are quoted by the authors to support the thesis that placing abused children in the homes of grandparents or other relatives is bad practice.

33. For a discussion of the concept of differentiation, see Murray Bowen, "Theory in the Practice of Psychotherapy," in Philip J. Guerin (ed.), *Family Therapy,* pp. 65–70.

34. Ibid., p. 84.

35. For a provocative discussion of the preservation of family ties, see Fernando Colon, "Family Ties and Child Placement" (unpublished paper, May 1976). Dr. Colon mentions he discovered, as an adult, at least six branches of his extended family who, given the opportunity, would have taken him in, thus eliminating the need for permanent foster care.

36. Michael Garber, "Neighborhood Based Child Welfare," *Child Welfare* 54, no. 2 (February 1975), pp. 73–81.

37. David Fanshel, *Foster Parenthood* (Minneapolis: University of Minnesota Press, 1966), p. 15.

38. Trudy Bradley Festinger, "The Impact of the New York Court Review of Children in Foster Care: A Followup Report," *Child Welfare* 55, no. 8 (October 1976), pp. 515–44.

39. Phyllis Johnson McAdams, "The Parent in the Shadows," *Child Welfare* 51, no. 1 (January 1972), pp. 51–55.

40. The genogram is also particularly valuable in guiding foster and adoptive home studies, as the worker is able to quickly gain a sense of family patterns, forces, relationships, losses, and myths.

41. The writer is indebted to Jean Felton, Sherry Miller, and Doris Stagg of the Branch County Department of Social Services, Michigan, for sharing their ideas and experiences.

42. James K. Whittaker, "Causes of Childhood Disorders: New Findings," *Social Work* 21, no. 2 (March 1976), pp. 91–96.

43. Florence Kreech, "A Residence for Mothers and Their Babies," *Child Welfare* 54, no. 8 (September–October 1975), pp. 581–92.

44. Robert Jay Lifton, "Foreword," p. 6.

45. Annette Baran, Reuben Pannor, and Arthur D. Sorosky, "Open Adoption," *Social Work* 21, no. 2, p. 97.

46. Rita Dukette, "Perspectives for Agency Response."

47. Betty Jean Lifton, *Twice Born: Memoirs of an Adopted Daughter* (New York: Penguin Books, 1977), p. 13.

48. Ibid.

49. Robert J. Lifton, "Foreword," p. 1.

50. Baran et al., "Open Adoption," p. 97.

51. Ibid.

52. Ibid.

53. Betty Jean Lifton, *Twice Born,* p. 247.

54. Annette Baran, Reuben Pannor, and Arthur D. Sorosky, "Adoptive Parents and the Sealed Record Controversy," *Social Casework* 55, no. 8 (November 1974), pp. 531–36.

55. See, for example, Amuzie Chimezie, "Transracial Adoption of Black Children," *Social Work* 20, no. 4 (July 1975), pp. 296–301; Amuzie Chimezie, "Bold but Irrelevant: Grow and Shapiro on Transracial Adoption," *Child Welfare* 56, no. 2 (February 1977), pp. 75–86; Deborah Shapiro and Lucille J. Grow, "Not So Bold and Not So Irrelevant: A Reply to Chimuzie," ibid., pp. 86–91; Dong Soo Kim, "How They Fared in American Homes: A Follow-up Study of Adopted Korean Children," *Children Today* 6, no. 2 (March–April 1977), pp. 2–6 and 36.

56. Mary Kathleen Benet, *The Politics of Adoption,* p. 20.

2 CONCEPTUAL DEVELOPMENTS

7 Social Networks, Mutual Aid, and the Life Model of Practice

CAROL SWENSON

Swenson undertakes to develop the concept of social network as a significant ecological variable in the life space of people, and to apply it to practice. She discusses some definitional problems inherent in the newness of the idea, and reviews the growing literature appearing outside of social work. A differentiated conception of social networks brings a richness to the whole idea of environment, especially when the network is viewed both as a behavioral setting and as a potent environmental instrument for helping.

Biologists and psychologists alike have called attention to the adaptive imperative for human relatedness. From birth to old age, human beings must adapt to other human beings if their needs are to be met. The infant is totally dependent upon his environment for survival. Yet dependence or, better, interdependence continues throughout life as the human being achieves and maintains his humanness and his very sense of identity from his relationships with other human beings. The price of failure in relatedness is the marasmic death of the infant, the profound loneliness of the isolated and the bereaved, the anomie of those not valued by their society, and the fear of attachment, self-hatred, and despair of the unloved. The artist has depicted these states even more tellingly than the theorist. Who can doubt that unrelatedness led to the destruction and death of Camus's Mersault, Kafka's Gregor, or Melville's Bartleby? The psychiatrist Otto Will once observed, "relatedness is a requirement of human life, the potential for its full development being a part of the biological equipment of man. One does not so much seek for relatedness or somehow develop it in others; it is there already. Relatedness is of man: without some semblance of it he will not survive." [1]

The attention of social workers has been called to the influence of the client's social network in the application for service and in the client's remaining in service. Questions have been raised about figures in the client's environment who may suggest, support, and encourage the application—and conversely, who may denigrate or discourage the application. Similarly, the question is raised as to who are the substitute figures in the environment making it unnecessary or less likely that the client will either apply for help, or if he applies, that he will remain engaged in the helping process? [2]

Swenson enables us to take the next step of actively engaging such figures in the professional service. Over evolutionary time, systems of mutual aid have been essential to the survival of diverse species, including human beings. [3] *Thus such systems represent adaptive environmental mechanisms to be considered by social work practitioners. They may provide for the exchange of resources, contribute to self-esteem and a sense of belonging, and hence furnish nutriments to the sense of personal identity and humanness. As a self-help group, network figures can provide opportunities for action, competence, and autonomy. Networks also, of course, can have a negative impact: they can undermine self-esteem and the sense of identity, they sometimes withhold resources and information, or uphold deviant values, thus having a disruptive effect on the functioning of individuals, groups or families. Practice issues then relate to how to firm up boundaries between the individual, the group, or the family, and noxious networks in the life space, how to mobilize potentially supportive networks, how to forge or renew linkages to such networks, and, when needed, how to create artificial networks to be added to the life space.*

—C.B.G.

SOCIAL WORK practice has been undergoing scrutiny and change, stimulated from within the profession and from society itself. Within the profession, new knowledge has become available to conceptualize practice. From without comes the challenge of ongoing rapid social change.

The ecological approach to practice establishes the person as an adapting and coping creature, striving for growth, mastery, and interaction with his environment. Helping relationships are based on a concept of the client and persons in his life space as active participants in progressive change, and of the worker as catalyst. Thus, helping relationships become more flexible and mutual and less important as an end in themselves. The objectives of treatment include providing an environment where the person's progressive forces are encouraged and the nutritive qualities of the environment itself are enhanced. Service arrangements allow for meeting people in their life space and for adjusting environments without requiring the potentially stigmatizing role of "clienthood."

Two concept clusters which seem to have particular relevance for this reformulation are social networks and self-help/mutual aid. These concepts offer potential for development in each of the significant aspects of a model for practice. These dimensions include: how the "problem" is defined, the philosophical view of the person, the worker-client relationship, the goals of helping, and service delivery arrangements.[1] First we will examine some of the theoretical material on social networks and mutual aid. Then we will look at ways in which network and mutual aid concepts have been used, either implicitly or explicitly, in practice settings. A systematic overview of diagnosing the network and planning interventions will follow. And, finally, we will look at connections between these concepts and the life model of practice.

SOCIAL NETWORKS

While there is a substantial body of knowledge available to social workers concerning social networks, it may be worthwhile first to underscore its significance. Sociological theory has been highly influenced by the Weberian arguments that informal or primary groups would wither away in urban society when faced with the powerful technologies and specialization of formal organizations. Then Talcott Parsons "rescued" the nuclear family from the fate of other primary groups, assigning it the tasks he felt were unsuited to formal organizations: procreation, child socialization, and adult tension maintenance. Parsons maintained, nonetheless, that the structures of the primary group and the formal organization were antithetical and that they should remain structurally isolated if each were to be most effective at its functions. These structural conflicts included such issues as the operation of the merit system within formal organizations but not within the family, permanence in family roles but impermanence in formal organizations, affectivity within the family but emotional neutrality at work, and so forth.[2]

Social work theory has developed consistently with attention given primarily to individuals and secondarily to the nuclear family. Theories of naturally occurring groups and communities fall far behind. While attention is given to the delivery of services through formal organizations, there has been very little systematic attention to informal mechanisms for provision of services, such as neighbors providing child care, or errand service for the elderly.

More recently theoreticians and researchers have come to question the notion of the disappearance/isolation of the primary group in modern bureaucratic societies. There is an increasing body of data which suggests that many kinds of groupings remain vigorous in an industrial society, and that these groupings have flexible boundaries and diverse composition. Some revolve around traditional units such as the extended family, others arise from shared interests or propinquity.

First, let us consider the extended family. Significant ongoing connections with many instrumental and emotional exchanges have been found among urban working class kin in London and in Boston's Italian neighborhoods. Leichter has reported extensive and often highly organized relationships within Jewish extended families in New York City. She also found that family members positively valued contacts with close and extended kin, whereas social workers tend to define these relationships as "problems" and sought to increase client's independence from family.[3]

There is a large literature on the "work group" or primary-group-like units which form within the workplace. These may initially be groups with tasks delegated by the organization which gradually take on nurturance functions. They can serve as highly important support groups. Though much of the writing on this subject has viewed the work group as a "problem" for the organization, more recently work groups have been seen as a positive factor, not only for the workers, but also for organizational purposes.[4] For some people, such as artists, professionals, scholars, and some businessmen, relationships formed through "work" are among their most important relationships with critical impact upon their self-image as well as their success or productivity.

Friendships and support groups develop as people come together around shared interests. Grandmothers, Democrats, school parents, chess players all "find" each other, often with a formal organization or physical location, such as a playground, serving as the initial catalyst or contact. There is even a "network process" whereby people of approximately matched interests or skill levels are "connected." Certain cliques may form in a senior citizen center as they discuss memories of the Depression or the New Deal. If Mary knows that both Sara and Jane play better tennis than she does (perhaps from defeat) she may introduce them to each other.

A similar argument can be made for the neighborhood, or in this day of urban concentration, the apartment building. Some relationships develop most highly under conditions of propinquity. For most children the neighborhood is the locus of play and finding playmates. Much socializing among adults occurs with near neighbors, or those located at "traffic points" in the daily round.

Furthermore, there are people whom the individual or family encounters as they interact with the formal organizations directly. These people would not be expected to abandon their organizational roles and functions in order to be helpful to a family. Thus, a family doctor who is reserved and competent may be in a family's network because the family positively regards his competence and helpfulness. Likewise, a welfare worker who is scrupulously fair may be a source of emotional as well as financial support for a family without there being any question of special favors.

Ms. H. needed birth control. She asked a friend to recommend a doctor. He's not a specialist, warned her friend, and he moved his office to a rather inconvenient location, but he is very thorough and he really cares about his patients. Ms. H. not only received a complete physical, but the doctor also spent almost an hour discussing her questions and concerns. She concluded that she would do just fine with Dr. G., even if his office was hard to get to.

Far from needing isolation, Eugene Litwak has suggested, primary groups and formal organizations can exist in interdependence and maintain their unique attributes and strengths.[5] In fact, to maximize effectiveness of most tasks, a combination of primary groups and formal organizations is best. For example, the care of an infirm elderly person: he may need a neighbor, not a policeman, to notice him fall;

a son or daughter, not a restaurant, to care for his daily needs while incapacitated; a social worker to arrange Medicare, rather than a relative to pay medical bills; and a hospital emergency room, rather than a friend, to tend to a broken leg.

Accordingly, a conceptual scheme which offers a "fresh start" to the analysis of social groupings is very much needed. Social network concepts seem to meet that need. The word "network" suggests flexibility of boundaries, interconnectedness of varying magnitude, and so on. This very flexibility presents some difficulties: "social network" has some of the same ambiguity as the word "community." [6] I am going to use it to mean a person's subjective community, that is, those individuals, groups, and parts of formal institutions which have meaning, actually or potentially, for a person.

Networks serve many functions for persons. A large proportion of these functions can be conceptualized as mutual aid, which can include both instrumental support and nurturance. Instrumental support is assistance in accomplishing a task: showing someone how to do something, providing goods or services, giving directions or financial assistance. Nurturance is emotional support in its various forms: offering encouragement, listening, giving advice, "being present," to name a few. While these are not always distinct in practice, a conceptual distinction may be useful. [7]

Ever since he lost his job, Mr. R. had been feeling more and more blue. He wasn't as young as he used to be, his children all went their own ways now, no one hired old guys like him. Finally, he became so depressed that his doctor recommended psychiatric hospitalization. Over the weekend, a deluge of relatives, friends, and neighbors trooped to his hospital room. On Monday, he told the staff that he really felt fine again and that he'd like to go home and start job hunting. The staff was aghast. Nothing had changed, had it? Why did he feel and look so much better? Well, Mr. R. said, I began to realize how many people really cared about me; I guess I was feeling pretty sorry for myself. And, you know, I was embarrassed to tell people I was laid off? Well, a couple of the people who came to visit had leads on jobs!

The social network can include a great variety of groupings, such as the extended family, "work groups," a college residence, the neighborhood, an ex-patient club, and more. The whole unit or only parts of it may be meaningful for the focal person. The latter is especially true with large formal organizations: one might have a significant relationship with only one person or a small subunit in the system. Hospitals or the welfare system are good examples.

An apartment building superintendent called the community mental health center. He was worried about Mrs. T., an elderly lady in his building. She was always alone, seldom went out, and recently had called with several "strange" complaints about neighbors—they were stealing her food, they were saying nasty things about her, they were coming into her apartment at night and rearranging the furniture.

Mrs. T. was, indeed, an isolated, paranoid lady who needed better food, medical care, human contact, and so on. Her apartment had been her home for 36 years and changes in tenants upset her, but she wouldn't think of moving. The super was eager to be helpful: he would drop by to visit, take her to the doctor, remind her to fix lunch, check whether she had enough food.

After a thorough physical and mental health evaluation, the staff decided to offer consultation to the super as the primary helping modality, offering him emotional support and professional backup to continue doing what he was already doing well. The social worker visited the super at his building, and could "drop in" to see Mrs. T. at the same time. Over a year later the plan was continuing to the satisfaction of all.

The term "social network" was first used rigorously in 1954 when Barnes used it to refer to kinship, friendship, and social class variables in his study of a Norwegian town. Shortly thereafter Elizabeth Bott used it in her study of working class English families. She said, "The research families did not live in groups. They 'lived' in networks, if one can use the term 'lived in' to describe the situation of being in contact with a set of people and organizations some of whom were in contact with each other and some not." [8]

Bott's study is one of the most evocative in the field. She was interested in sex-roles within the conjugal pair, and the relationship of these roles to the larger social context of the family. She found that the extent to which roles were separated along rigid sex lines was related to how close-knit the couple's social network was. Roughly, close-knit refers to everyone associating with everyone else, and loose-knit means there is not much contact between various persons in the network. In situations where network members were less apt to associate with each other, conjugal roles were more flexible. Bott has been interested in expanding this type of analysis to other types of groups. She says "my aim was (and still is) to understand how the internal functioning of a group is affected not only by its relationships *with* the people and organizations of its environment but also by the relationships *among* these people and organizations."[9]

Various dimensions of networks have been conceptualized for network analysis.[10] These include both structural and content variables. Structural variables include: *range* (size or number of people in the network); *segmentation* (areas of contact, such as family, school, neighborhood); *reachability* (access of individuals within a network to each other and the number of intervening links necessary); and *density* (the ratio of actual linkages to possible linkages). "Content" variables include: *frequency* (ratio of interactions between two people to the norm of network interactions); *uniplex-multiplex* (number of content areas or foci for a relationship); *intensity* (subjective evaluation by the focal person); and *directedness* (whether the relationship is symmetrical or asymmetrical). All of these differences can have profound effects. For example, two women are not likely to maintain their friendship over large geographic distances unless their spouses are moderately congenial; an adolescent whose "school" friends and "church" friends live in different towns and have divergent value systems is likely to have more difficulty achieving a sense of personal integration than an adolescent whose friendship groups are more congruent; a person with a limited number of relationships, all focused on the "work" segment, becomes highly vulnerable if his company lays him off.

If a social worker were to see a person who complained of feeling alone and cut off from people, he might focus on the feelings of distance and might possibly postulate a schizoid character style. On the other hand, he might well do a network analysis. He might find, for example, that a client had recently moved.

After moving, Mr. C. had experienced a sharp contraction in the *range* of his available network. Fancying himself "independent," and being not much of a letter writer besides, the *density* of contacts with family and friends at home markedly reduced. Furthermore, *reachability* was diminished, as he no longer directly contacted his father and sibs, but instead sent messages through his mother, who took on the role of "communication center" for distant family members.

In his new location, Mr. C's friends were concentrated in the work *segment*. These were relatively *uniplex* (work-focused) and *infrequent* contacts, compared to the lively social interactions among the rest of the group. He felt the lack of *intensity* keenly, adding that some of their shared interests felt quite alien to him. What is more, the relating seemed *asymmetrical*, with himself always being the initiator. The worker might conclude that Mr. C. needed to expend some efforts to reestablish connections with family and old friends, in a form which took account of the geographic distance. He might help the client moderate his eagerness to initiate relationships at work somewhat, and simultaneously help him decide whether he wanted to learn bowling, or backgammon, or pool, whatever "in" activity that the client felt uncomfortable about. He might encourage Mr. C. to become involved in a civic association, or amateur dramatics, or union activities—something to expand the range of his network. He might also point out that the client had some skills or qualities that his new compatriots would value, and help Mr. C. consider how he could gently bring these to their attention.

Networks may be described from two basic vantage points. First, a person's network can be analyzed in terms of himself as the "focal" person. This has been called the personal or egocentric network. Secondly, an ecological unit may be described—a rural town, a hospital ward, a nursing home—this is known as a "total" network.

Other dimensions of networks have received less attention. Networks might fruitfully be examined in terms of the fundamental ecological dimensions of space and time: such as the gradual expansion of the social network of the growing child, the contraction of the network of the aged, the impact of rapid travel and communication on geographic size of networks, or the differences in networks of people who have comfortable space to entertain as opposed to those who do not. There may be considerable variation in personally and culturally valued network configurations. For example, some cultural patterns support working, relaxing, and living with kin, whereas others do not. Personal choices may likewise cover a wide range, depending on preference and on circumstances. These ecological, personal, and cultural variables all bear further study.

Numerous techniques now exist for mapping networks, ranging from variants of sociometric techniques which can quickly be learned to very complex mathematical theory and techniques. Researchers using such techniques have investigated the whereabouts of natural helpers and attempted to clarify differences between stressed and nonstressed helpers. Research has also been undertaken to chart the relative locations of instrumental and emotional support in networks, with the tentative conclusion that instrumental support is offered in hierarchical relationships within formal organizational structures while emotional support is found in informal structures.[11]

In the following example, a Hispanic family experienced considerable expansion of their network following the death of one of its members. Shifts in relationships and changes in the paths of communication led to increased complexity in the network's functioning. Both positive and negative aspects can be observed.[12]

The identified patient, Mrs. L., was a middle-aged mother of four grown children who had been unable to recover from the death of her 28-year-old son Mervin six months previously. Then it became clear that her three daughters were also having trouble resolving their grief. One daughter, Sandra, became involved again in a self-defeating relationship with a former

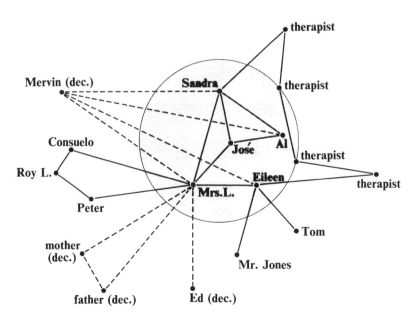

Fig. 1. Diagram shows the social network of Mrs. L. The circle represents the family group being seen by the family therapists. Broken lines show "ghost" relationships.

boyfriend Al who had been a friend of her dead brother. A second daughter, Eileen, began talking about marrying her boyfriend, Tom, of two months and began to separate herself from her family by inducing her boss, Mr. Jones, to act as a buffer. Sandra's eight-year-old son José emerged as 1) the "consoler," and 2) the object of a struggle between the mother and daughter. Sandra and Eileen each sought individual treatment in the midst of a crisis, then fled in furor. (There were already two family cotherapists.) In the midst of all this was also Mrs. L.'s ex-husband Roy with whom the third daughter, Consuelo, lived with her son, Peter. There were also, importantly, several "ghosts": the dead son Mervin, the mother's mother and first husband Ed (who died of the same form of cancer as Mervin), and her dead father. The children seemed less influenced by these other "ghosts" than Mrs. L., though they seemed equally troubled about their brother's death. By now there were, at a minimum, eighteen network members, including four therapists and four "ghosts," and without taking into account numerous others—relatives, friends, and neighbors. (See diagram of Mrs. L's network.)

MUTUAL AID

Concepts of mutual aid and self-help extend back in the professional literature at least to Petr Kropotkin, who dignified mutual aid as a positive factor in evolution. He said,

Sociability and the need of mutual aid are such inherent parts of human nature that at no time of history can we discover men living in small, isolated families, fighting for the means of subsistence . . . men used to agglomerate into *gens,* clans, or tribes, maintained by an idea of common descent and by worship of common ancestors. . . . [Then] a new form of union, territorial in its principle—the village community—was called into existence by the social ingenuity of man. This institution, again, kept men together for a number of centuries, permitting them . . . to make further steps in their evolution and to work out a number of secondary social institutions. . . . In [mutual aid's] wide extension, even at the present time, we also see the best guarantee of a still loftier evolution of our race.[13]

Mutual aid has been of particular concern to those who are interested in social change and the creation of a just society. It is a recurrent theme in the Bible. It has been a central theme in the writings of Mao Tse-tung and the Chinese revolutionaries. Its reality has been reported by Margaret Bacon. One of the Chinese told her: "Here I do not believe we need social workers; here we all serve the people."[14] There are neighborhood supportive services for the aged who do not have families nearby. Simultaneously, functions such as supervising children's recreation are assigned to the elderly so that they remain an integrated and important part of the community. Retarded children and other handicapped people can be maintained at home because the family is constantly helped out with the responsibility. Apparently the neighborhood committee serves as a catalyst for these efforts.

Mutual aid is a concept which is antithetical to such American values as competitiveness and individualism, but is highly consistent with some early American traditions, like barn-raisings and quilting-bees. It is also consistent with recent challenges to the dominant ethos posed by various social experiments, where people have tried to live in more personally meaningful ways.[15] This has generally included an ideological commitment to a less competitive, more personalized and sharing society where alienation and regimentation are overcome. Mutual aid is usually substituted both for individual ownership and for the market economy. Many have found that it is a rigorous lifestyle—requiring a good deal of discipline, conviction, and austerity.

From a very different perspective, Mark Zborowski wrote about the mutual aid in the Jewish community life of an Eastern European *shtetl*.[16] In this instance the community was separated from the larger society as much by prejudice as by choice. Hard times for all led to a mutual interdependence which achieved the best possible life for each family.

Mutual aid does not, however, require a situation of adversity. Litwak has studied exchanges between kin, friends, and neighbors.[17] He finds that significant mutual aid goes on, and that it can be related to the characteristics of the various relationships. For example, kin are permanent, and kin are likely to help out in long-term difficulties such as illness. Neighbors, on the other hand, are nearby, but are often temporary. They are available for emergencies and for short-term help, and also serve as "experts" on local matters, such as the best teachers in the local school or which butcher has the best meat. Friends often provide a peer age, sex, or status group which can provide emotional support around common life tasks, such as entering college, marriage, coping with adolescent off-spring, or dealing with bereavement.

A house-bound middle-aged woman became the nucleus of her apartment building. She would accept packages, take messages, share her knowledge of the neighborhood. Her door was always open, and many tenants dropped in to "chat." Sometimes they would do an errand for Mrs. M. Sometimes they got to know each other through visiting Mrs. M. Mrs. M. had turned her limitation into an asset: her friendliness and helpfulness "drew" others to her, and in helping them she also helped overcome her own potential isolation and helplessness.

SOCIAL NETWORKS AND MUTUAL AID IN PRACTICE SITUATIONS

In the literature there are many intervention strategies based implicitly or explicitly on the concepts that I have been describing. It is conceptually useful to think of interventions in two main areas: those which engage existing networks and seek to enhance their functioning, and those which create new networks, or "attach" a formerly isolated person to a network. These are not totally distinct in practice, but the distinction is useful for discussion.

One main body of "enhancing" intervention strategies relates to the family. "Family network therapy" has been developed largely by Ross Speck and Carolyn Attneave, in their work with families where ordinary family therapy has failed. They suggest that the family involve "everyone who is important to them." They may include forty to fifty people in the meetings. The helpers are a team which spans age-sex-role dimensions. They often include as helpers people who have been participants in previous networks. Networks not only develop approaches to the problem for which they originally came together; they also may continue meeting, either to deal with other problems, or to enjoy their new-found/rediscovered relationship.[18]

Nebraska's program of supporting families to care for retarded children at home is an instance where the family's emotional and instrumental resources can be expanded by a kind of formalized mutual aid. In this case, support might range from counseling an upset parent, to weekend caretaking, to home remodelling, to specialized medical equipment. The network, then, would expand to include people whose jobs are as social workers, "parent substitutes," carpenters, medical equipment repairmen, and so on.[19]

Several authors discussed the neighborhood as a locus of helping. Alice Collins and her associates have described an innovative approach of supporting informal caretakers. These are the people to whom everyone turns for help. The caretakers are not expected to change their roles into more formalized caretaking, but they are provided with consultation. The examples given earlier of the housebound woman and the concerned building superintendent are examples of informal caretakers, and the consultation to the super are examples of this approach. An interesting aspect of Collins's work is the articulation of the process of finding caretakers. This is a key part of any effort by formal helping organizations to serve as a catalyst to informal caretaking processes.[20]

Joan Shapiro reports work within a naturally occurring network of very troubled persons. She describes the ecology of a single-room occupancy hotel: moderately interdependent social groupings, natural leaders, processes for caring for the most damaged members, and ways of negotiating the outside world. She describes in some detail how a social worker can function as a catalyst to mutual aid and sharing of resources within even a socially marginal and troubled group. Her conceptualization would be applicable to many other ecological units, such as mental hospitals, nursing homes, or some apartment buildings.[21]

Hyman Weiner's report of interventions in "the world of work" is a final example of utilizing existing networks within a social system. This application of mutual aid and social network concepts focuses on maximizing job functioning rather than identifying pathology or treating "illness." Strategies include a wide range of interventions, from training union stewards in early case finding, to meeting troubled workers surrounded by fellow employees at their job site. Weiner and his associates devote a good deal of attention to the processes of gaining entry and legitimation in an organization with its own goals and purposes.[22]

In the area of creating a new network or "attaching" isolated persons to a network, there is an equally large range of interventions, but with a slightly different slant. First, these approaches are more likely to be focused on the "total network" of an identifiable group, say, ex-mental patients or the recently widowed. The terminology undergoes a shift from mutual aid to self-help, perhaps partly as a reaction to stigmatizing and other phenomena.

There are clear successes achieved by such groups in situations where professionals are less effective.[23] Alcoholics Anonymous and its related organizations, such as Weight Watchers and Recovery, Incorporated, come immediately to mind. Other groups come together around minority status and/or discrimination, such as women's groups, gay liberation groups, ethnic and religious groups. The possible role for a professional is sometimes questioned in relation to these groups. Some highly militant groups may refuse to allow professionals to be involved. However, in most instances it would seem that professionals could have a very effective catalytic or consultative role.

Many strategies have been designed to replicate a home life for troubled or isolated persons. Ali Keskiner reports on an innovative program in New Haven, Missouri where mental hospital patients are "fostered" by a community. In this case community leaders, individual families, the patient, and the hospital enter into a multilateral agreement. It provides for gradually expanded time in the community; the patient begins by visiting and eventually boarding with a family, or he may find an independent apartment. The plan is to move toward maximum social competence, and chronicity is not assumed.[24]

One program for children, called *Unitas,* has been developed using mutual-aid/social-network concepts in naturally occurring settings. It is located in the midst of a "burned out" section of the South Bronx and occurs where children are—on the streets, in school, in playgrounds, or at a settlement house. It incorporates helping-healing principles into the ordinary living and playing of children. Teenagers are taught how to be 'helpers' through discussion and activity groups and by observing the social workers as role models with the younger children. The children, when asked, identify the teenagers as their helpers, demonstrating that the mutual aid process really occurs.[25]

Carlos was 14 when the guidance counsellor referred him to "Doc Ed." He had been acting-up when he was in school and truanting. Doc Ed began having lunch with Carlos in the school yard. As Carlos's friends wandered over, Dr. Eismann began to know them too. Soon they were involved in the *Unitas* recreation activities and the "Family Circle," where teenagers and younger children talked over things that were bothering them . . .

Months later, Dr. Ed was able to verbalize a helping skill to Carlos and underscore Carlos's competence at using it. "You remember how you said José needed help? Well, you've really been helping José yourself. . . . You helped him deal with his dislike for Victor. You brought them both into this group, and you were the one who was able to find an interest they both could share. . . . And I saw them deep in conversation about it today!" Carlos smiled from ear to ear. "Do you mean it? I helped José!"

Some of the existing literature which demonstrates concepts of mutual aid or social networks in practice settings has been summarized above. It by no means covers all that has been written but was selected to show the range of practice applications.

DIAGNOSING THE NETWORK AND
PLANNING INTERVENTIONS

There is very little written about systematically diagnosing the social network or criteria for choosing among the intervention strategies described above. Such diagnosis becomes crucial for a practice where individuals are matched with environments which will uniquely maximize their growth. The following is a beginning effort in this direction.

First, it is important to analyze the nature and the location of the trouble. Where trouble manifests itself, of course, is not necessarily where it is basically located. However, any plan must bear in mind the poor fit between person and that part of their environment where trouble is noted.

A child who is inattentive in the classroom may be 1) hungry, 2) daydreaming, 3) scared, 4) unable to read what the teacher writes on the blackboard. Hunger may be based on a) no money for food, b) no time for breakfast because no alarm clock, c) a fight with mother who said "get out", or d) preparing the younger kids' breakfast. Being scared may relate to a) a teacher's threats, b) a class-room gang, c) an alcoholic stepfather with a strap. Even if the "location" of the trouble is the home, the neighborhood, or the welfare office, the "inattentiveness" still needs to be addressed with the teacher.

Secondly, one would want to assess the person's stage in the life cycle. Certain parts of the network will have special meaning for persons of different ages. For example, for an infant the nuclear family and available kin, neighborhood, and friendship supports for his mother would be important. Peer groups in the neighborhood are important for a latency-age child. The work group might be most important for a single adult.

Dealing with transitions may mean giving up a part of one's network. This is a factor which may be readily overlooked.

While we tend to notice the "loss" of nuclear relationships, such as the child going to first grade, or the separation from parents of going away to college, we overlook the loss of the high school peer group for the college student, the work group with a job change or promotion, the single-sex socialization groups with marriage, the child-related network for parents as children grow up and leave home. For the aged, networks shrink as mobility and activity decrease and as peers become ill or die.

As a third step, it is important to investigate in some detail the personal social network of a troubled person. Questions might involve: Who is important to you? Do they support you or provoke conflict? Do they tend to be in agreement with one another? What kind of support do they provide? Do they, for example, increase self-confidence, offer to help alongside you, offer to teach you, take over from you, or counsel you about realistic difficulties? A recent study has suggested that perceived social support can be an intervening variable between the experience of double bind communication and the development of clinical schizophrenia. Alfred Clark and William Cullen found that persons who experienced double bind communication and did not become schizophrenic also had strong social supports.[26]

Techniques for this type of investigation are available to some degree in the research literature, but there is considerable need to develop useful techniques for practice settings. Just as the mental status examination was developed because a person cannot always tell us directly about his thought processes, we need to develop a "network status evaluation." Sociometric techniques offer some clues. Extensive interview guides such as those developed by Bott, by Edward Laumann, and by John Lofland may also prove useful.[27] The problem is to be broadly ranging and at the same time intensive. Many available techniques can do one but not the other.[28] We may find that a systematic survey of possible network areas by open-ended probes is most successful:

Can you tell me a little about where you work? What sort of atmosphere or mood does the place have? Do you like to go there or dread it? What about the people you work with? Who do you particularly like and dislike there? Any idea what it is about them that you like (dislike)?

We will need to accumulate considerably more experiences with this kind of analysis before the best techniques become clear and we can do it parsimoniously.

A systematic overview of a person's (or family's) meaningful social network would need to include both formal and informal aspects of a number of sectors. It is very important to look at both sides of these spheres without slighting one or the other.

Sector	Formal Examples	Informal Examples
Family, nuclear	marriage, natural or adopted children	consensual and gay marriages, "families" in institutions
Family, extended	family rituals and reunions, cousins clubs	"adopted kin," foster grandparents, lodgers
Education	teachers, schoolmates	"street learning," mentors
Religion	religious leaders, congregations	folk-religion, prayer
Politics	political parties	influentials
Ethnicity	ethnic pride, self-help, and anti-discrimination groups	ethnic "recognition"
Work/Profession	company, union, professional associations	work groups, colleagues
Social Welfare	settlements, day care, family agencies, etc.	informal mutual aid, child care, errands
Health	doctors, clinics, hospitals	faith healers, folk remedies, druggists
Recreation	organized interest	informal groups—street
Friendship groups	groups, clubs, lodges, tournaments	groups, bridge foursomes, friends, or kin "dropping in"
Neighborhood	block clubs, tenant councils	"neighborliness"

People are perhaps more likely to talk about what I have called "formal" aspects of their network than about informal ones. A Puerto Rican is not as likely to discuss his spiritualist beliefs as he is to claim Roman Catholicism as his religion. A person is more likely to talk about conflict with his boss than the fact that his coworkers provide ongoing "marital counselling" which has been effective until this most recent crisis. Someone may say that he has no contact with the extended family, but overlook the fact that the childless couple down the street are functional "grandparents," give holiday presents to the children, babysitting, and so on.

It is important to consider what areas are salient; for example, where the trouble lies or what units of the network are most important at this stage in the life cycle. It is equally important to search for areas *without* trouble, looking for strengths from which to build. In assessment it would be important to evaluate the range, depth, and quality of the social network, paying special attention to gaps or over-concentration in one segment.

In order to assess where social networks exist which might be of potential use for "disconnected" persons (such as immigrants, long-term mental patients, orphans, isolated elderly), it becomes necessary to know the community in considerable detail—where and how much mutual aid is going on and where it can be developed. This involves a different type of diagnostic ability: being able to observe a community and identify supportive networks. Collins and Pancoast provide many ideas about discovering the intimate details of community life and identifying natural helpers. Another model is the Puerto Rican Family Institute's use of established immigrant "sponsors" to assist recent immigrants. Eismann's work in the South Bronx is another example of the effective use of resources in a network.*

Developing new networks for mutual aid depends a great deal upon the resources available within the group. For example, women's support groups and peer counselling programs for college students tend to draw on resource-rich populations. On the other hand, the process of establishing a mutual aid network of chronically hospitalized mental patients is a very difficult task. The former might be able effec-

* See notes 20, 23, and 25 for references on these programs which have been discussed earlier in the text.

tively to utilize a modest amount of professional consultation and back-up, while the latter will require massive inputs of resources.

Sometimes an effective intervention in a network on behalf of a troubled individual can lead to an invitation from the network to help it enhance its effectiveness as a mutual aid system. It might be possible to describe the ideal progression as moving from 1) introduction around a troubled person, 2) development of a consultative relationship to catalyze most effective mutual aid, and finally 3) using the strengthened network as a resource for other troubled people.

Peter was referred to a child guidance clinic because of behavior problems at home and in school. In the process of the evaluation, the social worker met several times with the teacher. They developed a good deal of mutual respect as they struggled to untangle what part the environment of the school played in Peter's troubles. About six months later, when a child in another classroom had difficulties, the social worker asked the first teacher if she would help the second teacher devise a classroom strategy.

It may be worthwhile at this point to deal explicitly with the issue of destructiveness in social networks. While there are obviously many constructive elements which can support development of human potential, at the same time it is important to be aware that networks can serve to undermine identity, to narrow choices, or to offer undesirable options.

One indication of awareness of these destructive effects is the increasing reluctance of executives to accept multiple geographic moves dictated by the corporation. A husband's troubled relationship with his mother may negatively influence the wife's relationship with their child. A spouse's career choice may create conflict within the extended family. A tightly knit network may make it very difficult to develop or express independent points of view.

A perspective on the functioning of the whole family has provided additional diagnostic understanding of individuals and suggested new techniques for intervention. Likewise, understanding the functioning of social networks may enhance the understanding of its subunits, such as the nuclear family, and suggest further interventions. Helping the network increase its competence at supporting rather than undercutting members may often be possible. In some situations, however, helping a person separate from a destructive network and begin to join or construct a new network may be necessary.

Evaluating total networks, rather than personal networks, has received a considerable amount of attention. The literature generally uses the language of "social environments" rather than social networks. Work in this complex and fascinating area has proceeded in quite different directions. Some of these techniques may eventually prove useful in assessing various segments of a person's social network, or in assessing the potential of a social environment for offering support to a troubled person. Currently, these techniques have been applied to units such as psychiatric wards, patient homes, and half-way houses. One interesting technique, developed by Rudolf Moos, maps an environment on a variety of dimensions with a rather straightforward questionnaire. These dimensions include organization, support, anger, autonomy, involvement and so on.[29]

SOCIAL NETWORKS, MUTUAL AID, AND THE LIFE MODEL OF PRACTICE

It may be clear from what has been said previously that social network theory and mutual aid concepts are at the heart of a life model of practice.[30] In order to make the connections more explicit, let us consider each of the five elements of a practice model in turn.

The definition of the problem: A life model of practice views the "problem" as a lack of good fit between the coping capacities of the person and the qualities of the impinging environment. Social network theory extends this concept by clarifying the nature of that environment, and by making explicit the need to consider relationships between the persons and objects in the environment as well as relationships between the environment and the person. This can be seen in practice strategies such as the "foster community" in New Haven, Missouri. Careful work with community network to enhance its competence at social support precedes relationships between the community and the mental patient. Mutual aid is a transactional concept which allows the individual an opportunity to give as well as to receive. The teen-age children in *Unitas* not only receive from the social worker but are able to give to each other and the younger children.*

The view of the person: Mutual aid is a reciprocal concept which supports the interactive, mastery-seeking view of the person inherent in the life model. It offers a humanistic vision of the nature of man—as a sharing, giving person. Social network theory suggests directions for analysis of the context in which people live and its impact upon their lives. Self-help groups are a particularly clear example of practice applications of concepts of mutual aid and social networks which serve to enhance the dignity and competence of persons.

The worker-client relationship: Mutual aid redefines exchanges as mutual and reciprocal, allowing consideration of the worker as receiver as well as giver. This brings home the common humanity of worker and client and undermines worker-client relationships which are based on an unequal distribution of power. It supports the life model view of the social worker as a helper in the life space of the person. Social networks open up the range of potential helpers to include a variety of persons in the life space of a troubled person. The use of indigenous homemakers, neighborhood teenagers, and community residents as "helpers" have all been described.

Goals of helping: In the life model, helping is conceptualized as providing an environment where the person's progressive forces are encouraged and the environment is enhanced. Mutual aid supports the person's growth and at the same time increases the competence of the social network at caring for its members. Social change at the level of social networks is an effective approach to enhancing the qualities of the environment. The progression of consultation to social networks to support a troubled person, increase the network's competence, and develop new "attachments" for isolated persons is a cyclical process of attention both to the person and to the environment.

Service delivery arrangements: Social network concepts help clarify the nature of the life space of the person. They allow for attention to problems without necessarily defining individuals as "clients."

---

* See notes 24 and 25 for references to these programs which have been discussed earlier in the text.

Mutual aid suggests a widened range of helping persons who may be located strategically in networks. Social work "catalysts" will need to be out of their offices and in the community, working with networks and identifying places where mutual aid is vigorous or can be fostered. In these various ways social network and mutual aid concepts give substance to the interest generated by the life model of practice in providing services in the life space of persons.

NOTES

1. Otto Will, "Human Relatedness and the Schizophrenic Reaction," *Psychiatry* 22, no. 3 (August 1959), pp. 1205–23.
2. John E. Mayer and Aaron Rosenblatt, "The Client's Social Context: Its Effect on Continuance in Treatment," *Social Casework* 45, no. 9 (November 1964), pp. 511–18.
3. Mutual aid has long been a prominent theme in the work of William Schwartz. See, for example, William Schwartz, "On the Use of Groups in Social Work Practice," in William Schwartz and Serapio R. Zalba (eds.), *The Practice of Group Work* (New York: Columbia University Press, 1971), pp. 3–24.

---

1. Carel Germain, unpublished lectures, Columbia University, 1975.
2. Max Weber, "The Essentials of Bureaucratic Organization: An Ideal-Type Construction," in *The Theory of Social and Economic Organization,* ed. Talcott Parsons, trans. A. M. Henderson and Talcott Parsons (Oxford: Oxford University Press, 1947), pp. 329–40; Talcott Parsons, "The Social Structure of the Family," in *The Family: Its Function and Destiny* (New York: Harper & Row, 1944), 173–201.
3. Michael Young and Peter Willmott, *Family and Kinship in East London* (Baltimore: Penguin Books, 1957); Herbert J. Gans, *The Urban Villagers* (New York: The Free Press, 1962); Hope Leichter and William Mitchell, *Kinship and Casework* (New York: Russell Sage, 1967).
4. See, for example, Edgar Schein, *Organizational Psychology* (Englewood Cliffs, New Jersey: Prentice-Hall, 1965).
5. Eugene Litwak and Henry Meyer, "A Balance Theory of Coordination between Bureaucratic Organizations and Community Primary Groups," *Administrative Science Quarterly* 11, no. 1 (1966), pp. 31–58.
6. Hillery, for example, reports 92 definitions of community. See George A.

Hillery, *Communal Organizations: A Study of Local Societies* (Chicago: University of Chicago Press, 1968).

7. I am indebted to George Brennan for this distinction, discussed at the "Support and Coping Symposium," American Psychological Association, Chicago, Illinois, September 1, 1975.

8. John A. Barnes, "Class and Committees in a Norwegian Island Parish," *Human Relations* 7, no. 1 (1954), pp. 39–58; Elizabeth Bott, *Family and Social Network* (New York: Free Press, 1971), p. 313.

9. Bott, *Family and Social Network,* p. 249.

10. See, for example, J. Clyde Mitchell, "The Concept and Use of Social Networks," in *Social Networks in Urban Situations,* ed. J. Clyde Mitchell (Manchester, England: University of Manchester Press, 1969), pp. 1–50; J. A. Barnes, *Social Networks* (Reading, Mass.: Addison Wesley Modular Publications, Module 26, 1972), pp. 1–29; "Support and Coping Symposium," American Psychological Association, Chicago, Illinois, September 1, 1975.

11. See, for example, "Support and Coping Symposium," American Psychological Association, Chicago, Illinois, September 1, 1975; F. Harary, R. Norman, and D. Cartwright, *Structural Models: An Introduction to the Theory of Directed Graphs* (New York: Wiley, 1965).

12. See Mitchell, *Social Networks* for the use of simple visual techniques for demonstrating principles in network functioning.

13. Petr Kropotkin, *Mutual Aid: A Factor in Evolution* (New York: New York University Press, 1972), pp. 141, 251.

14. Margaret H. Bacon, "Social Work in China," *Social Work* 20, No. 1 (January 1975), pp. 68–69. See also, Joshua Horn, *Away With All Pests* (New York: Monthly Review Press, 1969).

15. See Robert Houriet, *Getting Back Together* (New York: Avon, 1973); Rosabeth M. Kanter, *Commitment and Community* (Cambridge: Harvard University Press, 1972).

16. Mark Zborowski, *Life Is With People* (New York: International Universities Press, 1952).

17. Eugene Litwak, "Primary Group Structures and Their Functions: Kin, Neighbors, and Friends," *American Sociological Review* 34, no. 4 (August 1969), pp. 465–81.

18. Ross Speck and Carolyn Attneave, *Family Networks* (New York: Vintage Books, 1973). See also a series of articles appearing in *Family Process* written by these authors in 1967 and 1969. Other theorists start with the family and move rapidly to identify salient network members in order to deal with crisis. For example, Edgar H. Auerswald, "Interdisciplinary vs. Ecological Approach," *Family Process* 7, no. 2 (September 1968), pp. 202–15; John Garrison, "Network Techniques: Case Studies in the Screening-Linking-Planning Conference Method," *Family Process* 13, no. 3 (September 1974), pp. 337–54. Another expansion of family treatment is multiple family therapy. It is especially useful where there is a shared family pathology which is highly resistant to professional intervention, such as the families of some

psychotic adolescents. See Peter Laqueur, "Mechanisms of Change in Multiple Family Therapy," in *Progress in Group and Family Therapy,* ed. Clifford Sager and Helen Kaplan (New York: Brunner-Mazel, 1972), pp. 400–15; Elsa Leichter and Gerda Schulman, "Multi-Family Group Therapy," *Family Process* 13 no. 1 (March, 1974), pp. 95–110.

19. Ed Skarnulis, "Least Restrictive Alternatives in Residential Services" (Eastern Nebraska Community Office of Retardation, mimeo, 1974). Some may question whether the concept of mutual aid should be extended to include persons who are paid for their help. It is my view that it is the personalized quality of the help offered or the interdependence between the people which is most significant rather than whether or not money is exchanged. However, this is an area which needs further exploration. Of course, the concept of the indigenous homemaker is an older type of formalized mutual aid in social service delivery. See, for example, Gertrude Goldberg, "Non-Professional Helpers: The Visiting Homemakers," in *Community Action Against Poverty,* ed. George Brager and Francis Purcell (New Haven, Conn: College and University Press, 1967), pp. 175–207.

20. Alice H. Collins, "Natural Delivery Systems: Accessible Sources of Power for Mental Health," *American Journal of Orthopsychiatry* 43 no. 1 (January 1973), pp. 46–52; Alice H. Collins & Diane L. Pancoast, *Natural Helping Networks: A Strategy for Prevention* (Washington, D.C., National Association of Social Workers, 1976). Others have conceptualized neighborhood figures such as bartenders, as caretakers. Matthew P. Dumont, *The Absurd Healer: Perspectives of a Community Psychiatrist* (New York: Science House, 1968).

21. Joan Shapiro, *Communities of the Alone* (New York: Association Press, 1971). Also, Elliot Studt dealt at a conceptual level with naturally occurring networks in her work in correctional settings. Elliot Studt, "Social Work Theory and Implications for the Practice of Methods," *Social Work Education Reporter* 16 (1968), pp. 22–24, 42–46.

22. Hyman J. Weiner et al., *Mental Health in the World of Work* (New York: Association Press, 1973).

23. James M. Jertson, "Self-Help Groups," *Social Work* 20, no. 2 (March 1975), pp. 144–45; Alfred H. Katz, "Application of Self-Help Concepts in Current Social Welfare," *Social Work* 10, no. 3 (July 1965), pp. 68–74. In some situations, even though a professional may serve as a planner, catalyst, or convenor, the main helping is perceived as coming from others who are, or have been, experiencing similar situations. The Widow-to-Widow program is one example. Gerald Caplan, *Support Systems and Community Mental Health* (New York: Behavioral Publishers, 1974). Cardarelle reports a somewhat similar effort, utilizing group processes, which are particularly important in view of his concentration on children with deceased parents and the school context. James A. Cardarelle, "A Group for Children with Deceased Parents," *Social Work* 20, no. 4 (July 1975), pp. 328–30. Another very creative project has capitalized on the coping skills of recent Puerto Rican immigrants who have successfully adjusted to life in New York. They serve as "foster families" to newly arrived Puerto Ricans. In this instance, the cultural values attached to main-

taining extended kin ties maximizes legitimation of the program. A. Gonzalez, "The Struggle to Develop Self-Help Institutions," *Social Casework* 55, no. 2 (February 1974), pp. 90–93.

24. Ali Keskiner et al., "The Foster Community: A Partner in Psychiatric Rehabilitation," *American Journal of Psychiatry* 129, no. 3 (September 1972), pp. 283–88. An extensive literature is available on providing home care for the mentally ill, extending back into the Middle Ages, and including reports of efforts as far away as Africa. Matthew P. Dumont and C. Knight Aldrich, "Family Care After a Thousand Years—A Crisis in the Tradition of St. Dymphna," *American Journal of Psychiatry* 119, no. 2 (August 1962), pp. 116–20; T. Adeoye Lambo, "Patterns of Psychiatric Care in Developing African Countries," in *Magic, Faith and Healing: Studies in Primitive Society Today,* ed. Ari Kiev (New York: Free Press, 1964), pp. 443–53; Lynne Riehman and Carolyn O'Brien, "Project in Apartment Group Living," *Social Work* 18, no. 3 (May 1973), pp. 36–43; George Fairweather et al., *Community Life for the Mentally Ill* (Chicago: Aldine, 1969).

25. Ed Eismann, "Children's Views of Therapeutic Gains and Therapeutic Change Agents in an Open-System Therapeutic Community" (Bronx, New York: Lincoln Community Mental Health Center, mimeo, 1975); also personal communications.

26. Alfred W. Clark and William S. Cullen, "Social Support: A Counter to Pathogenic Communication," *Interpersonal Development* 5 (1974–75), pp. 50–59.

27. Bott, *Family and Social Network;* Edward O. Laumann, *Bonds of Pluralism: The Form and Substance of Urban Social Networks* (New York: Wiley, 1973); John Lofland, *Analyzing Social Settings* (Belmont, Cal.: Wadsworth, 1971).

28. One notable exception is the Environmental Transactions Inventory. See Western Interstate Commission on Higher Education, "The Eco-Systems Model: Designing Campus Environments" (Boulder, Colo.: WICHE, 1973).

29. Rudolf H. Moos, "Systems for the Assessment and Classification of Human Environments: An Overview" in Rudolf H. Moos and Paul Insel (eds.), *Issues in Social Ecology* (Palo-Alto: National Press Books, 1974); Rudolf H. Moos and William Insell, "Psychological Environments: Expanding Human Ecology," *American Psychologist* 29 (1974), pp. 607–13; John R. Graham et al., "Home Environment Perception Scale," *Journal of Community Psychology* 3 (1975), pp. 40–48; P. A. Moxnes and H. A. Engvik, "Diagnosing the Organization: The Psychogram," *Interpersonal Development* 4 (1973–74), pp. 1977–89.

30. Carel B. Germain and Alex Gitterman, *The Life Model of Social Work Practice* (New York: Columbia University Press [forthcoming]).

8 The Extended Family as a Resource for Change: An Ecological Approach to Family-Centered Practice

L. ANN HARTMAN

Hartman is interested in the extended kin as a presence in the ecological context of an individual or a group or a family. Real and fantasied events and relationships with salient figures in the past represent life processes that exert a positive or negative force on current functioning. Thus Hartman views the extended family as a resource for change. Its relationships and linkages become environmental instruments for helping people to fulfill their adaptive needs for relatedness, autonomy, self-esteem, and for providing space and time for action. She develops the genogram not as a technique but as a dynamic process for beginning the engagement with this powerful force in the life space. The process becomes "a study of continuities, of consequences, of how [a family] perpetuates [itself], and how each generation helps to doom, or helps to liberate, the coming one—the action of love, or the effect of the absence of love in time." [1]

In a less direct way, perhaps, this mapping of one's family in time and space is a way of helping people come to terms with the adaptive challenge of rapid social change. Mead has stated the case in her conception of three kinds of societies. The postfigurative is a culture in which social change occurs at a snail's pace, as in agrarian societies of the past; and children see their own future in the ways of their grandparents and parents. The cofigurative is a culture rather like our own before the 1960s where social change has picked up considerably in tempo; and children must now learn from the experiences of their peers since their future will be different from their grandparents' and even from their parents' experience. The prefigurative culture is likely to exist in a society where the rate of social change accelerates so rapidly that never again can children understand and learn about the future from their parents' experience. They must, in fact, take the hands of their elders and, in joint commitment, lead them gently into the unknown future. [2]

Families must nevertheless continue to socialize and to enculturate their members, despite the enormity and poignancy of the task in our prefigurative society. Hartman points out for us that social workers and clients can learn and grow together in their attempt to know their origins in time and space, transcending the temporal barriers of past, present, and future in family life, and the spatial barriers of here or there.

Milton Mayeroff has developed a useful metaphor for the adaptive balance between separateness and connectedness, in the conception of being "in-place," as opposed to being "out-of-place." [3] It is both a spatial and temporal metaphor; and because of its poetic nature it tells something of the quality of experience that Hartman has identified as coming out of the shared work on the genogram. Through caring and being cared for, the human being becomes "in-place." Being in-place is not only a return to a place from which one had been estranged, for it demands constant renewal through responding to the need of others to grow. It is not a specific location although it may partake of many places and many times. "Past and future, instead of being fixed and laid out for me, have an unknown and promising dimension. My awareness of the present is deepened by reflecting on the past, on what was and could have been, and reflecting on the future opens me to rich possibilities that move me to act on their behalf." [4]

The genogram as used by Hartman, and the professional philosophy that underlies its use, appears to be a way to "go home again," in order to untie the binds and retie the bonds, and savor the old loved places. It can help to achieve a liberating present—of being, at last, in-place.

—*C.B.G.*

"Man's working image of himself is anchored in his sense of intimacy" [1]

AN ECOLOGICAL PERSPECTIVE directs us to understand events and behavior in the context of the many influences and variables that impact upon and have a part in the production of those events and behaviors. It encourages us to focus on the adaptive balance that may exist between living beings and their environments. It leads us to understand and evaluate events and human responses in terms of their contribution to adaptation, integration, and differentiation.

These ecological principles suggest that this chapter should begin with some description of the intellectual context in which it is immersed and at least some of the personal and professional influences that have framed my thinking.

We have all lived through a period of rapid change. We have been exposed to arguments and conflicting opinions about both the nature and the future of the family. We have seen the weakening of family ties, a renewed emphasis on individualism, increased family breakdown, and serious questions as to whether the family can or should survive as a social institution. On the other hand, more recently we have been witnessing a strong reawakening of interest in and commitment to the preservation of the family, a growing concern about family connectedness, and increased interest in the relationship between family roots and the individual's definition of self. As is generally true of dialectical actions and reaction, both trends continue to exist simultaneously, leading to considerable confusion and inconsistency in our national attitudes toward the family. My thinking about the family has developed in this context of paradoxes and contradictions.

In terms of my professional development within this context, three major interests have influenced my approach to social work practice. These interests have, of course, been stimulated and enriched by many teachers, fellow learners, and clients. First, my habit of thought has always been holistic and synthetic rather than analytic and partializing. From my college days as a philosophy major, when I was fascinated by the writings of William North Whitehead, to the present time, my effort has been to think systems, to focus on relatedness rather than on the essential nature of separate entities.[2]

A second and closely related interest has been a concern with the relationship between the human being and the natural world. I have tended to take a strong "environmentalist" approach to social work practice, with my thinking enriched by the work of Edgar Auerswald,[3] Carel Germain,[4] Carol Meyer,[5] and others who have utilized ecological principles in the development of practice models.[6]

Finally, as a clinician, my main interest, since beginning practice over 25 years ago, has been in helping families. Marital work, parent groups, and parent-child counselling came fairly early in my professional life. Association with Sanford Sherman in the early 1960s led to conjoint work with the total nuclear family. The foundation had been laid when I came across and was particularly drawn to the ideas of Murray Bowen,[7] primarily through his writings and the writings of his students.[8] Since then, my effort has been to integrate and adapt these many influences to a family-centered social work practice.

My conviction continues to be that there are many sources of help in the ecological environment that can be made available to individuals and families for enhanced mutuality and growth. The chapters in this volume detail the uses of these many sources of help and nurture. This chapter will focus on just one part, albeit a very important part, of the individual's or nuclear family's environment as a resource for help and change, and that is the extended family as it has developed vertically through time and horizontally in space.

THE FAMILY

The family is a powerful biological, emotional, and social system that exists in space and through time. Most psychological theories have attested to its importance in human growth and development and literature is replete with family sagas which portray individuals living out family themes, attempting to resolve family tragedies and guilts, fulfilling family destinies. My starting point is that all people are deeply immersed in their family systems and that who they are, how they think and communicate, how they see themselves and others, what they choose to do and to be, whom they choose to be with, to love, and to marry is very largely a function of that complex family system that has developed over the generations. Therefore, in thinking about people, about function and dysfunction, about change and growth, I place the family in the center of my vision. Such a focus is highly consistent with the traditions of social work practice.

Social workers share a long history of family orientation. In the early years of the profession, the family was assumed to be the unit of attention[9] until the mental hygiene movement of the 20s began to shift attention to the individual.[10] It was no accident that the first social work practice journal was called *The Family!*[11] In health and mental health settings, as social workers began to have sanction for studying and attempting to remedy noxious elements in the patient's environment, the obtaining of family histories and work with the patient's family as a major influence in the social environment became the social worker's special professional role. I am not sure we ever realized the richness of our opportunity. Back in the 50s, young social workers sometimes felt like second class citizens because they "only got to work with the families," instead of the patients. They mistakenly felt that they weren't really where the action was!

By the mid-50s, the family therapy movement had begun and with it came the development of a growing range of exciting and innovative approaches to the family system, both as the primary unit for assessment and as the arena for treatment. Accounts of the work of the creative leaders who pioneered in the development of family treatment are available elsewhere and provide an excellent background for understanding the richness and diversity of this intellectual and professional movement.[12]

In the midst of this diversity, it strikes me as neither useful nor necessary to become involved in professional debates around which approach to helping individuals and families to change and to grow is "the best." If one holds a systems orientation one subscribes to the principle of equifinality, which suggests that, because all of the variables in a system are in transaction, a variety of interventions may well produce similar outcomes. Opening up and altering the communication system, refashioning the family structure, encouraging increased affective sharing and expression, working with the total family or with subunits within the family, surfacing family secrets or family losses and promoting operational mourning, making use of paradoxes to unbind double binds, using the transference, carefully avoiding the development of transference, joining the system, staying out of the system; the variety of approaches and techniques continues to expand. Questions about which is faster, easier, more efficient, or more lasting await careful research. At this point, those interested in helping people to grow and to change have many options.

This chapter will focus on one way of helping individuals and families to change, a method which appears to be particularly congruent with an ecological perspective, namely an approach to helping which makes primary use of the extended family as the arena for or instrument of change. This approach was developed by Bowen, among others,[13] growing out of his research on schizophrenia, his work with his own extended family, and his training of family therapists.[14] The goal of such work is "differentiation of the self" whereby the individual becomes increasingly aware of and free of powerful "ego syntonic" family proscriptions and commands. As a person becomes more differentiated, he or she becomes less immersed or fused in the family emotional system. Differentiation of the self out of the "weness" of the nuclear family is a natural process which starts at birth, continues throughout life, but is never totally complete. The regressive appeal of continued fusion in the face of overwhelming challenges of the world, the anxiety of parents, themselves insufficiently differentiated, traumatic cut-offs from important family members, all kinds of life and human exigencies can slow or interrupt the process of differentiation. A major goal of treatment, then, is to help a person begin to remove the obstacles to growth, to become increasingly defused from the family system, and to move to a higher level of differentiation.

People who are sufficiently differentiated can be away from their families without emotionally cutting themselves off, and can be close to their families without becoming lost in the system. They may be different from their families without being rejecting or fearing rejection. They may be like their families without losing a sense of self. They can love without fusing and can maintain a person-to-person relationship with each member of their family system without seeking closeness with one at the expense of another.

If a person has achieved this level of differentiation in relation to his or her family of origin, he or she will maintain similarly differentiated relationships with his or her family of procreation and others in the here and now world. Such a person can maintain intimate and satisfying relationships with a minimum of anxiety and has the energy and interest available for productive, goal-directed activity. This high level of differentiation must be considered an ideal and growth may be conceptualized as movement toward this ideal.

The following story, told by a woman attending a family assessment seminar, seems to illustrate, at least in part, the notion and the process of differentiation.

"For thirty years I've always ironed in the dining room," the participant explained, "My mother always did and I always did, and I never thought anything about it. A month ago, I loaned my ironing board to my married daughter who had just moved into a new apartment. I went up to the attic and brought down my mother's old ironing board. I set the board up in my dining room and as I used my mother's ironing board, I felt so close to her, so in touch with her again! I remembered her ironing and got to wondering why she had always ironed in the dining room. The answer was simple. We lived on a farm with no electricity. My mother used to have to heat the irons on the wood stove in the kitchen. She didn't iron in the kitchen because it was too hot with the stove going and thus she ironed in the dining room which was the closest room.

"And suddenly it struck me—I didn't have to iron in the dining room! I had an electric iron—and could iron in any room in the house. Since then, I sometimes iron in the dining room but I also iron in the living room in front of the television or in the kitchen. I really became free to iron anywhere I wanted to!''

This little vignette portrays the relationship between people and their families and points out how we may come to do the things we do and become the people we are. It also illustrates some interesting and important characteristics of those family forces which are so important in all of our lives.

First, much of the impact of the family system exists outside of awareness, not because it has been necessarily repressed or relegated to the unconcounsious but because it is so much a part of the self. As Frederick Duhl has pointed out, "that which is constantly experienced as neutral to awareness, being so immersed in the identity, so 'ego syntonic,' is rarely open to observation or challenge."[15]

So it is with family proscriptions. One step, therefore, in the process of differentiation is to find ways to objectify these family proscriptions, to step outside of the system so that these family rules can be recognized in the family and in the self. The affective accompaniment of such a process can vary considerably. Often the searcher laughs, expressing amusement and pleasure in the discovery. Some of the sense of pleasure may be related to the heightened sense of mastery and of freedom. The woman above was positively gleeful when she announced, "I can iron anywhere." She had freed herself, in this one area of functioning, from the control of transmitted family proscriptions and was now able to make a choice, based on her personal preferences and the circumstances of her life.

Other feelings may also be experienced. Sometimes the affect can best be described as an affectionate amusement toward the self. Of course, at other times there may be sadness and anger as a person comes face to face with the extent of tragic and debilitating constraints that have resulted from enmeshment in the family system. One young woman had been estranged from her father and his family following the bitter divorce of her parents when she was twelve. In her early twenties her father died in an automobile accident, making the "cut-off" complete. She struggled with feelings of depression throughout her twenties and finally sought help. It was with considerable anger and unhappiness that she realized how she had "bought into her mother's family system," questioning neither the cut-off from her father nor her mother's and the maternal extended family's characterization of her father.

Anger can also be directed at the self. Repeatedly, as family patterns become obvious and subject to challenge, students of their own families will exclaim, "How can I have been so stupid? How could I have not seen that before? Why didn't I question that?" Again, this response points to how completely the family world view has become a part of the self. Anxiety, of course, is almost a universal accompaniment of the search and the stronger the prohibition against looking at family information, against delving into family "secrets," the greater will be the anxiety about "finding out." Whether the feeling involved in discovery is sadness, or pain, or anger, or even ironic amusement, it is also almost always coupled with a sense of relief.

The ironing board story also illustrates the importance of emotionally connecting with the source of the family proscription. Our ironer, through handling her mother's board, felt close to her mother and was led to wondering about her mother and to wanting to understand her mother's behavior. Out of that understanding of the meaning and circumstances of her mother's life came the realization that she, herself, was a different person living in different circumstances. It is often that combination of closeness and empathy which can lead to a more realistic view as well as an acceptance of family figures and thus to the ability to recognize and feel comfortable with one's own difference.

In some respects, the ironing board story can serve as an example of a model of change. It includes the objectification and the growing understanding of an aspect of the family system. It includes the immediacy of experience in emotionally connecting with a primary figure instrumental in the development and propagation of the proscription being challenged. It includes the enhanced understanding of an empathy toward that key figure and ends with the family explorer having taken one more step in the process of differentiation. The following pages describe in greater detail this approach to interpersonal helping.

OBJECTIFICATION OF THE FAMILY SYSTEM

I have called the first step in this change strategy, "objectification of the family system." My choice of this term is an attempt to convey a process whereby a person begins to see his family system as a complex object for study, to slowly replace the family as it is subjectively experienced with the objective family that can be looked at "out there." Anyone who visits home usually has a brief experience of seeing the family more objectively, as an outsider might, during the first few moments after returning. Father seems to have shrunk. Sister's voice has gotten louder. Mother seems particularly preoccupied with her own concerns. Everyone seems different. Very quickly, however, one once again becomes a part of the family system, objective awareness fades, and the person feels at home with his or her familiar comforts and discomforts. A similar experience occurs when one fails to recognize oneself when suddenly presented with an unexpected reflection in a mirror.

Many experiences can enhance objective awareness but one method which I have found to be most useful and use regularly is the careful gathering of extensive factual information about the family over time and the organization of that data through the construction with the client(s) of a genogram. The genogram is an expanded family tree, modeled after the genetic charts used in biology, but including a wide range of social and demographic data. Instructions for preparing a genogram have appeared elsewhere,[16] but since it is such a key tool in this model and practitioners have developed their own variations, it may be useful to present the way I construct and use a genogram.

The skeleton of the genogram tends to follow the conventions of genetic and genealogical charts. A male is indicated by a □, a female by a ○, and if the sex of a person is unknown, by a △. The latter symbol tends to be used, for example, when the client says, "I think there were seven children in my grandfather's family but I have no idea whether they were males or females," or "My mother lost a full term child five years before I was born, but I don't know what sex it was."

A marital pair is indicated by □————○, and it is useful to add the marital date, □—m. 6/7/54○. Offspring are shown as follows:

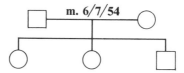

They are generally lined up according to age starting with the oldest on the left. This family has an older son followed by a set of twins.

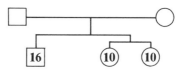

A divorce is generally portrayed by a dotted line, and again, it is useful to include dates.

A family member no longer living is generally depicted by ⊗ d. 1967. Thus, a complex, but not untypical reconstituted family may be drawn as follows:

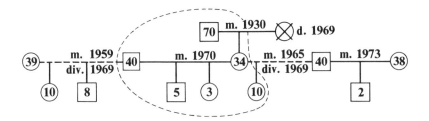

It is useful to draw a dotted line around the family members who compose the household. Incidentally, such a family chart enables the worker to quickly grasp "who's who" in complicated reconstituted families.

With these basic building blocks, expanded horizontally to depict the contemporary generation of siblings and cousins and vertically to chart the generations through time, it is possible to chart any family, given sufficient paper, patience, and information. As one charts the skeletal structure of the family, it is also important to flesh this out with the rich and varied data which portray the saga of the particular family being studied. The following kinds of information may be gathered:

Given names, first and middle, identify family members and indicate naming patterns and surface identifications. An exploration of the meaning of names may bring to light and objectify some surprising family projections. For exammple, in doing a genogram with Tony, a young man who was struggling with identity issues and a complex tie to his mother, naming patterns were discussed. Tony's American soldier father had met his mother abroad and immediately after their marriage, the couple came to this country. The move and subsequent political events resulted in the young wife being completely cut off from her family. Tony was born a year after his parents married. When asked whom he was named after, he replied, "I wasn't named after anyone in the family. I was named after St. Anthony . . . the saint of lost objects." Although Tony had never made this connection before, it now became apparent to him that he had really been named after everyone in his mother's lost family!

Dates of birth and dates of death record when members joined the family, longevity, and family losses. Birth dates indicate the age of family members when important events occurred, and chart each member's place in the sibship of each family. They indicate how early or late in a marriage a child came and the age of the parents at its birth. In a sense, birth, marriage, and death dates mark the movement of the family through time.

Place of birth and current place of residence mark the movement of the family through space. Such information charts the family's patterns of dispersal, surfacing major immigrations or migrations, and brings attention to periods of loss, change, and upheaval. On the other hand, such information may point to the fact that generations of a family have stayed within a fairly small radius, except perhaps for a particular individual in each generation who moves away. If your client happens to be this generation's "wanderer," that could be a valuable piece of information.

Occupations of family members acquaint one with the interests and talents, the successes and failures, and the varied socioeconomic statuses that are found in most families. Further, occupational patterns point to identifications and can often tell a good deal about family proscriptions and expectations.

Finally, facts about members' health and causes of death provide an overall family health history and also may say something about the way individuals are prophesying about their own futures. These prophecies may well have some power of self-fulfillment.

The above demographic data can take us a long way toward understanding the family system. However, I find also that gathering associations about family members can add to the richness of the portrayal. I often ask "What word or two or what picture comes to mind when you think about this person?" These associations tend to tap another level of information about the family as the myths, role assignments, characterizations, or caricatures of family members pop into the reporter's mind. Assignments such as "lazy," "bossy," "martyr," "beautiful," "caretaker," are likely to be contributed. This question also often brings forth reminiscences or stories that have become a part of the family biography and mythology.

Finally, certain aspects of the family's communication structure can be indicated. Parts of the family that have been "cut off" become quite obvious because the reporter generally has very little information about them. "Cut-offs" can be portrayed by drawing a fence where the cut-off exists whereas tight communication bonds can be demonstrated by drawing a line around portions of the family that form close linkages. It helps to keep things clearer if a colored pencil is used to indicate communication linkages and cut-offs so as not to confuse these with the basic genealogical structure.

Next it may be useful to explore some of the practical and technical issues in actually doing a genogram with a client or clients. First, in terms of timing, there appears to be considerable variation in practice. Some practitioners start the genogram, or complete a limited genogram, in the first or second contact. Although different occasions demand varied and flexible responses, I find I tend to work with the client on the genogram over many contacts but may devote only part of the interview to it. The attempt here is to maintain an easy flow between current issues and concerns and a search for the possible roots or reflections of these concerns in the family system. In the initial session, I generally begin the genogram by quickly sketching out the demographic data on the current household in lieu of completing a traditional face sheet. This immediately demonstrates a way of thinking and a way of working. Further, as a part of the contracting process in the initial phase of work, I explain my family orientation and my conviction about the importance of studying the extended family. I say that I will want to do a family tree with them, and mention that, in all likelihood, we may want to consider joint meetings with extended family members in the future.[17] This kind of preparation helps clients to understand the worker's approach and helps them consider whether this is what they want. Further, when the focus is shifted from current pressures to family study, the client is not surprised. In fact, considerable eagerness and interest is almost always evidenced. Incidentally, the furor over Alex Haley's *Roots* and the subsequent popularization of family study has made the task of introducing an intergenerational family orientation very much easier.

In terms of materials, I use a large tablet, at least 2′ by 3′, and have such a tablet always within reach. Some family practitioners suggest that the individual or family take the genogram home and work on it. I find that too much information, particularly about the process of discovery, can be lost in this way. Clients, of course, are encouraged to gather information on their own but then bring it to the office. Together we add it to the genogram. This process often continues throughout the entire contact. Usually, when extensive family work is being done, there are two working copies of the genogram, the client's copy and the one we work on together and keep in the office to be always available. It is important to use a large enough piece of paper and to be as neat and as clear as possible in entering material. This is not a matter of aesthetics. The advantage of a genogram over the same historical and social material as presented in the usual descriptive narrative is the fact that the genogram orders facts in a way that may be visually examined so that threads, relationships, themes, and patterns may emerge. A certain amount of orderliness in the presentation contributes to visual clarity and begins to systematize and give clients a sense of mastery over what has often seemed to be a chaotic collection of bits and pieces of facts.

Another management issue arises from the use of genograms in conjoint work with marital pairs and with family groups. Every marriage is, in a sense, the joining of two genograms and the new family thus formed flows from and is emotionally tied to the two extended families. Much of the negotiation and adaptation that must take place in the beginning of marriage revolves around developing some kind of compromise or resolution where family rules are in conflict. Stressful differences can range from major issues in role expectations and family boundaries to relatively minor but nonetheless important conflicts over such questions as, "Do you open your Christmas presents on Christmas eve or Christmas morning?"

Helping a marital pair do their genograms together has the major advantage of the couple sharing in the objectification of each family system. Such sharing leads to enhanced understanding and empathy between the couple. For example, as a wife begins to learn more factual information about the women in her husband's family, she begins to gain more understanding of the nature of some of her husband's expectations of her. One unanticipated consequence of shared genogram work can be a marked decrease in tension between the marital pair and the respective mothers- and fathers-in-law. As the extended in-law system is understood, the parent-in-law begins to be seen in the context of his or her family saga. Thus tension and resentment tend to become diffused throughout the system rather than being carried by the in-law as the sole author of all the spouse's most difficult characteristics.

Technical problems do arise, however, in sharing genogram work. One problem that appears to be common is the heightened competitiveness over time in the joint sessions that begins to develop between the marital partners. "We've talked more about your family than my family!" is a frequent comment, and there never seems to be enough time. At first, it was assumed that this was an expression of the spouse's jealousy about the other's interest in their own family. However, in an unrelated adult group focused on doing family work, the same intense competition over time developed. Although competition over time and attention is always an issue in work with groups, in my experience, I have never seen it so intense. In exploring this, it appeared that although the husband or wife and the group members were interested in the others' family work, they became so excited about and caught up in their growing understanding of their own families, it was difficult to wait and to share time. As one young woman said, after considerable shared work with her husband on their respective families, "John's been very interested in listening to me about my family and I've been interested in his, but I guess neither of us can listen as much as each of us wants to talk about it."

Considerable negotiation must take place over the use of time in these conjoint and group sessions. Further, there must be negotiation about the other's participation when the focus is on one family. When individuals work on their genograms, they may become irritated as the spouse interrupts with comments. This is usually experienced as highly intrusive, a commonly heard comment is, "Look, this is *my* family." Often couples agree that the other will be a quiet observer and may give feedback after the person discussing their family has finished a certain point.

The more fused a couple is, the harder it is for each to stay out of the other's time and space when the other is working on his or her genogram. However, the experiencing of this difficulty in the conjoint session and attention to this part of the process can be very useful in helping the couple to see and begin to deal with their difficulties in establishing and maintaining appropriate boundaries in their relationship. Even with all the complications and tension, I continue to feel that in most situations, the advantages of sharing the work outweigh other considerations. If, on the other hand, the extent of the couple's fusion and competitiveness keeps retarding progress, one solution is to do family genogram work with each partner alone but record the session on tape for the spouse or the couple together to listen to at home. This device facilitates separateness without closing the communication system.[18]

ANALYSIS OF THE GENOGRAM

An assessment of the family system over time through an analysis of the genogram develops step by step as the genogram is constructed. Fact gathering and thinking about the meaning of and relationships between the facts are complementary processes. If there is some pressure to ''finish'' the genogram in early sessions, the assessment process may be curtailed and some of the richness of the experience lost.

Each family genogram contains so many facts, so much information, it is easy to miss meanings and connections without some guidelines or tentative hypotheses to direct the study. A few suggestions about things to look for in thinking about the facts are presented here. As we continue to study the intergenerational patterns of families, we will learn more about the kinds of connections that could be salient and develop more hypotheses to be tested.

One key area of investigation centers on the intergenerational identification processes. Families seem to have a rather universal tendency to identify members of the current generation with members of previous generations. Often these identifications, while exerting considerable influence, are out of the family's awareness. A variety of things can promote these linkages. For example, a child born around the time of the death of an important member of the family frequently becomes a replacement object for that person and goes through life carrying the emotional burdens and the expectations connected with that salient figure.

The universality of the replacement phenomenon is rather touchingly demonstrated in the following story: A family's beloved German shepherd was killed by an automobile. Four days later, the family cat gave birth to a litter of kittens. The next day, a friend of the family was talking on the telephone to Billy, the five-year-old son. She inquired after the kittens and asked what they were like. "Well," he replied, "they look sort of like German shepherd puppies."

When a person has identified a family figure with whom he has been strongly linked, it is useful to find out as much as possible about that person and the circumstances of his or her life. This process of gathering factual data makes the person more real and understandable and also aids in the process of becoming differentiated from that person, and from the family projections and expectations which have resulted from the linkage. Such identifications seem to be particularly troubling when the family figure is shrouded in vaguely ominous mystery. One young man, around whom there had always been considerable anxiety in the family and expectation of eccentricity or even dysfunction, had always been told or had assumed that he was named after his paternal grandfather, and, indeed, he was. But there was another shadowy namesake. On a visit to the family graveyard, usually a rewarding experience in family study, he discovered, next to the graves of his maternal grandparents, a stone marking the grave of an uncle about whom there had been considerable family secrecy. Over the years, it had been communicated to him that this uncle had gone off somewhere, had somehow been "a bad lot," had married out of the faith and had died when the client was in his late teens or early twenties. In fact, there was so much mystery around his death that the client really wasn't completely sure his uncle was dead. He was amazed, there in the graveyard, to discover that this uncle, also with a name beginning with the same letter, had died two months before the client was born. Although this mystery has yet to be unraveled, it became clear that the client was very much involved with this highly toxic event in the life of the family—an event so toxic that the family for over thirty years had colluded in totally mystifying the figure of the uncle and had unconsciously denied the event to the point that there was even uncertainty communicated about whether the uncle was dead or alive. The importance of the event—

and of the uncle to this client—lies in the possibility that in the emotional life of the family he became the uncle's replacement, with far-reaching consequences in terms of family expectations, attributions, and the client's own sense of self.

Linkages between current family members and members of the family of origin can develop in other ways. Perhaps the single most powerful factor in this linkage or identification process is the place occupied by individuals in the set of siblings. Parents tend to identify their children with others who occupy the same sibling positions in the parent's generations. Family study should investigate these connections. Walter Toman[19] has developed a series of ten personality profiles which he felt tended to characterize different sibling positions. My own observations have led me to approach this issue in a somewhat different way. Although certain patterns may be widespread, it may be even more useful to discover how each particular family describes those occupying specific sibling positions. It may be that families are rather idiosyncratic but internally consistent in making these assignments.

For example, in one family, the second daughter was defined as mother's caretaker. Frequently, throughout the family, this daughter carried her mother's first or middle name. The pattern appeared to be quite consistent over four generations, a period of 100 years, and repeated horizontally across cousins and second cousins. In another family, second sons have consistently been alcoholics. A study of almost any family begins to suggest some of these patterns.

Clearly, one way of helping a person organize and assess the data from the genogram and to learn more about its personal relevance is to attempt to discover the sources of family expectations and projections through identifying links with particular members of the family of origin. These links may be forged through replacement, through the occupation of the same position in the family, and sometimes through striking or idiosyncratic physical characteristics. However the linkages have been formed, the student of his or her own family will do well to focus particular attention on these linked figures.

Another way to assess data is to search for family themes. Themes may be represented by behaviors repeated throughout the generations. For example, in one family the male line for three generations went away to war, met their spouses and married far from their origins, started new lives, and became part of their wives' families while cutting off from their own families. Another family seems to have a concentration of fragile, ailing women who need protection. And yet another family had more than its share of tragic losses, is preoccupied with loss, constantly and anxiously expecting the next blow.

Family themes may also surface through a discussion of family heroes and heroines. Generally, such larger-than-life people around which family mythology develops express a personification of the family's explicit or implicit values. Sometimes the communications about these heroes or heroines are double-binding as the family shakes their heads over great uncle George who left his family and ran off to the Klondike where he became a millionaire. While the heads are shaking, the family may smile with admiration and pride over his independence and resourcefulness. The telling of such tales, frequently a favorite family occupation, transmits values to the young in a powerful and colorful fashion. Anti-heroes are used in the same way where "cautionary tales" are told of ancestors who took certain paths which led to no good end.

One highly successful professional woman sought help following the ending of her marriage of many years. After her children reached school age, she returned to school to complete her professional degree. The more successful she became, the more ready she felt to leave what had been a suffocating marriage in which, for many years, she had allowed herself to be dominated by a rather limited and rigid husband. Now she was free—and miserable! She had not adequately dealt with the loss, and the work of mourning had to be completed. Mourning, however, did not appreciably lighten her depression. On turning to genogram work, family themes became apparent as she talked about three generations of women in her family. She spontaneously described each woman with superlatives: "brilliant," "creative," "extremely competent." The men in the family were seen as rather narrow and simple. They were frequently controlling and hid their wives' light under a bushel. Only one woman had failed to marry and, although seemingly quite active and fulfilled, was throughout the family an object of pity and scorn. The family myth became clear. "Women in our family have much more talent and creativity and competence than the men they marry, but they must supress their wishes for self-expression and achievement in order to get—and keep—a husband. This self-denial, however, is necessary and, indeed, worth it, because there is nothing worse than a woman without a husband!'' It became clear that this woman was painfully living out the family theme and in these terms, it was a "no win" situation.

THE PROCESS OF
INFORMATION GATHERING

Gathering family data is an arduous and often time-consuming task. However, the process is not merely a prelude to change but itself can bring about considerable change in the family system. This change can occur in a variety of ways. First, as the seeker sets out to gather information about the family, lively and significant communication lines are opened. Such opening of communication around important and shared realities is a major medium for relationship building. This is most dramatically seen when young adults visit aging relatives to gather family information. They may live in different worlds, disagree on many subjects, and they may have struggled with stilted exchanges for years. The one thing they share is that they belong to the same family and as the family pictures and letters and mementoes begin to be pulled out of chests and bottom drawers, a genuine exchange begins to develop. Bowen has suggested that the differentiation process is enhanced by the gathering of factual family information and by the development of a person-to-person relationship with each member of the extended family system. Both things can occur together with resulting system and individual change.

Harry, a 45-year-old man, had never talked alone with his father. His mother had successfully maintained her central positions in a father-mother-son triangle since Harry's boyhood and communications between the two men were transmitted through her. Harry knew almost nothing about his father's early life or family. The father, who was in his eighties, had emigrated from Europe as a young man and been separated from most of his family. Harry planned a visit to his father on an evening when he knew his mother would be out. His evening with his father not only brought forth fascinating and valuable information about his family but also resulted in a kind of closeness and sharing that had never existed between father and son. When Harry left, his father held his hand, and with tears standing in his eyes, thanked him over and over for coming. Harry was jubilant! This major change, however, was not without repercussions. First, the prohibition against direct communication between father and son was demonstrated by the fact that Harry "forgot" to mention the visit to his mother. He finally did mention it to her in a phone call. Two weeks later, when Harry went to have another talk with his father, his mother managed to provoke an argument between father and son. Father became depressed and went to bed. Harry left, angry and let down, and several days passed before he realized that the function of the explosion was to reestablish the old unhappy but familiar equilibrium.

Family study appears to be contagious and this contagion enriches the process as family members begin to share the search. The father of one client, a man in his 70s, responded to his daughter's search by getting reconnected to and gathering information about his own family, from which he had been quite cut off. "I want to do it for you and the children," he said, "but I also want to do it for me."

INTERVENTION

Although gathering family data is both a precursor to and a beginning of personal and family change, the extended family may be a resource for change in other ways. Change strategies may include identifying and overcoming resistances and obstacles to form genuine person-to-person relationships with family members, opening up closed lines of communication, surfacing secrets, demystifying mysterious family members, breaking through cut-offs, altering the family role arrangements by assuming a new role or even sitting in a different seat at Thanksgiving dinner. All of the interventions can bring about system change as well as individual change and enhanced differentiation.

Several issues must be considered when helping a client to embark on such a program for change, or, for that matter, when working on one's own differentiation. Although the route to personal growth may lie in precipitating a change in the total family system, the final objective must be change for the self.[20] The minute people adopt the attitude that they are going to fix up their families, they have probably been caught in old patterns. The families will also experience the change efforts as manipulative or even hostile, and move toward a more rigid and defensive stance.

However, because of the power of the family system and because of the ego syntonic nature of the very things that must be changed, people need to plan and check out their efforts at change and differentiation with someone who is outside the family system, someone who understands family system principles and can help with the objectification process. The internal and external forces against change take many disguises! Without support and help in standing outside the system and in identifying and challenging these forces, it is difficult for people within a system to select and carry through an intervention that may bring about change. The role of this helping person has been variously labeled as coach, family consultant, family therapist. The tasks of a person occupying this role include offering information about family systems, helping to objectify the family system, identifying obstacles to change, helping to devise strategies to bring about change, giving support through the interventive process, and helping to evaluate the change process. The role is as teacher and enabler. The client carries the responsibility for change.

PLANNING AND EXECUTING
CHANGE STRATEGIES

An intervention into the family system should be planned on the basis of a study of the family system and an identification of targets for change. For example, if a major cut-off is surfaced, then a plan may be made for breaking through that cut-off and opening up that part of the system. Careful anticipatory planning with a coach-consultant is also useful because such a move will give rise to considerable anxiety on the part of the client and the family members and all kinds of strategies may be employed to interrupt the process. Careful planning and checking of actions to be taken can help the client recognize and counter these attempts at interruption. For example, in the situation of Harry opening up communication with his father, it would have been useful had he been warned to watch for his mother's attempts to sabotage.

Planning, however, usually cannot take place on the basis of specific long term objectives. Family systems are so complex, the interrelated variables so numerous (and often unknown) that prediction is difficult if not impossible.[21] This suggests that change strategies must be planned on the basis of general hypotheses relating to the nature of family systems but with considerable uncertainty concerning outcome. An intervention can be assessed after the fact when outcomes become observable. The more we learn about the way family systems tend to operate, the more hypotheses we can develop to guide interventions. For example, one hypothesis about family system function is that cut-offs in a family tend to keep family members caught in and unable to integrate whatever is on the other side of the cut-off. On the basis of this, it is possible to plan interventions which involve helping people move across cut-offs and reconnect with family members from whom they have been alienated. Such an intervention, however, will in all likelihood start a chain of reactions reverberating throughout the system. It is just this kind of reaction that leads to the old adage, "Let sleeping dogs lie." However, another hypothesis about family systems suggests that sleeping dogs, though ostensibly quiet, may have major impact on the functioning of the family and its members.

Even what appears to be a very small intervention may start a process leading to considerable change. The following example of what would appear to be a rather minor intervention illustrates the point. One young woman, Carol, whenever she called home, called collect. If her stepfather (who had been married to her mother for 25 years) answered the phone he would accept the charges and immediately call his wife. When the client's mother was not home, he would refuse the call. This pattern is not unusual. Mothers frequently manage a family's communication switchboard. Carol had been thinking about the way her family communicated and the next time she called home, her mother wasn't home, and her stepfather refused the call.

On impulse, Carol called right back and said, "Why is it you will never talk to me? I'd like to talk to you—I don't have to only talk to mother!"

This small intervention set off quite a chain reaction. The stepfather and the mother had a fight about the relationship between Carol and her stepfather. He accused her of not allowing him to share Carol. She accused him of not being interested. Carol's mother attacked Carol for "going behind her back." The upshot of this was that the mother's guilt and unresolved feelings about the death of Carol's father 26 years earlier were surfaced. Carol began to learn more about her biological father and became reconnected not only with her stepfather but also with her biological father's family, from which she had been estranged. In embarking upon systems' intervention, one must be prepared for unanticipated consequences and learn to live with a certain amount of uncertainty.

A second general operating procedure for system change might be phrased "Although the shortest distance between two points is a straight line, a circuitous route is often easier to manage." Frequently the central toxic issue or the major relationship to be altered lies right in the heart of the nuclear family of origin. Although client and coach may agree that it is the ultimate point of intervention, the thought of a direct approach to the person or the issue creates so much anxiety that the client is immobilized and becomes discouraged. An oblique approach via more distant family members seems to diffuse the tension and ready the client eventually to tackle the problem directly. I have a visual image of a person circling in on a sensitive area of the system. The diffusion of nuclear family tension through opening up channels to the extended family appears to be a rather general phenomenon and has led me to encourage people to start family work with a somewhat remote part of the system.

CONCLUSION:
FAMILY SYSTEM WORK—
AN ECOLOGICAL PERSPECTIVE

This model of practice, which uses the extended family system as a resource for and arena of change, is one way of translating ecological principles into practice.

The basic framework and the unit of attention is conceptualized in ecological terms. The individual is understood in the context of his or her social and emotional environment. A salient portion of that environment is the family, and individuals and families are seen as open systems in transaction. The person is in the family and the family is in the person. The focus of study and of intervention is on the transactional relationships between the person and the family in space and through time and the assumption is made that a change in either family or person will interrelate and bring about changes throughout the system. Change is seen as a natural growth process. Differentiation is a process which begins with birth and continues if unobstructed throughout life. Increasing differentiation is a natural phenomenon when living systems are appropriately open.[22] This explains the recurrent emphasis in the model on opening closed communication, breaking through cut-offs, uncovering secrets, etc. On the other hand, again in an ecological perspective, family work is boundary work. Although the effort is to help boundaries remain open, it is also important to strengthen them, to clarify the nature of those boundaries and mark where they exist. Although this may seem like an inconsistency, the aim is for firm but open boundaries. In human interchange, it is people with firm and clear boundaries around the self who can risk openness and intimacy because such intimacy does not pose a threat to the integrity of the self.

Problems or difficulties are seen as the result of interrupted growth and development, as dysfunctional transactions, and as adaptive strategies rather than as disease processes located within the individual. Because of the complexity of causal processes in multivariable systems, no effort is made to find "the cause" and hence "the cure." Rather, interventions are made and tested through monitoring the system's response, primarily through naturalistic observation.

Life experience is the model and the primary instrument for change. Every effort is made to mobilize and employ natural systems for change rather than to develop new or artificial systems. For example, the client is encouraged to work through troublesome relationships with major figures in life, with the people involved, rather than with the therapist through the medium of the transference.

Finally, an ecological model of help, modeling itself on growth and on development, should be progressive rather than regressive.

This has considerable significance in the nature of the interchange between worker and client, leading one to question anything that reduces client autonomy and to seek ways of helping which enhance differentiation. This not only implies avoiding the use of transference but also encourages a move toward a more egalitarian relationship where less authority and power is vested in the helper. Rather, the relationship is redefined as one in which two people are working together on a shared project. Each brings a special expertise to the task. The helper has a certain expertise on the way family systems operate and how they might change. The client is the expert on himself and his own family. Further, there is no hidden agenda and it is the client, not the helper that makes the basic decisions, carries the responsibility for change, and actually performs the change strategies. The helper has knowledge about family systems and also has the advantage of not being a part of the family system being studied. Thus, it is the ''worker's'' role to help the client objectify the family system, help identify, plan and rehearse change strategies, and help discover and overcome obstacles standing in the way of change.

NOTES

1. James Baldwin, review of *Roots* by Alex Haley, *New York Times Book Review,* September 26, 1976, pp. 1–2.

2. Margaret Mead, *Culture and Commitment: A Study of the Generation Gap* (Garden City, New York: Natural History Press/Doubleday, 1970).

3. Milton Mayeroff, *On Caring* (New York: Harper & Row, 1971), chapter 4, ''Special Features in Caring for People.''

4. Ibid., p. 58.

———

1. Jerome Bruner, *On Knowing* (New York: Atheneum, 1966), p. 161.

2. See Ann Hartman, ''To Think About the Unthinkable,'' *Social Casework* 51, no. 8 (October 1970), pp. 467–76.

3. Edgar Auerswald, ''Families, Change, and the Ecological Perspective,'' *Family Process* 10, no. 2 (September 1971), pp. 202–15.

4. Carel Germain, ''An Ecological Perspective in Casework Practice,'' *Social Casework* 54, no. 6 (June 1973), pp. 323–31.

5. Carol Meyer, *Social Work Practice: The Changing Landscape,* 2d ed. (New York: The Free Press, 1976).

6. This interest is expressed in Ann Hartman, "The Generic Stance in the Family Agency," *Social Casework* 55, no. 4 (April 1974), pp. 199–208.

7. Murray Bowen, "The Use of Family Theory in Clinical Practice," in *Changing Families,* ed. Jay Haley (New York: Grune and Stratton, 1971).

8. A paper which had particular meaning to me as a former foster care worker was Fernando Colon's, "In Search of One's Past, an Identity Trip," in *Georgetown Family Symposia,* Vol. I, ed. Francis D. Andres and Joseph P. Lorio (Washington: Georgetown University Medical Center, 1971–72). Also see the other papers in this volume and J. O. Bradt and Carolyn Moynihan, *Systems Therapy* (Washington: Groome Child Guidance Center, 1972).

9. For example, see Mary Richmond, *Social Diagnosis* (New York: Russell Sage, 1917).

10. See E. E. Southard, "The Individual versus the Family as Unit of Interest in Social Work," *Proceedings of the National Conference of Social Work,* 1919, pp. 582–86.

11. *The Family,* published by the Family Welfare Association of America (the national organization which grew out of the Charity Organization movement), began publication in 1919. Its name was later changed to *Social Casework.*

12. See the following accounts of the Family Treatment movement: Murray Bowen, "Family Therapy After Twenty Years," in *The Handbook of Psychiatry* (New York: Basic Books, 1974); and Philip J. Guerin, Jr., "Family Therapy: the First Twenty-Five Years," in *Family Therapy Theory and Practice,* ed. P. J. Guerin, Jr. (New York: Gardner Press, 1976). However, my own impression is that neither of these accounts gives sufficient attention to the contributions made by social workers, for instance in the Jewish Family Agencies in both New York and Chicago. Perhaps a social work doctoral student will be challenged to track down this segment of the sociology of mental health knowledge and practice. For a beginning look at social workers' relationship with the Family Therapy movement see Frances Scherz, "Family Services: Family Therapy," in *Encyclopedia of Social Work* (New York: National Association of Social Workers, 1971), pp. 398–404.

13. Bowen's first presentation on the differentiation of the self in the family of origin and his work on his own family system was given at a conference for family researchers and family therapists in March 1967 at Eastern Pennsylvania Psychiatric Institution in Philadelphia. This paper was later published anonymously in *Family Interaction,* ed. James L. Framo (New York: Springer, 1972). Bowen reports his experience with training in "Toward the Differentiation of Self In One's Family of Origin," in Andres and Lorio, *Georgetown Family Symposia.*

14. One is in a quandary when presenting work influenced or suggested by the work of another. First, differentiation of the self through work with the family of origin is only a part of Bowen's extensive contribution to the field and should be understood in the context of his total theoretical structure. A recent summary of his theory is presented in Murray Bowen, "Theory in the Practice of Psychotherapy," in Guerin, *Family Therapy.*

Second, although influenced by Bowen's writings, what I present here is filtered through my own learning and experience, and as such cannot help but be altered. I would not presume to speak for Bowen but cannot proceed without discussing some of his key concepts. In a sense, an appropriate metaphor for the kind of relationship that exists when practitioners borrow, use, and alter the work of others and then report their efforts can be found in music: I might have called this chapter "Variations on a theme by Bowen."

15. Frederick Duhl, "Intervention, Therapy, and Change," in *General Systems Theory and Psychiatry,* ed. William Gray, Frederick Duhl, and Nicholas Rizzo (Boston, Little Brown, 1969).

16. Philip Guerin, Jr., and Eileen Pendagast, "Evaluation of Family System and Genogram," in P. Guerin (ed.), *Family Therapy.*

17. James Framo has pointed out how useful it is to mention this possibility in the first session, even though it may stimulate some anxiety and resistance. See James Framo, "Family of Origin as a Therapeutic Resource for Adults in Marital and Family Therapy: You Can and Should Go Home Again," *Family Process* 15, no. 2 (June 1976), p. 193–210.

18. Framo uses this method when he has conjoint sessions with one member of a marital pair and members of his or her family of origin. The spouse does not come but the session is recorded and later shared.

19. Walter Toman, *Family Constellations* (New York: Springer, 1961).

20. Edwin Friedman's creative and entertaining tour de force "The Birthday Party, An Experiment in Obtaining Change in One's Own Family" in *Family Process* 10, no. 3 (September 1971), p. 345–60, is a case in point. Friedman, a family therapist and Rabbi plans and executes an elaborate series of manipulations and reversals to bring about change in his family system. He has always occupied the role of "Family Therapist" and "Family Rabbi" in his own family. Throughout the intervention, he ostensibly steps out of these roles through the use of reversals and allows movement for other family members. But it seems to me that Friedman has fallen into the therapy trap. While he seeks to avoid the role of Family Therapist/Rabbi, his objective is nonetheless to bring about change in his family system, thereby continuing the role of Family Therapist.

21. Paul Watzlawick, Janet Beavin, and Don Jackson, in *Pragmatics of Human Communication* (New York: W. W. Norton, 1967), pp. 43–44, discuss the Black Box concept. This concept first originated in World War II when captured enemy equipment could not be opened for study because of the possible danger of triggering an explosive device. The concept has gained wide usage in electronics and more recently in thinking about complex human systems. The point is that when dealing with tremendously complex systems, it may well be expedient to focus on input-output relations rather than to attempt to make predictions on the basis of a knowledge of all the variables within the system.

22. In general systems theory, this phenomenon is called negative entropy. See Ludwig von Bertalanffy, "General Systems Theory and Psychiatry," in *American Handbook of Psychiatry,* ed. Silvano Arieti (New York: Basic Books, 1966).

9 Black Language as an Adaptive Response to a Hostile Environment

BARBARA JONES DRAPER

Black English is not a distortion of Standard English, but is a separate language having its own complex history and autonomous rules.[1] Its speakers, like any speech community, share a set of social conventions about strategies to be used in verbal communication, and rules about the use of metacommunications to signify intent, hidden messages, emotionality, etc. In this essay, Draper considers language as an ecological variable, and takes the position that, among blacks, language functions as a coping maneuver that is highly adaptive in a hostile environment. Viewed ecologically, any language serves to relate its speakers to one another and to the environment in which they are situated. This is particularly clear in the case of Black English, which serves to strengthen the bonds among its speakers, enhance their sense of identity and autonomy, and keep firm the boundary between its speakers and the larger environment. Even though some black slang has crossed over the boundary and become part of the language of the white community, whites still fail to understand Black English and the nonverbal communication patterns of black speakers. Similarly, the formal vocabulary and construction of Standard English used by the middle-class white or black social worker may bewilder or even anger the poor black client.[2]

Whites' unwillingness to consider Black English as a separate language that needs to be learned is nowhere so clear as in the educational system. Here the teacher and the social worker have often regarded the poor black child as unteachable because he does not speak Standard English and has trouble learning to read it. Since he comes with a rich language of his own that does not prepare him for the expectations and tasks of the school setting he needs to be taught Standard English as a second language just as the children of European immigrants needed to become bilingual. His learning task involves mastering two dialects that happen to share some words but are characterized by very real differences that have long been sustained by the caste-like division in the social structure.[3]

In her approach to black language, Draper also makes clear the transactional nature of coping and adaptation and their interdependence with environmental processes. While social and psychological disorganization exists at all levels of the social structure, it has become increasingly clear that behaviors among poorer groups in society, previously interpreted in characterological terms laden with white and middle-class biases, are realistic adaptations to a harsh environment. More importantly, however, black anthropologists and social workers are teaching their white colleagues about the diversity of creative coping mechanisms that flourish in poor black communities. These include the black church, mutual aid systems and processes of neighboring, music and dance, and the warmth and intimacy of language itself—all are bridges to human relatedness and reflections of human strengths.

—C.B.G.

THE RAPIDLY DEVELOPING literature on the structural validity of Black English underscores the logic of its syntax and grammar and the distinctiveness of its vocabulary. Like all other languages, Black English needs to be understood on its own terms and not in comparison with other forms of speech including Standard English. While the work on structure is interesting and pertinent to social work practitioners, it is the functional aspects of language as used by black Americans which I wish to begin to identify in this paper.

Prior to the 1960s, when the slogan ''Black is Beautiful'' helped to universalize a more positive self-image and assertions of group identity among black Americans, the following ironic jingle was well known among blacks:

> If you're white, you're all right;
> If you're yellow, you're my fellow;
> If you're brown, hang around;
> If you're black, stay back!

This verse poignantly and pointedly defined the perceived degree of acceptance of blacks by the larger white society. It demarcated possible levels of entry into the society based on ranges of color visibility. Despite having been an integral part of American life since the early 17th Century, blacks have been forced, until recently, to "stay back," or "keep your place." The force has been exerted through segregation laws and, more insidiously, through overt and covert discriminatory practices.

Stress theorists have pointed to the extremes of disturbance brought about by unusually threatening, damaging, or demanding life circumstances. They have also, however, emphasized the role of personality factors in reaction to stress.[1] These two aspects thus require that stress be defined in terms of the transactions between individuals and situations, rather than in terms of either alone. While there are commonalities in people's behavior under stressful conditions, there are also many variations. If, for example, motivational patterns and belief systems based on cultural values and social experience differ, then the exact conditions that produce psychological stress in one culture may differ from the conditions that produce stress in another culture.

Coping abilities and "adjustment" have traditionally been considered chiefly in terms of the intrapsychic factors which allow people to control psychologically the external stimuli impinging upon them and to maintain a state of personal equilibrium. It is becoming evident, however, that emphasis must be placed on such environmental features of coping as incentives and rewards, social supports, and available information.[2] Thus coping, like stress, reflects the relation between external physical and social demands and the individual's potential to deal with those demands. How the stress is appraised by the person and what coping abilities are used will affect the quality of the adaptive process.

Yet it is assumed that the standards of the dominant white middle-class structure provide the norms by which subcultures may be appropriately measured. Rationalizations for restrictive measures against blacks thus range from inferior genetic and physiological endowment, to intellectual deficit, to the now recently popular, "socially oppressed." These and other catch phrases cast blacks' behavior in pathological terms, as in "culturally deprived," "disadvantaged," "multiproblemed," and "socially handicapped." Such labels become code terms of pseudoclinical entities which disparage the psychological characteristics of the group itself—its levels of perception, cognitive styles, and uses of language.

Chestang attempted to construct a conceptual model for understanding black character structure as it develops in response to a hostile environment that does not consistently provide the supports necessary for effective coping and, indeed, withholds many of them.[3] He cites three conditions as being socially determined and institutionally supported: (1) social injustice; (2) societal inconsistency; and (3) personal impotence. Chestang believes that to function in the face of any one of these does cruel and unusual violence to the personality. To function in the face of all three subjects the personality to severe crippling or even destruction. Yet these three crucial conditions confront the black person throughout his/her life, and in Chestang's view, they determine his/her character development.

I believe, however, that Thomas and Sillen may be more accurate when they point out that

the psychological toll of second-class citizenship and a sense of powerlessness in American society is undeniable. Yet it is profoundly wrong to assume that black people have been overwhelmed by the destructive influences of that racist society. It is one thing to recognize the social handicaps that impede the fulfillment of an individual's potential. It is quite another thing to conclude that the handicap has "crippled" him. . . . Stress may also stimulate healthy coping mechanisms.[4]

An ecological approach to understanding the interaction between an oppressed people and an oppressing society suggests that in order to survive and function, the oppressed group must develop special coping capacities and resources. The sheer ability to survive and cope calls for a kind of adaptive strength that I think is indigenous to being black in American society. Coping patterns reflective of this strength have too often been "clinically" assessed as reflective of deficient character structure or due to faulty social structure (e.g., the black family). Few attempts have been made to define objectively the positive strategies which have enabled blacks to survive and grow within a hostile, ambiguous, and racist environment. Blacks have utilized, for example, the strong primary supports of extended family networks, relying on natural grandparents and/or on "aunts," a familiar, sometimes affectionate title which may or may not have to do with genetic ties. Strong church involvement is another important factor for many. The church socializes and it reaffirms belief in a higher power that can make things better. Then there is a sense of fatalism which is not always negative. For example, "What can I do?" implies a kind of "I can't fight City Hall," so one gets on with the business of *daily* living rather than making future plans. This day-to-day quality, while not "middle-class American," contributes to survival especially among the poor. The ability to go to a neighbor and ask for a few dollars, and to go to another with whom one can leave children while going to the clinic or to the welfare office, is also important. Even the hope of hitting "the number" makes for some stimulus and the possibility of having extra change to buy things otherwise not possible.

In a similar way, blacks have utilized language (along with music and humor) as a basic strategy for coping with the stress of living in a racist society. The use of Black English serves to create and sustain a sense of identity both for the individual and group. Moreover it is also a mode of adaptation that preserves a degree of autonomy from the demands and assaults of the larger society. As a boundary-strengthening or distancing device Black English enables its speakers to communicate safely within the group while effectively shutting whites out of the communication process.

This distancing phenomenon was experienced by two white students working with groups of black adolescent junior high school girls. Interestingly both students recorded a feeling a being "excluded" at some point in the group interaction. One illustration highlights this:

. . . All through their project they talked (loudly!) about all the fights they'd had or were going to have. They talked "around" me and K. (an unusually quiet member who was "strange" to the others and isolated by them) as if we were not there. As we moved from the kitchen into the front room, the same behavior continued and got increasingly raucous and excluding. . . . I knew I had to draw the group's attention. I could doubtless have done this by leaving, but I didn't want to leave K. "alone." I went back to the front room with the N.Y. *Times* in hand. I sat near K. and I whispered to her that I felt left out and she might too. She did. . . . I told the group that if they want to have a discussion, they can meet on a corner after school and do the same thing. I asked the girls to think about how this group is different. "What are we supposed to be doing here?" B. said, "I don't know . . . have fun and talk to each other." I said, "and listen." I told them I didn't enjoy conversations I could not understand and was not included in. They got serious almost immediately.

Both groups terminated abruptly after these exclusionary sessions despite outreach attempts. It seems unlikely that the same result would have happened with a black worker. The white workers literally could not understand the language being used and could not reproduce it in process recording for supervisory purposes. It would be interesting and helpful to have similar processes taped and interpreted by black and white workers to determine if there is a real difference in perception and understanding of language content in Black English.

Haskins and Butts have referred to the complication of the interface between oppression and verbal behavior:

One may consider verbal behavior in blacks as serving several functions: (1) as a defense against individualized and institutionalized racist behavior in whites; (2) as an aspect of the black life-style reflecting a healthy group narcissism, cohesive bonds, and affections; (3) as an avenue for the release of rage, fear, guilt, and other affects on an individual basis.[5]

The aforementioned example of the adolescent group illustrates one of these functions. In addition, the group's verbal behavior served a territorial function by defending the group's boundary against intrusion into the members' physical and social space by the two white students. Phrases such as "Keep in your place" and "If you're black, stay back" refer to the boundaries around social space exerted by whites.

Immigrant parents commonly use their native language when discussing adult concerns before their native-born children, nations utilize linguistic ciphers to protect matters involving national security, and even children create secret languages such as Pig Latin as devices for separating themselves from an out-group or in-group. Culturally based linguistic features such as pronunciation, rhythym, duration, and pacing of speech, its pitch and volume, along with nonverbal body behaviors, may be used by blacks as boundary-maintenance functions. They protect the integrity of the speaker's or the group's social and physical space. In the process, identity and autonomy are enhanced, thus strengthening adaptation.

While discussing language as a common speech, as a symbol of social solidarity, Edward Sapir acknowledged the existence of sub-forms of language among groups of people such as families or ethnic groups who are held together by ties of common interest.[6] Subgroups tend to develop their own peculiarities of speech which have the symbolic function of distinguishing the group from the larger group into which its members might otherwise be too completely absorbed. The use of specific words peculiar to the group declares the speaker to be a member of a perhaps unorganized but psychologically real group. The really important function of language, in Sapir's view, is to declare constantly to society the psychological place held by all its users. It can serve as a substitute means of expression for those who are barred from taking primary action upon their environments.

A classic cartoon which originally appeared in the now defunct black newspaper, *The Chicago Defender,* depicts two black street characters. They are busily gesticulating to each other as they leave two white police officers who are leaning against a patrol car after "apprehending" them and then letting them go. One character says to the other:

Alright, alright! So what if I did sing a couple of stanzas of Dixie and cut a few buck and wing steps back there. It saved the both of us from going to jail for vagrancy. The trouble with you is that you don't know how to differentiate between tomming* and progressive maneuvering.

It is often difficult for white people, who believe they are liberal and aware of the negatives inherent in a racist society, to understand the reason for the persistence of humor in black language or the ironic way in which blacks speak of themselves with a directness that would not be tolerated coming from a white counterpart. For example, whites rarely understand how the word "nigger" coming

---

* A servile manner before whites.

from them may evoke a possible reaction of physical violence but can be so loosely used among blacks themselves. *The Dictionary of Afro-American Slang* explains why:

Nigger: (possibly from the French negre), when used by a white person, usually it is offensive and disparaging; used by black people among themselves, it is a racial term with undertones of warmth and good will—reflecting, aside from irony, a tragi-comic sensibility that is aware of black history.[7]

Such a term used among blacks, then, in contrast to the usual interpretation of professionals, does not necessarily convey "self-hatred," or a "negative self-image." The burden of proof is on the person doing the labeling, and interpretation should always be related to the context of the specific situation.

A young white student was seeing a 14-year-old black adolescent who was experiencing many stresses: separation of parents, increased responsibilities towards his mother and siblings with whom he lived, split alliances with his father, father's girlfriend and their new baby, loss of a social studies teacher who taught black history, as well as undergoing expectable adolescent confusion. In the context of one interview, the student/worker noted:

. . .C. calls *some* blacks "niggers" when he thinks they "act up," and he may therefore have a low self-image. He wants to move where there are no "niggers." Through black history books and discussion he may improve his self-image.

While the worker has some awareness that the word "nigger" was used in this context to define those perceived as bad or undependable, which is one of the dichotomies in urban street language, it is in no way safe to generalize this to the person's own self-concept. C's wish to know more of black history also should not be interpreted primarily as a means of improving a negative self-image since he had not expressed such denigrative ideas. Rather, he had genuinely wanted to understand more of that knowledge which had been withheld from him.

Sapir[8] considered language to be a homogenous medium for the handling of all references and meanings of which a given culture is capable, whether these are in the form of actual comunication or such ideal communication substitutes as thinking. Once the form of a language is established it can discover meanings for its speakers which are not simply traceable to the given quality of experience itself but must be explained to a large extent as the projection of potential meanings into the raw material of experience. Sapir suggests, for example, that the choice of words in a particular context may convey the *opposite* of what they mean on the surface. The same external message is differently interpreted according to whether the speaker has this or that psychological status in his personal relations, or whether such primary expressions as affection, anger, or fear may inform the spoken words with a significance which completely transcends their normal value.

Similarly, Grace Sims Holt, a black professor of speech, has called this apparently paradoxical process "inversion," a process by which minority groups protect their individual and cultural identity against the caste definitions imposed by the dominant culture.[9] In her view, the phenomenon of inversion is a practical necessity for people in subordinate positions. Once the physical and legal chains on black people were removed, language became the major vehicle for whites to continue subsequent stages of oppression. White verbal behavior toward blacks defines, forces acceptance of, and controls the existing levels of restraint. Blacks clearly recognized that to master the language of whites was, in effect, to consent to be mastered by it through the white definitions of caste built into the semantic/social system. Inversion therefore becomes the defensive or adaptive mechanism which enables blacks to fight linguistic and psychological entrapment. The traditional process of inversion was based on the concept that while black skin cannot be disguised, speech can be, which then permits one to turn the tables verbally on an unknowledgeable antagonist.

In practicing inversion, the skillfulness is in the creation of the manipulator. The burden of the interpretation is always on the person receiving the image reversal. . . . Though the function (of inversion) is self-assertive, the process is a hidden dimension which remains quantitatively reduced (abandoned by blacks when picked up by whites) but qualitatively great. . . . The objective is no longer mere survival, but cultural and racial self-assertiveness.[10]

Protective adaptive responses are not only reactive to a stressful society but, to some extent, they have developed independently of the response to racism. This aspect of the black experience is conceptualized in the word "soul," currently in black speech.

Soul is love, and it's fed by the Southern farm and the big city ghetto. It's being flexible, spontaneous. The soul brother is sensitive and frank. He's cool too; he judges things by what he sees, not just by what credentials say. Where black people meet, you find a special warmth that you don't find any other place. Soul brothers can communicate by using only the essence of the message—straight to the point. Results are an effort to achieve a life-sustaining culture, perpetuating intimacy and affection with other blacks.[11]

An aspect of black verbal culture, often overlooked, is that it is a vital organization which thrives on what would appear to be emotional paradoxes. Sapir alluded to this phenomenon in his notion that the external message of language depends upon the psychological status of the person/groups.[12] Historically, it did not take the black slaves long to understand that whatever they said to their white masters, or even to each other, must be couched in words with double meanings, as half-truths, or in other forms that would ensure their own personal safety. They quickly became adept at such survival mechanisms. Thus the black person, South or North, has learned to accommodate whites. I do not mean "accommodate" in its usual meaning of "going along with" but in the adaptive sense. Blacks learned to use the complete inventory of speech intonation (e.g., the range from the soft-spoken "mumblin' word" to the hostile, loud, aggressive distancing associated with whites' image of the so-called "hostile black male"), gesture, and facial expression (impassive) to produce whatever appearance would be acceptable and life-saving. Most blacks, consciously or unconsciously, have developed a keen perception of what affects, motivates, and appeases the authority figures, usally white, with whom they interact.

This necessity for subtlety and deception probably also influenced the prolific production of black folklore and proverbs, the advantage of which is indirection. "Don Say No Mo Wid Yo Mouf Than Yo Back Kin Stan,"is a pointed illustration.

Too many professionals coming from narrow theoretical or practice viewpoints that emphasize a certain kind of communication skill have considered the black client to be "nonverbal." Black people themselves have always known differently. As Dr. Joseph White, former Director of Black Studies at the University of California at Irvine, pointed out, black culture *is* an oral culture.[13] Such oral expressions as the blues, the gospel songs, the heavy rap,* the sermon, and other oral traditions must be considered in order to reach an understanding of the psychological functioning of black people.

As a social worker, I believe there are profound implications for practice as the profession attempts in a more consistent way to understand and work with those adaptive mechanisms or coping abilities, including language, that are necessary to meet environmental and intrapsychic demands. In this connection, it is important to remember that social work has its own language system which not only has had the positive function of helping to maintain professional identity and a sense of belonging for its practitioners, but also has had the negative consequence of excluding a large proportion of poor blacks and other minorities from its services. The first task is to bring into awareness the pervasive ways in which black clients' cultural differences have been defined: "deviant,' "pathological," "culturally deprived," "nonverbal," "unmotivated." The second is to realize that the white worker, too, is a product of having grown up in a racist society. Prejudices and stereotypes are often just out of the awareness of even the most well-meaning worker who sincerely believes he/she is not racist at all. I recall a senior white faculty member who, in regard to my entering a doctoral program, asked me an apparently innocuous, "Can you write?" The question was insulting, and reflected the unfortunate general assumption in education circles that blacks can't "write." The question told me, as it has done for so many other blacks, that I was not an individual but just another piece of blackness!

---

* To hold conversation in long, impressive monologues.

At another time, as the supervisor of a bright, liberal, white, graduate social work student who had worked with another minority group in the midwest, I was discussing the pros and cons of growing up in a small Southern town. Her perky and well-meaning response was, "Well, I guess it was better than growing up in the ghetto!" Implicit here are two assumptions: first, that all or most blacks grow up in the ghetto and second, that this is necessarily a demeaning and generalizable experience.

Again, another white student made a home visit to a minority client who had a well-kept, well-appointed apartment. Upon returning to the agency, the student firmly stated in a relevatory manner that she *knew* the client was *into* something (i.e., some illegal activity) or how else could she have such a nice apartment!

A similar lack of understanding can be expressed by some blacks. In a mental health agency serving primarily black clients, a middle-class black psychiatrist, himself unfamiliar with some black expressions, explained in a team conference the "schizophrenic thought process" of a client who frequently used the word "evil" to describe a family member. The black workers looked at each other in disbelief, since "evil" usually does not imply deep intrapsychic disturbance but refers to someone who is ill-tempered or with whom it is difficult to get along.

These few examples I believe illustrate the lack of understanding such use of language conveys. When we professionals use terms such as "unmotivated client," we might rather reverse the application to "unmotivated worker." It is often the worker who lacks motivation to understand the unique cultural differences of the client group with which he works. How blacks use or don't use traditional professional services (usually set up under white middle-class professional standards) is determined by the way in which blacks perceive their existence in this society. With the motivation to understand, white professionals could become more open to learning from black culture. Interaction between black client and white worker could then become a two-way process instead of the one-way process it has been historically.

There has been a polite avoidance of discussion of behavioral, cultural, and ethnic differences even when they were most apparent.

Since these differences have been viewed as deviant by most social scientists, to discuss them in great detail was assumed to be rude. Another more pressing reason why both middle-class blacks and liberal whites have been reluctant to discuss these differences is fear that such discussions will be used maliciously by racists to support their theories of black inferiority.

Baratz and Baratz[14] caution that there is a two-fold difficulty inherent in this reasoning: (1) not talking about differences does nothing to make them disappear, and (2) not recognizing the distinctive behavior within a particular cultural model leaves the liberal with only one alternative, that of calling the black American a sick white man—sick in the social rather than genetic sense.

For the white worker who deals with black clients, it is essential that the black client be met on his own terms, that his own modes of communication be accepted and understood. The black client must not be judged by a normative middle-class white standard, one which is now proving not to have been that viable even for whites. To begin to understand the black experience, the white worker must try to enter the life space of the black client. He/she must listen to the expressions of black language, its sounds and meanings. Read black literature, and newspapers. Listen to black radio stations to get with the tempo and temper of blacks' feelings. Leave the office and walk around in black neighborhoods—look at the parts that are slums, but also acknowledge the blocks that are kept with pride. Look at the addict and pimp but also see those who carry themselves with dignity. Look at the hustler but also see the shopkeeper, the dentist, the doctor. Go with the black client to the hospital and the social service center. Notice the very real differences in the way services are often given to black and white clients. Really listen and observe, and you will readily see that in the use of language, blacks touch and feel, hurt, cry, and laugh. Most of all, learn to individualize. There is infinite variety among blacks whether in the metropolis or the small town.

Communication primarily through the interview is, after all, a basic social work tool. We teach our students interviewing skills and techniques; how to become cognizant of verbal as well as nonverbal clues. In addition to the form of the language used in communication, we might also learn to pay more attention to the content inherent in the communication. For example, the heavy "rap" or "calling the dozens" of the street kid may not necessarily represent grandiosity, overcompensation, circumstantiality, hostility, etc., but a style which indicates sheer satisfaction from telling a good story or getting the best of a peer, or keeping the worker at a distance.

Most schools of social work now have at least one elective course on one or more minority cultures. Such courses should be required. Either in these electives or in practice courses, sensitivity exercises could be given to heighten awareness of student attitudes. Minority vocabulary tests could be given at some point to determine the level of understanding of subgroup language. It would be interesting to note the experience of failure in those who do not score high, the same sense of failure that many blacks and other minority group members feel when confronted with the demands of communicating according to white middle-class expectations.

As the profession moves away from the deficit model or the culture-of-poverty model towards emphasis on looking at the transactions between clients and their environments and between worker and client, less emphasis will be placed on deviance from a supposed normative standard. More emphasis will be placed on seeking out and understanding adaptive mechanisms uniquely suited to particular environments and stages of the life cycle, and on generating environmental supports when they are lacking. If attempts are made to understand the uniqueness of the black experience from a black perspective, we may begin new ways of service delivery to the black community through active cooperation rather than imposition, and we will utilize the creative survival mechanisms of black people.

NOTES

1. J. L. Dillard, "General Introduction: Perspectives on Black English," in *Perspectives on Black English,* ed. J. Dillard (The Hague: Mouton & Co., 1975), pp. 9–32.

2. Peter Farb, *Word Play: What Happens When People Talk,* (New York: Alfred A. Knopf, 1974). See especially chapter 7, "Linguistic Chauvinism."
3. Dillard, p. 27. See also J. L. Dillard, *Lexicon of Black English* (New York: The Seabury Press, 1977) for a helpful discussion of the use of terms in various sociolinguistic domains.

1. Richard Lazarus, *Psychological Stress and the Coping Process* (New York: McGraw Hill, 1966), pp. 2–23.
2. David Mechanic, "Social Structure and Personal Adaptation," in Coelho et al., *Coping and Adaptation* (New York: Basic Books, 1974), pp. 32–47.
3. Leon Chestang, "Character Development in a Hostile Environment," *Occasional Paper Number 3,* University of Chicago School of Social Service Administration, November 1972, p. 2.
4. Alexander Thomas and Samuel Sillen (eds.), *Racism and Psychiatry* (New York: Brunner/Masel, 1972), p. 47.
5. Jim Haskins and Hugh F. Butts, M.D., "Don Say No Mo Wid Yo Mouf Than Yo Back Kin Stan," *The Psychology of Black Language* (New York: Barnes and Noble, 1973), p. 13.
6. Edward Sapir, *Culture, Language and Personality: Selected Essays*, ed. David Mandelbaum (Berkeley and Los Angeles: University of California Press, 1956).
7. Clarence Major, *The Dictionary of Afro-American Slang* (New York: International Publishers, 1970), p. 85.
8. Sapir, *Culture, Language, and Personality.*
9. Grace Sims Holt, "Inversion in Black Communication," in *Rappin' and Stylin' Out: Communication in Urban Black America,* ed. Thomas Kochman (Urbana: University of Illinois Press, 1972), pp. 152–59.
10. Ibid., 158–59.
11. Haskins and Butts, *Don Say No Mo,* p. 26.
12. Sapir, *Culture, Language.*
13. Quoted in Thomas and Sillen, *Racism,* p. 65.
14. Joan Baratz and Stephen Baratz, "Black Culture on Black Terms, a Rejection of the Social Pathology Model," in Kochman, *Rappin,* pp. 3–16.

10 Promoting Competence Through Life Experiences

ANTHONY N. MALUCCIO

Maluccio revives the notion of the therapeutic potential of life events first enunciated by Grete Bibring and by Lucille Austin in the 1940s.[1] Overlooked in subsequent theoretical developments until recently, the idea is presented by Maluccio in the light of new knowledge bearing upon the ecological perspective. The author demonstrates, across various areas of practice, the practicality of utilizing life events for the development of creative adaptation and competence.

Grete Bibring, a psychoanalyst and consultant to social workers, acknowledged that psychotherapy represents an imitation of life processes, and she believed that both life and psychotherapy achieve similar results in similar ways.[2] She declared that just as changes in real life conditions can create neuroses, they can make neuroses disappear. Such changes are not necessarily time-limited.

Lucille Austin, in her analysis of the various forms of casework treatment, suggested that stimulating growth experiences in the environment is an important part of psychotherapy.[3] Constructing positive experiences in the social reality of life itself can lead to more adequate functioning, increased satisfaction, and ego growth.

Bernard Bandler, a psychoanalyst, writing in the early 1960s, was the first to propose a life model of practice for social work.[4] He underscored the importance of working with the progressive forces in the personality, while simultaneously helping to remove blocks and obstacles to growth. A singular contribution lies in Bandler's suggestion that helping procedures be patterned on what parents do to raise well-adapted children rather than on what the physician does with patients. It might be added that helping procedures modelled on the ways people in real life actually cope with stress, adapt creatively and actively, and incorporate new attitudes and values, will also help in the design of more effective help to those whose coping and adaptive efforts have not been successful. There is also work to be done on developing procedures for influencing the environment to be more responsive to human needs, although Bandler did not himself refer explicitly to the environment, except for a brief reference to interpersonal conflict.

Genevieve Oxley developed a life model approach to therapeutic change in the person, related to how change occurs naturally in life situations.[5] She identified five ways in which personal change occurs: maturation, interaction, action, learning, and crisis resolution. This is a significant contribution, although the onus for change seems still to remain largely with the individual, and the necessary nutriments from the environment are not given explicit attention. Herbert Strean applied life model ideas to casework, but retained medical model ideas so that important distinctions were blurred.[6]

In the essay that follows, Maluccio relates the therapeutic potential of life experiences to the context in which they occur. He makes clear that promoting adaptation through action in the life space requires environmental supports. At times, perhaps, the most effective help lies in restructuring the situation so that inner needs are met and inner conflicts avoided or contained.

—C.B.G.

To get along is not to be "sick" and in need of "treatment" or to be in psychiatric jeopardy and in need of "support" or "evaluation." To get along is to live, to manage from day to day—which means one is not a case history, but rather has a life-history.

—Robert Coles [1]

THE "LIFE HISTORIES" of human beings who come to the attention of social workers reflect varied and creative strivings *to get along* while subject to a complex and changing array of environmental challenges. Consequently, social workers have long been concerned with enhancing the dynamic transaction between people and their environments. In particular, in their practice with individuals, families, or groups, they have relied on the purposive use of life experiences such as activities and relationships.

Leading theorists have also recognized the critical role of life experiences and events in social work intervention and have stressed the

I wish to thank Ronald Fleming, Bonnie Heilig, Karen Holzman, and Susan Pokorny, who provided some of the case illustrations included in this chapter.—A.N.M.

importance of changing the person's environment in order to mobilize natural opportunities for growth.[2]

Despite the long-standing professional interest in life experiences, the full potential of this type of intervention has not been realized, partly because of the lack of an appropriate conceptual framework. Through a focus on the adaptive fit and reciprocal processes between people and their environments, the emerging ecological perspective and life model of practice offer guidelines and action principles that can enrich the planful use of life experiences in social work.[3] In this chapter, I will discuss and illustrate how social work practice based on these guidelines and principles can facilitate natural adaptive processes and promote human competence in dealing with environmental challenges.

THE CONCEPT OF COMPETENCE

We begin with an overview on the concept of *competence,* since it has attracted limited attention in the social work literature. By competence I mean the repertoire of skills, knowledge, and qualities that enable each person to interact effectively with the environment. To be useful in practice, this concept must be examined in its multiple bio-psycho-social dimensions.

Theorists from diverse disciplines stress the importance of competence in human growth and development. From the perspective of ego psychology, Robert White,[4] a psychologist, defines competence as the person's achieved capacity to interact effectively with his environment, or the cumulative result of the history of his transactions with the environment. In his formulation, the key features of competence are self-confidence, ability to make decisions, and trusting one's judgment. The ego is strengthened through the cumulative experience of producing desired effects upon one's surroundings.

Thomas Gladwin,[5] an anthropologist, believes that social competence develops along three interrelated axes: 1) "the ability to learn or to use a variety of alternative pathways or behavioral responses in order to reach a given goal"; 2) "[the ability to comprehend and use] a variety of social systems within society [and in particular to utilize] the resources that they offer"; and 3) "effective reality testing [involving] broad and sophisticated understanding of this world.'' Gladwin's formulation differs from White's in its emphasis on the knowledge and skills needed by the individual in order to deal with societal requirements and to use social systems for the purpose of achieving personal goals. Gladwin also adds the essential factor of social feedback or social reinforcement to White's notion of the intrinsically rewarding and motivating aspects of the person's actions.

Embodying the symbolic-interactionist tradition in sociology and social psychology, Nelson Foote and Leonard Cottrell[6] conceive of competence in interpersonal terms and define it as the ability to perform certain kinds of tasks and to control ''the outcome of episodes of interaction.'' They argue that competence consists of the following components, found to some degree in everyone: health; intelligence; empathy; autonomy; judgment; and creativity. In their view, these abilities govern interpersonal relations.

M. Brewster Smith,[7] a social psychologist, proposes an integrative conception of competence. In his formulation, competence involves intrinsic as well as extrinsic motivation, social skills as well as personal abilities, and effective performance for *self* as well as *society* in one's social roles. Competent human functioning is influenced by a number of factors in the personal system of the organism and in the social structure. The key factors in the personal system are: the sense of efficacy or potency in controlling one's destiny; the attitude of *hope;* and a favorable level of *self-respect* or *self-acceptance.* Corresponding environmental inputs or components in the social system are: *opportunity* (e.g., supports or resources), which stimulates and reinforces the sense of hope; *respect by others,* which provides the social ground for respect of self; and *power,* which guarantees access to opportunity.[8]

These varying formulations highlight the notion that the drive toward competence is an important force in human behavior. As noted by Gordon Allport:

It would be wrong to say that ''a need for competence'' is the simple and sovereign motive of life. It does, however, come as close as any need (closer than the sexual) to summing up the whole biological story of development. We survive through competence, we grow through competence, we become ''self-actualizing'' through competence.[9]

The quality and level of competence in each human being contribute to his or her coping capacities and to the dynamic process of adaptation.

SIGNIFICANCE FOR SOCIAL WORK

Concepts of competence help to focus attention on the person's life space or environmental context. As indicated by Gladwin,

Competence is most effectively achieved when intervention is directed toward an ecological unit, consisting of a person and his immediate social environment.[10]

The outcome of the human being's efforts to cope successfully with life tasks depends not only on his or her qualities and needs but also on the availability and purposive use of varied environmental resources and social supports. Consequently, a major function of social work intervention is to provide opportunities for enhancing the mutual fit between people and their environments.

The dual focus in social work practice is on restructuring the environment and setting in motion natural adaptive processes in the client system. Toward this end, there is emphasis on opportunities for enhancing autonomy, on client tasks and activities, and on life experiences. In particular, life experiences play a major role in individual adaptation and the quest for competence.

Bobby, age 9, had been referred to a child guidance clinic by the school because of his acting out behavior in the classroom. He was living with his 34-year-old mother and a 5-year-old sister. His parents had been divorced for over three years and he had no contact with his father, who had moved to another state. The family was receiving public assistance.

Mrs. Cain worried about Bobby's "wildness." He had been on sedatives for a year and was subdued but withdrawn and depressed. When he was not medicated, Bobby's wild and destructive behavior (e.g., breaking toys) evoked in his mother a fear that he would grow up to be "vicious" like his father. Bobby looked terribly sad for a 9-year-old boy; his tightly curled dark hair and tight posture augmented his frightened, lonely appearance. He was seen by his teachers as incorrigible and aggressive, thus leading to his being rejected by teachers as well as peers. In addition, he suffered from learning difficulties.

Play and group therapy were used initially to enhance Bobby's sense of self. At the same time, the social worker and psychiatrist met on several occasions with the school staff to discuss Bobby's special needs and to facilitate coordination of services within the school setting. Through this process, his teachers gained some understanding of the particularly frightening experiences in Bobby's early life. They shifted their views and expectations of him and altered the program to suit his learning needs and styles.

Meanwhile, the worker used sessions with Mrs. Cain to support her efforts to act in several directions. She and Mrs. Cain met regularly with the school staff to review Bobby's functioning and discuss ways of coping with him. With the worker's encouragement. Mrs. Cain successfully petitioned the local Board of Education to provide busing for Bobby, who formerly was required to walk a difficult route of nearly one mile. Mrs. Cain also permitted Bobby and his sister to play with neighborhood children under her supervision. Her more active involvement increased her enjoyment of her child. As Mrs. Cain was helped to understand the perceptual difficulties that were interfering with Bobby's learning, she also became more tolerant of his slowness and frustration in the school setting. At the same time, she was less threatened by Bobby's "wildness" and became his advocate in the family and the neighborhood.

As Mrs. Cain's energies were mobilized in concrete tasks, her sense of adequacy as a single parent increased. She worked to disentangle herself from an in-law system which pressed feelings of shame and embarrassment on her and the children. She was able to mourn her lost marriage and to vent her rage at the broken marital contract. She sought legal counsel in efforts to obtain support payments from her former husband. At the same time, she made the father less of a phantom for the children by talking about him and listening to their feelings and concerns regarding separation from him.

With Bobby and his mother, the worker eventually arranged for a special education teacher to work informally with Bobby and his family after school. The worker supervised this relationship until there was a clear contract between the family and the teacher. The teacher gradually became an important family friend. He included Bobby in his own family's recreational activities and cultural and outdoor pursuits. There were also opportunities for Bobby to meet and play with a new and less threatening peer group. Bobby's demands on his mother became less intense with this additional "parenting" and his relationships with neighborhood children improved.

During more than two years of contacts with the clinic, there were significant changes in these people's lives. Bobby received an award as Most Improved Student. Along with his academic progress, he was involved in the Cub Scouts. The family moved to a more adequate dwelling, following a long struggle to find one they could afford within the real limitations imposed by the welfare allotment. Mrs. Cain went to work part-time. She began to think of her own future. She went back to school, determined to escape from the dehumanizing conditions of welfare dependency, and following upon her recent engagement to a man who got along well with her children. As her own future broadened, so did her ability to help her son to grow and develop.

The social worker located the sources of stress in the inadequacies existing within the social situation rather than in the personalities of family members. She therefore concentrated on helping them to create new resources and find better environments. Concrete changes such as moving to a new dwelling helped to create a more nurturing environment. There was some restructuring of the family's internal environment, as the worker held family meetings including Mrs. Cain, Bobby, and his younger sister. These sessions helped to alter communication patterns within the family and to make family interaction more positive. Bobby's school milieu was enriched and rendered more responsive to Bobby's needs, as reflected in the more positive attitudes of school personnel and the timely introduction of a supportive, special education teacher in his life space.

A major thrust in the worker's efforts was to help the mother identify and mobilize her own resources. By being involved in explicit contract negotiations with the worker, mother and son were able to sharpen their capacities for decision-making and to increase their control over their own lives.[11] In addition, through the worker's encouraging her involvement with the school staff and Board of Education, the mother further developed her sense of autonomy and became more competent. Her expanded ego functioning in a variety of roles, especially in that of single parent, reflected a more satisfying adaptation in the face of real life demands.

Mother-child interaction became more constructive and mutually rewarding, especially as Bobby achieved positive changes in his functioning in response to a more nurturing school and home environment, the individual relationship with a male teacher, and more satisfying transactions with his peers. In short, as they gained opportunity, respect, and power,[12] both mother and son engaged in more successful coping, which in turn led to further growth in their self-esteem and competence.

This case suggests a number of points for further consideration in each of the following areas: (1) using life experiences; (2) life space interviewing; and (3) restructuring the environment.

USING LIFE EXPERIENCES

In his discussion of the role of extratherapeutic experiences in psychoanalysis, Franz Alexander[13] stressed the value of "successful attempts at productive work, love, self-assertion, or competition." Similarly, the insights of ego psychology underscore the ego's growth through the person's involvement in activities that provide for need satisfaction, task fulfillment, crisis resolution, and learning of social skills. Engagement in purposive, goal-directed activities stimulates coping efforts and strengthens adaptive capacities. The experience of success in natural life activities enhances personal well-being and encourages new trials. "Effective doing" contributes to present competence and to versatility and effective coping strategies in future life situations.

Life itself is viewed as the arena of change: life experiences, events, and processes can be exploited for their "therapeutic value" as a means of providing effective help. Thus, action is used for enhancement of the client's self-image, development of autonomy, competence, growth, and mastery, and the release of latent potentialities and innate creativity.[14] Clients' own situations are used to generate opportunities for the productive use of coping, striving, and goal-directed action.

Mrs. Franklin, a middle-aged woman, was incapable of functioning on her own following her husband's recent death. After helping her to work through some of her grief reaction, the worker encouraged her to pursue a variety of activities, including arranging for a repairman to fix the oil burner, completing a clothes shopping program, and looking for a job.

As she slowly began these critical tasks with the worker's continued support, Mrs. Franklin enhanced her sense of autonomy, gained desperately needed feelings of competence, and improved her skills in dealing with her environment.

In another instance, an outreach social worker from a community mental health center became acquainted with a number of elderly persons who were living in fear in an inner city housing project. They were especially terrified by the youth gangs that roamed through the neighborhood committing acts of vandalism.

The worker established contact with several gang leaders and decided to try to bring them together with some of the elderly persons. After extensive, advance work with each of them, the worker succeeded in bringing together the gang leaders and older persons in a series of informal meetings.

Following a difficult initial confrontation, the meetings gradually became productive for both groups. The youth leaders gained some appreciation of the adults' fears and set out to develop ways of helping them not only to feel more secure but also to meet some of their daily needs such as shopping. In return, the "gang" members received modest financial compensation.

Resources to aid both groups were thus mobilized within their natural life context. The older people gained some control over their realistic fears by successfully confronting their youthful neighbors. The younger people learned to channel their energies into constructive and satisfying activities.

Social workers can help to bring out creative strivings and potentialities by providing diverse opportunities for action and facilitating the client's selection of the action most suited to his unique characteristics and adaptive capacities. Environmental diversity taps individual capacities and stimulates the development of alternative behaviors.

Natural life events can also be exploited to promote competence. Life transitions, life tasks, and new social roles provide opportunities for personal growth and learning of new social skills.[15] Human problems, needs, and conflicts need to be translated into adaptive tasks providing the client with opportunities for growth, mastery, and competence development. Thus, a couple experiencing marital discord were engaged in the task of identifying the factors leading to their persistent arguments. An older man facing eviction from his home was encouraged to look into the availability of other apartments. A recently widowed mother was helped to reassess her work skills and to explore various job possibilities. A neglectful parent was helped to learn skills in child care.

In these examples, tasks are designed to coincide as closely as possible with the client's needs and qualities, and to maximize possibilities for effective interaction. Such possibilities exist in many client situations, although they may be hard to find or obscured by the person's seeming resistance, lack of motivation, resignation, or helplessness. In the latter situations it is especially important for the worker to be persistent and imaginative in identifying latent strengths or creating new opportunities. As seen in the following case, individuals and families in impoverished environments need a great deal of help to restore their capacity to cope with life tasks, and to reexperience a state of hopefulness.

The Royces were a disorganized, inner-city family leading a marginal existence on public welfare. Since her husband's desertion several years before, 46-year-old Mrs. Royce had been struggling to care for her six children, who ranged in age from 7 years to the early 20s. The oldest son was in and out of jail in connection with various burglaries. A 20-year-old daughter was recently divorced and had returned to the family with her 2-year-old child. A teenage son was in a half-way house for retarded youth and frequently came home on weekends. The next child, a 16-year-old boy, periodically suspended from school, was awaiting placement in a residential treatment center for the emotionally disturbed. The two youngest children, a boy and a girl, were in first and third grade respectively. They were frequently absent from school and doing poor academic work. Both had been repeatedly involved in minor acts of vandalism in the school and neighborhood.

There was little evidence of competence on the part of family members. They were perceived as failures by the numerous agencies and institutions with which they were involved. They also viewed themselves as incompetent and inadequate—a view that was constantly reinforced by daily events in their chaotic lives. In short, the Royces exemplified the dehumanizing process through which social class factors and a debased status interact with harsh environments to produce vicious cycles of failure, frustration, and self-defeat. Ultimately the individual's spark toward competence motivation is dampened.[16]

The Royces were referred to a family service agency by the Protective Services Unit, after the latter received a complaint that the mother was neglecting the younger children. The reason for referral was to "help Mrs. Royce learn how to manage her children." Following several home visits, the family service worker was impressed by the mother's determination to keep the family together and by the children's affection for each other. With the family, she planned the following interventions: locating additional sources of financial assistance; family meetings to help the family introduce order into its interactions and to support Mrs. Royce's parental role; homemaker service to free Mrs. Royce to pursue her own interests for the first time in years; collaboration with school personnel to provide special services to several of the children; involvement of the children in recreational activities at a community center; and collaboration with a church to help Mrs. Royce and several other mothers to establish their own day care center in the community.

After a year of intensive work, the Royce family was less disorganized and its members were involved in their multiple and complex tasks. Mrs. Royce especially was more self-confident and active in her role as parent. Her greatest satisfaction was in receiving positive reinforcement from her children, neighbors, and school personnel that counteracted her long-standing sense of inadequacy and frustration. In short, Mrs. Royce and her children became more involved in active efforts to cope with numerous life tasks and challenges in the midst of an environment that was far from nutritive.

In this instance there was considerable evidence of personal and family disorganization. Nevertheless, the provision of opportunities and experiences was instrumental in the change and growth of the family's capacity for adaptive functioning. But perhaps of greatest importance for this family was the worker's shift from preoccupation with individual pathology to appreciation of diversity in human adaptation to environmental challenges and conditions. Anthropological research also has revealed the varied adaptive patterns, flexibility, creativity, and strength human beings manifest in coping with the inner-city ghetto as a nonnutritive environment. Such findings call into question the sometimes exclusive emphasis on social pathology and social disorganization. In their ethnographic study of inner city poor, for example, Charles Valentine and Betty Valentine found clear evidence of adaptive coping with adversity, of energetic activity, and aesthetic variety in residents' social functioning.[17] They noted, in particular, the restorative use of humor in the face of serious problems, renewed efforts in response to defeat, recourse to sacred and secular ideologies and organizations for psychological strength, and resourceful devices in manipulating social structures to achieve social change. The social worker's skill will lie in locating and engaging these personal and group strengths and coping styles.

LIFE SPACE INTERVIEWING

The *life space interview,* which was originally developed for treating pathology, can be effective in helping people to deal with life tasks or problems in living. Fritz Redl,[18] who pioneered the use of this technique, defines it as clinical exploitation of life events and provision of emotional first aid on the spot. As illustrated through the following examples, the life space interview is a powerful means of helping the client and worker to take advantage of the therapeutic potential of natural life experiences.

Mrs. Atkins, a young mother, was receiving help from the public welfare agency while her husband was hospitalized for several months following an automobile accident. In his absence she found it difficult to meet the needs of her three preschool children. She provided only minimal care and supervision. The children were frequently left outside on their own late at night. When a neighbor complained to the police, the protective services worker visited the home and found it a shambles. Dishes and clothes had not been washed for weeks; dirt was piled up in each room; and the children had been eating irregularly.

With Mrs. Atkins' permission the worker organized a work party: she and a group of friends came the next weekend and cleaned and reorganized the apartment. Mrs. Atkins, at first a passive spectator, gradually became involved in working with the others. She had obviously been feeling alone and helpless, and now came through as an alive person who cared about herself and her children.

The interest and concern demonstrated by the worker and her friends, coupled with the remarkable change in the physical appearance of the apartment, led to Mrs. Atkins' growing hopefulness and self-esteem. She became engaged with the worker in developing more constructive ways of coping with her child-caring responsibilities during Mr. Atkins' remaining time in the hospital.

The work party organized by the social worker represents an interesting use of the life space interview. A young mother, overcome by situational stress, was helped by direct action that blocked further deterioration in her physical and social environment and mobilized her own latent resources for active coping. In the real sense, too, the work party helped to straighten out Mrs. Atkins' life situation.

In the following example, 12-year-old Carl, hungry for attention, provoked rejection from his peers and teachers by his demanding behavior. The school social worker used "split-second" life space interviewing to demonstrate her caring and to provide some structure for a troubled child. She made use of casual contacts with him in the school corridors, the cafeteria, and on the street for such life-space interviewing.

When I first started seeing Carl, every time he passed me in the hall or even saw me from a distance, he would run up to me and ask me the day and time of our next session. It was always the same day at the same time, and he knew exactly when it was but he had a compulsion to repeat this question over and over. When I gave him the answer, he would then beg to come sooner or immediately and get angry and call me names when I refused.

Eventually, I turned these moments into split-second life space interviews. He would confront me with the question. Silently, I would look at him for a second, then put my arm around him and ask him how his spelling test went or tell him I liked his new shirt. He would respond appropriately and walk away, satisfied, saying he'd see me at——and name the exact day and time of our appointment.

These informal encounters were more productive than our individual sessions, which were frustrating me because Carl's anxiety interfered with his ability to stay with any topic for more than a few seconds at a time. As the year progressed, Carl was often able to pass me in the hall with merely a smile and a normal hello, secure in the knowledge that I cared about him.

In the next example, the social worker turned trips to the clinic into a series of tasks and challenges that enabled a frightened young woman to regain a sense of adequacy and mastery. Phyllis Gerardi, a woman in her mid-twenties, had a history of periodic psychiatric hospitalization for depression. She was immobilized following the recent sudden death of her mother, on whom she had been extremely dependent. Among other symptoms, she was having serious difficulty walking. When extensive testing ruled out any organic reason for this condition, Phyllis was referred to a psychiatric clinic. She was diagnosed as suffering from an "anxiety neurosis with depressive features" and was assigned to a group led by a social worker.

During the first few weeks, each session with Phyllis took on the flavor of the life space interview. Since Phyllis was unable to drive, I went to her home weekly to bring her to the clinic for our group sessions. She was ready every time I arrived. I used the driving time to encourage her to become more actively aware of the surrounding area as well as to discuss what was happening in her life.

Gradually it emerged that Phyllis suffered from acute anxiety attacks in public places. She would request that I do some shopping for her, but I encouraged her to accompany me into the stores. She did this successfully and I praised her ability, commenting on the enjoyment it brought her. There appeared to be some carryover during this period. Phyllis began accompanying her sister to the store, went to church on one occasion, and generally appeared more alert and active.

During the drives, I tried to engage her in showing me the area since it was well known to her and not to me. Our most interesting adventure was the day we got lost when Phyllis was trying to show me a new way back to her home. In the face of her concern, I commented that it presented a challenge. When we soon entered familiar territory, I accidentally missed the turn and Phyllis again took over the directing. She was able to show me a new way that took us by the home of one of her relatives. She seemed to enjoy our adventure and to appreciate the fact that she helped to solve the problem.

During this period I saw my tasks as providing the time and transportation to get Phyllis to the group; providing a supportive atmosphere in which Phyllis could discuss her fears; and encouraging her interest in the world and developing her sense of power in her life. Phyllis and I agreed on tasks for her. First, she had to be ready on time. Second, she had to make the decisions about how we would use the time together on our way home. Third, she was to talk about the meaning of each experience for her.

As in the previous cases, this worker used life space interviewing as an effective means of enhancing Phyllis's self-image and sense of competence.

RESTRUCTURING THE ENVIRONMENT

Environmental modification has been neglected and in general has had limited prestige in social work.[19] It has been viewed as appropriate largely for specific groups of clients, such as those who seem "poorly motivated" or who are not responsive to insight-oriented procedures. In reality, it is an intricate and promising modality that requires renewed attention in theory and practice.

Frequently, life situations need to be manipulated if they are to become growth-producing for the person. In such instances, the client's environment needs to be restructured in order that life experiences and events will support rather than undermine adaptive functioning. This is especially important since the fit between environmental demands and social supports is a major determinant of successful social adaptation:

Man's abilities to cope with the environment depend on the efficacy of the solutions his culture provides, and the skills he develops are dependent on the adequacy of the preparatory institutions to which he has been exposed.[20]

Through restructuring, the environment can be used as a primary means of helping, as a dynamic force for promoting people's efforts toward competence and adaptation.[21] A critical function of the worker therefore is to aid the client in seeking, modifying, or creating significant environmental opportunities.

In the illustration that follows, a depressed woman is helped to seek a new environment, that is, a new work situation which is more advantageous to her in her struggle toward adaptation.

Mrs. Thompson, a recently divorced 36-year-old woman, sought counseling at a family service agency because of frequent suicidal thoughts. She was an unhappy, withdrawn person with a long history of depression that was triggered again by her husband's abandonment and their subsequent divorce. For the previous seven years, she had been employed as a psychiatric aide in a large state hospital.

Initial counseling sessions centered on Mrs. Thompson's dissatisfaction with her job and especially her frustration in working day after day with people suffering from chronic schizophrenia. With the worker's encouragement, she began to consider other jobs and eventually obtained a job as salesperson in a florist shop. Mrs. Thompson found satisfaction in selling flowers, tending plants, and enjoying their beauty.

She talked with the worker about her pleasure in making people happy, her eagerness to go to work in the morning, and her sense of satisfaction at the end of the day. While the underlying depression was still present, there was no doubt that the new work environment was more positive and rewarding for Mrs. Thompson than the psychiatric ward where every day served to reinforce her depression. With the environmental change and improved feelings about herself Mrs. Thompson showed a new readiness to work on other factors involved in her depression.

The next example continues the case of Carl described in the preceding section on life-space interviewing. Carl had been referred to the school social worker by his sixth-grade teacher. He had received several years of intensive psychotherapy, and the child guidance clinic reported that little progress had been made. Furthermore, his functioning could be viewed as having deteriorated, since he was older and bigger and his infantile behavior was becoming increasingly inappropriate and unacceptable. While Carl and his parents continued in therapy at the clinic, the school social worker focused on restructuring his school environment:

1) Special arrangements were made so that Carl could go to the library to read or look at films or just sit quietly when he was upset. He subsequently developed close relationships with the adults who worked in the library and also became proficient in using the audio-visual equipment there.

2) Although Carl did not have organic learning disabilities, the learning disabilities specialist agreed to see him for a half hour every morning to help him organize his schedule and to give his classroom teacher relief while she got the rest of the class started for the day. Carl developed a close relationship with this woman, whose previous experiences as a special teacher of emotionally disturbed children enabled her also to provide helpful suggestions to Carl's classroom teacher.

3) Despite Carl's poor behavior, we arranged to have him put on safety patrol, in the hope of increasing his feelings of competence and pride in achievement. He was stationed next to one of the adult crossing guards who was asked to work closely with Carl.

4) The principal sometimes let Carl sit in his office with him and gave him little jobs to do or errands to run. The principal had a special fondness for him and Carl liked talking with him.

5) On a daily basis, Carl helped one of the first grade teachers to correct papers, run off dittos, fix the bulletin board, etc.

6) I led weekly classroom meetings which gave me an opportunity to observe Carl and relate to him as member of a life space group, i.e., his class.

Despite some continuing difficulties, Carl's transactions with the environment improved enough to prevent his suspension or expulsion. He was more comfortable with himself and less inclined to act out, as he received acceptance and attention from adults and as he participated in activities in which he experienced success.

The case examples suggest that life situations can be structured so that characterological difficulties or intrapsychic conflicts are minimized or contained and competence enhanced through natural feedback processes. In each case, environmental changes provided the client with opportunities for greater satisfaction, new social roles, and more positive interpersonal relationships. Modifications in the client's social context helped to produce changes in status, self-image, and response from others. With Carl in particular, resources in his social network were enlisted as key instruments of help.[22] In short, social work intervention created a more nutritive environment for each of these people and helped them to move toward more active coping with life challenges.

Milieu therapy also highlights the importance of restructuring the environment. John Cumming and Elaine Cumming[23] illustrate how the social structure of the hospital can be changed to make it more conducive to the growth of each person. They observe:[24]

Whereas psychotherapy sets out to make "basic"—that is, intrapsychic—changes usually expecting social improvement to follow, milieu therapy sets out to make social changes and trusts that ego growth will ensue.

As an example, Richard Boettcher and Roger Vander Schie[25] report marked success in shortening the hospitalization of chronic psychiatric patients and helping them to adapt to community living. The therapeutic program provided satisfying social roles and opportunities to acquire skills in problem-solving and in social interaction.

Ideas from milieu therapy have been extended to include work with families in open or community settings. In a demonstration project with severely disorganized families in an inner city area, the program included provision of day care and other resources and participation of parents in a variety of group experiences. The results showed that, given appropriate environmental inputs and opportunities, parents formerly viewed as disorganized or hopeless could improve their parenting skills. They were able to provide more nurturing environments and more competent care for their children.[26]

Competence and adaptation frequently requires new information and concepts; hence social work intervention often involves an instructive process. The worker provides information, stimulates new ideas and concepts, and encourages new actions on the part of the client system. The worker consequently plays an educational role—a role that is beginning to be effectively exploited in diverse practice contexts. For example, some family counseling programs have shifted from a clinical-medical to an educational model of intervention; the focus is on using the strengths and competence of family members and teaching interactional skills.[27] Family life education is used increasingly as a means of helping people to learn or strengthen skills in communication, decision-making, problem solving, and life planning. Group services are useful in the coping efforts of people facing major life transitions or crises such as marriage, divorce, relocation, or retirement.

Through such programs, people acquire information and develop skills that can promote their coping efforts, increase their ability to select the 'right'' ecological context for themselves, and develop their capacity to negotiate their environment.[28]

CONCLUSION

Social workers can contribute significantly to the promotion of competence in their clients through the use of life experiences and restructuring the environment. Their ability to do so depends to a large extent on the availability of nutritive social systems and supports in an environment that provides rich and diverse opportunities for growth and self-fulfillment.

In today's perplexing world and in the light of the inadequacies of many social institutions, it may seem naive or fanciful to think about social work practice in these terms. But our heightened awareness of the gap between the ideal and the reality can be constructive if it leads to renewed individual and collective commitment to the necessary restructuring of society and redefining of social work practice. As a beginning step, such a commitment would represent an important adaptive response on the part of each of us.

NOTES

1. Meyer suggests that Mary Richmond's *What is Social Case Work?* was a forerunner of the life model. Carol H. Meyer, "Purposes and Boundaries—Casework Fifty Years Later," *Social Casework* 54, no. 5 (May 1973), pp. 268–75.

2. Grete Bibring, "Psychiatry and Social Work," *Journal of Social Casework* 28, no. 6 (June 1947), pp. 203–11.

3. Lucille N. Austin, "Trends in Differential Treatment in Social Casework," *Journal of Social Casework* 29, no. 6 (June 1948), pp. 203–11.

4. Bernard Bandler, "The Concept of Ego-Supportive Psychotherapy," in Howard J. Parad and Roger R. Miller (eds.), *Ego-Oriented Casework: Problems and Perspectives* (New York: Family Service Association of America, 1963), pp. 27–44.

5. Genevieve Oxley, "A Life-Model Approach to Change," *Social Casework* 52, no. 10 (December 1971), pp. 627–33.

6. Herbert Strean, "Application of the 'Life Model' to Casework," *Social Work* 17, no. 5 (September 1972), pp. 45–53.

1. Robert Coles, *Farewell to the South* (Boston: Little Brown, 1972); pp. 6–7.

2. For example, several decades ago Gordon Hamilton identified the "living experience" as a distinguishing characteristic of treatment in her classic formulation of psychosocial casework. Cf. Gordon Hamilton, *Theory and Practice of Social Casework*, 2d ed., rev. (New York: Columbia University Press, 1951); pp. 246–49.

3. Cf. Carel B. Germain, "An Ecological Perspective in Casework Practice," *Social Casework* 54, no. 6 (June 1973), pp. 323–30; and Alex Gitterman and Carel B. Germain, "Social Work Practice: A Life Model," *Social Service Review* 50, no. 4 (December 1976), pp. 601–110.

4. Robert W. White, *Ego and Reality in Psychoanalytic Theory* (New York: International Universities Press, 1963).

5. Thomas Gladwin, "Social Competence and Clinical Practice", *Psychiatry* 30, no. 1 (February 1967), pp. 30–38.

6. Nelson N. Foote and Leonard S. Cottrell, Jr., *Identity and Interpersonal Competence* (Chicago: University of Chicago Press, 1965), pp. 51–57.

7. M. Brewster Smith, "Competence and Socialization," in John A. Clausen (ed.), *Socialization and Society* (Boston: Little, Brown, 1968), pp. 270–320.

8. Ibid., pp. 312–13.

9. Gordon W. Allport, *Pattern and Growth in Personality* (New York: Holt, Rinehart and Winston, 1961), p. 214.

10. Gladwin, "Social Competence and Clinical Practice," p. 37.

11. Cf. Richard J. Estes and Sue Henry, "The Therapeutic Contract in Work with Groups: A Formal Analysis," *Social Service Review* 50, no. 4 (December 1976), pp. 611–22; and Anthony N. Maluccio and Wilma D. Marlow, "The Case for the Contract," *Social Work* 19, no. 1 (January 1974), pp. 28–36.

12. Smith, "Competence and Socialization," pp. 312–13.

13. Franz Alexander, "Extra-therapeutic Experiences," in Franz Alexander and Thomas M. French (eds.), *Psychoanalytic Therapy* (New York: The Ronald Press, 1946), p. 40.

14. Anthony N. Maluccio, "Action as a Tool in Casework Practice," *Social Casework* 55, no. 1 (January 1975), pp. 30–35.

15. Cf. Orville G. Brim, Jr., "Adult Socialization," in John A. Clausen (ed.), *Socialization and Society* (Boston: Little, Brown, 1968), pp. 182–226.

16. Smith, "Competence and Socialization," pp. 302–16.

17. Charles A. Valentine and Betty Lou Valentine, "Making the Scene, Digging the Action, and Telling It Like It Is: Anthropologists at Work in a Dark Ghetto," in Norman E. Whitten, Jr., and John F. Szwed (eds.), *Afro-American Anthropology* (New York: The Free Press, 1970), pp. 403–18.

18. Fritz Redl, "Strategy and Technique of the Life Space Interview," *American Journal of Orthopsychiatry* 29, no. 1 (January 1959), pp. 1–18.

19. Cf. Richard M. Grinnell, Jr., "Environmental Modification: Casework's Concern or Casework's Neglect?" *Social Service Review* 47, no. 2 (June 1973), pp. 208–20.

20. David Mechanic, "Social Structure and Personal Adaptation: Some Neglected Dimensions," in George V. Coelho, David A. Hamburg, and John E. Adams (ed.), *Coping and Adaptation* (New York: Basic Books, 1974), p. 33.

21. Cf. Germain, "An Ecological Perspective in Casework Practice."

22. Cf. Carol Swenson, "Social Networks, Mutual Aid, and the Ecological Perspective" included in this book.

23. John Cumming and Elaine Cumming, *Ego and Milieu* (Chicago: Aldine-Atherton, 1962).

24. Ibid, p. 271.

25. Richard E. Boettcher and Roger Vander Schie, "Milieu Therapy with Chronic Mental Patients," *Social Work* 20, no. 2 (March 1975), pp. 130–134.

26. Eleanor Pavenstedt (ed.), *The Drifters—Children of Disorganized Lower-Class Families* (Boston: Little, Brown, 1967).

27. Cf. Joseph H. Golner, "Home Family Counseling," *Social Work* 16, no. 4 (October 1971), pp. 63–71.

28. Cf. Gitterman and Germain, ''Social Work Practice,'' p. 607; and Rudolf H. Moos, *The Human Context: Environmental Determinants of Behavior* (New York: John Wiley & Sons, 1976), pp. 394–431. Moos stresses the role of information about the environment in human coping and adaptation.

3 PRACTICE ISSUES

11 Participation and Practice

CHARLES F. GROSSER

Grosser poses a humanistic challenge for democratic participation in the affairs of society by all citizens, and a scientific concern about the technological means that can make participation possible in today's complex bureaucratic environment. His interest is in the personal and social benefits to accrue from such participation.

Human beings must adapt to the very environmental changes they have themselves created. We are painfully aware of the physiological, social, and emotional demands placed upon all of us by the social institutions we have created. An especially disturbing aspect is the steady upward flow of power in large bureaucratic structures. Such organizations become less and less able to individualize people, as they become more and more dependent upon rules, computers, and labelling processes. Loci of policy- and decision-making are increasingly removed from direct contact with the users of service and lower-level staff who are directly engaged with service users. The depersonalization to both becomes even more apparent as organizations take on goals of self-maintenance and no longer perform their manifest functions.

Meanwhile, new sources of environmental stress are continually generated by rapid social change so that the lag between environmental demands and institutional responses to them grows wider, and the goodness-of-fit is diminished still further. In Grosser's view all citizens must participate in the effort to keep these man-created institutions responsive to human needs and aspirations. The task is to maintain mastery not only over our scientific technology, as a life and death matter, but also over our social technology.

Social workers of a reformist bent have suggested that clients are themselves a neglected human resource for achieving organizations' intended functions.[1] Redesigning their organizational roles from passive recipients to citizen participants in policy-making, service provision, and other organiza-

tional tasks can help change the character of the organization.[2] *Usually this position also includes an emphasis on the corrective experience provided to the client in his having control over matters that profoundly affect his life.*[3]

The adaptive task of maintaining the responsiveness of institutions, however, introduces a political dimension, as issues of economic and social power come to the fore. The differential access to power and opportunity in social systems means that those who are most dependent upon the services and functions of a given social structure have fewer means to influence it. Some would declare that such corrective experiences as milieu therapy and patient self-government, for example, rarely involve real transfer of power and decision-making. Others believe that consumer participation at board levels of large or small, public or private institutions is often illusory, not only because of difficult issues in representation but because of the tendency toward log-rolling and reciprocity with more powerful members and groups.[4] *Some social workers take the position that the practitioner's reluctance to incorporate a politicized stance in practice is itself a political act of social control, obscured by a professional ideology of objectivity and neutrality. Others go further to suggest that the only appropriate function for social work is to direct its practice to the fundamental issues of oppression and inequality. Anything less supports the status quo.*[5]

In the face of this dialectic, Grosser achieves a synthesis, tolerating the tension between stability and change, conservatism and radicalism. He accepts neither the absolute immunity of social structures to real change, nor the demand to overthrow them. And he is interested in participation as a human right, not in participation as therapy. Thus he is concerned with participation, not primarily as a corrective experience for the client (although he agrees that may be a welcome side effect), but primarily as a corrective to democratic institutions and processes that have gone awry. Furthermore, Grosser includes the practitioner's participation as stemming from the same two imperatives of human rights and democratic advance.

—C.B.G.

DEMOCRATIC TRADITIONS AND BENEFITS

DIRECT PARTICIPATION by citizens in the life of their communities has been historically and currently seen as an integral component of a democratic society. Where few take part in decisions there is little democracy; the more participation there is, the more democracy there is. Participation, which is simply the engagement of the rank

This article is a section of a larger work on participation in the Welfare State currently in progress.

and file in political and social community processes, has also been viewed as most salutary to the participants themselves.

The theory of participatory democracy is built around the central assertion that individuals and their institutions cannot be considered in isolation from one another. The existence of representative institutions at the national level is not sufficient for democracy; for maximum participation by all the people at that level socialization, or "social training," for democracy must take place in other spheres in order that necessary individual attitudes and psychological qualities can be developed. This development takes place through the process of participation itself. The major function of participation in the theory of participatory democracy is therefore an educative one, educative in the very widest sense, including both the psychological aspect and the gaining of practice in democratic skills and procedures.[1]

Participation heightens the capacity to contribute to and be enriched by society, induces feelings of belonging, and provides a sense of control over life, all of which are seen as contributing to good mental health. The ideal type of such activity, direct participation as exemplified in the Greek city-state or in the New England town in the 16th century, appears to be no longer possible. Indirect participation in the affairs of large nation-states by means of chosen representatives has become the mode of citizen engagement in democratic societies. This transition, which has occurred inevitably as nations have become larger and more complex, is viewed by many as the source of much of the dislocation and alienation experienced by those who live in present-day urban, industrial, democratic countries.

Apart from the personal benefits to be realized by engagement in direct participation and the benefits that accrue to the democratic state, it has been suggested that the absence of participation is likely to produce a state of affairs where the interest of the nonparticipants will be ignored. The Greeks themselves apparently were aware of this pitfall. Coulanges quotes the Greek historian Thucydides, who commented, that "democratic government was needed to give the poor a refuge and the rich a check." He goes on to point out the expedient nature of Greek society, noting that the ruling class would have avoided the advent of democracy "if they had been able to found the government for a few and liberty for all. That the poor might be protected in their personal interests it seemed necessary that they should

have the right of suffrage."[2] In these two qualities of the participatory process—the psychological and social benefits inherent in the
activity itself and its function to assure the equitable distribution of
the communities' goods and resources—we have a familiar dichotomy which is represented in the direct service and community organization components in the field of social work.

SOCIAL WORK

It is not unexpected that social work, reflecting its concern with the
adjustment of individuals in society, has become interested in participation. That the advent of this interest has been recent reflects social
work's historical function of maintaining social equilibrium as it provides services to people—a function, as shall be noted later, which is
changing in emergent welfare states. The programs through which
social work has acted on this interest are very different, as for example the early settlement movement over a half century ago and the
provisions for participation mandated in the 1977 federal Title XX
legislation. Over time social work practitioners, particularly those
who came to be referred to as community organizers, paid attention
to the processes necessary to facilitate citizen participation and
brought them into the rubric of social work practice. Community organization and direct practice developed as unrelated, sometimes an-
tagonistic, components of the same field. The genesis of both took
place however in the same national environment: the burgeoning capitalist republic characterized by social Darwinism, selective noninter-
ference by government in the affairs of citizens, and Elizabethan
judgments regarding those deemed unable to cope.

THE WELFARE STATE

The national context within which social work now exists is the
welfare state of which the United States, despite disclaimers to the
contrary, is one. This characterization is used advisedly in this article
bearing in mind the emerging nature of the welfare state in the U.S.
and the fact that the nation's attitudes and policies are far from unani-
mous in their commitments to this trend. For purposes of discussion,

however, the welfare state is being considered as an ideal type rather than a set of current policies and attitudes.

Within a welfare state social service programs become institutionalized as functions of government. Social work is experiencing the trauma of this transition as its location shifts from an entrepreneurial matrix of quasi-voluntary organizations to welfare state institutions. This change in the locus of social work makes for some fundamental alterations in the nature of its practice. In a welfare state it is the failure of the various agencies (e.g., those providing social services, insurance, and utilities, or those charged with meeting education, health, and recreation needs, or those which support populations at risk) which call forth the bulk of the problems in which social workers intervene. The field is finding that conventional practice is not well suited to the service delivery imperatives produced by this new environment. New practice models are being articulated and developed [3] which update the social work experience and develop techniques to deal with the disjunctures that occur between citizens of the welfare state and the institutions of that society.

The concept of participation as an integral component of direct service practice is timely as a result of the emergence of the welfare state. The absence of participation from practice in laissez-faire society has, in the minds of some critics, vitiated practice. But since, in such a system, the distribution of social work services is essentially a market place phenomenon, the final consequence is in the choice as to who will use social workers' services. In contemporary practice those who can use a rehabilitative service focused on the individual, wherein technician cures patient, often turn out to be members of the urban middle class. The fact that social workers were primarily serving the middle class and not the poor became an issue of contention during the early sixties. Though, in addition to denying the fact, attempts were made by various voluntary agencies to serve poor populations they hadn't been in contact with and though numbers of public agencies endeavored to professionalize their staffs, the characterization remains valid. Graduate schools which train social workers are chosen by those seeking the best, least expensive, and quickest route to careers as therapists in private practice or voluntary psychiatric and family agencies. This trend has accelerated of late as various public subsidies for social work students available during the sixties have been withdrawn.[4]

In the welfare state, however, given the changed locus of social work and the institutionalization of social services, the absence of participatory interventions in practice is impossible. In the welfare state public systems have been created to provide for human needs predicated on the assumption that the roots of individual dysfunction lie in social organizations as well as in human failings. For this reason the populations to be served are not determined by the market place but consist of various categories of citizens whose designation is a matter of public policy. These categorical groups are ubiquitous and overlapping and theoretically include all citizens. A further result of this quality of a welfare state is that a practice is developed which operationally distinguishes between personal and institutional failures and makes assessments and constructs interventions accordingly. That society assumes responsibility for providing the good life for its citizens suggests that participation is perforce an element in the process of assisting those who have been unable to utilize the social mechanisms for achieving the good life or from whom the good life has been withheld. In other words, those not receiving their proper share of vested welfare state entitlements can be seen as "nonparticipants," or, engagement through participation in the service systems of the welfare state is a form of participation.

DIRECT SERVICE

The purpose of this article is to consider some of the ways in which issues of participation become relevant in the transition of social work in the welfare state. The central thesis which will be presented is that an integrated social services* practice model establishes a context wherein participation is an integral part of direct social work practice. Participation in this context, as a component of direct practice, is not a moral or political activity ancillary to social work. Nor is it a speciality of those engaged in social action or social

---

* This term is used to subsume, but not reconcile, three forms of practice referred to in the literature as generic practice, case management practice, and practice based upon an ecological-systems perspective.

change or a device to enable unrepresented groups in the community to become a part of local pluralistic political processes from which they have been excluded. Community organization practice seeks to facilitate participation as one of the ways to fulfill these and other social functions.

As a part of direct practice participatory activity, though it draws on many of the skills and strategies of community organization, is a process whose goal is service delivery. The reference to participation as an integral part of practice reflects the importance of participation at every point, e.g., at assessment (identification of problems and choice of the one to be addressed), when determining the nature of the intervention, and when determining the nature of the collaborative relationships between the worker, recipient, and others. This integration is made explicit by the definition of social work under which an integrated service model is conceived. This definition locates social work at the point of dislocation between individuals and the social systems with which they regularly engage.[5] In order to deal with the problems which arise at this juncture between individuals and societal systems, practice emerges which can both enhance the ability of individuals to cope and address the problems produced by malfunctioning social institutions.

The description of practice appended to this article is a sample of what the integrated social work model might look like. The participatory activity of the worker (that is, where the worker and/or members of the family with which he/she is working interact with environmental institutions to get service) is an intrinsic part of her practice. This activity involves engagement with the school, Housing Authority, Veterans Administrations, NAACP and Urban League, elected officials, and the local television station. The worker's and family's objectives with regard to these institutions were directed in some instances toward affecting administrative and decision-making processes; in other instances the worker attempted to get one organization to influence another or to hold an organization responsible under the law. The worker's activity involved aspects of public life which hold democratic institutions accountable. Such activity as this could well be defined as active citizenship. In this instance, however, it was direct social work practice, as a result of which a family was housed. That the father in this family was hospitalized and the mother cared for a large household precluded active collaboration by them with the worker. More direct activity by recipients would be characteristic of participation in the model under consideration.

It should also be noted that of the family's various entitlements under existing public legislation, education and housing policy were the basis on which they and the worker came together. These categorical statutes which derive from citizenship affect the nature of practice in that they are enforceable rights. This both legitimates and makes effective participatory practice and facilitates a collaborative relationship between worker and recipient in the "exercise of citizenship."

Facilitating engagement between persons and social institutions is, in fact, participation. Accomplishing this engagement, as will be elaborated later, involves a number of skills and processes heretofore excluded from the repertory of direct service. These processes, when separated from direct practice, were seen as purely instrumental; they can now be viewed as a means of inducing personal growth as well. Participatory behavior then is engaged in by and on behalf of the service recipient in an effort to resolve a particular problem. The efficacy of such interventions is determined by the extent to which they achieve short-term practice goals and service delivery, rather than institutional or political outcomes.

SOCIAL ACTION

Community organization, planning, and other interventions oriented toward political and social change are not rendered obsolete by the emergence of the welfare state. On the contrary, the experience of sich established welfare states as Sweden and Israel, where social welfare institutions often lose touch with service delivery and recipient, demonstrates the imperative of participatory processes as devices to keep human bureaucracies responsive to those they are designated to serve.* Participation in political terms then is not the

---

* In both Israel and Sweden the defeat of the Labor governments in 1977 after lengthy terms in power was attributed in part to voter dissatisfaction with the stultifying bureaucracy of welfare state institutions.

focus of this discussion because it is no longer timely. Nor is it not being considered because a clear relationship between political participation and participation as a component in direct practice does not exist.* It is rather that our discussion here is concerned with direct service wherein priorities and accountability are measured in terms of fulfilling recipients' needs.

The delivery of service is the raison d'être of the participation we are discussing; and this is different in important ways from political participation where social or institutional change is sought. Participation as part of practice is, as are all other aspects of direct service,† unique to the individuals involved. The nature of participation is determined by the needs and capacities of the recipients and shaped by the nature of the service delivery problem and the particular interventions necessary to resolve it. Strategies of problem-solving and the impact of various persons outside the immediate situation but significant to it further influence the process, as does the quality of the partnership that has been contracted between the recipient and the worker. Political participation, by contrast, is shaped by the need to accommodate the social and political forces surrounding a particular change objective. In any social change action the effect of practice decisions on groups outside the worker and the recipient such as supporters, resistors, neutrals, and influentials must be considered. All this, of course, reflects a process which is essentially instrumental, geared to long-range-collective (rather than personal-immediate) goals. Though engagement in this process has personal meaning for, and may be self-enhancing to, those who engage in it, this is clearly not its focus as it would be in direct practice participation.

An analogy for political participation can be drawn to a legal test case where one seeks out or even provokes the grievance to be tested. The intent is to benefit a category of persons, and not only the particular individual in whose name the litigation is undertaken. It is interesting to note that the most frequent way in which an institution subjected to a test case protects itself is to yield the point at issue before

---

* Note that in the appended practice description precedents were set which were applied on behalf of other families in similar circumstances.

† Or at least as all aspects of direct service *should* be: e.g., agency interest, staff convenience, political expedience, notions of recipient "worthiness" or "humbleness," should certainly be irrelevant to the nature of the service-giving process.

legal or administrative precedent can be established. This defeats the social change objective but, of course, fulfills a service objective. In the direct service analogue all efforts would be geared toward avoiding the grievance in any way possible, or failing that, to resolve it quickly and efficaciously without regard to precedent or to establishing a record to facilitate future action. This is an important distinction because the same practice may be either effective social action and poor service, or the reverse. Achieving direct benefit to recipient and achieving social change do not necessarily coincide. If clarity about the distinction is not maintained, the interests of the beneficiary are apt to be forgotten. When this is the case the likelihood is that the vulnerable will once more be ignored and it is of no comfort to them that this time it occurred ''for a good cause.'' This abrogation can also occur when individual leaders or representatives forego social change objectives and use social action strategies to obtain personal benefits.

ABSENCE OF DIRECT PARTICIPATION

Facilitating participation in community organization requires the social work practictioner to use skills in conflict management; negotiating, bargaining, and other skills in dealing with organizations; skills in gathering and using information; and other special skills.* Such community organization generally involves activity on the part of a few who act as representatives or leaders for a larger group (e.g., a neighborhood, the elderly, welfare recipients, the tenants of a given building). In a sense we have here the same indirect participation that we referred to earlier; the alienating way in which democracy was experienced when small communities give way to large complex nations. What we have in effect is a social work intervention which replicates the problem that it has been called forth to resolve. The small percentage of social workers engaged in organizational work, even when involved with a broad constituency, seek out those in the

---

* These are not the skills which have been included as a part of conventional social work practice. In fact some of them have been viewed as antithetical to good practice in that they were seen as directive, manipulative, or based on premises which did not see client failure as the source of the problem to be resolved.

recipient groups who tend to have such skills as mentioned above, are acknowledged leaders, or are seen as having the capacity for leadership. Organizers become engaged with such activists in order to be successful in social action. Social work organizers do not reach the vast rank and file of beneficiaries; direct service workers who do reach them are not knowledgeable regarding skills in participation nor do they believe that such skills are properly a part of the helping process. As a result the vast majority of the recipients of laissez-faire-sponsored social work have gotten no experience learning how to locate opportunities for participation or for acquiring the skills with which to engage in the process. The absence of participation from traditional practice reduces the ability of workers and recipients to negotiate service delivery systems as well, since these are skills essential to the practice interventions necessitated by the welfare state.

PARTICIPATION AND PRACTICE

There is much potential in the integrated social service practice model for finally bridging the separatist tradition of the field of social work. Healing this breach will certainly provide possibilities for dealing more efficiently with delivering individual services in the welfare state and will offer many opportunities for enrichment and growth of practice. From the perspective of this article there is yet another exciting and most compelling possibility suggested by the integration of participation and practice. It may well be that the welfare state, which transposes egalitarian democratic traditions into human service benefits, provides an opportunity for direct participation once again. Such an opportunity, thought by some to be no longer available, does in fact exist despite the size and complexity of modern nations. This opportunity for direct participation arises from the relationship between the citizen recipient and the agencies of the state which distribute its social welfare resources. If there is any merit in the argument that participation is a central component in this relationship between state agency and recipient, then facilitating this component through the collaborative assistance of service-providing practitioners will, in addition to providing for more effective service, utilize categorical benefit systems as opportunities for rank and file recipients to participate directly in their social environment. At the risk of sounding grandiose it would appear that the service model under discussion can provide a viable role for social work in the welfare state, enhance the quality of democracy by increasing the amount of participation that takes place, provide the morale and psychological benefits experienced by participating citizens, and utilize the nature of the participatory process to monitor service systems. There are a variety of points of view as to the meaning of the term "generic" as it applies to a practice model for social work; the one in this article encompasses such service and institutional perspectives as noted above.

CITIZEN-PARTICIPANT: "CLIENT"

"Clients"[6] in the ancient Roman city were an inferior servant class living under the protection of a patron family who acted on their behalf in the affairs of the city and to whose authority they submitted. In contemporary society, social service institutions and social workers (among others) use the term client to designate one who receives service. In the last decade it became apparent to some, most particularly Charles Reich,[7] that those designated as clients (welfare clients particularly), were treated as inferior to the rest of the population in a variety of ways and were deprived of such basic constitutional rights of citizenship as privacy and the freedom to travel. In addition to this direct abrogation of citizenship, access to engagement in electoral politics and in the public and voluntary organizational life of their communities was obstructed as well. They were, for example, not represented on such local citizen advisory bodies as draft boards, Boards of Education, governing boards of voluntary medical, recreational, and social service agencies, advisory committees to elected officials, and the like. Essentially clients in the laissez-faire, capitalist republic, like their Roman and Greek antecedents in the city state, are less than citizens.

Given its derivation and its literal meaning, "client" is an inaccurate and inappropriate term for designating those who receive social welfare benefits. (While the inappropriateness of the term has been evident, unfortunately social work practice and welfare agency policy have made it distressingly accurate.) The point is not semantic; central to the thesis of participation as part of service is the assumption that entitlements in a welfare state are vested in the status of citizenship. Citizens who can utilize the benefit systems on their own do so. Citizens who are not able to utilize the benefit systems on their own are assisted in a variety of ways to acquire the knowledge, skills, and personal and social resources necessary to do so. Neither citizens who participate on their own in the acquisition of the benefits of the welfare state, nor those who do so with assistance, are clients. The process by which assistance is provided, the nature of the relationship between service workers and recipients and the knowledge and skills which comprise this practice is centrally shaped by the fact that the beneficiary is a citizen, not a client,[8] for citizens participate and clients do not. In addition, workers who hold common citizenship with recipients in the welfare state participate as well.

CITIZEN-PARTICIPANT: WORKER

Social work practitioners have been characterized in many ways, reflecting different aspects of the genesis and sociology of the field. Practitioners were early on, and are sometimes still, seen as do-gooders (a term for which, in my mind, no apology is needed). Another perspective, reflecting the functional tradition in the profession, saw the practitioner as an instrument of agency purpose. Public administration called forth practitioners as good bureaucrats while clinical traditions stressed a highly trained, self-aware, disciplined professional who, albeit with continuing supervision, would function independently. These somewhat haphazard designations reflect laissez-faire social work practice. In welfare state social work, another context for practice is added, the one which is the theme of this discussion, the practitioner as citizen and participant.

The arguments put forth with regard to opportunities for service recipients to participate in their society apply to service workers as well. Class, ethnic, and racial differences between workers and recipients certainly reflect differential opportunities for indirect participation. Middle-class social workers are more active in electoral politics and local organizational life than are lower-class service recipients. However, insofar as direct participation is concerned, recipients and workers appear to be equally estranged. Direct participation is of importance to practitioners even though they engage in established democratic rituals. Indirect participation by way of representative government provides little opportunity for practitioners to influence institutions which directly affect their lives. These institutions include the benefit systems of the welfare state, some of which they do or will engage in as recipients as do all citizens. The institutions with the more ubiquitous relevance for practitioners are the agencies within which they work and those ancillary to their practice. Instrumentally, their employing agency dispenses a variety of rewards. Workers have generally regularized their relationship with employers in this regard by forming mutual benefit organizations which then negotiate on their behalf. The expressive activity of the employing agency as reflected in the quality of its program, is generally given little attention. Nevertheless, when a welfare institution withholds services or provides them inappropriately it corrupts its workers as it victimizes its intended beneficiaries. Practitioners cannot retain personal or professional integrity in a benefit system whose social welfare objectives have been subverted. The participatory aspects of direct practice provide an opportunity for workers in partnership with recipients to engage in professional practice in a way which helps to hold the social welfare institutions, particularly the one in which they work, accountable to their substantive purposes.

Since the raison d'être of participation in practice is insuring the benefit received by the recipient, political, bureaucratic, or economic sensitivities are secondary. As a result the recipient and the worker in collaborative participation are able not only to gain personal benefits, but also to provide the welfare state with a much needed addition to its systems of accountability untempered by the inhibitions which so often characterize the bureaucrat or planner. Legislatures, government agencies, and other instruments of representative government take responsibility for political and bureaucratic accountability. Experience in this country and elsewhere makes it clear that the exclusion of the rank and file from participation in institutional accountability threatens the integrity of the welfare state. Again participation as a part of practice is suggested as an option worth trying in an attempt to integrate citizenship into the day-to-day activity of residents of the welfare state. Meeting this national need unites workers and recipients in an attempt to insure the integrity of the state and provide additional checks and balances for the welfare institutions with which they are directly engaged. The social and psychological benefits which attend such activity will also be enjoyed by workers as well as by recipients.

SOCIAL WORK PRACTICE:
AN ILLUSTRATION

The following account was written by a masters student at the Columbia University School of Social Work as part of her work for a course in Case Advocacy. The student's major was social casework, and the paper was written to describe case advocacy, not general practice. This account is offered as an illustration of the kind of practice of which participation can become an integral part. The illustration does not contain the kind of recipient participation projected in this paper. It does illustrate, however, the way in which service provision interacts with and affects various public and voluntary institutions, and acts to hold them closer to the rank-and-file service user. The case example is designated by the writer as advocacy. This designation is, I believe, simply an expedient way to emphasize a component of general practice which had, for a time, been overlooked in social work practice. Participation, as it is being argued here, is not a component of case advocacy, but of general practice. It is in that sense that this account is offered as an illustration.

Last year I was placed as a student social worker in an integrated public elementary school located in a suburban and predominantly white middle- to upper-class neighborhood. I assumed an advocacy role on behalf of the F. family with little agency support, little knowledge of the law, and even less knowledge of the role and skills of the advocate.

Initially, I became involved with the F. family when the twins, Kathy and Karen, were referred to the school social work department by their kindergarten teachers because of their apathy and lack of communication in the classroom. I observed the twins in their classrooms and made an appointment to visit Mr. and Mrs. F. in their home.

The F's are a poor, large, black family. The household consists of eight children, one grandchild, and the parents. Derek, three years old, is the only boy; the twins are five years old; the other children are Patricia, age 9, Yvonne, 11, Felician, 12, Donna, 15, and Jackie, 16. Jackie is an unwed mother of a 7-month-old baby girl.

While we were talking about the twins' difficulties in school, Mrs. F. suggested that their problems were probably related to their housing situation. Mrs. F. was very upset about her family's present living condition and explained to me that their house had been condemned over one year ago. She explained that they do not qualify for public housing due to the large number of children in the family. The housing authority to date has apparently been unable to locate suitable housing at a price the F. family can afford to pay.

Their living conditions were atrocious. There were numerous health and safety hazards throughout the house. There were large rats and cockroaches, faulty plumbing, large holes in the walls, open and exposed wiring, missing bannisters from the already unsteady railing, broken windows, broken front door lock, uncollected garbage in front of the house, and an open gas heater was the sole source of heat. I could easily see why Mrs. F. was so upset—I was shocked and horrified by these conditions.

I asked about Mr. F., and Mrs. F. burst into tears, explaining that Mr. F. had been taken to the hospital a few days ago. This had been the first time that they had been separated since they have been married. Mrs. F. quit her job so that she would be able to care for the children and so that she would be able to visit Mr. F. while most of the children were in school. Mr. F. worked the evening shift and had taken care of the children while Mrs. F. worked during the day. Mrs. F. told me how frightened she felt without her husband. She stayed up all night, fearing that men would break into the house, knowing that Mr. F. was away. The family lives in what is generally considered the worst and most dangerous section of the city. I felt that Mrs. F.'s fears were justifiable and very real.

I asked Mrs. F. what was wrong with her husband and she replied that she didn't know, except that it was serious. The children were taking the separation from their father very hard. "We are a very close family," Mrs. F. commented.

Mr. F. has tried very hard to keep the family together. He has refused any public assistance (his salary is just above the eligibility requirements). Mrs. F. confided that Mr. F. is a very proud man who has managed to keep his family off welfare. Both Mr. and Mrs. F. are worried about their present financial state. They have not been required to pay rent since their house was condemned, nor were they instructed to keep it in escrow. Mr. F. has been steadily employed, has an excellent work record and his employer thinks highly of him.

Social Work Intervention and Advocacy:

I alerted all of the children's teachers and their social workers to the father's hospitalization so that they would be better able to understand and to deal with the children's emotional needs.

I called the V.A. Hospital and spoke with the social worker who was assigned to Mr. F. We discussed Mr. F.'s condition and I explained the family's housing situation to the worker. The hospital felt that Mr. F. should not return to living conditions that would be harmful to his health. The hospital's position became a resource that would contribute to solving the problem of housing. The hospital social worker is also helping Mr. F. with facing the realities of his financial situation (i.e., the need for financial assistance).

I suggested to Mrs. F. that perhaps the hospital's concern regarding their housing situation was a blessing in disguise. Perhaps, with the hospital backing us, the housing authority could be pressured to find suitable housing. Although agreeable to my trying, Mrs. F. was not very hopeful, and I soon realized why. I began calling the housing authority and talking with various people who had been involved with the F. family. I was generally given the "runaround" and conflicting information. I made a notation of whom I called, the date, and a summary of our conversation and sent a copy to the person I had called so that I would have a complete record if I needed this as a resource in the future.

I was beginning to experience what large, poor black families continually face. One man, Mr. R., who worked for the housing authority, told me that the F. family really did not want to move. I asked him if he could explain his feeling and he replied that he had shown the F's several suitable apartments. I later learned that the apartments that were shown to Mr. and Mrs. F. were renting for $400–$600 per month. The F's themselves were looking for apartments but were continually faced with high rents and discrimination against large poor black families. I tried to enlist the aid of the Urban League and of the NAACP. However, both organizations were facing internal disorganization and were of little help.

Finally I reached the director of the housing authority, who replied with exasperation at the mention of the F. name. She explained that the problem was the *number* of children, that according to housing regulations (HUD) only *two* children of the *same sex* could share *one* bedroom. She suggested that it would be easier to find housing if the oldest girl moved out with her infant daughter and also if she would take Derek, the youngest boy, with her since he would require a bedroom of his own (he was the only boy). I was outraged. It seemed that the only way to obtain decent housing for this family was to break up the family. What effect would this have on Jackie? on Derek? on Mrs. F.? on the entire family? I was beginning to understand Mrs. F's resentment toward authority. I asked the director of the housing authority if perhaps a wall could be knocked down to combine two apartments; I had heard that this had been done before. She refused to even consider this.

I was unsure of my role and what I should do next. I had never been an advocate for a client before but felt very strongly that I *should* be in this case. I decided to call the State Representative, attempting to go one step higher along the bureaucratic ladder. He was quite upset about the situation, especially when I suggested that I wanted to call him before I contacted the local television station, which had done a human interest story on the F. family's housing situation last year when their apartment had initially been condemned. By contacting the state representative I was able to schedule a meeting with the mayor and all interested parties.

I also continued to gather support from other agencies who have become involved with the family. I made an attempt to involve as many agencies as possible in an effort to increase ''our'' power and influence. I also asked Mr. F's doctor if he would write a letter to the mayor and to the director of the housing authority, which he did immediately. The medical social worker apologized for not becoming more involved, stating that since she was a government employee she was not allowed to engage in any adversary actions.

I continued to apply pressure to various officials through persistent and continuous phone calls and letters. I called Legal Aid concerning the legal rights of the F. family. They advised me that the F's could sue the city for discriminating against large families in terms of housing, especially since the city was given federal funds to construct or make available housing for just such families and has not, as yet, done so.

The housing authority finally agreed to knock down a wall and combine two apartments. It took six months to get this far. However, I recently heard that my efforts have helped other large families obtain housing and that the city, threatened by law suits, is beginning to purchase two-family housing for large families.

While I was working with the F. family, many questions arose in my mind concerning my role. First, I wasn't sure if my agency would support me (at least I couldn't be fired!) or to what degree they would become involved. I discovered that the principal of the twins' school would cosign letters but nothing beyond that. My supervisor offered no assistance in acquainting me with the power structure of the city and the various agencies with which I had become involved. I was, however, allowed to assume an adversarial role on my own. Quite frankly, I feel that public schools have the responsibility to become involved in the community and to support the children.

I also felt acutely my lack of knowledge and skill: 1) knowledge of the law; 2) knowledge of the institutions with which my client interacts; and 3) knowledge concerning how to effect change—strategies and tactics, how to use the power system within the community.

With hindsight I think I would have done things differently. First, I would have thoroughly studied and evaluated the nature of the problem, the character of the organization that was to be the target of our efforts, and the availability of resources to support our efforts. Had I done this in the beginning, I think I might have attained our objective much sooner and I might have affected a larger population, rather than just one client.

I would have identified the sanctions for advocacy earlier and felt more confident knowing I had sanctions to support and justify my actions. The legal sanctions were quite powerful. The city was violating the law and also my client was *eligible* to receive public housing.

I identified my resources "as I went along"; with hindsight had I identified potential resources earlier, I might have been more efficient and effective in obtaining our objective. I would have examined the service network more closely in an attempt to discover possible allies. Our resources included all the agencies that I tried to involve in order to obtain the power and influence which I lacked. These included the V.A. Hospital, the school, Catholic Charities, the State Representative (political power), Family and Children's Service, Legal Aid (legal sanction). Mrs. F. was also a resource who applied pressure in terms of persistent phone calls, etc. I think I would have examined the receptivity of the housing authority more carefully. I had identified the housing authority and its director as the target system, which I now feel was perhaps not fair. And I assumed from the beginning and without sufficient evidence that they were not receptive to my objective.

My method of intervention involved *negotiating, informing* various agencies of the problem, *pressuring* with persistent phone calls and letters, and evoking the power and influence of superiors along the hierarchical ladder; *coercion* via legal action was used as well as threatening to use unfavorable publicity (television and newspaper coverage that would be embarrassing to the city). In retrospect I should have examined more closely the risks involved in employing the various methods of intervention that I chose. I could easily have alienated the state representative, for instance, by threatening publicity and by immediately assuming an adversarial role when, perhaps, this was not necessary.

Luckily, I achieved my objective. As stated earlier, I feel I could have achieved my objective sooner had I possessed advocacy skills and knowledge of the laws. My supervisor was given permission to assume my role for follow-up. I was pleased to hear this and felt that this signaled a change of policy within my agency. I subsequently heard from my supervisor that my work on behalf of the F's did affect poor large families in general, for the city is now purchasing housing for these families.

Many would say that interventions of this kind have always characterized good practice. There is, however, little evidence that such good practice does indeed prevail. Yet such statements are offered as reasons for not changing existing curricula or service programs. It might be argued that the failure of the field to engage in this good practice is primarily the reason why a new model for practice is needed. If it is "old wine in new bottles," so be it, for it has become increasingly more difficult over the last few decades to locate old wine in any kind of container.

NOTES

1. Elliot Studt, "Social Work Theory and Implications for the Practice of Methods," *Social Work Education Reporter* 16 (June 1968), pp. 22–24, 42–46.

2. See, for example, Gordon Hearn, "Social Work as Boundary Work," mimeographed paper presented at the Third Annual Institute on Services to Family and Children, School of Social Work, University of Iowa, April 1970. Some formulations include participation in advocacy programs within service systems, and in this respect Hearn draws on Daniel Thursz, "Consumer Involvement in Rehabilitation," *Rehabilitation Record* (September–October 1969).

3. For an early example of this important emphasis in contemporary practice, see Irma Stein, "The Application of System Theory to Social Work Practice and Educa-

tion,'' mimeographed paper presented at the Annual Program Meeting of The Council on Social Work Education, New York City, January 1966.

4. Bruce C. Vladeck, "Interest-Group Representation and the HSA's: Health Planning and Political Theory," *American Journal of Public Health,* 67, no. 1 (1977), pp. 23–29.

5. I am indebted to Professor Pierre Racine of the University of Montreal School of Social Work, in particular, for materials and references relating to this position, including his own paper, "On a Rationale for a Politically Conscious Practice in Social Work," mimeographed.

---

1. Carol Pateman, *Participation and Democratic Theory* (New York: Cambridge University Press, 1970), p. 45.

2. Fustel DeCoulanges, *The Ancient City* (Garden City, New York: Doubleday, 1960), p. 328.

3. See, for example, Ruth Middleman and Gale Goldberg, *Social Service Delivery: A Structured Approach to Social Work Practice* (New York: Columbia University Press, 1974); Howard Goldstein, *Social Work Practice: A Unitary Approach* (Columbia: University of South Carolina Press, 1973); Allen Pincus and Anne Minahan, *Social Work Practice: Model and Method* (Itaska, Illinois: F. E. Peacock, 1973); Alex Gitterman and Carel Germain, "Social Work Practice, A Life Model," *Social Service Review* 50, no. 4, (December 1976), pp. 601–10.

4. For an elaboration of this assertion, see Charles Grosser, "Laissez-Faire Social Work in a Welfare State," mimeographed (Louisville: University of Kentucky, Kent School of Social Work, 1977).

5. William E. Gordon, "Basic Constructs for an Integrative and Generative Conception of Social Work," in *The General Systems Approach: Contributions Toward an Holistic Conception of Social Work,* ed. Gordon Hearn (New York: Council on Social Work Education, 1969).

6. DeCoulanges, *The Ancient City.*

7. Charles Reich, "Individual Rights and Social Justice: The Emerging Legal Issues," *Yale Law Journal* 74 (June 1965), pp. 1245–59.

8. Charles Grosser, "A Polemic on Advocacy," in *Shaping the New Social Work,* ed. Alfred J. Kahn (New York: Columbia University Press, 1973).

12 Social Prevention: An Ecological Approach

MARTIN BLOOM

René Dubos tells us that the ancient Chinese paid their personal physicians to keep them healthy. The really good doctors were believed to be not those who treat the sick, but rather those who instruct people on how not to get ill.[1] In contemporary America, our health care system is foundering because of the emphasis on treating the sick, at greater and greater cost with less proportionate benefit, while little attention is given to keeping well.[2] Despite their cost-effectiveness, preventive services receive little or no financial support from third party payers, including medicaid.[3] The government itself is ambivalent about prevention as the Department of Health, Education, and Welfare issues warnings about saturated fat while the Department of Agriculture marks fat-laced beef with its prime stamp of approval. DHEW campaigns against smoking while DA subsidizes tobacco growers.

Educational measures to help people modify hazardous life styles stir minimal responsiveness among many segments of the citizenry. New groups of young persons and women continue to join the ranks of smokers. Others of us are unwilling to control the factors involved in our own obesity, hypertension, and tooth decay despite the fact that these and other health problems are largely within our power to control. Measures requiring individual action in matters of health seem generally to be less successful than those which depend on mandate, such as vaccination and pasteurization, or on people's passive presence in an arena of concern as, for example, in fluoridation of drinking water, improved highway design, and sanitation.[4] Even so, the elimination of environmental pollutants that cause illness and disability is hampered by vested interests and public lethargy.

Personal and social factors combine to make primary prevention difficult in the domain of health. Primary prevention in the social realm may be even more difficult because causal factors and their interaction are less well understood. Mandated "social innoculations" seem impossible to imagine. Some attempts to devise passive measures for mental health protection in the schools are appearing, however, which is cause for optimism. Creative social workers and innovative agencies provide crisis intervention services and family life education, although these do not always represent primary prevention.

Bloom delineates the issues and tasks in social prevention by means of a carefully conceived framework. He neither minimizes the difficulties nor skirts the revolutionary implications in carrying out the conception. But the steps for moving into primary prevention at programmatic levels, and guidelines for research to underpin social policy and program planning, are clearly identified. Readers will respond to different aspects of Bloom's presentation according to their own professional concerns, but of general interest is his repeated stress on promoting positive growth and preventing negative outcomes. These are complementary aspects of an ecologically oriented practice as well.

Within the discipline of ecology, emphasis is placed on social planning to make the environment safe for living organisms, to safeguard resources, and to assure adaptive balance. It follows that when an ecological perspective is applied to social work, then we take on the challenge to promote adaptive interchanges between people and environments, not limiting our function to entering situations after the damage has been done. This requires the incorporation of a preventive point of view into even a residual or rehabilitative service.

Bloom's analysis suggests that "interventive practitioners" allow themselves to feel uneasy and perplexed about the conditions they observe, and maintain an action-oriented, problem-solving attitude toward them. Thus medical social workers arrange to have parents stay with hospitalized children. School social workers offer group meetings to all interested teen-agers to discuss the common concerns of adolescents. Workers in touch with the very young or the very old in bland environments suggest means for increasing sensory stimuli. A community guidance clinic offers "Programs for People Without Problems." [5] A pediatric clinic provides a "Professional Grandma." [6]

Above all, Bloom underscores the need for collaboration with others in the continuing effort to promote the growth-producing qualities of the environment. In so doing, we may make our own modest professional contribution to enhancing the quality of health care, nutrition, housing, employment, education, and opportunity for all people. To paraphrase Dubos, it may then be said that the really good social workers are those who not only help people already having problems in living, but who also work to prevent such problems and to release potentialities.

                                                         —C.B.G.

How is one to go about a professional practice which involves preventing a problem that hasn't yet occurred? Or encouraging some equally unrealized but desired event to take the place of the predicted untoward one? Or maintaining a balance of obviating the undesired and promoting the desired over long periods of time? And how should the helping professional provide empirical data regarding the success or nonsuccess of such longitudinal programs when the persons involved, not to mention the environmental contexts, are constantly changing? Prevention is paradoxical because in spite of these very serious programmatic hurdles, there are few who would disagree in principle with President Kennedy: ". . . 'An ounce of prevention is worth more than a pound of cure.' For prevention is far more desirable for all concerned. It is far more economical and it is far more likely to be successful." [1]

Yet there are relatively few who have taken these statements seriously, and have carried them through to their logical conclusions in theoretical, empirical, and practice activities. Goldston estimates that about 5.2 percent of the total staff time in 400 operating, federally funded, community health centers was devoted to legally mandated types of preventive activities. [2] One looks in vain for even the subject heading "prevention" or "primary prevention" in the *Cumulative Index* (1965–1974) of *Abstracts for Social Workers.* Curricula of schools of social work which abound in many types of interventive and rehabilitative methods courses can scarcely muster one course in prevention. Our words, our deeds, our impact regarding primary prevention of social and psychological problems have had relatively little impression on society.

This bleak picture is not wholly accurate. We can retrace the steps of social work's contribution to primary prevention of social problems with Wittman who reminds us that Mary Richmond's "long view" did not include a society wise enough "to apply knowledge about human behavior and social systems to develop humane policies and to create mechanisms that would eventually prevent the onset of problems for individuals, families, and communities." [3] Perhaps such dreams inspired the social reformers who helped to develop child

This paper was supported, in part, by HEW Grant No. 1 T32 AA07130-01, National Institute on Alcohol Abuse and Alcoholism; and NIMH Grant No. 1 T21 MH 14980-01, Social Work Education Branch, Division on Manpower and Training Programs.

labor legislation and other social mechanisms that were preventive in nature, whether or not that label was applied.

Without that label, without the planned conception of what was involved in primary preventive activities, these efforts were often of short duration or mixed with and perhaps coopted by interventive and rehabilitative efforts. This is not to minimize the pioneering activities of social workers such as Rapoport, Wittman, Buell, and others, merely to set their efforts in perspective of the entire profession and the society which it serves.[4]

In the last few years, theorists and researchers have established a national forum—the Vermont Conferences on the Primary Prevention of Psychopathology; and practitioners from many disciplines are developing their organization—the National Association of Prevention Practitioners. Government efforts in funding preventive programs and in providing training grants appears to be picking up momentum.[5] Some books have appeared in the social work literature, as well as a number outside of that profession, which contain the word prevention in their titles, while presentations at national social work meetings, for the first time in many years, likewise contain this term—used in various ways.[6] This may just be the time to reconsider President Kennedy's challenge to fulfill the claim that prevention in social affairs is more desirable, economical, and successful than attempted cures.

This paper presents some concepts toward a working language for preventive social work. Through such a framework, social problems and potentialities may be logically addressed: prevention of negative outcomes and promotion of positive outcomes may be implemented and evaluated.[7] These concepts are largely borrowed from other disciplines and sciences—indeed, from an international array of preventive experiences and experiments—and are recombined into models which we are currently testing in field situations, at The George Warren Brown School of Social Work, Washington University, St. Louis.

THE PUBLIC HEALTH TRADITION

In contrast to private practice or even conventional medical institutions, public health is oriented toward community-wide or population problems appearing in and dealt with in the community. It has tradi-

TABLE 1. COMPARISON OF PREVENTIVE MEDICINE AND SOCIAL PREVENTION MODELS

Preventive Medicine (Medical Model)		Social Prevention (Ecological or Systems Model)	
Stages of Disease *	*Preventive Medical Approach* †	*Steps of Problem Solving and Value Determination*	*Social Prevention Approach*
1. *Stage of susceptibility:* in which the prerequisite conditions for the occurrence of the disease emerge.	1. *Health promotion:* Furthering health and well-being through general measures like education, nutrition, provision of community services, etc.	1. *Orientation* to general forces bearing on a class of specified events with recognition of the values of special interest groups.	1. *General prevention:* Identification and action regarding social policies and programs which promote or obviate broad classes of events.
2. *Preclinical stage:* No symptoms visible but analytic tools could reveal pathogenic events.	2. *Specific protection:* Measures applicable to a particular disease in order to intercept the pathogenic agent.	2. *Definition of the problem and concomitant potentialities* for the population of persons affected.	2. *Differential prevention:* Actions taken toward specific units of risk or of potentiality as discrete units of action.
3. *Acute clinical stage:*	3. *Early recognition and prompt treatment:*	3. *Formulation of preventive theoretical framework:* The most probable and optimally valued set of hypothetical solutions from the available knowledge base.	3. *Systemic prevention:* Actions taken toward units of risk and of potentiality within a social-ecological system.
A. Prodromal (early warning).	A. Screening & periodic exams.		
B. Manifest (patient aware of symptoms).	B. Disease control.		
C. Remission (possible disappearance of symptoms but not disease).	C. Surveillance of pathogenic conditions.		

4. *Post-acute clinical stage:* Residual effects of disease continue to be present and problematic.	4. *Disability limitation:* Preventing or delaying the consequences of clinically advanced or noncurable disease.	4. *Concomitant measurement of the preventive project:* Includes monitoring the process and evaluating the outcome, with feedback to correct preventive action.	4. *Systematic evaluation:* Comparison of actions relative to norms or standards of reference generated by population in question.
5. *Termination of clinical stage:* Either patient is rehabilitated to the best level attainable, or patient dies.	5. *Rehabilitation:* Bring affected person back to useful place in society as far as possible.	5. *Termination and/or institutionalization:* The methods of solution and the products of the solution may be ended or incorporated into standard social procedures.	5. *Systematic publication and promotion of program:* Successful prevention includes incorporation of the program into some social institution available to everyone.

* Adapted from Judith S. Mausner and Anita K. Bahn, *Epidemology* (Philadelphia: W. B. Saunders, 1974).
† Adapted from Hugh R. Leavell and E. Gurney Clark (eds.), *Textbook of Preventive Medicine* (New York: McGraw-Hill, 1953).

tionally followed a version of the medical model which seeks specific causal agents for particular diseases located within congenial environments, such as mosquitos living in swampy areas carrying the organisms which cause yellow fever. Bloom vividly describes the triumphs of this tradition in cleansing 19th-century Europe and America and reducing the incidence of many communicable diseases—albeit for reasons unrelated to the miasma theory under whose guidance the cleansing was performed.[8] We are heirs to the public health concept of host and victim, agent and carrier, and the biophysical-social environments in which these events take place, although we have to convert this inheritance into coinage suitable to the psychosocial realm.

Table 1 summarizes the public health approach to prevention. This table should serve to remind the reader of the well-developed literature regarding this approach and its demonstrated results, particularly in regard to certain acute diseases, but now extending beyond its beginnings.[9] The first column on the left summarizes stages of disease, a conceptual interpretation of the general way in which a person and a specific pathogen come together. Not all diseases, particularly chronic disorders, fit this model, but it is common enough to be used productively for many acute diseases. Such a conception draws together the set of assumptions which direct attention to certain problems and appropriate solutions to them.[10]

The second column summarizes the preventive medical approach which stems from Leavell and Clark's contributions.[11] There is a rough correspondence between stages of diseases and the types of preventive medical approaches; this suggests that the assumptions underlying one may be used to interpret the other. For example, health promotion might be directed toward points in the social order where persons are susceptible to pathogenic agents. If we know that children of the poor are likely to suffer from malnutrition, then we should undertake to augment the presently existing states of health so as to obviate the predicted deterioration that results from long-standing poor nutrition.[12]

There are so many points at which people are first susceptible to what could become problems that it might be more feasible to wait until a preclinical stage occurs in order to offer specific protective measures, such as giving a vaccine to high risk groups for a specific pathogen, in contrast to nation wide programs such as the swine flu effort in 1977. As we approach the acute clinical stage, we leave behind the possibility of primary prevention in favor of "secondary prevention," or treatment. When disability limitation and rehabilitation are the central concerns, we are engaged in "tertiary prevention"—an unfortunate euphemism.[13]

For Leavell and Clark, the point of specific protection is prevention in the strictest sense. Much is known about the natural histories of specific diseases and the contexts in which they occur. This knowledge has led to many preventive medical approaches such as those which strengthen the would-be victim (for example, immunization), or which attack the pathogenic agent (such as renovating the insides of houses by removing peeling lead-based paint), or which act to ameliorate a deleterious social and physical environment so as to minimize contacts between the would-be victims and pathogenic agents (for example, developing rules regarding occupational hazards and designing machinery to decrease them). Specific protection requires considerable expert knowledge and skill, and as a consequence, persons working in this area are afforded high status and power. Public funding for research and development is heavily focused at this juncture.

We must now inquire as to what paradigmatic view is likely to be most useful in addressing psychosocial problems and potentialities. A particular conception of a primary preventive approach to social and psychological problems is set forth on the right side of Table 1. Although the paradigm is influenced by the public health tradition, the differences in underlying assumptions needed to deal with social concerns must be recognized. Whether workers in social prevention have a sufficient knowledge base to focus their efforts in this way remains to be determined.

PREVENTIVE SOCIAL WORK

The subtitle of this section of Table 1 refers to an ecological or systems model.[14] This subtitle summarizes a perspective in which social situations are characterized by networks of large numbers of events which may be agents, hosts, or environments for other events, all at the same time. Whether one is rooting for rats, lice, or men during the Black Plague makes all the difference in attaching labels. Moreover, these large numbers of events are continually flowing and changing, like a Joycean stream of consciousness, while the whole tends toward balanced interchanges among the diverse elements. What the medical model has done is to pick out some discrete events in this flow which have been found to have relatively predictable relationships with other events, particularly those having some physical existence. Other public health writers recognize the complexity and relativity of these relationships; for example, people who carry the tuberculosis bacilli do not necessarily become ill. The outcomes are determined by peoples' physical constitutions, states of health, and other environmental factors interacting with the bacilli.

The ecological model of primary social prevention, however, faces a more challenging task of finding some conceptually identifiable arrangement of events within the flux of everyday life that may not have already demonstrable influences on some other set of events. For example, Grannis retrospectively examines the "wide-spread, long-term use of a trivial yet subtly noxious agent"—cigarette smoking—with regard to demographic characteristics of the older population of the United States.[15] Using current information that heavy smoking shortens one's life span between seven and twelve years, Grannis demonstrates how this factor *alone* is sufficient to account for the demographic structure that currently exists—an excess of 2.5 million widows over the number of likely widows predicted on the basis of chance. Even knowing such critical information is not sufficient to have a wide-spread impact on the behaviors of large numbers of persons, especially young people and women.

Likewise, using powerful prospective tools does not necessarily influence decisions on how we shape that future. Levin, Hirsch, and Roberts, using a computer simulation, illustrate how various elements of community action regarding narcotics are likely to work in interaction.[16] The addition of more police, methadone clinics, education of potential addicts, and a community awareness program have predictable effects on crime rate, the numbers of addicts on the street, and the socioeconomic stability of the community. Yet there are many other factors—political, ideological, psychological—which compli-cate the task of the would-be preventer. How, then, should a social work preventer proceed?

In place of a neat natural history of specific diseases, the social preventer has a *method of approach,* a sequence of preventive prob-lem solving steps derived from the common scientific method, but in-tricately mixed with values and value decisions. As outlined in Table 1, the first step of preventive problem solving involves *orientation,* what are the general forces bearing on the specific event in question? It is important to note—and perhaps this is one of the distinctive fea-tures of a social prevention approach—that events are moving toward positive as well as negative combinations, that some forces are *pro-moting desired outcomes* as well as *obviating undesired ones,* de-pending on the perspective of the observer. These orientational issues help to provide some broad patterns to the flux of events; they also help to identify value positions of those who seek or oppose the proj-ect goals. Indeed, for any one party, there may be both positive and negative factors involved in the decision; each subsystem has its own systemic calculations operating within its own value perspective.

The next step in preventive problem solving is to *define the prob-lem* specifically. This involves locating *units of risk*—those clusters of events which are predicted to lead to untoward outcomes for some specified population of persons—and *units of potential*—another clus-ter of desired events which may be predicted to occur if certain ac-tions are made to take place. It is important to note that this approach assumes that the population at risk or with potentiality is currently functioning in a relatively adequate manner in regard to the specific project goal, although this does not assume perfect functioning per-sons in all regards. It is also assumed that the units of risk and the units of potential and the negative and positive goals are system-atically interrelated so that definitions of the situation, and con-sequently plans of action and evaluation, must necessarily deal with both.

The third step of preventive problem solving concerns the analysis and construction of the *most probable theoretical framework,* that is, that empirically-based system of hypotheses which appears to offer the strongest probabilities of outcome within the values and costs that relevant parties are willing to pay. Like any other theory, it is an abstract guide to practice and requires translation into specific strategies.[17] The preventive theorist must give full weighting to desired and undesired events, and to the contingency planning with which one lives through each successive stage of development. But more than most theories, a preventive approach requires a concomitant measurement system both to monitor the process and to evaluate the outcome, since no problem is currently visible and serious questions can be raised about whether the results would have happened by natural events without the preventive or promotion project. This *measurement process* is part of the fourth step. It also includes a feedback mechanism which is very important to *both* the *theory* and the *practice*—perhaps another distinctive feature of social prevention.

For example, within the limits of present knowledge, certain general developmental norms are available as milestones against which the changes in targeted groups can be compared. However, there are many difficult questions in using such theoretical materials: Should the targeted population be "adjusted" to the majority? How is heterogeneity and innovativeness to be included in the preventive project? How are the values of relevant parties to be fitted together? An evaluation system requires the practitioner to be very specific about project goals and how well they are being attained. Ongoing data collection enables the practitioner to assess not only the preventive practice but also theoretical models which guide that practice. It should be expected that more frequent shifts of strategy will take place within the conceptual perspective than in relatively unchanging, larger theories of personality or society.

The last step of preventive problem solving involves *incorporating the results* into the ongoing stream of social life, since presumably the current targeted population will be replaced by another generation who will face the same social issues and challenges all over again. Prevention as promoting the desired and obviating the undesired is a continuous task faced by society and should be integrated into the social fabric as part of the expectable social environment.[18]

The social prevention approach is derived from the preventive problem-solving method as well as the public health model. Table 1 shows three modes of approach: *General prevention* involves iden-

tifying and acting in regard to social planning, policies, and programs which either promote or obviate broad classes of events, for their own purposes, rather than for any specific preventive goal. Education, for example, has its own agenda, whether or not preventers see in education the vehicle for instilling lifetime skills. Preventers must therefore work with educators to help them achieve their goals, especially those consonant with preventive objectives.

Differential prevention involves actions taken toward specific units of risk or of potentiality, regarded as discrete units of action. For example, programs identifying parents who are potential child abusers typically have a specific focus; although narrowly conceived, such projects receive wide support because, in part, society has become accustomed to piecemeal programming in social welfare.[19] Nevertheless, it is possible to evaluate the success of such programs within their own scope of reference. Considerable specialized knowledge and practice wisdom does build up in a particular program, and workers come to be identified as specialists.

But in the ecological perspective, these characteristics of differential prevention are short-term gains, and may stand in the way of more fundamental changes. *Systemic prevention* seeks to take into consideration the inevitable interaction when one both promotes and obviates various events in units of risk and of potentiality regarding some targeted project. For example, if we provide school lunch programs to promote health of children, then we had better be prepared for healthier young persons who mature earlier. If some of this early maturity is expressed in sexual behavior, we had better be prepared with the appropriate educational programs and accessible contraceptive technologies. If some young unwed adolescents have children of their own, then we had better be prepared with social support systems to aid in the child-rearing process. No one of these programs—school lunches, sex education, family life skills—operates in a vacuum, even if it appears so in the separated institutions which provide for them. Prevention may be the quintessential practice of social coordination, of identifying and acting on the expected interventive effects of promoting and obviating some set of events relative to some goal.

Regardless of which preventive approach is taken, *systematic eval-*

uation and *promotion* of successful programs should be involved. Indicators of quality of life are very complex when set within complicated longitudinal programs. It may be that the negative events in one program are a necessary precursor to positive events in another which may lead to an overall advance for both sets of events in the long run. That adolescent pregnancy is increasing may force the awareness of the rights of infants as well as the rights and responsibilities of young people, and the larger question of what is a meaningful total life may be advanced.

ILLUSTRATION

The social preventive aspects of work in lead poisoning contain all of the essential ingredients of any preventive project. Lin-Fu points out that lead poisoning is somewhat unusual because as a medical-social problem it is entirely under the control of society—both in regard to causing the condition and treating it, and in attempting to prevent the disease.[20] The first step of the social prevention model asks for general orientation to the project: what larger social forces are involved in the circumstances labeled lead poisoning? Focusing on the most common victims of this problem, young children in the inner city, we can quickly call to mind a number of major factors: the manufacture of lead-based paint, its application on the inside walls of places where young children are growing up—in spite of laws to the contrary; the deterioration of the paint resulting in peeling, the presence of children who are not closely monitored and who eat the paint chips; the fact of less-than-adequate medical services which may not recognize the early symptoms of lead poisoning, which are in fact common to many other conditions etc. This brief list calls attention to a number of factors: economic issues; legal issues; social factors regarding landlords or deteriorating property as well as the segregated patterns of social life which force certain racial, ethnic, and social class groups to occupy these deteriorating areas of cities; social-psychological issues (who is raising the child and what emotional relationships are present between parent/surrogate and child); medical issues regarding pica (the tendency to ingest inedible substances); etc.

Some of these issues engage social norms at the highest levels—the profit motive, racial attitudes, and the like—which no one project is going to affect significantly without coordination from many quarters. But in specific instances, changes in local ordinances may affect the profitability of deteriorating housing or challenge segregated housing—issues not related directly to lead poisoning per se—so that even such broad issues can have preventive considerations.[21] One of the barriers to social prevention is the question of whether, fundamentally, it is an applied science of revolution, as it frequently raises questions about basic social relationships. The ecologist recognizes that any basic social change—or nonchange—may have revolutionary impact in the long run; the question is whether we are to be aware of this or to attempt to influence it toward an optimal configuration of valued goals.

Other orientation factors are aimed more directly at specific occurrences of the problem: the training of professional groups to recognize signs of lead poisoning, and the education of parents to preventive considerations, from repair of the physical structure to other forms of psychosocial interactions between parents/surrogates and child; etc. With the focus on this level, we have moved to the second step in preventive problem-solving, locating the specific units of risk and of potentiality. The usual response to recognizing units of risk is to develop a program for each. For example, some progressive public health departments organize campaigns to canvass neighborhoods presumed to be in high risk so as to provide information to parents with very young children.[22] Less frequently, special educational programs are directed toward local medical units to increase their awareness of lead poisoning symptoms. Very rarely are landlords informed of the hazards to young children and the corresponding legal risks they might face—if indeed there is any significant legal risk to be found in local ordinances.

Unfortunately, there are few programs directed toward the strengths which these same populations at risk possess. Poverty does not totally determine child neglect.[23] In other literatures the strengths of poor black families and other ethnic minorities are being recognized.[24] The viability of existing social and cultural structures and natural helping networks are being explored.[25] The tandem development of young inexperienced parents and their children represents another point of entry for primary prevention.[26] Indeed, even when an older child in a family is in treatment for one problem (delinquency), the younger siblings may be the objects of primary preventive efforts as well.[27] Whole families are brought together in these primary preventive efforts with sensitivity to ethnic and cultural conditions.[28]

Thus, as we begin to identify both the positive and negative units, we can begin to merge programs dealing simultaneously with both. This is the next step in social prevention, a combined approach attempting to deal with obviating negative outcomes and promoting positive ones, each set viewed as reciprocally influencing the outcomes of the other. Such integration forces the helping professional to consider the knowledge and skills of other professionals and paraprofessionals. It pushes the entire activity out into the community, and seeks clear evaluation methods by which all relevant parties can contribute to the definition, the maintenance, or the change of the program.

Cost/benefit analyses are clearly a part of this social prevention program. For lead poisoning, Lin-Fu suggests some very provocative figures: if one child becomes retarded as a result of lead poisoning and spends his/her entire life in an institution for the retarded at public expense, the cost is estimated to be over $200,000.[29] This sum, multiplied by the numbers of affected individuals, raises the question of distributed values within the larger social order. Who pays this money and is there a clear choice of paying it after the fact (for treatment and rehabilitation) or for paying (some of) it before the fact, in preventive efforts? It is the task of the social preventer to make these choices clear, based on the best available evidence. Complicating these cost issues are many value issues so that the social preventer becomes, in effect, a publicist, an educator, a politician, an economist, a medical expert—in short, a generalist with a specific program. It may be argued that this is the historic role for social workers, one which yet needs to be fulfilled.[30]

EDUCATING A PREVENTIVE
SOCIAL WORKER

Just as a person trained in preventive medicine must first learn general medicine—and then unlearn parts of it so as to be psychologically oriented to promoting states of health rather than patching up states of disease and disorder—so the student of preventive social work must learn some basic knowledge, skills, and values, and then move to a different helping plane in order to use these and other forms of information in a new way. Whether the difference between interventive social work and preventive social work is merely a matter of quantitative degree or qualitative difference may someday surface as an important educational issue. It is still too early, however, to do more than build on a common base of social work concepts, information, and procedures, as well as concepts borrowed from other disciplines, while being sensitive and alert to differences.

Students of preventive social work, for example, must learn about human growth and development in the physical and social environments. However, in place of normative use made by the intervention worker (comparing a current state of a person's malfunction or maladaptation with the norm for that type of person), the preventive social worker uses the norms as anticipated goals against which to compare current developments, so as to keep the person within the range of progression toward some goals which can be prejudged by relevant parties (including the person himself or herself in some cases). This use requires some specific understanding of the states of individual development and particularly of tandem developments when parents and children are facing interrelated challenges such as the first entry into school or adolescence. It also requires a clearer understanding of variations in the sex, race, class, and age of persons involved, as these are the major categories which influence the form of that development.[31]

Another major domain of social work education is social welfare policy, planning, and programs. This macrolevel perspective is equally important to preventive social workers who might be taking a direct part in planning for populations at risk or with positive potential. Does this mean that such students are required to be generalists, having training in both micro- and macrolevel areas? In part, yes. Prevention appears to take so many forms that some training in the range of possible social work roles seems advisable. But the preventer is not simply a generalist; rather, some specialized set of skills seems most advisable for practical work in depth.

As social work faculties have long known, it is difficult to be or to teach one how to be both generalist and specialist. However, there is another approach which tends to resolve this dilemma: a team approach in which generalists with a variety of particular specializations come together on a given project and coordinate their individual contributions so far as possible. To attain this goal, the preventive social work program at the George Warren Brown School of Social Work has designed a curriculum that has some courses on a generalist base and latitude for electives to meet students' career interests in specialized areas. Then teams of students take their field placements together, designing coordinated proposals for what they seek to learn and how they can contribute to the agency's functioning as a team. Moreover, given the structure of the training grant on which this work is based, it is possible to experiment by allowing different teams with successive generations of students to continue in the same agencies. This allows for continuity of projects and diversity of experiences for students.

A third major component of social work education is learning research. For the preventive program, this is interpreted as learning to monitor the progress and to evaluate the outcome of the prevention as a practitioner, not as a specialist in research.[32] Thus, master's degree students are instructed in single-system designs as approximate methods of measuring longitudinal events as they occur in practice. Doctoral students apply their skills to preventive programs as well. With the enthusiastic cooperation of several community agencies, this mix of master's and doctoral level training for preventive social work provides an extraordinary challenge for the helping professions.

NOTES

1. René Dubos, *Man Adapting* (New Haven: Yale University Press, 1965), p. 226.

2. For discussion of contemporary issues in health care, see "Doing Better and Feeling Worse: Health in the United States," *Daedalus* (Winter 1977).

3. Marvin M. Kristein, et al., "Health Economics and Preventive Care," *Science* 195 (February 4, 1977), pp. 457–62.

4. "Resolutions and Policy Statements Adopted by the Governing Council of the American Public Health Association, Oct. 20, 1976," *American Journal of Public Health* 67, no. 1 (January 1977), pp. 76–107.

5. The Sheldon Community Guidance Clinic, Inc., New Britain, Conn., Spring 1977. Evening sessions were held in the public library, with child care provided by library staff. Three such sessions were for single parents, and a fourth considered a full-length movie about a multihandicapped child. Professional staff led the sessions.

6. Sharon Johnson, "Professional Grandma Counsels Parents," *The New York Times,* October 6, 1977, a report on a La Jolla, California pediatric group.

---

1. President John F. Kennedy, Message of the Congress of the United States on Mental Illness and Mental Retardation, February 5, 1963.

2. Stephen E. Goldston, "Primary Prevention: A View From the Federal Level," in George W. Albee and Justin M. Joffe (eds.), *Primary Prevention of Psychopathology. Vol. 1. The Issues* (Hanover, New Hampshire: University Press of New England, 1977).

3. Milton Wittman, "Preventive Social Work," *Encyclopedia of Social Work* (New York: National Association of Social Workers, 1977).

4. While the list of social work contributors is not complete, mention should be given to Lydia Rapoport, "The Concept of Prevention in Social Work," *Social Work* 6, no. 1 (1961), pp. 19–28; Milton Wittman, "Social Worker in Preventive Service," *Social Welfare Forum, 1962* (New York: Columbia University Press, 1962); Bradley Buell, "Implications for Social Work Education of Conception of Prevention," in *Proceedings of the Annual Program Meeting of the Council on Social Work Education,* 1960. See also Kurt Reichert, "Prevention: Social Work's Historical Challenge," a paper presented at the 104th Annual Meeting of the American Public Health Association, Miami Beach, 1976.

5. Herbert Staulcup, "Primary Prevention of Alcohol Abuse: A Literature Review" (unpublished manuscript).

6. For example, Alice H. Collins and Diane L. Pancoast, *Natural Helping Networks: A Strategy for Prevention* (Washington, D.C.: National Association of Social Workers, 1976); Carol Meyer (ed.), *Preventive Intervention* (Washington, D.C.: National Association of Social Workers, 1975). See also Emory L. Cowen, "Social and Community Interventions," *Annual Review of Psychology,* 1973, pp. 423–72; Marc Kessler and George W. Albee, "Primary Prevention," *Annual Review of Psychology,* 1975, pp. 557–91; James G. Kelly, Lonnie R. Snowden, and Ricardo F. Muñoz, "Social and Community Interventions," *Annual Review of Psychology,* 1977, pp. 323–61.

7. See, for example, Walter B. Simon, "Some Issues in the Logic of Prevention," *Social Science and Medicine* 6 (1972), pp. 95–107.

8. Bernard L. Bloom, "The 'Medical Model,' Miasma Theory, and Community Mental Health," *Community Mental Health Journal* 1 (1965), pp. 333–38.

9. See, for example, L. E. Burton and H. H. Smith, *Public Health and Community Medicine for the Allied Medical Professions* (Baltimore: Williams and Wilkins, 1970); James F. Jekel, "Communicable Disease Control and Public Policy in the 1970s—Hot War, Cold War, or Peaceful Coexistence?" *American Journal of Public Health* 62, no. 12 (1972), pp. 1578–85.

10. Thomas S. Kuhn, *The Structure of Scientific Revolutions,* 2d ed. (Chicago: University of Chicago Press, 1971).

11. Hugh R. Leavell and E. Gurney Clark eds., *Textbook of Preventive Medicine* (New York: McGraw-Hill, 1953).

12. Herbert G. Birch, "Malnutrition, Learning, and Intelligence," *American Journal of Public Health* 62, no. 6 (1972), pp. 773–84.

13. Cowen, "Social and Community Intervention."

14. See, for example, Carel Germain, "An Ecological Perspective in Case Work Practice," *Social Casework* 54, no. 6 (1973), pp. 323–30; James G. Miller, "Living Systems: Basic Concepts," *Behavioral Science* 10, no. 3 (1965), pp. 193–237.

15. George F. Grannis, "Demographic Perturbations Secondary to Cigarette Smoking," *Journal of Gerontology* 25, no. 1 (1970), pp. 55–63.

16. Gilbert Levin, Gary Hirsch, and Edward Roberts, "Narcotics and the Community: A Systems Simulation," *American Journal of Public Health* 62, no. 6 (1972), pp. 861–73.

17. Martin Bloom, *Paradox of Helping: Introduction to the Philosophy of Scientific Practice* (New York: Wiley, 1975).

18. Alfred J. Kahn, "New Policies and Service Models: The Next Phase," *American Journal of Orthopsychiatry* 35, no. 4 (1965), pp. 652–62.

19. Compare the systemic approach of David G. Gil, "Unraveling Child Abuse," *American Journal of Orthopsychiatry* 45, no. 3 (1975), pp. 346–56.

20. Jane S. Lin-Fu, "Childhood Lead Poisoning: An Eradicable Disease," *Children* 17, no. 1 (1970), pp. 2–9.

21. See, for example, Elihu D. Richter, Selma Jackson, Solomon Peeples, Courtney Wood, and Roberta Volante, "Housing and Health—A New Approach," *American Journal of Public Health* 63, no. 10 (1973), pp. 787–83.

22. See "Facts About Lead and Pediatrics," (New York: Lead Industries Association, n.d.); Jane S. Lin-Fu, "Lead Poisoning in Children," Children's Bureau Publication no 452, 1967.

23. Jeanne M. Giovannoni and Andrew Billingsley, "Child Neglect Among the Poor: A Study of Parental Adequacy in Families of Three Ethnic Groups," *Child Welfare* 49, no. 4 (1970), pp. 196–204.

24. Robert Hill, *The Strengths of Black Families* (New York: Emerson Hall, 1972).

25. Collins and Pancoast, *Natural Helping Networks.*

26. For example, see Phyllis Levenstein, "Cognitive Growth in Preschoolers Through Verbal Interaction With Mothers," *American Journal of Orthopsychiatry*

40 (1970), pp. 426–32; Susan W. Gray and Robert A. Klaus, "The Early Training Project: A Seventh-Year Report," *Child Development* 41 (1970), pp. 909–24.

27. Nanci Klein, James F. Alexander, and Bruce V. Parsons, "Impact of Family System Intervention on Recidivism and Sibling Delinquency: A Model of Primary Prevention and Program Evaluation," *Journal of Consulting and Clinical Psychology* 45, no. 3 (1977), pp. 469–74.

28. Dale L. Johnson, Hazel Leler, Laurel Rios, Larry Brandt, Alfred J. Kahn, Edward Mazeika, Martha Frede, and Billie Bisett, "The Houston Parent-Child Development Center: A Parent Educational Program for Mexican-American Families," *American Journal of Orthopsychiatry* 44, no. 1 (1974), pp. 121–28.

29. Lin-Fu, "Childhood Lead Poisoning."

30. Martin Bloom, "Explorations in Preventive Social Work," paper presented at the 5th Biennial Professional Symposium of the National Association of Social Workers, San Diego, 1977.

31. See Martin Bloom, *Life Span Development: Sex, Class, and Racial Variations Relevant to Preventive and Interventive Helping* (New York: Macmillan, Forthcoming [1979]).

32. Martin Bloom and Stephen Block, "Evaluating One's Own Effectiveness and Efficiency," *Social Work* 22, no. (1977), pp. 130–36; Martin Bloom, "Toward Ultimate Measures of Student Competence in Field Performance," paper presented at the 1st Big Sky Summer Symposium, Big Sky, Montana, 1977.

13 *People Cannot Go It Alone*

Sister Mary Paul Janchill

Sr. Mary Paul's article presents a programmatic example of Bloom's conception of social prevention. Having a grant-supported mandate to prevent and control juvenile delinquency in an impoverished area of Brooklyn, a group of energetic social workers engaged in primary preventive efforts through the provision of developmental services. They engaged in secondary preventive efforts through early intervention at the first signs of trouble, and tertiary preventive efforts through a range of rehabilitative and restorative services. All efforts were, ultimately, directed to the child and his family, school, and neighborhood context. The social workers, through education and experience, possessed a knowledge-based orientation toward the complicated interactions associated with the eruption of delinquency in such ecological contexts. After a year of additional study of the existing social problems and the resources and strengths in the community, they were ready to begin their tasks with respect to specific "units of risk and of potentiality." [1]

The Park Slope experience also illustrates the town-meeting approach to citizen participation as referred to by Grosser. [2] *The many segments of a living neighborhood—residents, schools, police, merchants, civic associations—were mobilized to undertake the creation of a network of services and resources for all residents. Many took part in forums and task forces to identify needs, establish priorities, locate strengths, release human potentialities, plan action, allocate tasks, and exchange resources, information, and energy. All of this generated a sense of caring and interdependence that comes out of active participation in events and processes that touch intimately on one's life. In reciprocal fashion, the new sense of self-esteem and competence are spurs to further effective action. The beginning efforts of the social workers and the community set off a spiraling of achievement by both.*

Some readers may see in Sr. Mary Paul's account a similarity to the set-

tlement movement of an earlier day, buttressed by modern knowledge and commitment. The settlers had hoped to create a "helpful, friendly life among the poor," by processes of good neighboring. Summer outings to the country for children and their mothers, clubs for boys and girls, classes for their parents, penny banks, and public baths were a few of the diverse activities provided by settlement houses. Increasingly, the good neighbors moved beyond the walls of the settlement to undertake action on industrial conditions, consumer problems, tenement reform, overcrowded schools, and sanitary needs. They pioneered in the use of the schools as neighborhood centers.[3] The greatest similarity may lie in the fact that the Park Slope staff were living and working in the ecological context. Like an emergency room of a busy general hospital, the Family Reception Center was in a position to receive calls for help and to respond to them 24 hours a day, every day of the year, and the staff could move in and out of schools, police precincts, family courts, businesses, and homes as shifting life forces demanded.

No matter how much one is tempted to draw parallels to earlier days, however, these devoted social workers of the 1970s remain uniquely themselves. Knowledgeable, highly skilled in a variety of helping approaches, deeply committed to human potentiality, these social workers exemplify the ecological perspective on practice.

—C.B.G.

In Park Slope we believe that helping services cannot afford the dichotomy that addresses the individual while ignoring the tapestry of his environment. That is equal to considering a fish out of water or a tree out of soil. We would then have removed each from the source of life and growth, identity and understanding which defines and validates the existence of each. Nothing is more absurd than man or woman alone. Nothing perpetuates mental illness more than the segregation of man from his field, ideologically or practically.

Our response to human need must essentially be framed in an ecological understanding. All systems connecting and responding will create profound changes in the quality of life in Park Slope.[1]

FAMILY RECEPTION CENTER

A YOUNG, vibrant staff, convened by Sisters of the Good Shepherd Residences in the fall of 1972 to initiate the *Family Reception Center* in the Park Slope neighborhood of Brooklyn, New York, thus articulated its self-understanding and mission. A mandate had been given this agency by the Law Enforcement Assistance Administration in funding a program of "court diversion" for troubled youth of the area. The mandate followed on nearly a year of our knocking on the doors of community residents, merchants, clergy, school guidance counselors, police, nurses, physicians, social service providers, and Family Court judges, to search out their perceptions of problems and needs.

There had been near universal agreement in these discussions that the strategy of comprehensive, family-centered services proffered by the agency would be an appropriate and welcome response to an accelerating ''youth problem.'' The neighborhood of over 100,000 residents was estimated to have 42,600 people (some 35.7 percent) under 21 years of age. Local studies had shown rising juvenile delinquency and venereal disease rates. In addition, the city's Office of Special Services for Children had undertaken to locate by zip code the addresses of natural families who had lost their children to foster care, as well as the locations of substitute family homes and group care settings. This study revealed that out of 37 zip code areas that covered the city's boundaries, the two that comprised Park Slope were eighth and ninth highest in risk. One of these areas, for example, had sent 159 children into substitute care while only 26 foster homes were located in that sector. Park Slope was extremely underserviced, having no group home or group care setting and no outpatient mental health clinic or family agency for the neighborhood.

On the other hand, Park Slope is in many ways a microcosm of New York City, diverse in its ethnic and class representations and typical of many other sections in each of the boroughs. The well-known attractiveness of rehabilitated ''brownstones'' on the upper slope of the Prospect Park border has drawn a small fringe of professional and middle-class families along one boundary of the neighborhood. However, other sections of the community reflect poor housing conditions and incipient blight. Abandoned and razed buildings have multiplied in recent years, creating sites for exploitation and abuse. Racial and ethnic tensions have been high. Strong ethnocentric orientations have tended to generate segregated recreational, social, and social service programs in the area. Despite an ethos of racial and ethnic integration proclaimed by ''brownstone'' residents in Park Slope, such integration has been accomplished only within that professional and middle-class arc of the neighborhood, while there has been little crossover from "up slope" to "down slope" stores, schools, recreation centers, or activities.

Locating ourselves a bit "down slope" but at the horizontal center of the neighborhood, we were helped by a philanthropic foundation to renovate an unoccupied four-story building: unoccupied at least by official tenants, although we discovered we were displacing a group of youngsters who had set up their cots on the top floor and had made this their home while they "stole for a living." We soon came to know these displaced youth who had been extruded by the schools. They were no longer sought by attendance officers nor counted among the categories of "handicapped children" requiring special educational programs, since they were not "brain-injured," or "neurologically impaired," "mentally retarded," or "emotionally disturbed"—just simply truants and nonreaders. There were other youth and families we met in sizeable numbers who had become marginalized and labeled, and were waiting for extrusion from home and community. There were school suspensions, court petitions of neglect, PINS (Person in Need of Supervision), or delinquency.

Our task was clear, for as social workers we found ready made for us a whole client population constituted by marginalization in interaction with impinging social systems. Such marginalization tends to generate cycles of events, reinforced by new inputs and reactions and then reinvested with new energy.[2]

As Robert White stresses, the inherent drive of the organism to have effect calls on and requires a mutual presence of the individual and the environing system in which the spending of energy is reciprocated and reinforced.[3]

Accordingly, the Family Reception Center developed a twofold set of goals: (1) provision of a comprehensive range of personal and social services aimed at supporting the developmental tasks and competence of children and families living in the neighborhood; and (2) reduction of marginalization in any social system in which it was an operating dynamic, whether in the family, school, or other community institution. The program would be integrative because it would itself be related to human service systems throughout the neighborhood; it would be comprehensive because it would provide a range of helps most immediate to life management concerns of neighborhood residents while also helping to generate those helps it could not directly provide, e.g., medical and legal services. Accepting the initial mandate for juvenile delinquency and control which brought us funding, we nevertheless defined our strategy as one of universal availability in a noncategorical approach, in order to avoid isolating a particular client group which then would run the risk of alienation of that very group. Throughout, our approach to juvenile delinquency prevention and control would be guided by the conviction that a community's health, strength, and safety must be measured by its capacity to sustain its children.

The design of the Family Reception Center, therefore, became that of a *primary access system,* open seven days and seven evenings a week, available to give service to any family resident in Park Slope which had at least one child of school age, without fee, by self-referral or at the request of any social agency or community group, or the request of a parent or interested party. In addition to individual and family casework, there are therapy and activity groups planned for children, youth, and parents, according to their interests and needs. Parents and children are brought together to new understandings and knowledge through discussion groups, communication workshops, family life education programs, film and speaker programs (in Spanish and English) on human problems and special subjects—housing, legal rights, and the like. Parents develop and run their own social and recreational programs. They also sponsor a dance-theatre workshop for neighborhood children and youth. Teenagers also plan recreations. There are informal activities as well as special outings and occasional camping weekends. An educational advocate works with the educational system, helping to resolve school-student conflicts and to locate, when necessary, appropriate programs to match the special needs of children. Where particular diagnostic help is needed by a child or family member, psychological testing and psychiatric evaluation can be provided. Linkages with legal, medical, housing, and financial assistance resources are created according to need.

In addition to these modalities, the Center includes a short-term residential component (one floor of its building) known as a "crash pad" for back-up in emergency situations where a child or group of siblings require temporary removal from a conflicted home situation. At times a whole family has been housed here briefly. The "crash pad'' has been a valuable resource in the service of runaways until family equilibrium can be restored. Exerting strenuous efforts to maintain children within their own community and families, the Center staffs call upon least restrictive alternatives within the neighborhood and within the city in those cases where child placement is a requirement. The purpose in this is to minimize the loss of familiar ties and grounding for the child and to maximize family contacts toward the earliest possible reconstitution of the family unit.[4]

Simon, a 16-year-old boy, was referred to the Center by Special Services for Children (of the New York City Department of Social Services) for exploration of placement and diagnostic assessment in our "crash pad." Both his parents died suddenly of heart attacks—the father in 1974 and the mother two months before the "crash pad" admission. Placement seemed inevitable as Simon was allegedly disruptive of his older sister's marriage, physically abusive to her, rivalrous with her infant son, and was keeping late hours and truanting.

We found that intense depression was underlying this hostile and despairing behavior. With supportive services to an aunt residing in Park Slope (including recruitment of public assistance payment of support for Simon), she agreed to take him into her home where there would be a friendship with her own 20-year-old son. The social worker slowly but steadily engaged Simon in a reconnection with school and preparation for part-time employment.

In another situation:

The Aguirrez family was referred to the Family Reception Center by a neighbor during a crisis of eviction from their apartment. Separated now from her older, married children, Mrs. Aguirrez came with the four remaining at home, ages 16, 9, 5, and 3. As they were homeless, the mother and four children were admitted into the "crash pad" and the social worker helped to secure a new apartment. For some time there were major problems in stabilizing the financial situation of the family, and approaches toward individual treatment of the mother were unsuccessful. However, Mrs. Aguirrez gained specially from attending the Parents' Night program each week. She applied herself to completing a high school equivalency curriculum and currently attends a Project Chance program designed to move her to college later. Mrs. Aguirrez is also a member of a women's group at the Center dealing with female sexuality. Though the children initially appeared quite neglected, substantial improvements occurred.

In still another situation:

> Mrs. Olds at age 21 is the mother of three children, the oldest of whom is 7. The social worker responded to a call from a school guidance counselor who planned to press a Family Court neglect petition because 7-year-old Anna was not attending school. Mrs. Olds was helped to obtain an order of protection against her husband who was threatening her, to obtain medical help for the relief of pain from a congenital hip condition, and to formulate a realistic budget with the help of the welfare center. The worker pressed the landlord to accomplish needed repairs in the apartment, and helped Mrs. Olds with some furniture. Beds were particularly important as one child was sleeping on two chairs facing each other. Mrs. Olds was helped to locate a good day care arrangement for the children, which would allow her to finish her high school education as she desired to do. The care of the children improved as Mrs. Olds experienced the steady support of the Center.

At the end of the first year of the Center's inauguration, service had been given to 252 families, and to 198 additional families during the second year.[5] During the third year 212 more families received direct assistance, and through May 1977 the total had gone beyond 950 families. Help consisted of service to from one to ten family members. Also, information and referral services had been provided to many more, and a staff person outstationed at the Brooklyn Family Court gave immediate counseling and aid to numerous others. Many Park Slopers, then, had found a neighbor's response and in turn had opened themselves to others' needs.

Basic to the work of the Family Reception Center is the concept that personal and intrafamilial difficulties are not simply problems on an *interactional* level (though such problems are often presented and do become the focus of skilled help), but they have to be understood in an ecological frame of reference: persons interacting within an environment of impinging systems. The enabling work therefore involves the development of greater *access*—person to person, person to community institution, and community institution to person, as well as access from one group to another—so that children and families are included, are helped to *belong* and to have stakes in a community rather than their becoming marginalized.

The specific services offered at the Family Reception Center reflect the staff's conviction that service means helping: 1) to buttress emotional and social strengths of individuals so they may better deal with stresses that impinge on them; 2) to open the way to growth opportunities and to increase social experiences and relationships which contribute to the quality of life; 3) to facilitate opportunities to participate in one's neighborhood and to develop stakes in that neighborhood; 4) to enhance access to roles through family, school, work, and recreation; 5) to provide remediation and treatment of emotional and personal conflicts and of social disabilities and problems; and 6) to advocate for the support of environmental systems (medical, vocational, housing, civic associations, recreational centers, income maintenance, and schools), without exclusions.

Such service requires assessing and working with the full range of need, not overlooking those social system problems which contribute to stress or to symptomatic behavior.

THE PARK SLOPE MINI-SCHOOL

One segment of our population needed more from us. In the early months of the Center's life we found not only the displaced stealing gang who preceded us in occupying our building, but many others of latency and teenage years who had long been away from school, and could not readily accept or be accepted by another school. Six months after the initiation of the Center program, we asked the Board of Education of the City of New York to enter into a partnership with our agency wherein they would send teachers to work with 21 such troubled, alienated, and truant children and we would provide a child care specialist to help the teachers relate to the children and shape a therapeutic school milieu in a location we would rent; in addition, we would provide a range of supports to the children and their families through the Family Reception Center. Thus, within the first year of the Center's initiation, the Park Slope Mini-School opened with 21 children, three teachers, and our child care specialist. The children's prolonged alienation from school and unsocialized behavior led to the resignation of five teachers within the first five weeks and a request by our landlord that we find space elsewhere. Within the next six months, however, the experience of social belonging by the children relieved the heavy demands for social control. The youngsters' anxiety and aggression subsided as they learned to read and perform in "life skills" tasks designed for them, and as they were inducted in the rewards of caring for each other. Guidance counselors of the area began to find other such children, as did our own staff as they worked in the neighborhood.

The four children of the Burris family, ages 10, 8, 7, and 6, came to the attention of the Center because of severe learning and behavioral difficulties manifested in school. Recently transferred to the care of maternal grandparents, they had previously known gross neglect and abuse as their mother was and still is heavily drug-addicted. The children had often been subjected to beatings, left for days without supervision or food, and disciplined by being put in closets. The school guidance counselor was particularly concerned about the oldest boy, Jaime, who was unable to form peer relationships, often withdrew into fantasy, and would frequently leave his seat in a classroom to crawl on the floor. He was accepted into the Mini-School and provided with both individual and group treatment; progress was notable and Jaime is now able to read on grade level. Socialization improved with decreased recurrences of regressive behavior. However, he continues to need the Mini-School's small individualized classes, as well as individual and group counseling; and probably will for some time.

Eight-year-old Tommy has been out of school for more than a year on home instruction, diagnosed as autistic with retardation. He was also admitted to the Mini-School, beginning with a half-day program, to allow him to make a gradual adjustment to the school setting and the other children. His academic and relational gains improved, and he showed potential for other advances. The situation of 7-year-old Bess, who was able to stay in a regular school class, was monitored, and the youngest child was accepted into a special speech class. Regular supportive contacts with the grandmother were maintained. The individualization of the Mini-School, the nurturance of that therapeutic setting, combined with individual and group treatment of the children and close liaison with the school psychologist and with the grandmother, helped sustain four children who were at high risk when we originally met them.

The Park Slope Mini-School doubled its enrollment after the first year to accommodate latency-aged children with very conspicuous emotional and behavioral problems associated with learning impairments. The next year the population of the program again doubled, and in June 1977 the Park Slope Mini-School numbered over ninety children, most of whom were by then in classes situated within neighborhood public schools. Planning was also then completed for the original rented site to be dropped so that all the children would have the more normalized situation of public school location, while our child care specialists and social work services of the Center staff would follow them there. The model of a public-voluntary partnership wherein staff, who are experienced in child care and therapeutic group leadership, aid and support the work of teachers, and the educational functions are further buttressed by the Center's wider services to the children and families outside school hours, has proved to be an economic and far-reaching strategy in preventive services. For the school district, it has presented alternatives to the exclusionary process of transferring children labelled as "socially maladjusted," "neurologically impaired," or "mentally retarded," to special schools or classes. Strategies to strengthen the capacities of parents and to increase the responsiveness of the school also contributed to the children's academic progress; and their belonging *in school* is an important factor in improved behavior.[6]

THE BARBARA B. BLUM RESIDENCE

Soon after the opening of the Park Slope Mini-School program we needed to begin the development of a neighborhood group home accommodating, at any one time, eight boys and girls who needed placement for a longer period because of a particularly noxious set of environmental factors. The Barbara B. Blum Residence, a family-type dwelling next door to the Center, makes it possible for such children to receive intensive casework services while they attend community schools and socialize normally with their friends. They also have unrestricted access to their own families, who are free to visit in the group home. The group home's social worker (supported by consultative clinical staff of the Center) also works extensively with each child's family. Currently this group home remains the neighborhood's only treatment-oriented group care setting for adolescents.

CHILDREN AND YOUTH
DEVELOPMENT SERVICES

Meanwhile, as these three programs were unfolding and developing, the agency had embarked (toward the end of the first program year of the Family Reception Center) on still another set of strategies focused more specifically on the community of Park Slope as a human ecological system. Children and Youth Development Services was inaugurated in August 1973, with a federal grant, once again given with a mandate of "delinquency prevention." Now there were to be new levels of intervention as we would try to be a catalyst in building the capacity of the neighborhood itself to sustain its children and families. A youth services system or network, we hoped, would grow out of the conscious interfacing of social groups and institutions of the community: youth and parents, schools, police, churches, block associations, civic organizations, merchants' associations, recreational leaders, and service groups. CYDS would promote the sharing of resources and facilities, ideas, information, and staff consultation, as well as active case and policy advocacy. It would initiate and develop many more direct services to youth and families of the neighborhood. All of these, however, would be constructed by CDYS staff *with* other neighborhood social systems, and all would be open universally to Park Slope residents without reference to financial need.

Some of the methods utilized included:

A. Maintenance of three neighborhood task forces on recreation, education, and youth employment. These help to focus attention on primary support systems, often the family, which impinge on youth development.

B. Convening neighborhood-wide forums or meetings for sharing information about activities and resources, for recruiting new opportunities, and for eliciting exchanges of facilities and assets among groups.

C. Linking groups with each other through program tasks as well as offering consultation to community groups and acting as enabler in the development of their capabilities.

A youth employment program was developed, for example, by a CDYS staff member working with merchants' associations and many other neighborhood residents as a Jobs Task Force. Together they created an "odd job market" which gave teenagers a steady stream of entry level work experiences leading to gains in self-confidence, work habits and vocational readiness. Neighborhood service groups worked together to provide youth with meaningful sites and tasks for federally funded summer jobs so that these would not be mere hand-outs for attendance but good learning experiences. And CDYS took responsibility, out of its own grant, for partial funding of a Career Exploration Center for youth sponsored by five Protestant churches of the neighborhood. The youth employment program, then, was an outgrowth of grass roots participation and intergroup sharing.

The Educational Task Force gained the approval of the District Superintendent of District #15 schools to adopt a district-wide "Committee on Children with Special Educational Needs." The particular focus of this representative group is on meeting the needs of children with learning disabilities and problems of truancy through the recruitment of community supports and resources for the use of schools and parents, avoiding as far as possible the stigmatizing process of "certifying" the children to residual and segregated programs. The Recreation Task Force formed a Basketball League of eight junior division teams of twelve players each, ranging in age from 14 to 16. Each of the eight teams is sponsored by a local merchant or civic group.

Through the Children and Youth Development Services system there is an intergroup effort of civic service organizations, clergy, schools, professional associations, police, and others to focus on the potential of all systems (educational, recreational, health, mental health, business and employment, and social services) to sustain youth and increase social belonging, thereby effectively curbing delinquency.

CYDS also outstationed a worker at each of the two police precincts covering Park Slope so that we could serve within the neighborhood those situations involving runaways, neglect or abuse of children, and family assault complaints, as well as the less serious delinquencies which did not require arrest. Crisis-intervention at the police precinct level, and follow-up by a more experienced CYDS caseworker, resulted in diverting many residents from deeper penetration of the law enforcement and court routes by connecting them with social supports in the community.

Walter, 11 years old, walked into the 78th Police Precinct requesting emergency shelter. He had been involved in a fight at school and was sent home by the principal, but was afraid to return home. The social worker outstationed at the precinct interviewed Walter and learned that he had previously run away from home other times, had slept overnight on the subway train, and had been returned home by the police. Despite a new attempt to mediate the mother-son relationship in an interview at the precinct and Walter's agreement to return home, he later came back to insist that he wanted "placement in a home." Arrangements were made for brief residence in the Center's "crash pad," and Walter continued to attend his school while living there. Walter was found to be a depressed, conflicted child who had suffered a history of multiple parental separations. His mother, a West Indian, was concerned about him but oriented to a more punitive style of discipline. She responded to counseling sessions, recognized how the child might feel rejected by her, and agreed to reach out to him. Currently, Walter is continuing in individual sessions, and follow-up is maintained with the mother. Walter participated in the summer day camp program and continues to be sustained within his family.

As clergy from Park Slope called attention to frustrations in providing effective help and protection to battered wives, CYDS offered them defined helps in establishing a *Safe Homes Project* in the neighborhood. Our own staff would recruit and train volunteer counselors (almost all of them having had graduate training and experience in casework or psychology, and almost all living in the neighborhood) and would also develop linkages with legal and other needed resources, if the clergy would recruit from among their respective congregations families who would offer their homes once a year for a few days to give assaulted wives and mothers a "safe home" while the latter and their husbands received intensive help. The CYDS community developer trained 15 counselors (most of whom have graduate degrees in the human services) who volunteer counseling services with the women or their husbands. During the first six months of the program eight safe homes were recruited from the community itself to give short-term, free, emergency residence to such women, and training was given to the owners of these homes regarding appropriate ways of responding while giving shelter. In its first four months, the project gave assistance to twelve women: all received counseling, four made use of a safe home, two were relocated, and two returned to their husbands. The community developer gives continuous supervision to the volunteer counselor during the entire time a case is being carried for service. She also provides linkage of CYDS's "safe homes approach" with the larger, city-wide shelter facility which another organization sponsors. As this program has grown, the neighborhood is taking responsibility for its own families. The name of the project reflects the wider goal that every house in the neighborhood be a "safe home."

Persuaded that neither the family nor the school can alone be responsible for education of today's children, and that both need a supportive and contributing environment, CYDS adopted the "community school model" as a major strategy toward the creation of neighborhood itself. In this model the community public school becomes a veritable community for parents as well as children. In two elementary schools CYDS mounted this model in a three-pronged design of activities during and after the school day: (1) family life education programs in their broadest sense: all those issues which bear on family life and supports to families, including tenants' rights, negotiating health systems, public financial assistance, sex education of children, teaching handicrafts to children in the home, and many other topics; (2) after-school enriched play and socialization activities for children and youth; and (3) learning enrichments to stimulate growth in children and adults. Parent-centered programs have been held during school hours while their children are in classes, with other offerings in evenings. The model is created not only by the involvement of school and parents but by the contributions of experts from universities and special groups, making for considerable economy in a design that takes stigma and client status out of the service entirely! We believe that a school which is responsive to children and parents is a bulwark to families, and in turn it is enriched by parent and community participation.

CYDS has served thousands of individuals in these and other activities which are, characteristically, neighborhood-wide and generated from shared staff and resources. A variety of youth group leaders of the community, for example, are provided with free tickets to recreational and cultural events which have been gathered by CYDS. Occasional camping weekends reach many youth of the neighborhood through sharing the agencies' resources. CYDS staff have helped a new youth group, sponsored by local merchants, to become incorporated and to achieve funding. A community services project, involving 32 youth of the local public high school in giving volunteer services to human service agencies while receiving school credit, is still another CYDS program helping school staff give leadership training to students. Placement sites include a Senior Citizen Center, a program for mentally retarded children, a local hospital, and public schools for tutorial services.

Staff of CYDS become members of other agency boards in the community and, like staff at the Family Reception Center, hold themselves available to foster and augment the contributions of any group interested in giving service to Park Slope residents.

Program design has thus included advocacy, the coordination of services toward effective service delivery, direct services to youth for the provision of developmental opportunities, and the enhancement of personal and family effectiveness. All the time that it individualizes children and youth and their families, however, CYDS works toward the development of the neighborhood as a sustaining community. It sees the neighborhood as a bearer of values and source of human supports.

SUMMARY

Utimately it is in the neighborhood that youth must learn societal goals, develop human commitments, and achieve functional roles. Ultimately, also, it is in the neighborhood—in the matrix of interacting social systems of family, school, and social organizations that make up a community—that some children have become marginalized, set aside, rejected, and made "officially illegitimate." Delinquency is not only a personal status for a given child, but *it is a problem of the neighborhood*.

Our own staff living in Park Slope and working in any of the four programs described want to prevent this "fall-out" and alienation; they want to see an end to isolation of any individual; they work to develop a collective response in the neighborhood to enrich the lives of all its people.

> People do not "make it on their own"
> People cannot "go it alone"
> Even if it were possible—
> Why would anyone want to? [7]

NOTES

1. Martin Bloom, this volume.
2. Charles Grosser, this volume.
3. For an interesting historical analysis of the role of the settlement movement and the community center movement in using public schools as the sites of neighborhood centers, see Robert Fisher, "Community Organizing and Citizen Participation: The Efforts of the People's Institute in New York City, 1910–1920," *Social Service Review* 51, no. 3 (September 1977), pp. 474–90.

---

1. *Who Is My Neighbor,* a brochure describing the four Park Slope, Brooklyn programs sponsored by Sisters of the Good Shepherd Residences, 1974.
2. Sister Mary Paul Janchill, "Systems Concepts in Casework Theory and Practice," *Social Casework* 50, no. 2 (February 1969), pp. 74–82.
3. Robert W. White, "Motivation Reconsidered: The Concept of Competence," *Psychological Review* 66 (September 1959), pp. 297–333. See also, Nicholas Hobbs, *The Futures of Children* (San Francisco: Jossey-Bass, 1975), p. 150.
4. Sister Mary Paul Janchill, *Criteria for Foster Placement and Alternatives to Foster Care* (New York State Board of Social Welfare, 1975).
5. For evaluations and reports covering the first two years of the Family Reception Center program, see Edmund A. Sherman and Renee Neumann, *The Family Reception Center: Evaluation of the Program* (New York: Child Welfare League of America, September 1973); Ann W. Shyne and Renee Newman, *Commitment to People: Evaluation of the Family Reception Center* (New York: Child Welfare League of America, September 1974); and "Research Spotlight on a Neighborhood Program," *Child Welfare* 52, no. 10 (December 1973), pp. 677–81. Also, Robert Morris, Ilana Lescohier, and Ann Withorn, "Social Service Delivery Systems: At-

tempts to Alter Local Patterns 1970–1974—An Exploratory National Survey at Midstream'' (Florence Heller Graduate School for Advanced Studies in Social Welfare, Brandeis University, January 1975).

6. Michael Phillips, *A Neighborhood School for Children with Special Educational Needs: History of the Park Slope Mini-School* (New York: Community Trust, 1976).

7. *Who Is My Neighbor.*

Index

HV
95
.S62

HV
95
.S62